THE NEW COMMUNIST THIRD WORLD

THE NEW COMMUNIST THIRD WORLD

AN ESSAY IN POLITICAL ECONOMY

EDITED BY PETER WILES

CROOM HELM
London & Canberra

© 1982 Peter Wiles
Croom Helm Ltd, 2-10 St John's Road, London SW11

British Library Cataloguing in Publication Data

The New communist Third World.
  1. Underdeveloped areas — Politics and government
  2. Underdeveloped areas — Economic policy
  I. Wiles, Peter
  330.9172'4   HC59.7

  ISBN 0-7-0

ISBN 0-7099-2709-6

Typeset by Leaper & Gard Ltd, 32 Feeder Road, Bristol
Printed and bound in Great Britain
by Billing and Sons Limited
Guildford, London, Oxford, Worcester

CONTENTS

Preface

Abbreviations

Afghanistan's new leftist government has asked the United States
to step up its foreign aid program. A senior State Department official
said today the Administration was considering the request. It was made
last month after Afghanistan signed about thirty aid agreements with
the Soviet Union. The official said: 'They would like quite a bit more
aid. They said if we gave more it would be accepted.' The official told
newsmen that although the country's new leaders were obviously
oriented towards the Soviet Union, the request was a sign that
Afghanistan intends to remain non-aligned and preserve good relations
with the United States.

Reuter, Washington, 3 August 1978

PREFACE

This book is the result of a two-year project, 'The Commercial Policies of the Communist Third World', financed by the Social Science Research Council. I take this opportunity to thank the Council and my own parent institution, the London School of Economics, for their administrative competence and tact.

Our preliminary results have appeared in a much shorter version: Edgar Feuchtwanger and Peter Nailor (eds.) *The Soviet Union and the Third World* (Macmillan, 1981).

The project had a double origin: Adi Schnytzer's perpetual insistence that small peripheral Communist countries are of great interest and, from time to time, importance; and my own mounting impatience with the unwillingness of Africanists and Arabists to take a new phenomenon seriously, or master the necessary background.

Each author is responsible as shown, except that disproportionately many tables on trade are the work of Alan Smith, and I have inserted, with permission, occasional passages in other contributions: e.g. on Maoist military doctrine in Chapter 13 and 'the Filioque Connection' in Chapter 3. Editorial policy was, however, to 'Let Thirteen Flowers Bloom' in the new garden of tropical Sovietology, subject to the presentation of certain standardised information.

Peter Wiles

ABBREVIATIONS

ACR	ed. Colin Legum, *African Contemporary Record*, N.Y. and London, 1979
ADB	Asian Development Bank
AIM	Agencia de Informacão de Moçambique
AKFM	Party favouring rapid independence in the late fifties (Madagascar)
ANC	Africa National Congress (South African Resistance Movement)
ARB	*African Research Bulletin*, Africa Research Ltd, Exeter, UK various years
AREMA	Avant-Garde de la Révolution Malgache
ASECNA	Agence pour la Sécurité de la Naviation Aérienne en Afrique et à Madagascar
ASOS	*Africa South of the Sahara*, Europa, London, tenth edn, 1980
b, bn	billion, i.e. one milliard or a thousand million
BOIS	Bundesinstitut für Ostwissenschaftliche und Internationale Studien
CEDIMO	Centro de Documentacão e Informacão de Moçambique
CEPII	Centre d'Études Prospectives et d'Informations Internationales (Paris)
CFA	Communauté Financière Africaine (the name of the franc in most of francophone Africa). Equals 2 French centimes, and is kept convertible at that rate
CIA	Central Intelligence Agency
c.i.f.	carriage, insurance, freight
CMEA	Council of Mutual Economic Assistance (Comecon)
CNPD	Conseil National Populaire pour le Dévélopppement (Madagascar)
CSC	Confédération des Sydicates Congolais
CSSR	Czechoslovak Socialist Republic
DAC	Development Advisory Committee (associated with OECD)
DPRK	Democratic People's Republic of Korea
EBM	*Etude de la Banque Mondiale, Evolution Récente et Perspectives Economiques*, World Bank, Washington, DC

ECOWAS	Economic Community of West African States
EDF	European Development Fund
EEC	European Economic Community
EFTA	European Free Trade Association
ETA	Euskadi Ta Askatasuna (Basque terrorists)
EUA	European Unit of Account
FAC	Fonds d'Aide et de Coopération (French agency)
FAPLA	Forças Armadas Populares de Liberação de Angola
FCO	Foreign and Commonwealth Office, London
FES	Friedrich-Ebert Stiftung. Serial: FES *Bericht: Entwicklungs-politik Kommunistischer Länder*
FLEC	Cabinda Enclave Liberation Front
FLOSY	Front for the Liberation of South Yemen
FNLA	Frente Nacional de Liberacão de Angola
f.o.b.	free on board
FPLM	Mozambique's People's Army
FRELIMO	Frente de Liberacão de Moçambique
FRG	Federal Republic of Germany
GDP	Gross Domestic Product
GDR	German Democratic Republic
GNP	Gross National Product
IBEC	International Bank for Economic Co-operation (the CMEA's 'IMF')
IBRD	International Bank for Reconstruction and Development (now the World Bank)
IDA	International Development Authority (the soft loan organisation of the World Bank)
IFS	*International Financial Statistics*, IMF monthly
IIB	International Investment Bank (the CMEA's 'World Bank')
IISS	International Institute of Strategic Studies (London)
IMF	International Monetary Fund
IMFB	International Monetary Fund, *Benin, Recent Economic Developments*, 4 June 1979
IMFC	International Monetary Fund, *People's Republic of the Congo – Recent Economic Developments*, SM/79/91
IRA	Irish Republican Army
JEC	Joint Economic Committee (of the US Congress)
JETRO	Japan External Trade Organisation
LIBOR	London Interbank Offered Rate
m	million

MAGIC	Mozambique, Angola and Guinea Information Centre (London)
MDRM	Mouvement Démocratique de la Révolution Malgache
METB	Monthly External Trade Bulletin (of the EEC)
MNR	Mouvement National Révolutionnaire (Congo)
MONIMA	Leftist peasant group (Madagascar)
MPLA	Movimento Popular para a Liberacão de Angola
n.a.	not available (note that '−' means 'insignificant' or 'irrelevant')
NCTW	New Communist Third World (Afghanistan, Angola, Ethiopia, Mozambique, PDRY)
NEP	New Economic Policy (in USSR 1921-8)
NFAC	National Foreign Assessment Centre
NLF	National Liberation Front (Yemen)
OAU	Organisation of African Unity
OCAM	Organisation Commune Africaine-Malgache
OECD	Organisation for Economic Co-operation and Development
OPEC	Organisation of Petroleum-Exporting Countries
PCT	Parti Congolais du Travail
PDRY	People's Democratic Republic of Yemen
PFLO	Popular Front for the Liberation of Oman
PLA	Party of Labour of Albania
PMAC	Provisional Military Administrative Council (Ethiopia)
PRG	Provisional Revolutionary Government (of South Vietnam)
PSD	Parti Socialiste Démocratique (Madagascar: Tsiranana)
RNM	Resistência Nacional Moçambicana
SAL	South Arabian League
SDR	Special Drawing Rights (IMF)
SNASP	Internal Security Service (Mozambique)
STABEX	The counter-cyclical import subsidy scheme of the EEC, in connection with the Lomé Agreement
STE	Soviet-type economy
SWAPO	South West African People's Organisation
SWB	*Summary of World Broadcasts*
th	thousand
UDEAC	Union Douanière et Economique de l'Afrique Centrale
UMOA	Union Monétaire Ouest Africaine
UNBM	*United Nations Monthly Bulletin of Statistics*
UNITA	União Nacional para a Independência Total de Angola

UNRRA	United Nations Relief and Rehabilitation Agency
UNTA	National Union of Angolan Workers
UNYITS	*United Nations Yearbook of International Trade Statistics*, New York, annual
VT	*Vneshnyaya Torgovlya* (the Soviet foreign trade statistical yearbook)
WBB	World Bank, *The Economy of Benin*, 31 May 1979
YAR	Yemen Arab Republic (North Yemen)
YD	Yemeni Dinar
YSP	Yemeni Socialist Party
ZOAM	Organisation of unemployed youth (Madagascar)

1 THE GENERAL VIEW, ESPECIALLY FROM MOSCOW

Peter Wiles and Alan Smith

Introduction. Purpose of the Study

1. The New Communist Third World (NCTW) is an area that defies precise definition. It consists of those developing countries that have recently proclaimed a Marxist-Leninist form of government (Angola, Mozambique, Afghanistan, Ethiopia and the PDR Yemen) plus a periphery of doubtful cases. Our choice of countries to study has been determined in the main by this essential question of definition, but we have also bowed to the constraints of time and finance, and the availability of scholars with the appropriate linguistic skills. We wish, too, not to duplicate country studies being conducted elsewhere. Our main assertion will be found in Part II of the book: the countries of the NCTW are substantially independent, especially in economic matters. They really can trade with whom they like, and their tempo of, say, agricultural collectivisation is also their own decision. *They, or rather their governments, are volunteers*, quite unlike Poland, Hungary and Czechoslovakia.[1]

This chapter concerns a matter less difficult to research: the economic policy of the Soviet Union and/or CMEA towards these countries. For the purposes of economic analysis, we can reasonably distinguish between three major types of Communist economy:

Group 1. Those countries that are full members of the Council for Mutual Economic Assistance (CMEA), subdivided into:
(a) The European 'core' (Soviet Union, Bulgaria, Hungary, East Germany, Poland and Czechoslovakia);
(b) Non-European members — Mongolia, Cuba and Vietnam. We are including aspects of these three in our study, to illustrate one possible outcome of membership in the 'Communist Third World';
(c) Romania, the 'core' member that has revolted.

A word here on peripheral types of membership. The NCTW and Laos are 'observers'. North Korea has been an observer, but seems to have lapsed in 1978-80, to become one again in July 1981. Albania did not formally resign from the CMEA until September 1968, when she appears to have done so by ceasing to pay her dues. She is however treated openly as a member in Czechoslovak and Polish, but silently as a non-member in Soviet, trade statistics. Yugoslavia is a 'participant' according to a highly specific agreement in 1965 with CMEA, rather resembling her formal 'association' with the EEC. The significance of observer status remains obscure and requires further study.

Group 2. Countries that have been Communist a long time and are designated as Socialist in official Soviet/CMEA statistics, but are not members of CMEA and currently beyond direct Soviet influence — Albania, China, North Korea and Yugoslavia. We have included aspects of Albania and North Korea in our study, to illustrate yet other possible outcomes for the NCTW. There have been latterly almost overwhelming grounds for adding Romania to Group 2, but she is sufficiently studied elsewhere. If we may diverge for a moment into purely strategic/diplomatic matters, it need not be stressed how tolerable it would be for NATO, or 'The West', if all Group 3 countries took this road. Then, our major area of study is:

Group 3. The NCTW itself: those developing countries that have proclaimed Marxist-Leninist forms of government but are not yet officially designated Socialist by Soviet ideologists or in the foreign-trade statistics of CMEA countries, yet maintain close relations with the USSR, and receive substantial military aid from her. These countries are: Angola, Mozambique, the PDR Yemen and Ethiopia. To them we must now add Afghanistan, which went Communist (in 1978) too late for our project, and could hardly be said at present to have an economy; and Grenada, which we have omitted, as 'Cuba's Laos'. These six countries and Laos were the only ones outside the CMEA to vote for the USSR on the Afghanistan motion at the United Nations on 15 January 1980.[2] (We have omitted Laos and Cambodia.)

Group 4. There are also doubtful cases like Madagascar, Benin, Congo-Brazzaville and Guyana. We give brief studies of the first three, but have substituted for Guyana the 'one that got away', Somalia.

It is basic to this study that the proclamation of Marxism-Leninism by the group 3 countries is both voluntary and genuine, even though in some cases it concerns only small elites. The countries may or may not be satellites, but the elites do not feel that way (except, surely, in Afghanistan). Mozambique in particular is no more of a satellite than Romania. *Each country is different and must be studied from the inside.* This applies even more strongly to Group 4.

We reject the parallels, often urged, of Ghana about 1961-4, Egypt about 1968-72 or Guinea about 1959-61. These countries were simply allied to the Soviet Union. They never proclaimed themselves to be Marxist-Leninist, persecuted religion, founded or encouraged Communist parties, put up innumerable pictures of Marx and Lenin, etc. Their subsequent diplomatic turnabouts tell us much less about the future of, say, Mozambique than we can learn from Cuba and North Korea. Moreover USSR has learned a *little* tact from those early connexions, of which two ended in the expulsion of her ambassadors.

The distinction between temporary allies and permanent imitators is of great emotional and intellectual importance. When Sékou Touré was young and Nasser and Nkrumah were alive many knowledgeable people lost their heads and cried 'wolf'. There was no solid empirical justification for calling these people or their states Communist.[3] Therefore to-day many knowledgeable people refuse to cry 'wolf' when the wolf stands in plain undoubted view.

A rose is a rose is a rose. It is contrary to fact to speak of Agostinho Neto as if he had been a sort of young Sékou Touré when he was beyond any possible doubt a sort of Ho Chi Minh. Even the Foreign and Commonwealth Office (FCO 1980, Table 8A, which we quote below) continues to call Angola, Mozambique, Ethiopia, PDRY and Afghanistan 'non-socialist' in 1978! In the text at least there are beginnings of the recognition of reality, with the phrase 'CMEA' taking the place of 'socialist' more than once. The US Department of Commerce sternly persists, in a quarterly publication (1980), in listing as 'Communist' only the CMEA minus Vietnam and Cuba, plus Laos, Albania and China; but the reason[4] is that Cuba, Vietnam, North Korea and Cambodia are totally embargoed. The NCTW is not listed because 'no US regulations have specifically classified them as being a Communist country'. The CEPII in Paris (1979, p. 2), in a study of Soviet — Third World trade, states that 'All in all the Soviet approach to Africa seems to have changed only a little' in 1973-8, and remains 're-active and opportunist' in sub-Saharan Africa — without once mentioning the Communist form of government in Angola and Mozambique. Blinkers powerful enough to cut off that much vision must be ideological. We shall not here speculate on the reasons for this, except to say that one cause is surely a simple human failing:

Africanists and Arabists form distinct and honourable intellectual disciplines, and are unwilling to welcome 'tropical Sovietology' to their preserves. We hope to behave as modestly as intruders should — but we insist upon our rights!

It is amusing that the Russians too have difficulties with nomenclature and indeed concepts. These difficulties partly arise from diplomacy: the spread of imperial power should be veiled until it is safe to confess it. But ideology seems also curiously unable to cope. The old distinction of a 'country of national democracy' (e.g. Guinea) has dropped out of the literature. This concept was introduced by Khrushchev at the Twenty-first Party Congress, 1961, to describe such countries as Cuba and Guinea then were: probably what we have in this book called 'marginals'. Note that this was in Khrushchev's expansive period, when Full Communism was not far away, Mongolia was admitted to CMEA, and missiles were sent to Cuba. 'National (natsional'naya) democracy' was of course always junior to 'People's (narodnaya) democracy'. That phrase meant the East European satellites and Mongolia, all of which have now 'founded socialism'. Since this is recognised by USSR, people's democracy too has dropped out of Soviet use, though it survives in the titles of the PDR Yemen and the Korean PDR. The other countries treated here have the titles shown in their chapter headings. These are doubtless significant to them, but often Soviet official documents simply give the geographical name, except for the PDRY which must be distinguished from the YAR. Groups 1 and 2 are simply 'socialist' in Soviet parlance, and VT reproduces their official titles in all cases.

Thus there is no official terminology any more,[5] but our Group 3 does receive recognition in careful and unofficial phrasing. For instance Primakov (1979, our italics) distinguishes them in the third and fourth paragraphs of his article:

Thus it is for example significant that the abolition of the colonial system, which culminated in the bankruptcy of the last colonial empire, the Portuguese, has led to the emergence of anti-imperialistic regimes in the former Portuguese colonies which *orient themselves to scientific socialism*. This is not least thanks to the circumstance that the victory of the national liberation revolutions in these countries was preceded by long years of stiff fighting in which cadres of revolutionaries grew up and became strong — cadres who saw the future of their countries in organic ties with the other components of the *world-revolutionary process* (revolutionärer Weltprozess): the socialist community of states and the international workers' movement.

The revolution has won in Ethiopia, and the revolutionary-democratic leadership has also chosen the path of deep-reaching transformations of society under socialist banners (literally Losungen). *The revolutionary* movement in Afghanistan has had a historic *victory*. *Revolutionary changes have deepened* in the People's Republic of Congo, in the Democratic Republic of Madagascar, in the P.D.R. Yemen, in the People's Republic of Benin, in Tanzania, Algeria, Libya etc.

But at the same time differently directed shifts of power have occurred in Pakistan, Sri Lanka and Bangladesh. A rejection of the socialist orientation is to be observed in Egypt, a turn to the right describes also a number of other UDCs. What is the cause of these processes?

— and he continues for ten pages to describe the policies of multi-national corporations. We feel here no need to analyse the place of the multi-national corporation in Soviet demonology. We only observe that the NCTW, except for the PDR Yemen, is correctly described above as places where the final (Soviet-type) Revolution has won. We agree with Primakov.

2. What then exactly is a Communist state? The criterion might be a political or an economic one or a mixture of the two. From the political angle, a genuine people's republic can be described as a state ruled by a single Marxist-Leninist party. The substantive question then becomes what constitutes such a party. The economic test could be the presence or otherwise of thoroughgoing nationalisation, agricultural collectivisation and the central direction of the economy by a non-market plan. The dominant view, however, would probably incline towards a dual test involving both these elements to identify a genuine Communist state.

The difficulty with the economic test is that the degree of planning and state control which can be instituted by a revolutionary government shortly after coming to power in an underdeveloped country is severely limited by the usual objective constraints of under-development. When we add to these constraints the inevitable disruption which revolutionary change must bring with it, we can expect that the country will be forced to begin with a sort of NEP: the 'commanding heights' only will be nationalised, there will be a few experiments only in agricultural collectivisation, and planning will be confined to public-sector investment. All this is exactly what Lenin did himself: it is super-orthodox. But while this lasts (and it may last long) the economy's external appearance is not easily distinguishable from that of the average 'mixed' economy of Third World countries. But it may still be the government's *firm intention* to move towards planning as soon as it seems practicable. The problem is that policies applied to stabilise a new social and economic order may not be indicative of and, indeed, may be positively misleading as to the government's ultimate intentions. On these grounds we would tend not to rely on any simple *domestic* economic criterion to identify a people's republic. As to foreign trade and aid, however, two criteria can be laid down and are defended in each case in this book: a predominance of Soviet/CMEA aid and arms deliveries (while civilian trade continues in an ordinary manner).

We must then turn to the political test, namely that of the existence or otherwise of a Marxist-Leninist party. We would in fact argue that it is this aspect (i.e. the political rather than the economic) that is the more reliable for determining the nature of the state and society. Detailed direction of the economy presupposes, after all, political control before it can be effectively exercised. However uncomfortable to Western economists and to Marxists of all sorts this ordering of the 'political' and the 'economic' may be, there is no doubt that in this case the former precedes the latter: a poor country with an 'NEP' will develop in different directions according to its politics.

The political test must, however, go beyond the party slogans or it will degenerate into the earlier and simpler test of the previous section of what the state proclaims itself to be. It must extend to an examination of the party's organisation and its role in the political system. One-party states where an exclusive party pervades every area of social and economic life and is the origin of all important initiatives, and where the state apparatus is a close but subordinate parallel of the party apparatus are *prima facie* good candidates for designation as Communist. *Per contra* Ethiopia to-day, like Cuba in the 1960s, must remain somewhat doubtful.

But there is still a danger of confusion. Just as even a colonial government or an Arab monarchy can engage in extensive direction of the economy so can a 'nationalist' government find it convenient to institute a single-party apparatus. The party is however never in practice a 'vanguard' one, but always embraces a very large proportion of the people and allows internal disagreement (no 'democratic centralism').[6]

Moreover, such single parties disavow class war and accept only restricted parts of the Marxist-Leninist ideology. And in the same way as the Soviet model of economic development can be found useful (whether genuinely Marxist or not) so can the Soviet model of political organisation be found a viable political form in conditions of underdevelopment which would realistically rule out Western-style political evolution.

Prime evidence that a state is genuinely Marxist-Leninist can be derived from its treatment of religion. It is almost a definitional part of Leninism that (i) religion must be persecuted, and (ii) the *aktiv* — though not all the periphery — of the Party must be atheists. To (i) tactical exceptions are of course possible, but not to (ii) — the instrument of policy must remain sharp and bright even if the policy is in abeyance. But tactical exceptions have been few in number: mainly Stalin's relaxation during the Second World War. We could not even say that in Poland, where religion remains overwhelmingly strong, there had ever been a year without petty persecution of it; or any Christians in the Central Committee. Religious policy is a litmus test.

How does the NCTW measure up to this? The only even apparent failure is the PDRY, and this raises the question of Islam and Communism, recently made topical for the Soviet case itself by Carrère d'Encausse (1978). Islam is a tougher nut to crack than Protestantism or the Far Eastern religions, even than Catholicism. As Islam enjoys a few minor privileges over other religions inside the Soviet Union, we should not be surprised that the second independent Moslem Communist country (after Albania) deviates a little. In the words of the *New York Times* (27 May 1979), 'What is certain is that the Marxist leadership finds it necessary to keep Islam as the state religion, to continue to reach Islam in the schools and to appear in the Mosques on religious holidays.'

It is a progressive Islam, and a people not in any case noted for its Moslem piety. Notably there is nominally complete equality for women (as in the USSR). But such liberalising manipulations were practised by Lenin on Orthodoxy and by every Polish leader on Catholicism. The really striking point is the Politburo's attendance at the mosque: *Paris vaut bien une messe*.[7]

We must therefore end this general discussion rather inconclusively. But enough has been said to show how much ambiguity there can be about identifying a genuine Marxist-Leninist State and how necessary it is to consider all the possible dimensions of the character of the society, even if we are unsure about their relative weights.

3. We turn to the question of *irreversibility*. It is improbable that the NCTW will go back on the Marxist-Leninism that they have adopted. The principal impedimenta of this creed are precisely a set of efficient instruments for taking and keeping power, and a tightly knit, self-perpetuating elite with a workable ideology. Equally important, there is Soviet or Cuban force on the ground, except in Mozambique, and Soviet or East German penetration of the security system. On this account it is not surprising that Mozambique alone exhibits hankerings towards China — another Marxist-Leninist state. The initial choice of system and ideology was fairly free. But there is no going back. You do not 'unbecome' a Communist state. The case of Somalia is particularly instructive (Chapter 9); you can't escape unless USSR virtually declares war on you and you become very angry indeed.[8] Even then it is doubtful if Somalia would have escaped had the period of Soviet-type Communism been longer; the security police was already penetrated.

We must draw attention however to the 'marginals' e.g. Benin. What Colonel Kérékou (Chapter 6) can do he can also undo — if the Russians continue not to take him seriously and 'help' him to be a better Marxist-Leninist. Also an anti-Communist *coup* could unseat him. But it is precisely part of the definition of a 'marginal' that USSR does not take it seriously; and above all that it makes no attempt to infiltrate its state organs. Therefore these countries' position is reversible. This is as much as to say that the irreversibility doctrine is a proposition more about Soviet foreign policy than about the invincibility of a local Marxist-Leninist security police. Such forces are very far from invincible: every country of Eastern Europe except Romania and Bulgaria has already had to be 're-invaded' once — if we may count the many threats and compromises in the Polish case, unsettled as this goes to press. Afghanistan was only 're-invaded' because a more or less independent Communist *coup*, two years old, was clearly going down to failure. The 'Brezhnev doctrine' is nine-tenths of irreversibility. Since Stalin died there have been many 're-invasions' but no invasions. To be already Communist is the thing that is dangerous.

4. But irreversibility from what? It is not diplomatic independence that really worries the Russians, as Romania shows. Yet even in internal affairs Marxism-Leninism has become by now a house with many mansions. A separate African Road to socialism is more often talked about than, say, the Polish (or indeed the Vietnamese) Road. But in practice Polish Communist policies or wishes are specific and definite, spring in fairly clear ways from local circumstances and traditions,

and form a permanent though developing body of more or less coherent doctrine. But none of this can be claimed for any form of Afro-Marxism.[9] Africans, especially in Group 3 countries, are simply not educated enough, nor have they a long and impressive enough tradition, to found a viable native form of Marxism, or indeed any other all-embracing ideology.[10]

It is for instance often claimed that Afro-Marxism is distinguished by its rejection of class-war, and its restriction of hostilities to capitalist imperialism. Certainly the non-Marxist single parties (above) do exactly this. It seems at first also true of Angola and Mozambique; but they had practically only a Portuguese bourgeoisie. There was not even a native 'comprador bourgeoisie'.[11] In their circumstances, class war could only be directed against *kulaks*, and would therefore be counter-productive. But class war is definitely a feature of Ethiopian rule, and even in the pseudo-Marxist Congo, Ngouabi gave it lip service (Chapter 7).[12] In other words the genuine absence of class war in Angola and Mozambique is less due to an independent ideology than to the absence of 'exploiting' classes, once imperialism was defeated. In any case, once any Marxist-Leninist regime has liquidated its internal enemies it ceases officially to wage class war, and the issue passes into history. And certainly Soviet sources do not insist on the necessity of class war in the NCTW.

It seems more likely, then, that the NCTW will adopt specifically Soviet ideology and — with due regard to stages — Soviet economic organisation than it is that Poland will. Those who say it does not matter that African leaders 'mouth Marxist-Leninist phrases' do Africa too little honour, and reveal themselves as virtual racists: it matters what people think and, even if they do not altogether mean it, what they say. On the other hand, those who believe that an independent non-Soviet ideology or policy will emerge among the African countries we have selected do Africa too much honour. They must specify exactly what its present beginnings are; exactly which African traditions, country by country, are in conflict with exactly which Soviet traditions; and how these particular countries will get out of the trap which they seem to be in. All the above applies with lesser force, in our opinion, to the PDRY and Afghanistan: Islam is a most serious competing ideology with a long and respectable tradition.

It is true that some countries of the NCTW have gone Communist in very unorthodox ways. Mengistu of Ethiopia began as a hardly better Marxist-Leninist than, say, Castro of Cuba. But that is also true of Lenin himself! And precisely Cuba, the unexpected 'volunteer', was in the early 1960s the first country in the NCTW.

It cannot be stressed enough that there is nothing un-Leninist about the economic behaviour of the NCTW, whether it is their decision or USSR's. It is a virtually perfect copy of Lenin's own behaviour during the NEP, except that there are perhaps rather more state farms but rather less nationalisation in other sectors, and slightly more tolerance is extended now even than under Lenin to big foreign capitalist enterprises. All this accords, moreover, with current published Soviet advice. However, if the NEP cannot give us an exact parallel to the kind of tolerance extended by Angola or the PDRY to multi-national corporations, the USSR of the period of so-called détente is itself slightly more welcoming than during the NEP. On the other hand social and political arrangements were more tolerant under the NEP than in the NCTW to-day (or USSR to-day).

It is an empirical fact that no great social or political risk attends the Communist country that opens up its economy. No harm *has* been done to either the NCTW or to USSR itself — to-day or in the NEP. Certainly extremes of hostility prevent trade, but trade does not greatly 'corrupt' culture or affect the grip of the security police. Whatever Lenin once thought on this question during the NEP, he was wrong even at the time. To-day, now that USSR is a military super-power and has a whole empire of Communist satellites, she and they have every reason to be self-confident. The only exceptions are the two Stalinist powers, North Korea and Albania. These indeed stand to be corrupted, say by capitalist tourists or consumer goods. In their isolation paranoia is indeed appropriate.

5. What future awaits the NCTW if it joins CMEA? If we were Ethiopian planners, and looked at the matter coldly, at arm's length, what would we see? Or would the 'Group 2' policy seem preferable?

The CMEA and the Warsaw Pact are the only permanent inter-state organs in the Communist world that pretend to supranationality. There are of course very many multi-national production units, banks, research institutes etc., and the NCTW would have, as CMEA members, access to them too (indeed has it in part already). Strictly speaking the CMEA is not supranational, however, but an organ of sovereign Communist states in which each retains a veto. Romania regularly uses this veto, forcing the rest to pursue this or that joint scheme without her. The EEC has many more pretensions to, and attributes of, supranationality.[13]

One difficulty is that Communist states are run by ruling monopoly parties. These formed in principle a *camp*. 'Camp', however, President Tito is said to have said, 'that means to us a concentration camp'. Nowadays the approved Soviet word is 'commonwealth' (sodruzhestvo). A recurrent theme in Soviet long-term policy toward the economic relations between socialist states over the past sixty years has been their unification under a *joint economic plan*. Compare on this Article 96 of the Eighth Party Congress of 1919, reiterated by Lenin (1920), Bukharin and Preobrazhenski (1921, pp. 446-7), and Khrushchev (1962). Khrushchev aroused vehement opposition in Romania, and the issue was again put into cold storage until recently. The Soviet economists Alampiev, Bogomolov and Shiryaev (1973) referred to 'the final result – integration of all the socialist national economies in one international economy regulated under a common plan', but added that 'this goes beyond the framework of the foreseeable future'.

They may well say that. A detailed Soviet-type plan at CMEA level entails the absolute supranationality of the CMEA over member states; and this implies a single supranational party. But USSR would not wish to dilute the purity of its own party. Granted therefore that in the short run pragmatism excludes such far-reaching integration, the following questions would appear to remain concerning the external relations of the NCTW:

(i)   Will these countries (assuming no grand political reversal on their part) remain largely independent both of one another and the other Communist states, i.e. join Group 2 (with or without directing a greater proportion of their trade towards other Communist states generally), or

(ii) Will they eventually become members of CMEA – and if so, how integrated will they become with other members?

(iii) To answer (ii) we must also know the future relation of Mongolia, Cuba and Vietnam to the rest of CMEA – how integrated will they become with the European 'core'?

Although some of the evidence is conflicting, we feel that we can make a reasonable preliminary attempt to answer some of these questions, encompassing a period of perhaps the next ten to fifteen years, using both qualitative and quantitative evidence.

As we have seen, there has been renewed pressure in the 1970s to establish joint planning procedures within the CMEA which could ultimately form the basis of a joint plan. Although the Soviet Union (and in particular Gosplan) appear to be the main movers of these proposals, progress towards this goal has been cautious and has carefully avoided any reference to direct supranationality. Lately the dollar has increasingly been substituted for the transferable rouble within the CMEA; and this has a one-to-one relation to the making of deliveries not included in the annual planned trade protocols, moreover at 'world' not CMEA prices.[14] Furthermore, Soviet difficulties in establishing joint planning within the CMEA 'core' over a ten-to-fifteen year period make its extension beyond that 'core' over that time period unlikely, although this need not preclude the possibility of other countries following the example of Mongolia, Cuba and Vietnam and becoming full members of the organisation.

Therefore the critical questions in this regard would appear to be (ii) and (iii) above. Soviet attitudes to these questions appear to envisage a two-tier approach both to the time-horizon over which integration will take place and to the countries that will be included — but are sufficiently open-ended to permit variations in the pattern. Thus during earlier (abortive) attempts to introduce joint planning, Soviet economists argued that the European CMEA members would enter the stage of Full Communism under the direction of the CMEA before the Asian countries. This was echoed by Khrushchev who spoke of 'the need to . . . go in for planning at the level of the CMEA and *afterwards* at the level of the socialist world system as a whole' (our italics).

Currently it is argued (we take an early example from Alampiev *et al.*, 1973, p. 84) that the first stage of integration will cover roughly the next three five-year plan periods (i.e. up to 1990) and appears to apply to the existing CMEA countries only, whilst 'the second stage will be marked by a higher degree of economic and organisational unification of the national economies of the *socialist* countries in an international economic complex. From plan co-ordination the countries will go on to the formulation in one form or another of a common plan, for advancing the world socialist division of labour'. The role of non-CMEA countries in this process is left deliberately open:

> The stages of integration may be considered not only in terms of the development of economic ties between the countries which have now announced their intention to participate in it. Some stages in the advance of integration may also be connected with the involvement of new countries into the integrating community. Because the integrating community is not a closed one, other countries accepting its tasks and purposes may later join in. *However, it is not possible at the present time to anticipate such*

*stages . . . with various modes of inclusion of individual countries
in the integrating community* (our italics).

How then will this process affect the trade patterns of those developing
countries that are (or may become) members of CMEA and can we
predict which countries will become members?

The three main proposals to establish joint planning activity in
CMEA (enacted since 1974) are:

(a)   The long-term target programmes — basically an attempt to
      attempt to integrate members' perspective plans on a sectoral
      basis (which *could* considerably affect investment
      programmes);

(b)   The Agreed Plan of Multilateral Integration measures for
      1976-80 (i.e. improved integration of five-year plans, including
      specific joint investment proposals and measures to raise the
      living standards of the developing CMEA countries, especially
      Mongolia);

(c)   The inclusion of special sections in members' annual, five-year
      and perspective plans to ensure the national allocation of
      resources for CMEA agreements and projects.

Note that there is nothing strictly supranational about these
arrangements: they are inter-state plans, arrived at merely under the
umbrella of the CMEA. But note that all precede the accession of
Vietnam. That country is a very big one — the second biggest in the
CMEA. She brings with her two satellites that do not enjoy formal
membership. The integration of Vietnam is clearly a long way away.
We even understand that she uses bilaterally settled prices, not CMEA
prices; and foreign-trade roubles, zlotys etc., not the transferable
rouble, in her clearing accounts. Nay more, this applies to Cuba too.[15]

Currently Mongolia and Cuba are participating in all sections of the
integration proposals and have included special sections in their
national plans (which Romania has refused to do). The nature of their
participation does appear to differ from that of Eastern European
countries in that:

(a)   their trade relations with CMEA countries are more highly
      concentrated with the USSR.

(b)   as predominantly suppliers of raw materials and food products
      they will be net recipients of CMEA investment resources in

the first instance (like USSR!).

The Cuba of ten years ago was very like the NCTW of today. Where she stands now they will one day stand, barring the unlikely event that they will choose the Albanian model (see Chapter 10). Accordingly we do not feel that at the moment there is any attempt to introduce the four countries directly into 'core CMEA status' (although they all currently have observer status at CMEA). The logic of economic systems, Marxian analysis (to which their leaders subscribe), historical and cultural factors and factor endowments all point in this direction. For the present the NCTW has adopted the far more open trade policy described below (Chapter 1, sect. 7, and Chapters 2-5). As the Soviet Union is attempting to integrate CMEA through joint-planning activity and is eschewing market-type solutions this would limit the joint planning of the NCTW to specific (isolated) projects.

Furthermore, a revealing indication of Soviet intentions in this area may be that the payment agreements concluded in 1976 with Angola and Mozambique stipulate that payments between the countries will be made in convertible currencies (not transferable roubles). This strongly implies that the prices used are 'world' prices, and of course the bilateral protocols settling annual delivery are not made within the CMEA framework. Though without doubt the prices are distorted in favour of the NCTW they are surely not CMEA prices — from which poor countries do not in any case specially benefit (apart from oil).[16] This would appear to be a good confirmation of our hypothesis that full integration is not on the *tapis* for some time.

In the long run, however, we would expect the countries that become members of CMEA to join the integration proposals, and their investment plans to be affected accordingly. To the extent that this would limit convertible currency earnings, this would result in a reduction in their trade with the West.

Finally the simplest point of all: supranational planning constitutes the loss of national sovereignty. The central authority does not merely establish a free market and forbid you to interfere with it, as in the EEC; he tells you exactly what to produce. This notion is not attractive to ex-colonial, indeed to any, states!

6. *'Levelling Up' and the CMEA.* So the prospect of supranational detailed planning is a deterrent. But what of the prospect of aid? It seems wrong to us, perhaps particularly if we are Marxists, to try to integrate the poor with the rich. But, on reflection, there is nothing

impossible in it, any more than there is in the fact that they engage in classical trade (the simple exchange of commodities) with each other. Nor is there anything undesirable from the economic as opposed to the political view-point. Trade should, of course, continue to be based on comparative cost – and even under Communism this is more or less the case. Provided that this is so, co-operative projects can be rationally based on the trade that will result from them; and rational, even fair, supranational plans can be agreed upon, embracing eventually the whole economy. Only migration must be strictly controlled, for that takes place on the basis of absolute advantage and will go from poor to rich in all skill-grades. Indeed all of these points apply, *mutatis mutandis*, to capitalism.

Such integration does not necessarily raise the productivity or real income of the poor country to that of the rich one, but rather tends, if the experience of EEC and CMEA is any guide, to leave each member growing at its separate particular rate. It is only the ultimate form of integration – annexation or federation – that tends to the strict equalisation of incomes. For the unified state must permit migration; and being a welfare state, it pays out unitary social services, sets unitary health and schooling standards, levies unitary progressive income-taxes and even encourages or enforces unitary wage-scales. Such is the Central Asian case, and that of the Old South in the United States. But it follows that no rich state in the modern world will be willing to annex a poor one! All such collocations inside one boundary are inheritances of the past, when the state was not responsible for economic welfare and so for equality.

Annexation, then, implies *levelling up*.[17] Unlike a world plan, this doctrine is a late-comer. It is of enormous practical importance for the NCTW. This process is in no way implied by the original CMEA founding document, the brief communiqué of January 1949 (Kaser, 1965, pp. 11-12) – which does not even mention socialism! In 1958 the very authoritative Stepanyan argued that European CMEA members would enter the stage of Full Communism, under the direction of the CMEA, before Asian Communist countries. This implies levelling up at least in Europe. But the geographical distinction was abandoned by Khrushchev in 1959 (*Pravda*, 28 January) when he said that all Communist countries would reach Full Communism at about the same time (cf. Yowev, 1960). This was a very bold statement indeed, when we consider that the split with China was as yet by no means *chose jugée*. To level China up would take more resources than the USSR disposes of.

Not surprisingly, then, levelling up is present only in very shadowy form in the Charter of 16 May 1960: Article I on 'Purposes and Principles' lists 'the raising of the level of industrialisation in the industrially less-developed countries' (see e.g. Kaser, 1965, pp. 182 sqq.). It is equally absent in Satyukov, *Pravda*, 27 October 1961.[18] But then comes, rather surprisingly, the CMEA's own super-official Resolution, 'The Basic Principles of the International Socialist Division of Labour'.[19] This is absolutely explicit, and at some length, that levelling up will take place; moreover it is at this very meeting that Mongolia was admitted. This country then has received a most definite promise that it will be levelled up. No doubt the rapid volte-face is due to the definitive character of the Sino-Soviet split at this date.

It was after this meeting in November 1962 that Khrushchev proposed supranational planning, thus antagonising the Romanians who saw in it the suppression of their sovereignty. That he raised this issue at the same time is, we have shown, no coincidence.

However, there is a good deal of confusion about levelling up among Soviet experts. It is sometimes presented as just a purely factual statement about all Communist countries. If we confine ourselves to 'middle-class' countries like the Balkan members of the CMEA, or the Mediterranean members, or members-designate, of the EEC, we find them catching up equally well. Indeed they need not, under capitalism, belong to EEC! This is because their technology is backward but they can afford to buy better stuff and learn to use it. By the early 1960s Bulgaria and Romania had more or less levelled themselves up (Askanas *et al.*, 1976), while Albania had ceased to attend CMEA meetings (December 1961), and Mongolia had not been 'very poor' for a long time.

But even without a specifically CMEA policy of levelling up, the rapid growth of the NCTW would be a particularly grave challenge in the matter of economic development. Hitherto Communism has embraced only one very poor country: China, a country so large that no mere volume of aid, or lucky shift in the terms of trade, can help it. Neither Mongolia nor Albania nor North Korea was as poor in this century. It is also worth remembering that Angola and even Mozambique and the PDRY are at the richer end of the Third World. But there is real destitution in Ethiopia, Afghanistan and, for that matter, Indo-China.

Will these very poor countries, then, outstrip India, Indonesia, Bangladesh, even China? Capitalism has quite a good record since World War II in developing the richest poor countries, such as Taiwan, South

Korea, Hong Kong and Singapore used to be. These have actually outstripped Albania and North Korea, and possibly also Mongolia – the Communist countries at their level. They import the technology that suits them and educate their work force up to the required standard. They do not differ in the vital respects of technology importation from such more typically middle-rank nations as Mexico, Portugal or Greece (above). But at the bottom end of world poverty we are less sure; the record of capitalism and state capitalism is quite bad. We even learn that Tanzania has done slightly better than Kenya.

In the simplest terms, Marxism-Leninism is a good mobilising ideology and social system. Where the mobilising of the people is the main thing, and great personal competence or high technology a secondary matter, it may turn out to be the best system. This suggestion presupposes one thing: the government makes no gross strategic error, such as encouraging the people to riot instead of working (China 1966-76) or running down an immensely profitable and very large export industry (Cuban sugar under Guevara). Note that such extreme fanaticism and unwisdom have never manifested themselves in a CMEA member. USSR of course behaved very foolishly long ago in the experimental years 1918-33; but it is precisely her accumulated wisdom that now prevents aberrations in the CMEA.

But levelling up implies vast quantities of aid, even though straight capital transfers should for ideological reasons be small (see sect. 7). So it is not popular among existing members. Thus in July 1972 Cuba joined. Ptichkin's article on this stresses the levelling-up-as-policy commitment to Mongolia and surely extends it to Cuba, though not *totidem verbis*. His article on Vietnam's accession in May 1978 makes only one feeble mention of levelling up.

Historically Mongolia and Cuba are very different. Mongolia is USSR's oldest satellite: she only collectivised her nomad agriculture in 1955-9, but long before had got into step with history by going through the Great Purge in 1937-8, at the same time as USSR (as indeed did Catalonia; this again shows the primacy of politics over economics). With a population of only 1.4 million, and very many Soviet advisers, she is best described as a very poor autonomous *oblast'* in Siberia. She was admitted to CMEA in June 1962, when the restriction to Europe was erased from the statutes. This was also the height of Khrushchev's campaign for supranational planning; he included Mongolia in the countries that should reach Full Communism simultaneously with USSR (see above). After all, so few people could be lifted to the Soviet level without great expense. A small but important consideration, moreover, was surely to maximise unrest in Inner Mongolia. The 1.9 million Mongols in this mainly Chinese province are indeed two to three times as rich as the Han people in general,[20] but this leaves them very far below Outer Mongolia. At the moment this does not matter, since Beijing (? and Moscow) forbid contact. But the gap must in the end become a very awkward matter indeed for Beijing.

In 1962 Cuba still harboured Che Guevara, with his unorthodox ideas about centralisation, bonuses and money. The country was not yet trusted as properly Communist — indeed it did not have a duly constituted Party. Cuba, then, was a member of many subordinate agencies of CMEA for some time before she formally joined the Council itself, in 1972. By this time Brezhnev was in power and Full Communism was off the menu. Consequently Cuba's admission constituted no promise to raise her real income rapidly to East European levels. But it was a guarantee of economic aid and — indirectly but very certainly — military security for ever. Note in particular the aid-for-African-adventure deal which seems to have followed: as Soviet aid deliveries rose in 1975, Cuban troops played a role in Africa that would have been very dangerous for Soviet troops.

For the Vietnamese accession (June 1978) see Chapter 13. An important reason for the admission of both these countries to CMEA is clearly the wish of the USSR to impose some of their aid burden on the other members, nearly all of which enjoy higher consumption levels than herself (Askanas *et al.*, 1976). Rumours that, for instance, Czechoslovakia opposed the entry of Vietnam are extremely plausible, though they cannot be confirmed.

The cases of Cuba and Vietnam indicate that a rough uniformity of economic practice may be a condition of entry.[21] And yet more than uniformity is surely required: there must be an assurance of *internal* irreversibility. For like too many other white men Russians do not take Africans seriously, and do not believe in their commitment to this or that ideology. Admission to CMEA, so long delayed in the Cuban case, is an accolade. It will be noted that, relying on the interventions of Soviet arms, East German police, etc., the authors are more convinced of the irreversibility of Communism in the NCTW than, evidently, is the Soviet government. But then we are only academics and bear no state responsibility!

We conclude that if CMEA membership is no longer a guarantee of total levelling up, it still promises a good deal of aid. Table 1.2 shows with extreme approximation what a Communist country to-day may hope to win and lose by ceasing to be even formally non-aligned.

Broadly speaking, supranational planning is bad and fraternal aid is good. So 'Group 2' status remains a possibility, and we discuss it under Albania and North Korea (Chapters 10 and 11).

7. Diplomacy (e.g. the vote on Afghanistan) is a better indicator than the geographical distribution of foreign trade. A major reason for the NCTW's trade policy is that USSR and Eastern Europe simply cannot supply all that the group wants to buy, or use all it wants to sell. The Third World generally does not like Communist machinery, because it is not very good. Its members, even in this group, are particularly oriented to the markets of their ex-colonial masters, by language, custom, personal knowledge and industrial standardisation. They do not and are hardly meant to give preference to CMEA goods; and must be expected to choose what is in their own opinion their best interest, even against Soviet advice. However, that advice has become since the early 1960s fairly clear: the Soviet Africanists and Orientalists are of opinion that the NCTW should remain attached to the capitalist world market (Jeffreys 1974, Clarkson 1978).

And here again we need feel no surprise. If Poland may borrow as much as she can from Chase Manhattan, and keep an uncollectivised peasantry; if Hungary may run a half-market economy in her socialist sector, and buy 37 per cent of all imports and 34 per cent of machinery imports from capitalist countries and set up co-operation agreements for multinationals on Hungarian soil; if Cuba may draw 33 per cent of all her imports from the advanced capitalist countries except USA (or three times more than from CMEA except USSR); then why is Mozambique out of line in readmitting Portuguese workers?[22]

In short, NCTW countries have not necessarily more political independence than CMEA members because of the apparent independence of their economic policies. Actually CMEA members have great independence here too. The NCTW is simply doing what all very poor left-wing countries objectively must do, and there is plenty of Communist precedent for it. Their political independence must be judged separately, by their political actions at home and abroad. If to say this is bad Marxism, so be it — the Communist 'superstructure' was always independent of its 'base'. Moreover, gross differences in the ultimate economic order are surely less likely than political defections to Group 2 above, i.e. refusal to join CMEA but retention of a Soviet-type economy and polity.

8. Meanwhile the civilian trade patterns of the NCTW have not altered

much since they went Communist. This is very different from the early experience of Eastern Europe, when, in the first flush of the Cold War and the near-total US embargo, Stalin diverted 80 per cent of his satellites' trade inward. Nor is the striking difference irrational. For, then as now, the Third World of whatever political colour has little economic incentive to trade with USSR, and in the period of détente, capitalism is quite willing to finance or at least trade with the NCTW. Indeed, the sort of goods that such countries will want is certain to be compatible with the Western embargo (Cocom) on strategic exports to Communist states.

It follows that an essential part of Soviet policy towards the Communist Third World is the *divorce of aid from trade*. The difficulty with trade is that the Soviet Union, and indeed CMEA, can export almost nothing that advanced capitalist countries cannot export better. This is because Communist agriculture is, of its nature, very unproductive and Communist R and D is little better. So agricultural exports are simply unavailable, and industrial exports, though certainly available, are inferior. Moreover, it is remote from Soviet or CMEA tradition to import tropical products, the traditional luxury food exports of the Third World; and the indirect tax on such commodities is spectacularly high, even in comparison with that on other consumer goods. As to the Third World's new and competing exports of consumer-good manufactures, these are kept out by the administrative devices typical of the Soviet-type economy, which are surprisingly similar to the quotas whereby advanced capitalist countries do the same thing.

No wonder then, that Third-World-CMEA trade lags. It should be possible to concentrate such opportunities for expansion as the Soviet-type system allows on Cuba and Vietnam, and after them on the CTNW; but although this has to some extent happened, still the imports from these latter countries have not risen a great deal (Table 1.1). But aid is much easier to concentrate. Financial capital to lend abroad (i.e. savings surplus to domestic requirements) is, to the great credit of the Soviet system, almost as difficult to find as exports, domestic requirements being kept high by the large planned volume of investment. However, the concentration of the small sum available on a few countries does raise its importance a great deal.[23] More than 83 per cent of aid committed by Communist countries to the Third World in 1954-72 was concentrated on fifteen countries.

Of course, there must be *some* exportable commodity to back up financial aid, unless the latter is to be convertible. That commodity is,

Table 1.1: Soviet Visible Imports from the NCTW etc. (m foreign-trade roubles)

	1970	1973	1975	1976	1977	1978	1979
Afghanistan[d]	30.9	34.4	64.3	66.8	76.5	75.7[a]	139.7
Angola[e]	–	–	–[a]	14.4	10.4	9.6	11.8
Ethiopia	0.8	2.2	2.1	0.7	1.5	4.3[a]	18.6
Mozambique	–	–	–[a]	–	–	0.8	0.9
PDR Yemen	0.2	0.1	0.1	–	2.0[a]	0.5	2.6
Benin	–	2.1[c]	0.5	–	–	–	1.5
Congo	0.7	2.6	2.4	2.0	2.9	2.9	2.9
Madagascar	–	0.3	1.1	3.3	11.8	1.4	1.2
Somalia	0.4	1.1	4.3[a]	4.7	2.9[b]	–	–
Total	33.0	42.9	74.7	91.9	108.0	95.2	179.2
As a % of all Soviet imports	0.3	0.2	0.3	0.3	0.3	0.2	0.4

Source: *VT*, various years.

a. year of Communist take-over.
b. year of Communist expulsion.
c. Marxism-Leninism was spontaneously declared in 1974.
d. Imports are composed of wool, cotton and food products.
e. Imports are composed entirely of natural coffee..

in the Soviet and CMEA case, machinery (for after all bad machinery is better than none) and arms. We have little accurate idea of the volume of arms deliveries by any country in the world, still less of the method of payment; there is always some secrecy. But our preliminary estimates indicate that hard-currency earnings from such sources are not insignificant for the USSR, follow political opportunities rather than commercial relations, and need not depend on the recipient's export potential if he is a hard-line ally or if sympathetic third states with large hard-currency balances can be called upon to support him.

In this way the ordinary rule, that aid follows trade, high volumes of the one going with the other, is broken. We give in Table 1.1 Soviet imports alone, since Soviet exports, including, as they do, arms deliveries, are really unknown.

Afghanistan is a traditional and obvious trade partner, itself however negligible in Soviet terms. The others add up to three ten-thousandths of Soviet imports! They show, at this minimal level, quite satisfactory, political ups and downs. No notice, for instance, is expectedly taken of Kérékou's 'unilateral' declaration of Marxisim-Leninism in Benin (see Chapter 6). Few details are available for imports from the NCTW in East European sources, which presumably indicates negligible volumes. Poland and Romania commenced importing from Angola in 1976; Polish imports reached $8 million in 1976 and $16 million in 1977, Romanian imports were $1 million in 1976 and fell back to zero in 1977.

9. But the *geographical distribution of aid provenance* is an excellent indication of political allegiance. Table 1.2 sufficiently bears this out, but it is very inaccurate and many warnings should be made.

For capitalist countries the source is OECD 1978 and 1980. The figure is for 'Total Net Receipts', which includes: official loans; official grants; private long-term investment of all sorts; official transactions not having the character of aid. All these figures are net. Our reasons for including capitalist commercial loans are, first, that many Communist loans (especially in 1964-74) have commercial motives and, secondly, that the important question for poor countries is the total net flow from each competing system.

For Communist countries the source is the FCO 1980. Aid to Vietnam and Cuba is given both net and gross in the source (Table 1.4). It is overwhelmingly the greater part of all Communist aid. That to Cuba is mainly subsidies to Cuban commodities sugar and nickel, i.e. grants; and the subsidy that the USSR makes to all her CMEA partners by not raising her oil price to the OPEC level. Aid to other countries is only given gross in the source (Table 8a), and we have frankly guessed the amount of debt amortisation[24] to deduct. The basic figure of 50 per cent is very low when we consider that the percentage of net to gross disbursements for all those countries together ranges between 40 and 83 per cent (FCO, 1981, Table 4).

Note the *concentration* of Soviet aid to the Third World upon the NCTW. It is this concentration, not the quite small volume, that indicates allegiance. The other lesson of Table 1.2 is quite obvious; if you are a very left-wing country you must try to join the CMEA, since you will get many times more aid, even from the world as a whole, than before. But just for this reason the CMEA will be very hesitant (see section 6 above, and under 'Mozambique'). It must surely prefer to continue the present situation, in which OECD and OPEC finance the NCTW, and Communist aid, though growing rapidly, is very small.

Note furthermore that the aid is *meant* to be small. Countries get brotherly, not fatherly, assistance from each other. They are supposed to use it to pull themselves up by their own bootstraps, with aid, to change the metaphor, priming the pump only. The USSR, after all, had only her own bootstraps, and now she is rich she has not forgotten. Ideally aid is technical and military, not financial:

> The redistribution of national income among socialist states cannot be a leading form of their economic co-operation and cannot play a leading role in eliminating the essential differences in levels of economic development in individual states. Although credit facilities accelerate the economic growth of the economically less developed countries it diminishes the amount of capital investment in creditor countries.
>
> Mikulski, 1975, p. 39

They must not forget that the very name of the CMEA enshrines the concept of *mutual* aid. We are a far cry here from Mrs Thatcher's 'hand-outs' – a derogatory term. Of course, Communist aid is in fact as one-way as anyone else's, and not mutual at all. When its recipients harp on this word they are being hypocritical.[25] But words matter all the same, and the mutuality slogan shapes the character of the aid.

We summarise all this in Table 1.3. The abrupt Soviet switch to a total concentration on Communist countries at the moment of the Portuguese Revolution and the penetration of the Horn comes almost too pat to be convincing! It is also in part due to a very big shift out of

Table 1.2: Net Public Aid and Private Capital Disbursements ($USm)

		OECD bilateral	OPEC bilateral	Non-Communist multilateral	USSR	Rest of CMEA
Afghanistan	1973	31.9	–	14.2	?8[a]	–
	74	17.9	28.6	14.7	?11[a]	2[d]
	75	28.1	21.6	21.2	?13[a]	1[d]
	76	32.7	14.7	29.1	?10[a]	2.5[d]
	77	27.4	21.5	51.5	?12[a]	?2.2[b]
	78	32.7	18.4	44.4	?14[a]	?1.7[a]
(from USA)	79	68.2 (32.0)	8.3	52.5		
Angola	1973	22.0	–	–	–	–
	74	37.0	–	0.1	–	–
	75	36.5	–	0.8	–	–
(from Sweden)	76	40.6 (39.7)	–	7.0	1.5[d]	–
	77	–14.1	–	39.7	2.5[d]	–
	78	23.6	–	18.2	3.5[d]	–
(Italy, Sweden)	79	96.8 (43.7, 39.6)	–	17.7	–	–
Mozambique	1973	13.8	–	–	–	–
	74	9.8	–	0.1	–	–
	75	–8.4	–	9.0	–	–
(from FRG)	76	70.4 (59.0)	1.1	35.6	0.5[d]	–
	77	61.1	0.1	14.3	1.5[d]	–
	78	80.8	–	29.8	1.8[d]	–
	79	118.7	10.0	31.6	–	–
Ethiopia	1973	47.8	–	21.3	–	?0.5[a]
	74	69.4	1.3	39.1	4.0[d]	?1.0[a]
	75	67.4	1.2	62.8	1.0[d]	?0.25[a]
	76	71.2	–	65.9	1.5[d]	?–0.2[e]

Table 1.2: Continued

		OECD bilateral	OPEC bilateral	Non-Communist multilateral	USSR	Rest of CMEA
Ethiopia	77	54.2	—	51.4	2.5[d]	?−0.2[e]
	78	51.0	—	79.6	?2.5[b]	?0.6[b]
(from FRG)	79	121.0 (57.6)	—	99.8		
PDRY	1973	3.0	3.0	4.8	?1.6[a]	?0.25[a]
	74	7.4	23.5	17.3	?1.8[a]	?0.35[a]
	75	12.8	49.1	14.3	?1.5[a]	?0.35[a]
	76	8.6	135.1	20.9	?4.4[b]	?0.2[a]
	77	6.3	76.0	29.7	?6.0[b]	?1.1[c]
	78	15.7	40.2	48.0	?5.9[b]	?1.6[c]
(from Italy)	79	33.7 (30.8)	10.4	43.9		
Benin	1973	14.9 (9.3)	—	13.1		—
(French	74	16.8 (7.1)	5.8	15.0		—
sub-total	75	34.5 (21.9)	—	25.4		—
in brackets)	76	25.5 (8.6)	1.0	24.6		—
	77	30.5 (13.6)	—	25.5		—
	78	36.3 (19.7)	—	34.3		—
	79	57.8 (27.8)	2.1	36.9		—
Congo	1973	168.4 (140.6)	—	10.0	—	0.4[d]
(F.s.t.i.b.)	74	32.1 (22.5)	—	17.6	?0.4[b]	0.9[d]
	75	18.9 (21.4)	—	18.7	?0.3[a]	0.9[c]
	76	125.6 (99.5)	4.2	27.6	?0.2[a]	?0.3[c]
	77	39.1 (31.0)	3.3	15.9	?−0.1[e]	?0.3[b]
	78	53.1 (70.8)	11.1	42.6	?−0.1[e]	?0.1[a]
	79	34.3 (37.5)	4.0	24.8	?0.0[d,e]	?0.2[a]
Madagascar	1973	29.8 (24.3)	—	25.1	—	—
(F.s.t.i.b.)	74	36.0 (17.4)	7.3	31.9	—	—

Table 1.2: Continued

		OECD bilateral	OPEC bilateral	Non-Communist multilateral	USSR	Rest of CMEA
Madagascar	75	30.6 (19.2)	–	63.4	–	–
	76	25.6 (20.0)	–	36.1	0.1d	–
	77	17.7 (20.1)	1.0	35.3	0.4d	–
	78	60.1 (17.3)	4.0	54.4	0.6d	–
(France, Italy)	79	165.5 (47.4, 76.9)	13.8	43.0	?1.3b	–
Cuba	1973	–10.9	–	2.6	359	66
	74	31.9	–	4.7	70	–161
	75	157.9	–	6.7	1340	54
(from Belgium)	76	347.4 (140.6)	–	9.9	1848	143
	77	63.0	–	16.4	2380	131
(from Japan)	78	179.5 (159.8)	–	31.3	3030	167
	79	17.1	10.0	14.9		
Vietnam	1973	465.1	–	2.4	420	?100
	74	705.2	–	4.5	?450	?110
	75	284.8	40.0	30.6	?450	?120
(from Sweden)	76	161.4 (87.1)	6.1	18.6	?500	?142
	77	257.6 (113.0)	–	47.6	?500	?142
	78	297.3 (88.2)	–	161.2	?500	?142
	79	311.8 (69.7)	–	106.7		
N. Korea	1973	–	–	–	?145	–
	74	–	–	–	?145	–
	75	–	–	–	60	–
	76	–	–	–	4	–
	77	–	–	–	–	–
	78	–				
	79	–				

Table 1.2: Continued

	OECD bilateral	OPEC bilateral	Non-Communist multilateral	USSR	Rest of CMEA
Somalia 1973	15.0	5.5	16.7	?1.0[a]	?0.5[d]
74	–4.4	77.9	32.4	?6.0[c]	?0.2[d]
75	33.5	87.9	58.4	?7.5[c]	?0.4[d]
76	26.3	40.1	51.6	?9.6[c]	?0.1[b]
77					
(from Italy)	129.0 (109.3)	180.6	49.8	?2.8[a]	?–0.1[e]
78	61.5	66.8	49.5	?–5.0[e]	?–0.1[e]
79	126.2	75.9	62.6		

a. Communist disbursements are given gross in our source. In these cases 50% has been deducted for debt service since there has been a long and even flow of previous aid.
b. See (a), but 30% only has been deducted because of a recent increase.
c. See (a), but 20% because the recent increase was very big.
d. New flow; gross taken as net.
e. Little or no gross aid. Amortisation guessed.
f. Including non-Communist South Vietnam.

India, gross disbursements to which ran as follows ($m.): 1971, 42; 1972, 49; 1973, 160; 1974, 288; 1975, 30.

East European behaviour is very different. Half as populous as the USSR, and rather richer in terms of consumption, the East European CMEA bears one-sixth of the foreign aid burden, and about one-sixth of the defence burden too. It is also much more generous to the non-Communist world.

Tables 1.2/3 treat CMEA aid to Cuba differently from all other aid in the whole table: the extremely large subsidies on CMEA sugar purchases, and in the Soviet case also on nickel purchases and oil sales, are explicitly included. When the world price of oil rises (as at the end of 1973) Soviet subsidies rise; when the world price of sugar rises (1974) CMEA subsidies fall, even below zero. The world price of oil is a stable and meaningful quantity, that of sugar is very volatile since a quarter of international trade in sugar is tied up in long-term contracts. We feel nevertheless that it gives quite an unfair picture to leave out these immense sums. There appear to be no serious estimates of the grant element in other preferential trade, whether Communist or capitalist, and whether the prices or the quantities embody the preference. The conceptual difficulties are enormous, let alone those of fact-gathering.

10. A country's commercial policy is above all illustrated by the *international economic bodies* to which it belongs. Table 1.4 shows only serious grant or loan-making bodies, and covers a wide span of left-wing countries to make comparison possible. We have recognised as regional bodies which are 'serious' in the sense meant only the Asian Development Bank and the Lomé Convention. There are therefore no 'serious' European bodies, except of course the EEC and the CMEA itself. UN regional bodies clearly do not qualify.

When Communism began to spread from the USSR the new Communist countries, rich or poor, observed the Stalinist principle of belonging only to CMEA. China and North Korea have avoided even that. Yugoslavia and Albania left CMEA, the one to become part of the comity of nations, the other to cut herself off more and more. Within CMEA, Czechoslovakia, Poland and Cuba even abandoned the World Bank and the IMF. But since about 1970 new joiners have carefully maintained their outside links — as well they may, since beggars cannot be choosers. Also Romania has struck out on her own.

11.   The NCTW differs greatly from the 'core' CMEA as regards *inter-*

national migration. Romania, Poland, Cuba and Vietnam have an intermediate policy.

Communist migration is an offbeat subject, seldom systematically tackled.[26] The 'core' has since 1932 taken a strongly ideological and isolationist, i.e. Stalinist, position. People simply do not wish to leave the workers' paradise, so they must not be allowed to. Even the bourgeoisie has been converted, nay, easily converted; there are no irreconcilables of whom we are better rid. Or at least, should any one appear to be like that, further re-education (preferably in a *corrective* labour camp) will show him the error of his ways. Then too, would-be emigrants carry out knowledge that our enemies use to their profit. As to would-be immigrants, they are probably spies.[27]

Since the so-called détente began, the 'core' has relaxed these rules, especially in favour of Jews and Germans, who can claim nationality in a foreign, non-Communist, state. Romania has trafficked in ransom, and even allowed Jews out free, for a longer time. But Cuba and Vietnam have let people out on a grand scale, quite openly on security grounds, and with the full approval, albeit very grudgingly implemented at lower levels, of state and Party. Unlike the rather spotty and unofficial Romanian and Polish emigrations, we cannot say there were here any humanitarian grounds. On the emigrants' side, however, economic motives have been in all four cases at least as strong as political. Inter-Communist migration is yet another subject, which concerns us less. Mongolia used enormously many Chinese *Gastarbeiter* until the Sino-Soviet split, and there are now fair numbers of Polish and Bulgarian *Gastarbeiter* in other CMEA countries.

In contrast the NCTW is awash with immigrants and emigrants. This is simply because it is African or Arab: frontiers mean less in those parts of the world. Arabs are supposed to be one nation, African tribes are split by arbitrary imperialist boundaries. In consequence both economic and political migration is frequent and massive. In Southern Africa there is an added complication: emigration is towards the hated racialist power that sits at the bottom of the continent — and pays better wages.

The numbers are so large that the NCTW has taken the decision to do little about them. Illiterate nomads, peasants and workers flood out and even in, as if there were no Marxist-Leninist states. It would be very difficult to stop them, and they are not a great security risk. But it is certain that serious planning cannot begin until the frontiers are closed.

The *emigrant's remittance* is an enormously important element in many a poor country's balance of payments, for instance, in Yugoslavia, Algeria, Turkey. Communist countries are no exception if

Table 1.3: Geographical Distribution of Net Aid 1973-9 ($m)

	1973	1974	1975	1976	1977	1978	1979
USSR net disbursements[e]	1,217	1,051	1,973	2,457	2,959	3,687	
of which to Cuba	359	70	1,340	1,848	2,380	3,030	
Vietnam	420	450	450	500	500	500	
Total non-CMEA countries	438	531	183	109	79	157	
of which to Communist	145	151	108	60	32	110	
(N. Korea)	145	145	60	4	—	—	
(Cambodia)	—	—	—	—	—	50	
(Laos)	—	—	40	40	20	30	
(NCTW)	—	6[a]	8[a]	16[b]	12[c]	30[d]	
Non-Communist	293	380	25	-1	-3	-3	
East European net disbursements[e]	193	-15	251	366	343	375	
of which to Cuba	66	-161	54	143	131	167	
Vietnam	100	110	120	142	142	142	
Total non-CMEA countries	27	36	77	81	70	66	
of which to Communist	—	—	—	20	30	44	
(N. Korea)	—	—	—	—	—	—	
(Cambodia)	—	—	—	—	—	—	
(Laos)	—	—	—	20	30	40	
(NCTW)	—	—	—	—	—	4[d]	
Non-Communist	27	36	77	61	40	22	
DAC[f,g] total net disbursements	21,603	28,370	38,824	38,001	41,842[h]	60,031[h]	63,458[h]
of which to Cuba	-8	37	165	371	79	211	32
Vietnam	468	710	355	186	305	454	418

Table 1.3: Continued

	1973	1974	1975	1976	1977	1978	1979
OPEC[g] total net disbursements	1,352	4,074	6,659	6,761	12,660[h]	13,394[h]	14,384[h]
of which to Vietnam	–	–	40	6	–	5	1
Cuba	–	–	–	–	–	–	10

a. Somalia.
b. Somalia, Angola, Mozambique.
c. Ethiopia, Angola, Mozambique.
d. (c) plus Afghanistan, PDR Yemen.
e. All from FCO 1980, Table 7, as amended by their later exclusion of $50m. to India from USSR, 1974-8; and by my transfer of the NCTW (Table II) to the Communist side.
f. i.e. the OECD countries.
g. Includes private investment. OPEC-financed agencies have been added to OPEC, and all other multilateral agencies, *faute de mieux*, to DAC. Source: OECD 1978, p. 266; OECD 1980, pp. 6-9.
h. The totals in 1977-9 are for DAC bilateral and OPEC-plus-all-multilateral respectively.

Table 1.4: Membership of International Organisations (dates of joining unless otherwise stated)

	CMEA	World Bank[c,i]	IMF	Regional
Angola	never	never	never	never Lomé[l]
Mozambique	never	never	never	never Lomé[l]
Ethiopia	never	always[d]	always[d]	always Lomé[l]
PDR Yemen	never	71/72	1 Jan. 71	always Lomé[l]
Afghanistan	never	always[d]	always[d]	ADB Dec. 66[j]
Somalia	never	always[d]	always[d]	always Lomé[l]
Benin	never	always[d]	always[d]	always Lomé[l]
Congo	never	always[d]	always[d]	always Lomé[l]
Madagascar	never	always[d]	always[d]	always Lomé[l]
Mongolia	June 62[i]	never	never	never ADB[j]
Albania	? Feb. 47–Dec. 61	never	never	—
Vietnam	June 78	77/8[a,i]	c. 1 Aug. 76[a]	ADB Feb. 77[j]
S. Vietnam	never	up to 74/5 incl.	up to Aug. 75 incl.[f]	ADB Dec. 66[j]
Laos	never	always[d]	always[d]	ADB Dec. 66[j]
Cambodia	never	1970/71[i]	c. Apr. 70	ADB Dec. 66[j]
N. Korea	never	never	never	never ADB[j]
Cuba	July 72[h]	up to c. 1 Nov. 60[c]	up to c. 1 June 63[g]	—
Romania	Jan. 47	72/3[b,i]	15 Dec. 72	—
Poland	Jan. 47	up to Feb/Mar 50	up to c. 1 Mar. 50	—
Czechoslovakia	Jan. 47	up to 1 Jan. 54[c]	up to 1 Jan. 55	—
Hungary, Bulgaria	Jan. 47	never	never	—

Table 1.4: Continued

	CMEA	World Bank[c,i]	IMF	Regional
Yugoslavia	Feb. 47–July 48[k]	? always[d]	? always[d]	never EEC
China	never	never	never	never ADB[j]

a. Probably acceded on a successor-state basis, in view of South Vietnamese membership (UN Mission, p. 55); but note intermissions.
b. Not IDA.
c. Earlier years from *IFS* monthly.
d. Before 1969/70.
e. From *IFS*.
f. As printed in *IFS*. Taken literally, this means that the new 'independent' Communist government of S. Vietnam was a member for one year.
g. First moment of vacation of directorate.
h. Long previous membership of subordinate agencies.
i. Joined in fiscal year 1 July-30 June: from annual report.
j. Foundation Day was 19 Dec. Data on ADB from Huang, 1975.
k. But an application or invitation to rejoin was mooted in 1961-2 (Kaser, 1967, p. 100), and a formal association has been in force since 1965.
l. The Lomé convention is treated as essentially African. Of Portuguese ex-colonies, only Guinea-Bissau belongs. The two conventions are dated February 1975 and October 1979 (Euroforum, Brussels, 16/1979). The countries in this note also all belong to the African Development Bank except, apparently, Angola.

they allow emigration or can profit from a previous emigration, as in Poland. In the NCTW the fact of remittances is an incentive to *laissez-faire*. Notably Mozambique benefits enormously from its semi-skilled workers in South Africa, and the PDRY from its 'white-collar' workers in many other Arab lands.

Will these emigrants one day be so 'ideologically firm' that they pose a threat in the country of reception? It is very early to say. In Europe and North America the opposite is the case: Communism is intellectually inferior to capitalism since it denies freedom; and economically inferior mainly on historical grounds. Apart from individual spies the emigrants are good, even super-good, citizens. But the opposite may eventually hold in the Third World, where freedom is not a much sought-after commodity and Communist development policies may prove superior. It is still difficult, however, to imagine the NCTW continuing to accept immigration.

Another point must detain us before we leave migration. When judging the performance of revolutionary anti-colonial governments, we should not forget that the expulsion of the colonialists reduces income more than population. Unless the expelled people had much higher marginal products than incomes after tax, it remains entirely doubtful whether, once the initial chaos is over, the native population suffered any reduction in income at all; yet simultaneously any journalist can see deserted hotels and weeds in suburban gardens.

Thus the recent performance of the Mozambican (and *mutatis mutandis* the Angolan) economy can be represented very schematically indeed by these numbers:

	Y_1	P_1	Y_1/P_1	Y_3	P_3	Y_3/P_3	Y_6	P_6	Y_6/P_6
rich	20	$5(=1_a+4_c)$	4	2	1_a	2	12	$4(=2_a+2_c)$	3
poor	80	95	0.84	72	95	0.76	79	94	0.84
total	100	100	1.00	74	96	0.77	91	98	0.93
natives only	84	96	0.875	74	96	0.77	85	96	0.885

where Y is the total income of a nation or class and P its population, a = *assimilado*, c = colonialist.

The revolution is in 'year two', and in the chaos of 'year three' the elite consists of the very small number of *assimilados*: the original number minus those dispossessed, plus an about equal replacement of revolutionary managers. Their marginal product is halved; and the poor's productivity also drops 10 per cent, mainly because outside peasant agriculture it depended on good colonial management. In fact, had the poor remained in the colonial enterprises their productivity would have fallen substantially, since they were complementary with the rich whites. But actually they went back to subsistence farming. By 'year six' the colonialists have trickled back, a great number of natives have been promoted, and productivity has been restored: wholly in the case of the poor, partly in the case of the rich. *The natives are actually more productive than before*. But the hotels and suburbs are still crumbling, since $12 < 20$, and incomes are more equally distributed between the two classes despite the partial restoration of the productivity difference. In the case of Mozambique such a result may already obtain. In strife-torn Angola we must still wait for it. Angola is still in 'year three': the poor have suffered, but much less than the rich.

Technical Note

The foreign-trade participation ratio is the ratio (exports of goods and services) ÷ (GDP or GNP), taking both items in domestic currency, and both kinds of export gross of the corresponding import. It is supposed to measure a country's degree of participation in the international division of labour. This indeed it does by definition, except when indirect taxes and subsidies weigh differentially upon exports and other goods and services. In this case it is necessary to specify that both numerator and denominator be at factor cost. The main problem here is set by the so-called *Preisausgleich* in a developed Soviet-type economy. The *Preisausgleich* is a highly complicated system of *ad hoc* subsidies and taxes on foreign trade. Happily of all the countries here discussed it only affects Mongolia and North Korea, and the reader may be referred to other sources, for instance, Wiles 1968 and 1979.

The ratio pays no attention to the price- or income-elasticities of demand for imports or of supply of exports. It measures participation not dependence. Nevertheless it is clear that dependence tends to rise with participation.

It is important not to use US prices in the valuation of the denominator. Above all, non-traded services are a very large part of non-traded production, especially in poor countries, which do not export many services but may still export a large proportion of their goods. Productivity in such market services as restaurant meals and hair-cuts does not vary much internationally, so their prices are very low in poor countries. This applies *a fortiori* to the valuation of at-cost services, such as soldiers' and civil servants' labour. All this very greatly exaggerates GDP and so gives absurdly low participation ratios (Wiles, 1979).

The same exaggeration inspired the search of Kravis *et al.* (1978) for a *purchasing power parity* independent of the rate of exchange. The rate of course converts exported goods and services very adequately from their domestic value to their value in foreign currency. But for just the above reason non-traded goods and services must not be converted by the rate but only by the parity. This is why we use only the parities, which, it will be observed, yield results quite inconsistent with the multiplication of, say, GDP by the rate of exchange. The purchasing power parity is an index number: Kravis *et al.* have tried to approximate Fisher's 'Ideal' formula.

Notes

1. To give the rock-bottom minimum list of 'non-volunteers', excluding such nations as Lithuania and Georgia; annexed and so forgotten. Afghanistan clearly belongs now to this latter list. We have not studied Afghan economic policy as it is far too unsettled.

2. But we are happy to report that we had settled on this list (except Grenada) earlier! We consider this fact to be more than a minor research triumph; rather a vindication of our basic concept.

3. And the project director points out that at the time he was most careful to avoid this error! Cf. Wiles, 1967.

4. As they explain in their letter to us of 20 November 1980.

5. Negatives are hard to prove. We can speak thus confidently on the oral assurance of Professor Hans Bräke of the BOIS, Cologne.

6. In particular, it will put up more candidates than there are seats in state elections, thus allowing voters to feel democratic by turning candidates down. A possible exception are the Baath parties of Syria and Iraq. These are indeed elitist, monopolistic, non-Marxist parties (i.e. Leninist but not Marxist!). So of course were the Fascist parties in their heyday.

7. For more on Islam in or around the NCTW see the chapters on Somalia and Benin.

8. The only known case of a Communist country reverting to some other social form is Iranian Azerbaijan in May 1946. But this territory was part of Iran, an independent country that had not been conquered by USSR and had a cut-and-dried treaty-claim to her territorial integrity. Besides, Iran was clearly backed in her claim by President Truman, at that time the monopolist of the atomic bomb (Feis, 1970, p. 82). A still more doubtful example might be the Soviet zone occupation of Austria (liberated in 1955).

9. On this very vague concept cf. Legum, 1978.

10. On Nkrumah's failure to establish his version of Afro-Marxism even in theory cf. Wiles, 1967.

11. These are the small native capitalists who conduct local business for the white multinationals, on a substantial commission. Although of Marxist invention the phrase is a very precise description of a distinct but otherwise unnamed result of imperialism (including Soviet imperialism!).

12. Class war was practised by Amin in Afghanistan (the liquidation of 'feudalism'). It is absolutely safe to predict that Karmal will, as Tarakki intended to, engage in class war when the coast is clear. In the PDRY the YSP, as a 'vanguard' party, declares that class war is a fundamental part of its political concept and its ideology. Nevertheless, tactically, under present circumstances – when the formation of the working class is only beginning – the YSP stresses the necessity of a strong alliance between the working class, the peasants, the intelligentsia and the petite bourgeoisie.

13. For the origins of this difference cf. Wiles and Smith, 1978.

14. This information has been drawn orally from East European contacts, though it is not exactly secret. Note that each of the three elements thus combined could have been separated: e.g. non-protocol oil could be sold at world prices but for transferable roubles, etc.

15. Information from private East European sources. These sources are unable to guarantee its veracity.

16. Orally communicated by sundry East European sources.

17. The Russian is usually something like 'sblizhenie i uravnivanie ekonomicheskogo razvitia'.

18. And in a less authoritative place: Titarenko in *Politicheskoye Samoobrazovanie*, March 1962.

19. E.g. in *Neues Deutschland*, 17 June 1962.

20. Observations of Peter Wiles, Sept. 1979 (including Chinese official statements at various levels). The total population of Inner Mongolia is 19 m. The total number of Mongols in all Chinese provinces is 3.0 m.

21. When Hungary, once in, made great changes (1968), nothing of course could be done except invade again – and this was not done. Anyway, Hungary continues to use the command system for CMEA trade. In much more important ways Romania remains 'in' but is no longer 'of' CMEA.

22. This was written before Poland went still further out of line (in summer 1980) by being forced to concede semi-free trade unions. We know that this feature is as much disliked by the Polish Party as by other CMEA powers; and cannot be sure that it will long remain within the range of toleration.

23. Cf. ed. Nayyar, 1977, pp. 3-4; *UN Statistical Yearbook*, 1973, p. 715.

24. 'Net disbursements' (our concept here) are gross disbursements minus amortisation. 'Net transfers' (the alternative concept) excludes also interest.

25. Cf. President Machel as quoted here, as quoted on p. 158.

26. Cf. Wiles, 1968, Ch. 13.

27. Except the Armenians going back to Armenia in 1945 (Kolarz, 1952, pp. 217-20); and in every 'core' country pensioners who return to seek their roots – with pensions in hard currency.

PART ONE:

THE NEW COMMUNIST THIRD WORLD

2 THE PEOPLE'S REPUBLIC OF ANGOLA: SOVIET-TYPE ECONOMY IN THE MAKING

Nicos Zafiris

Introduction

Angola is 1,246,700 square km. in area and has a population of approximately 7,500,000. It has a long coastline of 1,650 km. on the Atlantic Ocean. With a *per capita* income estimated at $736 for 1978[1] it is among the richer of the 'low-income countries'. The main explanation of this is the country's mineral wealth, particuarly its oil, diamonds and iron ore, though copper, phosphate and manganese have also been discovered and are capable of more systematic exploitation. Otherwise the country is mainly agricultural (the sector contributing a steady 50 per cent of GNP).[2] Coffee (of which Angola was, before independence, the world's fourth largest exporter) sisal, cotton, tobacco, rice, sugar and palm oil are the main cash crops, but the fishing industry is also fairly developed. Angola's industrial output has grown considerably in relative importance from 8 per cent of GNP in 1960 to 21 per cent in 1977,[3] accounting in considerable measure for the country's substantial growth rate of 8-9 per cent in the decade preceding independence.[4] The industrial sector is, in addition, fairly diversified. Apart from food processing and beer and soft drinks, there is also cotton and tobacco processing, oil refining, and the production of cement, tyres, plastics, soap and paper. The foreign trade participation ratio has traditionally been around 25 per cent (exports/GNP) and 20 per cent (imports/GNP), the balance of trade being usually positive.

Although not as diverse tribally as other areas of Africa, Angola is far from homogeneous. The majority consists of Bantus (including significant numbers of Ambundos and Bakongos in the North) but there are also some 2 million Ovimbundus in the Centre and South. While almost all education takes place in Portuguese, the country's official language, tribal dialects are widely spoken. A large proportion of the population are christianised, but among the rest fetishism is the prevailing religion. The country is ruled by the MPLA — Workers' Party — under the Presidency of José Eduardo dos Santos. A former part of the Portuguese Empire, Angola is now an independent People's

Republic. Its unit of currency is the *Kwanza* ($1 = 27.62 Kwanza in October 1980).

Angola has recently attracted attention as the (literal) battleground of big power confrontation. Our main concern here is, however, to study it as a revolutionary state building socialism. The economy will remain our primary interest, so we shall not attempt to cover, except tangentially, events which have been the subject of extensive comment both in academic literature and in the world press. As will be seen, Angola's socialism in its first five years of independence has been fairly unequivocally Marxist-Leninist, both in terms of economic policy and political evolution.

The Colonial Background

During the centuries of Portuguese rule colonisation proper remained limited, the country having developed more as a centre for the slave trade. Perhaps as many as five million Africans were taken out of Angola from the fifteenth to the nineteenth centuries and sold as slaves on the other side of the Atlantic.[5] It was not until this century that colonisation got under way while the institutions of slavery were gradually giving way to forced labour on the infrastructure, on European-owned plantations, and in the mines. The transport infrastructure in particular was developed very unevenly. Two of the best ports in Africa, Luanda and Lobito, were built, the latter connected to neighbouring Zaire and Zambia through the Benguela railway. Otherwise the transport system remained underdeveloped for the most part.

Agriculture and industry also showed some development at the same time, particularly coffee-growing and diamond-mining. But the most spectacular developments involved foreign capital which the Portuguese government's generous terms began to attract from around 1960. Among these we must mention the concessions to the Gulf Company following the discovery of oil off the northern coast and the agreement with South Africa to start developing the water resources of the Curelai and Cunene river basins. The project, which aimed to provide electricity for the whole of Southern Angola and Northern South West Africa, was well under way at the time of independence.

Nevertheless, Angola's economy before independence remained predominantly agricultural. 85 per cent of the population was engaged in agriculture, the vast majority living in a virtual subsistence economy.

That stood in sharp contrast to the relatively developed capitalist sector which produced the main cash crops and extracted the mineral raw materials for export. The main exports in recent years were oil and coffee (see Table 2.1) which accounted, together, for 50 per cent of total export revenue. The exports were thus concentrated on a number of key products. The imports, on the other hand, were traditionally much more varied, as would have been expected, with machinery, transport equipment and capital goods in general broadly representing more than 50 per cent of the total.

Table 2.1: Angola's Principal Exports 1973-5

Product		Value ($m)	% of total exports
	1973		
Petroleum		209	31
Coffee		169	26
Diamonds		n.a.	n.a.
	1974		
Petroleum		595	48
Coffee		247	20
Diamonds		97	8
	1975		
Petroleum		472	52
Coffee		165	18
Diamonds		44	5

Sources: *Marchés Tropicaux*, 13 Sept. 1974; *Yearbook of International Trade Statistics*, UN, various issues. These sets of figures are, unfortunately, not fully consistent with one another, but there is no reason to expect that major discrepancies in coverage are involved.

In terms of trading partners, Angola's economy was for a long time fairly closely integrated with Portugal's. Almost all her cotton was exported to Portugal at fixed low prices. Portugal was, on the other hand, only one of the big recipients of the key exports of oil and coffee. The USA, Canada, and Japan also bought large quantities of oil (crude or partially refined) and the USA in particular was, in addition, a big importer of Angola's coffee.[6] The position with respect to trading partners can be seen in Table 2.4. The picture is, generally, one of vigorous trade with many capitalist countries in addition to Portugal, especially the USA (on the export side) and the USA again, W. Germany, South Africa, Britain and France on the side of the imports. During the decade 1965-75 exports to Canada, Japan and the USA showed the fastest growth (65 per cent, 53 per cent and 30 per cent respectively).

But significant trade was also taking place, before independence, with other parts of the Portuguese Empire like Mozambique, Cape Verde and Macao.

Table 2.2: Angola's Balance of Trade Before Independence

Year	($m) Imports	Exports
1970[a]	368.5	423.4
1971	428.9	422.5
1972	397.4	515.6
1973	542.0	779.5
1974	625.0	1229.3

Source: *Yearbook of International Trade Statistics*, UN, various issues.
a. Other estimates, however, prepared by the Government of Angola for the IMF, show a deficit for that year (private sources).

The possession of oil together with the other main mineral export — diamonds — and the country's virtual self-sufficiency in food usually earned a surplus on visible trade before independence, a fact of considerable significance for the Portuguese Treasury. The surplus peaked in 1974 to a massive $600m, as can be seen from Table 2.2.

The balance of payments was traditionally dominated by the trade account. On the invisibles side, there were considerable railroad receipts (mainly for the transport of Zambian copper on the Benguela railway) but the balance was often negative, mainly due to interest and salary remittances (Table 2.3). Increasingly adverse capital movements since 1973 contributed to reduce the overall surplus to a relatively small amount and meant that little remained available for addition to the reserves.[7]

On the whole, however, and despite reservations about the figures, we must conclude that Angola was more of a 'financier' than a 'beneficiary' nation of Portugal's late investment drive in the empire as a whole in the last 15 or so years before the empire's dissolution. The country's finances were closely integrated with Portugal's, a fact reflected in the administration of its external transactions which generally had to go through the Bank of Portugal. The Angolan escudo was pegged to the Portuguese and was in theory equivalent to it, although in practice it was inconvertible and represented legal tender only in Angola. The budget also had to be approved by the Portuguese

Table 2.3: Angola's Balance of Payments 1970-4 (SDR m)

	1970	1971	1972	1973	1974
Trade Balance	−37.4	−78.5	92.1	73.9	131.8
Services Balance	1.6	23.0	−27.3	−22.6	−61.4
Private Traders (net)	−11.5	−11.0	−7.7	−7.8	−16.2
Current Balance	−47.3	−66.5	57.1	43.6	54.2
Capital Movements (net)	20.9	2.4	−24.2	−33.4	−44.2
Private	(21.0)	(3.3)	(−22.7)	(−33.3)	(−51.3)
Public	(−0.1)	(−0.8)	(−1.4)	(−0.1)	(7.0)
Overall Balance	−26.4	−64.0	33.0	10.2	10.0

Source: Data provided by the Angolan authorities.

government and it was generally expected to be balanced. But budget deficits do not seem to have been a problem in the last few years before independence. Angola often made, in fact, a positive contribution to the Portuguese budget if we neglect Portugal's military expenditure to keep it in subjection. The reserves' position also seemed stable at independence, although reserves had fallen to barely three months' imports by mid-1975, partly due to capital transfer facilities granted to leaving Europeans. The foreign debt position was more problematic, although not in an immediate sense. There was at that time a private debt of some 72m SDRs outstanding[8] but the public debt position with Portugal was much more unclear, as Angola seemed to have claims on gold and exchange reserves held by the Portuguese Central Bank.

Not surprisingly, the Portuguese also had effective control of the vital oil and diamond sectors. The oil field was dominated by three Portuguese companies, although Gulf Oil (Cabinda) was acquiring substantial concessions, as we have seen. In diamonds the *Companhia de Diamantes de Angola* (Diamang) had a monopoly until 1971.

Turning now briefly to colonial society, independence inherited a situation of over 85 per cent illiteracy and an education system mostly city-based and geared to the needs of the settler elite. For a long time the vast majority of the indigenous population only had access to education in the form of scattered mission schools. Class and racial divisions were thus very highly correlated. Education started to become more widely available to meet the growing need for skilled labour and, more importantly perhaps, to create a class of native bureaucrats favourably disposed to colonial rule and capable of assisting it in administration and trade. The education of native *cadres* potentially useful to the regime was finally intensified after the outbreak of the armed struggle, giving rise to a small local 'petty-bourgeois' class of *assimilados*. There had indeed been some racial as well as cultural 'assimilation' and *mestizos* had begun to occupy positions in administration.

But these developments did not significantly break the fundamental native/colonial distinction. The binary nature of secondary education (with urban-based, university-oriented *liceus* in the provincial capitals and lowly-regarded technical schools elsewhere) played a large role in this. Effectively, only the colonial bourgeoisie had access to university education. At independence nine-tenths of the students at the university were Portuguese.[9] The myth of racial integration was finally exploded at independence. Hundreds of thousands of Europeans left the country and some of the *mestizos* joined them.

The Transition to Independence

The struggle for independence dates back to the 1950s. The main — and eventually victorious — liberation movement (MPLA) came into existence in 1956 with a commitment to armed struggle. Early acts of insurrection in the cities were defeated but the movement gradually established substantial operations and eventually controlled many country areas. It set up elementary administration, health and educational services, in which 'revolutionary instruction' was included. The movement's progress was aided by its ability to establish bases in neighbouring Congo-Brazzaville (since 1964) and Zambia.

There were, however, two more liberation movements on the field; the FNLA and UNITA. Both had a strong regionalist/tribalist character, the FNLA among the Bakongo people in the North and UNITA among the Ovimbundus in the Centre and South. In contrast, the MPLA always claimed to be a truly national movement. The war of independence, waged in parallel by these three movements, eventually led to war between them. The victorious MPLA calls that war the 'second war of independence', insisting that both of its rival movements had become heavily compromised with foreign interests. Certainly both the FNLA and UNITA did come to rely primarily on Western help while the MPLA turned to the Soviets. It developed at the same time into a Marxist-Leninist party. And, as the MPLA has finally won power, we must regard Angola as a Marxist-Leninist state.

In discussing the events up to the end of these wars our purpose will be a limited one. We should only highlight, that is, a number of points relevant to our analysis of the development of economic and political institutions in Angola since independence, as well as developments in its international trading position.

The history of the rivalry between the movements goes back to the very beginnings of the armed struggle in 1960. The ideological differences were not, however, entirely clear at the start and even now it seems difficult to identify either the FNLA or UNITA with clear ideological positions. But the existence of these two movements meant that currents and shades of opinion which might have been expressed within the MPLA, and thus made it representative of a wider spectrum of viewpoints, have found their expression outside it instead. All those movements have come to be characterised more by their alliances during the war. The FNLA and UNITA established in neighbouring Zaire the basis of their operations and UNITA has come to depend heavily on co-operation with South Africa. The MPLA had to move its headquarters from what was Leopoldville in the Belgian Congo (Zaire) to Brazzaville in the increasingly Marxist former French Congo. Followers of the FNLA and UNITA were eventually branded by the MPLA as representatives of the petty bourgeoisie who wanted no more than to replace the Portuguese bourgeoisie, and Zaire as a base of 'Western imperialism' installed to provide 'subversion' in progressive regimes.

Although the MPLA was recognised as the only representative of the Angolan liberation movement by OAU in 1968, the Portuguese Government was not prepared in 1975 to hand over power to it alone. Rather, the Alvor agreement signed in December 1974 provided for the surrender of power to the three movements together. It was in this way that the 'Transitional Government' started to function in January 1975 with the MPLA representing only a minority within it. The arrangement was of course highly unstable. More importantly, the continued existence of three fairly credible liberation movements through the independence war provided ample opportunities for big power involvement. One after the other, the USA, South Africa, China, the Soviet Union (mainly through its Cuban proxy) and Zaire found themselves involved in the conflict. The precise order in which these powers became involved is still a matter of dispute, but once the initial commitment was made extrication presented problems for all concerned. The extent of the various involvements and the details of the temporary alliances struck are also largely unclear.

A recent challenging thesis on the events in Angola (Stockwell,

1978) must, however, be mentioned at this point. Stockwell, who ran the CIA's operation in Angola in 1975/6, accuses the agency of serious misjudgement in mounting a limited programme to oppose, unnecessarily, an MPLA victory when it was clear that the MPLA was the strongest of the three movements and not particularly hostile to the USA. President Ford authorised the Angola Programme on 14 July 1975, and the first planeload of arms went to Kinshasa on 29 July. This would appear to be later than the first deliveries of Soviet arms (see below). But having provided the excuse for massive Cuban military involvement in this way, the USA soon found that a very big commitment would have been necessary to reverse the balance subsequently. Such a commitment being impossible in the climate of US public opinion after Vietnam, defeat had to be conceded. It was the same constraint of public opinion, in fact, that had kept the operation secret — and therefore limited — in the first place. The USA was thus guilty both of choosing its allies unwisely (the CIA had dismissed MPLA's leader A. Neto as a 'drunken psychotic poet' and had chosen to support FNLA's H. Roberto), and also of supporting them too feebly so that they could not win. The US strategy remained in fact limited to only ensuring a 'no-win' situation. The more ambitious aim of seeking victory would have been unacceptable to Congress, in terms of cost.

The South Africans are also regarded as having themselves blundered in their open support of the defeated side and in their own abortive invasion of Angola in 1976, which they quickly had to abandon. Of course the Soviet/Cuban involvement had begun earlier than this: the airlift of Soviet arms in the spring of 1975; Neto's appeal to Castro in July; Cuban military instructors in October; Cuban forces in December 1975.[10] The escalation was intense, with some 10,000 South African and 15,000 Cuban troops committed in early 1976. It is probable, however, that, but for the Cubans, the South African and American presence would have been decisive.

China, which had (along with Romania!) supported the FNLA, also emerged from these events with diminished prestige for having allied itself to the defeated side, and also severely embarrassed for having been caught in a pro-Western alliance, one which contained South Africa in particular. Zaire, which had supported the weak FNLA movement, also lost as it eventually found itself neighbouring a hostile nation under Soviet influence; also Zaire had close to 1 million refugees in its territory while some 4,000 of the enemy force of Katangese *'gendarmes'* operated against it from Angola. The latter group actually fought on the side of the MPLA, but this has been, in fact, another alliance which those concerned will probably prefer to forget in the long run. UNITA will similarly wish to forget its alleged collaboration with the Portuguese colonial army at one point,[11] and 'the West' as a whole cannot be too proud of its use of certain nondescript groups of mercenaries towards the end of the war.[12]

The length and acuteness of the confrontation, however, plus the fact that it did not, fundamentally, end in compromise may have been the important factors in fostering a rather radical and uncompromising attitude within the MPLA movement both before independence and since. It is an attitude which has been manifested both in political organisation and in economic policy, as we shall see in the next section. But as will also be seen, other factors have tended to dilute the MPLA's radicalism at the same time.

The Party and Political Development

The Central Committee Report to the First Congress in December 1977 (MPLA, 1979) clearly proclaims the constitution of the movement into a 'vanguard' party of the working class. Having fulfilled its 'historic mission as a national liberation movement' it is now ready to 'unite into a solid alliance the workers, peasants, revolutionary intellectuals and other working people dedicated to the cause of the proletariat.' The revolution is defined as a 'People's Democratic' one which will 'create the conditions for the transition to the stage of the Socialist Revolution.' Meanwhile, however, the revolutionary alliance 'will exercise a Revolutionary Democratic Dictatorship over internal and external reaction, creating the conditions for the establishment of the Dictatorship of the Proletariat.' The MPLA thus appears, as at December 1977, very explicit in the definition of its own Marxist-Leninist character. The Congress actually changed the name of the movement to *MPLA-Partido do Travalho* (Workers' Party).

The principal organisational norm is defined, somewhat vaguely, as Democratic Centralism and the commitment to maintain ideological purity against 'all manifestations of bourgeois, petty-bourgeois and colonial ideology' is affirmed. The roles of the Party Youth and of the Women's Organisation are emphasised. But much more importantly, a central role seems to be reserved for UNTA, the National Union of Angolan workers 'which organises the working class . . . defending their interests and fighting for their constant education.' We shall amplify later to see that Angola has been serious about instituting centralised control of the labour movement under party direction.

Furthermore, the document is explicit about the intention to control the media which 'under the leadership of the Party, will have the task of mobilising, instructing and educating our people in the objectives of the Socialist Revolution.' Of religion it states that it is 'by its very essence a distorted reflection of . . . reality.' It still guarantees freedom of conscience that is 'the right to profess religion or not . . . so long as he complies with the law and the norms of Socialist morality.' But 'with regard to religion as an ideology . . . the party will base its policy on the supposition that the struggle for a free, scientific and materialistic consciousness is an integral part of the struggle to build a new society.'

A further typical problem in Communist parties, namely that of factionalism, is tackled in the document. The problem is stated to have originally appeared in 1963, mainly in the form of 'leftist' groups. 'Always directed from abroad', factionalism finally assumed, according to the document, the dimensions of 'counter-revolution' in the form of the abortive coup of N. Alves (up to then Minister of Internal Administration) in May 1977. A brief digression into that incident may throw light on the regime's character and subsequent development.

The official view of the conspiracy is that it was an 'ultra-leftist' one with elements of (black) racism. Alves condemned the MPLA as class-collaborationists and declared himself 'champion of the struggle against the bourgeoisie', roughly identified as the whites and the *mestizos*. Alves's power base seemed to be in the 'People's *Bairro* Committees' in Luanda which had originally come into existence as the defence organisation of the black population against acts of violence by the settler community. In a sense they represented 'spontaneous' local political action outside the more formal structures of state power. Hasty elections held in 1976 under the 'Law on People's Power', initiated by Alves, consolidated his supporters' position in the *bairro* committees. At the same time, by adopting a rather purist pro-Soviet stance, Alves looked, momentarily, like 'Moscow's man' in Luanda.[13]

The defeat of the conspiracy was followed by the dissolution of the *bairro* committees and restructuring of all other organisations which had become infiltrated by Alves's supporters. These included the consumer co-operatives, some of which, it was alleged, had helped the conspiracy by creating artificial food shortages in Luanda, the trade unions, the women's and the youth organisations.

The change in climate is reflected both in the First Congress Report and in subsequent practice. The Report commits itself to the abolition of the People's Power Law and acknowledges that 'spontaneous' political action can also be used against the party. It reaffirms its faith in Democratic Centralism and explains, in particular, that the organs of people's power cannot be separate from the state apparatus. In the following months the MPLA as a party, rather than as a liberation movement, went on to establish much stricter conditions for membership, and to set up 'party cells' in workplaces and localities throughout the country. Applicants for membership had to satisfy not only the party but also their workmates.[14]

The MPLA movement had not, however, been unaware of the special role of the peasant class in Angolan conditions, and in this too it is eminently Leninist. For peasants represented the majority of the movement's membership. The MPLA had also shown itself appreciative of its lack of workers with a developed Marxist-Leninist consciousness. It had been, as a consequence, quite liberal, up until 1978, in automatically converting membership of the MPLA (Movement) into membership of the MPLA (Party).[15] It has maintained, on the other hand, a keen perception of the class enemy, particularly in the shape of the 'petty bourgeoisie' which seems, in the absence of a big capitalist class, to constitute the main element of opposition. This rather heterogeneous group in which the leadership has tended to include the small traders, artisans, civil servants, professionals, agricultural smallholders and even the students and intellectuals has been the subject of frequent attacks for being generally unco-operative in the economic sphere to the point of economic sabotage. The 'petty bourgeois' have also been attacked for blocking the ascendancy of workers and peasants in party organisation.

Two more recent internal political developments must be mentioned. The first was the abolition of DISA, the Secret Security police, in July 1979, in response to accusations of disappearances and 'arbitrary treatment' of prisoners. The transfer of security to the jurisdiction of the Ministry of the Interior may not prove of great significance in the long run but it may be an indication of willingness to move towards greater openness in the field of internal security.

More importantly, there was the gradual reorganisation of the state structures. The intention is to create a pyramid of elected assemblies going from the basic unit of the *bairro* or village up to the National Assembly. That has been conceived to be the supreme legislative body replacing the Revolutionary Council.[16] Elections were held through the summer of 1980 to a series of 'electoral conferences' which would in

turn elect Provincial Assemblies and the National Assembly itself.[17]
Nominations to these elections were made by the Party, the Youth
Organisation, the Women's Organisation and the Trade Unions.
Candidates nominated from the last two sources, as in USSR, need not
be party members, since neither organisation is a strictly party one.
But members of 'factionalist' organisations, FNLA, UNITA and
FLEC, are excluded. On the whole, the National Assembly appears to
be modelling itself on the Supreme Soviet, with the MPLA-party
retaining the classical stranglehold over the nomination procedure,
through itself or through front organisations.

The Continuing Armed Conflict

Ever since the end of the 'Second War of Liberation' on 27 March 1976
the MPLA has had to continue to combat internal armed resistance.
That has been represented by the remnants of the FNLA and UNITA.
The latter in particular has been very effective in the south of the
country, mainly through hit-and-run strikes, although its claim to
actually 'control' areas in the south appears very exaggerated. But it
does have one solid 'achievement' to show in having kept the Benguela
railway out of action throughout the period of independence. Since
the establishment of diplomatic relations with Zambia in mid-1976,
UNITA has been unable to operate from Zambian territory. It has also
been deprived of almost its entire Zairean support since the more recent
normalisation of Angola's relations with that country, too. As a result,
UNITA operations seem to have become entirely dependent on South
African support, to the movement's considerable discredit.

On the whole, the UNITA challenge seems to be fading. Large
numbers (around 1m, according to the government) of UNITA
supporters who had fled into the bush around 1976 have been returning
to the villages and towns. The re-integration of these *regressados* has
not been easy since many have returned in a poor physical condition
and still hostile to the MPLA. Remaining UNITA activity has been
increasingly used by South Africa as a counter to Angola's support for
SWAPO, the Namibian liberation movement, and its continued
operations along the border have kept the area in a state of tension.
Towns and villages have been changing hands between UNITA and the
regular FAPLA forces assisted by Cuban troops, UNITA occupying
them generally during the rainy season when landing strips are put out
of action and then withdrawing again when the rains stop.[18] But

UNITA activity has not wholly ceased elsewhere in the country. Arrests of some 120 alleged UNITA bombers were reported in August 1980 followed by 16 executions, in turn followed by a number of executions by UNITA in reprisal.[19] And UNITA can still claim, as indeed its leader J. Savimbi did, in London in the summer of 1980, that a regime which requires the continued presence of such a large Cuban military contingent (of which more later) cannot be regarded as stable.

Hostilities with the unfriendly neighbouring states themselves have been equally if not more unsettling. As far back as February 1977, the then President Neto was complaining that 'hardly a day passes without planes, helicopters, vehicles and troops crossing the border'.[20] The main threat at that time seemed to be from Zaire which was also accused of hijacking and stealing Angolan planes and of preparing, ultimately, a second invasion of Angola in co-operation mainly with the northern-based FNLA. This operation (Cobra 77) did not eventually come to anything and the two countries have progressed to normalisation of relations from that point on, as we shall see later.

More recently, however, and more seriously, there have been renewed and escalating hostilities from South Africa, which had always maintained considerable forces along the Angolan border with South-West Africa (Namibia) since the end of the war. The immediate cause of these hostilities has been Angola's support for SWAPO, which has been fighting against South African administration of Namibia, and the South Africans have been claiming only to attack SWAPO guerrilla bases situated in Angola. The attacks have mainly taken the form of air-raids, although there have also been ground attacks inside Angola's territory which the South Africans have been justifying in terms of 'hot pursuit'. The strikes which kept growing through 1978 and 1979 acquired the dimensions of an invasion in June 1980, involving unprecedented quantities of arms and men and resulting in South Africa's gaining temporary control of considerable areas in the south of the country. Angola's casualties and material damages have been reported high,[21] as the attacks have clearly not been limited to military targets. The hostilities have continued, although on a reduced scale in late 1980, but diplomatic initiatives for a solution have also been gathering momentum, as we shall see.

Theses on and Practice of Economic Policy

The first task facing the transitional government in 1975 was the

maintenance of production at around the pre-independence level,
following the disruption which came as the inevitable consequence of
war. The departure of hundreds of thousands of mostly skilled
Europeans was also responsible for a considerable drop in productivity.
The abandonment by these of large numbers of plantations and
livestock centres led to shortages of agricultural products. A little later,
the escalation of the military conflict between the movements ensured
that the task could not be accomplished, and production started to run
well below pre-independence levels. Coffee and diamonds, in particular,
slumped heavily and oil came to account for 80 per cent of total exports
in 1976.[22] Production difficulties continued, of course, even after the
takeover of power by the MPLA. The disruption in agriculture was
intense. The coffee harvest of 1976 was under particular threat, due to
massive labour shortages caused by the return to the south of tens of
thousands of Ovimbundu plantation-workers from the coffee-growing
central areas. A massive campaign to mobilise city dwellers into
harvesting teams was only partially successful and production was only
a third of the pre-war figure.[23]

In addition, the Civil War seems to have brought massive damage to
infrastructure. According to the Central Committee's Report,[24] more
than 130 bridges, more than 20,000 goods transport vehicles (80 per
cent of the total stock) and large numbers of buildings and agricultural machines were destroyed during those few months of
1975/6. There was also considerable damage to roads, railways and
airports. Economic sabotage by fleeing colonials included massive
slaughter for consumption or sale of thousands of head of cattle, as
well as considerable damage to vehicles. Theft was also rife. A massive
effort had to be undertaken in 1976 and 1977 to repair these damages.
According to the First Congress Report, from July 1976 to June 1977
about 12,000 vehicles were imported, with priority given to heavy
vehicles for goods and collective passenger transport. Ten aircraft were
also acquired in the same period and efforts were made to rebuild
bridges (about 45 in 1977) and to improve the port and airports.

Fishing was another sector which was affected particularly severely.
Due to damage to ships and crew shortages the 1976 total catch was
not more than ten per cent of the 1973 figure.[25] Taking industry as a
whole, production in most enterprises was running, at the end of 1976,
at between 10 per cent and 50 per cent of pre-war levels. The task of
reconstruction was clearly a massive one.[26]

Further, the problem of settling financial relations with abroad
had to be faced, initially by the Transitional Government and then by

the MPLA. The three liberation movements were able to formulate a common policy on this issue which was a generally 'mild' one. They promised for example, to 'honour foreign debts provided they had been incurred in the interests of the Angolan people'. In the event that was also, largely, the policy which was followed by the MPLA on its own, although the settlement of debts to and claims on Portugal proved a fairly contentious matter.[27]

During the months in which the Transitional Government gradually gave way to the MPLA a series of legislative measures were taken to lay the foundations of a planned economy and a socialist state. Free education and medical care had been established by the end of 1975. In February 1976 the Law of State Intervention was promulgated containing the first policy guidelines for nationalisation. The Law was based on that of the Transitional Government formulated in 1975 which had provided for a substantial amount of nationalisation, particularly in the financial sector. It had been envisaged, more specifically, that Angolan nationals would acquire a share of at least 70 per cent of the capital of banks and insurance companies within which the state's own share would be over 51 per cent. The establishment of new commercial banks had been prohibited and the whole reinsurance sector was to come under state control.

The Law provided for state intervention[28] in all enterprises where that was justified: basically, because of their strategic importance or their state of abandon. The strategic criterion was to include enterprises playing a major role in foreign trade and enterprises holding a monopoly position. Enterprises in which sabotage by the former (mainly Portuguese) owners was involved were also to be taken over.

However, the need for experts supersedes 'strategic' nationalisation, especially in the case of multinationals. The attitude towards these was not at all hostile. As early as February 1976 the then Foreign Minister, E. dos Santos, was stating that Angola was 'ready to respect their interests' if they 'aided the development of the country and were of benefit to the people'. Nationalisation of foreign enterprises was to be limited to those abandoned by their owners.

The general attitude on planning was outlined in the Law of State Intervention which defined three basic sectors: state economic units, co-operatives, and private enterprise.[29] The First Congress Report (December 1977)[30] reaffirmed later that the economy was to be a planned one, although it acknowledged that 'present concrete conditions do not as yet permit the drawing up of a single national plan for the period up to 1980, detailing implementation responsibilities and year', due to lack of experience, cadres and information. But 'instruments have to be created to ensure the control of mixed and private enterprises.' 'The patriotic petty bourgeoisie must also be led to positions in line with the interest of the most exploited strata.'

The report also contains a number of other theses on various matters of economic policy. On overall development strategy it lays down that 'agriculture is the base and industry the decisive factor in economic and social development.' The oil, fisheries and construction sectors are defined, interestingly, as 'sectors of short-term economic take-off', while the mining industry is designated as the 'medium-term economic take-off' sector. Studies are proposed to examine the longer-term strategic options.

As to trade it is proposed to strengthen state activity in distribution as well as to control commercial activity in the private sector, while the creation of consumer co-operatives is to be encouraged. The peasants must be progressively integrated into the cash economy. On foreign trade in particular the intention is to establish a state monopoly through 'the setting up of state-owned concerns specialising in imports and exports'. In the short term the part of foreign trade which is still in private hands is to be 'rigidly controlled'.

The report makes reference, in addition, to the need to reduce unemployment, increased as a result of rural migration to the towns, and undertakes to take steps to raise rural living standards, halt the exodus and encourage the return of the unemployed migrants to the countryside.

The ultimate objective of the abolition of exploitation is, of course, affirmed together with the distributive norm, 'from each according to his ability, to each according to his labour', during the transition to socialism. The desirability of collective production is also emphasised for both industry and agriculture, and strong words of encouragement can be found in the report for the formation of co-operatives in agriculture, fishing and industry.

In addition to the First Congress Report, theses on policy have appeared in other pieces of legislation as well as in official statements. Legislation and policy have been particularly interesting in the areas of workers' participation and trade unions. A law in 1977 abolished collective management of state enterprises, which had been experimented with and found ineffective, and substituted Soviet-style director-management but retained some provisions for worker participation. The workers would make suggestions in connection with the drawing-up and implementation of enterprise plans, working conditions, the management of the enterprise social fund, etc. But in the autumn of 1978, following a year of preparation, the restructuring of the whole labour movement was announced at the Third National Conference of UNTA (National Union of Angolan Workers). Individual unions were to be formed by sector of production, and Trade Union Committees were to be elected in every workplace to represent the work force. But the overall aim was 'to stimulate political activity among the work force in order to strengthen class consciousness and to help create the conditions for Socialism'.[31] Faith in 'democratic centralism' was reaffirmed and UNTA as a whole pledged to 'work for the fulfilment and overfulfilment of the National Plan for 1978'. The organisation was to represent the working class in discussions of salaries and working conditions with the relevant ministries, but also to mobilise it for mass literacy campaigns and political purposes in general, as we have seen. UNTA conceded, in particular, that strikes were unacceptable 'for the time being'.[32] Thus the general trend on unionism appears to be along the Soviet path.

Important developments also took place in legislation on foreign investments. On 5 July 1979 the Council of the Revolution passed a law which permitted these, provided Angola's independence was respected. They could only be authorised, however, if they were compatible with the National Plan, but they could then be guaranteed periods of operation of between 10 and 15 years. Foreign firms were also required to employ and train Angolan workers, whereas foreign workers could only be employed with specific permission. There were also provisions allowing profit repatriation, guarantees of compensation in the event of nationalisation and tax relief. But foreign capital was not to be allowed in the strategic areas of defence, banking, insurance, telecommunications and water supply.[33] On the whole, however, these moves seem to have consolidated a strongly pragmatic attitude to foreign investment.

We can now move to a brief survey of the actual application of these ideas over the period, starting once again with the effort to restore production to pre-independence levels. For production difficulties have continued throughout the period. The coffee crop in 1978 was still only one-third of the 1974 level while sugar was running at around two-thirds of the corresponding 1972 figure.[34] Cuban experts were brought in and mass mobilisation of coffee pickers was undertaken for every harvest. Even so, the 1979 crop was the worst ever recorded although the 1980 one, estimated at two and a half times the 1979 one, may mark the turning point. Angola has now slipped back to eighth place as a coffee exporter, but the government is hoping to improve on this soon through its own organisation which now has a monopoly on all coffee exports.[35]

On fish the improvement through 1977 was painfully slow, the catch still running at some 25 per cent of the 1973 level. In May of the same year the then President Neto complained that Angola was importing almost all classes of foodstuffs. And whereas there was, fortunately, the foreign exchange to pay for these, the trend was a disquieting one as export revenues were not rising fast enough, or were even falling.[36] The whole period since that time has, in fact, been littered with moral exhortations from the leadership to improve productivity in agriculture and industry. Both state administrators and the 'petite bourgeoisie' have come under fire for negligence or actual non-co-operation.[37] It seems difficult to generalise about the extent of improvements in production in relation to pre-independence levels, but for what it is worth the OECD (1980) estimate of post-independence GNP per head was as follows: 1975 = 100, 1976 = 87, 1977 = 87, 1978 = 89, 1979 = 86.

As regards agricultural organisation, the general policy has been to establish state farms on land abandoned by settler farmers, including a few agro-industrial complexes. The co-operative sector has also been developed alongside the state one, generally on a non-coercive basis. Peasants are first encouraged to group together in (loose) 'associations', mainly to use technical assistance collectively, and only later to form 'co-operatives' in which some collective farming is a requirement. Most co-operative development seems to be in the north, so far.[38]

On industrial nationalisation the preferred strategy seems to have become one of strong participation rather than complete takeover by the state. Something of a wave of nationalisation followed the legislation of early 1976, and 'Intervention Commissions' were appointed to run the abandoned firms in particular. By the end of 1976 the state was represented in almost every industrial sector although not to the same degree. Sugar, textiles, plywood and construction gravel are examples of sectors which had been taken over completely by the end of 1978. The state also took over 80 per cent of the shipyards, 85 per cent of brewing, 67 per cent of matches and 52 per cent of leather and footwear, but in other sectors the corresponding percentage was fairly low. New state organisations had been created in distribution and marketing, the role of which was intended to grow according to the First Congress Report.

The basic organisation of the entire distribution system seems to be the 'state shops' (*lojas do povo*) and the state distribution organisation *Coprope*, with monopoly powers over basic items.[39] Angola has consistently kept faith with these institutions and does not appear at any time to have given much encouragement to private traders. This is despite shortages which have necessitated the introduction of rationing. As noted in a recent analysis of the economy by the Political Bureau,[40] wage rises over the years of independence have been excessive in view of production difficulties and 'parallel' or 'speculative' markets have been flourishing as a result. In the cities the problem has been aggravated by the presence of large numbers of unemployed, as we have seen, and the government is now issuing ration cards only to persons with jobs. But food imports are continuing high, as low producers' prices and distribution difficulties are discouraging peasants from supplying enough to the industrial sector. A hazardous guess would suggest that Angola may soon be forced to make a turn in the direction of reform along the lines announced in Mozambique in March 1980.

Nationalisation has also covered the banking sector and control over the financial system was further assured by currency reform. A new currency, the *Kwanza*, was created to replace the colonial escudo but no exchange was allowed for holdings of escudos outside the country, thus wiping out the value of the currency which had left the country illegally. Bank balances of persons who had left Angola were also finally confiscated in May 1979.[41]

Meanwhile, the efforts have been continuing to settle Angola's 'reserves' in Portugal, as well as Portuguese claims on account of nationalisations. An immediate settlement of this problem does not appear to be in sight.[42] Angola is, on the other hand, fairly welcoming to the return of skilled settlers. On the whole then relations with Portugal seem to have developed in a business-like manner.

Actual policy towards foreign and particularly multinational companies reflects the pragmatic attitude which we saw earlier in legislation and official statements. The state has refrained from completely taking over any of them. The state took over in 1977 a majority (61 per cent) shareholding of *Diamang*, the diamond-mining monopoly, which had accounted, before independence, for some 8 per cent of total world output. The industry had been severely disrupted by the war and output in 1975 had fallen to around one-third of the pre-independence level. The government did allow, however, the remaining 40 per cent of the shares to remain in the hands of foreign investors, Portuguese, Belgian, US and Swiss.[43] But of these, the remaining Portuguese shares were nationalised in 1980, a fact which provoked much resentment and some retaliation by the Portuguese. The government is still trying, however, to retain the services of Portuguese marketing experts in particular and has invited more Western experts to reactivate some of the mines.[44]

Even before independence oil had accounted for some 40 per cent of Angola's export earnings, and that figure has gone up since, due to the price-rise and the crisis in Angola's other exporting industries. The main foreign company involved had been Gulf in the Cabinda area. After independence, the government attempted to replace Western involvement in the oil industry with Soviet and Cuban. Eventually, however, Angola found it impossible to dispense with Gulf's expertise and knowledge of the fields and, following negotiations, a mixed company (Cabindan Gulf Oil) was established. This has a 51 per cent shareholding by the Angolan state but the management and marketing have been returned to Gulf. In addition, Texaco of the USA, Total and Elf of France and Petrobras of Brazil are undertaking exploration in joint ventures with Sonangol, the Angolan state oil company.[45] More recently, similar agreements with Mobil, AGIP and the Yugoslav Nafta Gas have been announced.[46]

New Western investments have been arriving on a 51-49 per cent partnership basis with the Angolan state. On the whole, then, we cannot report any significant change in Angola's pragmatic attitude on the issue of nationalisation. The attitude towards foreign investment remains, fundamentally, an inviting one. This conclusion is supported by Angolan accusations that South Africa's military attacks might also have been aimed at frightening potential Western investors.[47]

In the general organisation of foreign trade, however, a considerable role seems to be reserved for state enterprise. An enterprise has been created to regulate imports (*Importang*) and another for exports (*Exportang*). The former is to handle almost all classes of imports with the exception of some machinery items, which were to be directly in the competence of particular ministries. The role and number of private importers seems to have been diminishing all the time. *Exportang* was similarly to co-ordinate the marketing of export products not under the control of multinationals and also their acquisition from domestic producers.[48] This is then a field in which the state appears, on the whole, to be assuming a controlling role, despite the special arrangements with the key foreign interests mentioned already.

As regards the international organisation of the economy we must then conclude, overall, that progress towards establishing a socialist economy has been partial. There has been peasant resistance to early attempts at collectivising agriculture, as well as worker resistance to close state control over trade unions. Although Angola's latest trade union laws still appear somewhat illiberal, as we have seen, there has been, by recent accounts, a growing awareness of the failures of 'overcentralisation' and increasing talk of 'decentralisation'. Similarly, in the domain of 'planning', although organs have been created both at national and ministerial level, more is being said about 'planning at the level of the productive unit'. The longer-term significance of these developments is not, however, easy to assess at present.

On the broader issue of development strategy, Angola's commitment to the Soviet model is difficult to assess. For Angola is, due to its oil and minerals, a somewhat atypical underdeveloped country, as indicated already. Mineral exports can provide development capital and the country is not so dependent on an agricultural surplus. This is clearly recognised in the First Congress Report, as we have seen, which designates the oil sector as one of 'short-term economic take-off'. At the same time the Angolans appear to be aware of the dangers of over-reliance on oil and of failure to raise productivity in agriculture and other industries.

Foreign Trade and Diplomatic Relations

The report to MPLA's First Congress is brief on the subject of foreign trade. The basic aim stated is to diversify exports as well as the number of countries with which trading relations are to be established, 'giving special priority to Socialist and non-aligned countries'. It is, on the other hand, fairly explicit on the political/diplomatic side. It contains extensive statements of gratitude for those powers which helped the MPLA militarily during the two wars of independence, particularly, of course, the Soviet Union and Cuba. But Yugoslavia, Guinea-Conakry, Guinea Bissau, Mozambique, Algeria, Tanzania and most countries of the Eastern bloc and the Portuguese Communist Party are also mentioned in the same vein. The document is also fairly illuminating as regards the country's future orientations in the sphere of international politics. Starting from a basic pledge of allegiance to the UN and the OAU, it moves on to a clear statement of its view of the international scene as amounting to a 'struggle between two social systems'. It is stated that 'the fundamental question is — either

Table 2.4: Angola — Main Trading Partner Countries (Visible Civilian Trade)

Imports ($m)								Exports ($m)					
1973	1974	1975	1976	1977	1978	1979		1973	1974	1975	1976	1977	1978	1979
51.5	63.9	55.0	39.6	42.3	34.7	101.8	USA	218.9	471.3	426.3	260.5	298.8	218.5	315.9
1.5	1.7	1.1	1.0	3.5	1.5	0.8	Canada	80.9	94.6	0.5	1.0	–	–	10.9
30.0	30.0	20.4	4.6	42.0	40.2	32.6	Japan	68.5	70.4	101.0	36.8	9.4	5.6	54.5
18.5	21.8	13.7	12.3	25.8	42.4	33.9	Belgium	8.6	13.0	27.7	14.1	2.8	5.4	15.4
36.5	42.5	40.9	10.4	36.4	30.9	53.0	France	11.6	19.0	17.8	10.7	8.8	4.5	3.6
70.6	80.4	39.6	27.5	80.8	87.5	87.4	West Germany	39.3	49.9	38.7	15.7	10.3	5.3	5.0
20.6	30.5	14.6	19.4	21.7	31.8	49.6	Italy	8.8	17.1	10.2	3.2	1.1	0.5	0.5
13.5	13.2	11.5	14.4	48.4	54.9	35.5	The Netherlands	19.7	17.5	12.1	14.7	16.7	40.3	9.9
8.9	8.7	8.6	15.8	47.6	29.1	61.3	Sweden	–	–	1.6	1.2	1.1	1.0	–
7.9	14.7	6.8	8.8	13.8	22.4	12.6	Switzerland	2.3	2.9	8.7	5.3	9.4	9.7	4.3
41.5	43.7	35.7	14.3	20.3	43.7	71.5	UK	22.3	3.5	13.8	8.2	8.6	77.8	95.6
142.9	137.3	76.9	31.3	69.8	72.1	128.9	Portugal	197.7	330.1	110.0	37.4	21.9	6.5	13.2
8.5	13.3	9.3	5.5	24.4	30.6	32.7	Spain	26.6	39.9	42.5	6.3	3.3	3.8	5.0
31.4	62.0	56.8	77.3	99.0	120.6	132.7	South Africa	8.7	12.8	11.4	15.4	19.4	21.4	25.8
–	–	–	–	–	–	–	Algeria	–	–	0.5	14.1	27.8	41.4	55.0
3.3	5.2	6.6	24.3	28.8	24.9	56.8	Brazil	2.0	0.4	6.9	0.1	1.2	1.3	2.6
–	–	5.0	0.8	11.0	14.9	32.6	Argentina	–	–	–	–	–	–	32.9
–	–	5.8	11.7	17.5	23.4	25.7	Chile	–	–	–	–	–	–	–
–	–	–	–	–	–	–	Virgin Islands	–	–	25.5	35.8	143.3	180.1	126.1
–	–	–	–	–	–	–	Bahamas	–	–	–	87.0	362.2	637.5	701.2

Table 2.4: Continued

	Imports ($m)							Exports ($m)						
	1973	1974	1975	1976	1977	1978	1979	1973	1974	1975	1976	1977	1978	1979
Zaire	0.4	0.3	–	–	–	–	–	14.8	4.0	–	–	–	–	–
Iran	13.8	8.4	–	–	–	–	–	–	–	–	–	–	–	–
USSR	–	–	–	c.7.5[a]	c.101.2[a]	c.75.0[a]	–	–	–	–	c.17.8[a]	c.13.1[a]	c.13.0[a]	–
Romania	–	–	–	2.5	6.2	8.9	9.8	–	–	–	–	–	13.1	14.4
Yugoslavia	–	–	0.2	7.7	22.4	39.1	38.9	–	–	0.3	9.1	2.5	16.2	1.9
Bulgaria	–	–	–	–	–	13.0[b]	–	–	–	–	–	–	–	–
Yemen PDR	–	–	2.2	–	–	–	–	–	–	4.2	6.3	8.4	10.5	11.6
China	–	–	0.4	–	0.3	2.5	–	–	–	1.5	1.3	0.2	–	–
Mozambique	8.1	8.2	3.7	–	–	–	–	7.8	6.3	4.6	3.0	1.4	1.5	–
Macao	6.5	3.5	–	–	–	–	–	–	–	–	–	–	–	–
Cape Verde	–	–	–	–	–	–	–	5.6	7.6	–	–	–	–	–
Totals[c]	542.0	625.1	451.6	360.6	747.8	815.2	1083.0	779.4	1229.3	906.6	620.3	980.4	1331.1	1557.3

a. Mirror trade figures from *Vneshnyaya Torgovlya*, originally in transf. roubles. The following conversion rates have been used:
1 R = $1.33 (1976); $1.36 (1977); $1.46 (1978). Imports have been raised, and exports diminished, by 7.5% to convert Soviet c.i.f. to Angolan f.o.b. and vice versa.

b. From FES *Bericht* I/1979.

c. Total also includes trade with countries not shown in table. Significant trade only shown.

Sources: 1973-4: *Yearbook of International Trade Statistics*, UN, various issues. 1975-8: *Direction of Trade Yearbook*, IMF, 1979.

socialism or capitalism', and that 'there is no other, third, way'. On this understanding, the non-aligned movement must 'develop even further its anti-colonial, anti-racist and anti-imperialist character'. Attacks follow against South Africa and the USA. But the conclusive commitment to Marxist internationalism is, perhaps, contained in the last paragraph of the relevant passage which states that 'there cannot be an African or a European Socialism, one Socialism for developed countries and another for under-developed countries — there is only Scientific Socialism, which is a fact in large areas of our world.'

The actual conduct of foreign trade, however, has followed a pragmatic pattern. Table 2.4 summarises the picture with respect to partner countries and overall, permitting a direct comparison of the positions immediately before and since independence. First, as regards the totals, there was in 1975 a significant overall reduction of trade in comparison with 1974 and a further reduction in 1976, until trade started to increase again in 1977. Secondly, the balance of visible trade remained in surplus throughout the period, although the excess of exports over imports was proportionately smaller than in the two years before independence.[49]

Turning now to trading partners, trade with some countries seems to have suffered a permanent decline compared with the period before independence. The drop was massive in the case of exports to Portugal and also very big in exports to the USA.[50] But while the USA continued to be among the biggest recipients of Angolan goods, Portugal seems to have now become an insignificant importer. On the other hand, exports to Angola from these two countries seem to have suffered only a small decline. Japan and the other Western European countries broadly maintained their positions as exporters but they seem to have ceased to be significant importers of Angolan goods. That position seems to have been occupied, surprisingly, by the Bahamas and the Virgin Islands. That was, however, the result of specific, and most probably *entrepôt*, agreements for the particular years with the state organisation handling Angola's (three) main export products. The present pattern thus may well not be maintained with these particular countries (or indeed with any others!). Angola's own imports from South Africa seemed to increase steadily throughout the period, indeed she has become her main supplier, and the same is true of exports to South Africa, although the scale of the latter is much less spectacular. Finally, trade gained momentum with certain new (or almost new) Latin-American partner countries: Brazil, Argentina and Chile, reflecting these countries' sentimental interest in 'Iberian' connections.

The artificial trade with the Portuguese empire fell away. On the export side alone, Algeria also gained.

In the Communist world we must note an increase in trade with Yugoslavia (mainly imports) and with Romania (only imports). More importantly we must note considerable trade with the USSR, especially on the import side since 1977, although the relevant figures appear only in the Soviet statistics. The USSR has exported, almost exclusively, machinery and transport equipment (planes, trucks, cars) and imported natural coffee.

As regards the commodity composition of the other imports, the Bank of Angola's estimates for 1977 were: food products, 42.4 per cent; other consumer goods, 16.4 per cent; machinery, 16.1 per cent; transport equipment, 13 per cent; and raw materials, 12.1 per cent. Given that the percentage of food imports was only 13.4 per cent in 1974 we can note a very big increase in their relative importance within the total, a fact which has caused some anxiety, as we have seen.

The exports have continued to be dominated, of course, by the three key products, oil, coffee and diamonds. The latest available figures for the values of exports of these are given for 1976 by *Yearbook of International Trade Statistics* (Commodity Tables, volume II, 1979) as $240m for oil, $165m for coffee and $10m for diamonds.

On the whole, the trade statistics do not show any great shift of Angola's trade towards the CMEA. But the figures are widely regarded as inaccurate and much essential detail is unavailable at the time of writing. The available figures may still underestimate, somewhat, the importance of economic links with the Communist World. We must, therefore, turn once again to other sources, particularly reports of trade and co-operation agreements.

In the civilian field, the most important of these has, perhaps, been the fishing agreement signed with the Soviet Union in April 1977. In exchange for fishing equipment (including ships and technical assistance) the USSR has acquired fishing rights in Angolan waters. But the USSR has also agreed to help with the construction and improvement of fishing ports.[51] Cuba too has entered into a fishing agreement with Angola.[52] The Russians and Cubans together controlled at one time more than 85 per cent of the catch, particularly the marketing. But a fishing agreement with Poland has also been reported.[53] The agreements have generally included help with the training of Angolans. For these reasons fish does not appear as a commodity in the visible balance.

Cuba has sold sugar[54] and has agreed to co-operate in the

construction field.[55] The Soviet Union has agreed to provide technical aid in agriculture and Soviet experts have been helping to set up state farms.[56] There is also an agreement for the Soviets to help with mineral exploration and numerous agreements have been reported yearly on the details of technical, economic and cultural co-operation. On the whole, however, the Soviet economic presence in Angola has not been massive.[57]

The Cuban presence has been comparatively more impressive, certainly in terms of personnel.[58] The Angolans have been gratefully acknowledging Cuba's civilian help, particularly during 1976/7 when it went a long way towards replacing the skills of the departing Portuguese, especially in coffee and sugar production and in health and education. More recently the Cubans have been aiding in construction. Some 3,000 Cuban construction workers are in Angola at the time of writing, or expected shortly, to help build, in particular, 2,000 houses in Luanda.[59] Perhaps the most valuable aspect of Cuba's contribution, however, has been training in practical and scientific skills.[60] Most other East Europeans have also entered into agreements with Angola and in some cases significant trade has started to take place as a result. Thus Romania has signed two trade and co-operation agreements in spring 1978 and sold rolling stock,[61] while she has been the only East European country to have offered a specific credit commitment of $75m.[62] Agreements with the GDR have provided for the assembly of modern cargo handling equipment in three Angolan ports, as well as for the supply of agricultural machinery.[63] A big co-operation/ assistance agreement has also been in force since 1977 in the field of budgetary, financial and statistical organisation and in those of transport and public health, while it is estimated that 6,000 East German trucks were in service by 1979.[64] An agreement with Hungary provides for the assembly of 9,000 buses by 1990,[65] in addition to co-operation agreements in the medical field. Bulgaria has also agreed to help in agriculture, among other things, with the setting up of state farms.[66] Co-operation has been increasing with Yugoslavia, mainly in the field of agricultural machinery,[67] while Czechoslovakia has agreed to sell 300 trucks and promised scientific co-operation.[68] Frequent visits to Angola by economic representatives of Eastern European countries are reported. Still within the Communist world we must mention the 'most-favoured nation' agreement with Mozambique signed on 2 July 1979, and a lesser one with Algeria, among the more marginally socialist nations.[69]

Similar agreements have been concluded, in the meantime, with a number of Western countries. Among these we must single out a 'general' agreement signed in July 1978 on trade and co-operation with Portugal and specific ones on maritime transport (i.e. use of Portuguese ships), on construction (particularly the sale of some $15m worth of prefabricated structures), and on electric power.[70] It would appear that trading links with the old colonial power have been reactivated a little recently and statements by Angola's Foreign Minister, visiting Portugal in the summer of 1979, convey an optimistic view of likely further developments of trade between the two countries.[71]

Among the other Western countries there have been significant increases in trade and/or economic agreements with Brazil, France, the UK, Sweden and Belgium. Brazil's exports to Angola, in particular, have been increasing spectacularly. Mostly consisting of industrial goods,[72] they must be seen in the context of Brazil's growing industrial power and her conscious policy of economic penetration in Africa. Reciprocally, Angola has itself increased its oil exports to Brazil. Sweden has sold Angola some 1,500 buses and lorries,[73] the UK has sold ships[74] and Belgium has entered an agreement on transport.[75] Renault of France has supplied a bus and car assembly plant,[76] a fact which has made French penetration look to some observers at least comparable to Brazil's, in terms of growing significance.[77] Finally, agreements have been announced with Zaire to increase trade and, more significantly, on the use by Zaire of Angola's railways and ports for the export of Zairean copper.[78]

Angola, like Mozambique, is outside the Lomé Agreement. But the EEC as a group has, also, despite disagreements among members, provided aid of some 8 million EUAs[79] towards repairing the Benguela rail line, the total cost of which has been estimated at some 63 million EUAs. Some US participation was even arranged by the EEC which had to be deflected, however, to Zaire's and Zambia's section of the line, due to the USA's continuing diplomatic differences with Angola. But there have also been contributions from The Netherlands (2 million) and Belgium (1 million). Finally a contribution of 7.7 million EUAs towards the same purpose has been received from the Arab Bank for Economic Development in Africa.[80] The EEC has in addition offered financial assistance for the relief of refugees.[81]

An idea of the relative influences of East and West in Angola can, perhaps, be gained by an examination of the respective numbers of personnel present in the country. The East is probably slightly ahead on numbers, and that is excluding the large Cuban military contingent still present. An estimate puts the number of Cuban military personnel at 19,000 (including troops, of course) in 1978,[82] plus about 7,300 civilians. The numbers of military and civilian experts from the USSR and Eastern Europe together are given by the same source as 1,300 and 1,400 respectively for the same year. That made a total of around 10,000 Communist technicians in 1978. Against them there has been a much smaller number of Western technicians, other than Portuguese, but a growing number of the latter. The number of Portuguese is, of course, only a small fraction of the 100,000 who left at independence.

Foreign trade and co-operation agreements are perhaps more indicative of attitudes on the international-political plane than ideological statements and even diplomatic relations. But as we have already seen some of the official views taken by the Angolan government on international relations, we must now examine the conduct of its practical diplomacy.

A major problem of Angolan diplomacy since independence has been the issue of recognition under the MPLA government. The issue split the OAU right in the middle in January 1976, with 23 countries in favour of the MPLA and 23 still in favour of a government of 'national unity'. But the MPLA did gain recognition, narrowly, soon afterwards. Then came the split with the USA and the American veto against admission to the UN. But that obstacle, too, was overcome on 1 December 1976, albeit more than a year after independence. There were difficulties with Portugal which had, on withdrawing, handed over power to the three liberation movements and refused to recognise the MPLA government alone, even after other Western powers, notably Britain and France, had done so. Portugal also became host to various anti-MPLA activities including those of UNITA and FNLA. But in June 1978 the two countries finally agreed to develop 'relations of friendship and solidarity . . . as well as economic and cultural co-operation'. The agreement was widely interpreted as meaning, among other things, that Portugal would take measures to restrict anti-MPLA activities and also seems to have led to something of a wave of applications by refugees to return to Angola.[83] Normalisation also took place with France which, again, seems to have undertaken no longer to support anti-MPLA activity in its territory. The relationship with the USA itself also appears to be getting warmer: a substantial trade continues. But diplomatic recognition is still being withheld by the USA as long as Cuban forces are still present in the country.[84] Certainly, the strategic objective of the USA with respect to Angola now seems to amount to little more than a reduction of the numbers of the Cuban military personnel stationed there.

The vast majority of the other countries have now recognised Angola. Significantly, perhaps, the first recognition, after the Soviet Union, of the MPLA as the legitimate government came from Brazil in 1975.[85] Angola's own diplomacy has been conciliatory as well, permitting, especially, normalisation with Zaire and trade with South Africa.

It seems necessary to distinguish four dimensions in Angola's political, economic and diplomatic position, not necessarily in order of importance. The first is the Marxist-ideological and military one which, as we have seen, orients the country towards the Communist bloc. The second is the regional, which draws Angola towards the rest of Africa and forges special links with Zaire and South Africa in particular. The third dimension is the historical one which has linked it to Portugal and, through that, to Brazil and the West in general. This link is particularly important, of course, in terms of the country's linguistic, religious and cultural development. But there is also a fourth dimension, i.e. the oil-producing one, which is now creating potential links with OPEC, which however she has not joined.

We have already discussed Angola's ideological commitment, its growing trade with the Communist world and its dependence on Communist military aid. It would thus not be surprising if the first of the four possible orientations outlined earlier turned out to be the dominant one in due course. The logical conclusion of that road is, of course, CMEA membership. But the other influences are also strong and *could* eventually take Angola away from that path. We must examine these in turn.

The regional dimension has two aspects. First there is the connection with South Africa. As we have seen, that country has now become Angola's ideological, political and military adversary and the differences seem, at first sight, irreconcilable. We have already discussed recent (and considerable) hostilities between them. As long as Angola continues to support SWAPO[86] South Africa can presumably be expected to continue supporting UNITA, creating a buffer zone between itself and the Marxist regime's forces. More fundamentally, South Africa may be hoping still to internationalise an eventual war with the Marxist regimes of Southern Africa.

But economic logic still pushes in the direction of reconciliation. Angola's trade with South Africa has been growing and, indeed, more rapidly than the average, as we have seen. That fact, in addition to the enormous cost for Angola of South African and UNITA hostilities, explains Angola's eagerness for a peaceful co-existence. She has indeed been seeking to establish a demilitarised zone along the Namibian border.[87] There have also been reports that Angola has been suggesting secret meetings with the South Africans to negotiate an end to border hostilities, and indeed reports that a meeting has already taken place.[88] We can venture the guess that as long as both the present regimes of Angola and South Africa remain stable a normalisation of relations can be expected.

The second aspect of the regional dimension is represented by the links with the other black states of Africa, particularly the neighbouring ones. Of considerable significance here has been normalisation with Zaire. It was not long ago, as we have seen, that Angola was denouncing that country as an outpost of imperialism and even as late as June 1978 President Mobutu of Zaire was declaring that 'reconciliation was out of the question for the time being'. But the need to resume shipments of copper on the Benguela line seems to have finally dictated an attitude of co-operation on Zaire's part. Angola, too, badly needs a secure Eastern border in view of hostilities with South Africa on its southern front. 'Reconciliation' finally came on 30 July 1978, and visits followed by the two Presidents to each other's capital. Zaire agreed to close FNLA and UNITA offices and appears to have ceased supporting these movements. Voluntary repatriation of the many mutual refugees has got under way.[89] But the most immediate task has been, of course, the restoration of the Benguela railway to full working. The line has in fact been functioning only intermittently due to constant sabotage by UNITA guerrillas.[90] But the incidence of such sabotage appears now to have been reduced.[91] The rhetoric also became a little more compatible as President Mobutu of Zaire condemned recently 'racist attacks by South Africa' and its 'illegal occupation of Namibian territory'.[92] Angola and Zaire have now established full diplomatic relations.

The potential links with other black African states (especially the southern 'front line' ones with respect to South Africa) are also extremely important. A conference of nine Heads of State from these countries in Lusaka in spring 1980 explored the possibilities of integrating their economies more closely and explicitly declared their intention to 'liberate their economies from their dependence on the Republic of South Africa'.[93] They saw transport as their first priority, noting that 'the dominance of the Republic of South Africa has been reinforced and strengthened by its transport system. Without the establishment of an adequate regional transport and communications system other areas of co-operation become impractical'.[94] The decline of trade between Angola and Mozambique (Table 2.4), despite the strong preference, which is of Portuguese origin, shows how right the heads of state were.

The Lusaka conference was followed by a meeting in Addis Ababa to discuss a proposal for a Preferential Trade Area in East and Southern Africa, and Angola signed the related draft treaty.[95] Policies of regional integration in Africa enjoy in any case the support in principle of the OAU, which has even been urging the formation of regional preferential trade zones. The Angola-Mozambique preference already exists, and the main effort has been directed towards expanding bilateral trade and co-operation in general with neighbouring countries. We have already discussed the recent development of such links with Zaire and Zambia. To these we must add the recent establishment of a joint commission in Lagos for trade and co-operation with Nigeria and a (third) visit by Congo's President S. Nguesso in autumn 1980.[96] It is worth noting that Nigeria, like the Congo, has supported the MPLA from the beginning of the armed conflict and actually offered financial assistance after independence.[97] Nigeria has also sent a small amount of exports to Angola but trade between the two countries still appears negligible at present.

The Western and Brazilian dimension, the third of the influences distinguished earlier, has been much in evidence, as we have seen already in the form of trade, co-operative agreements and aid. But aid in particular from the Western, or Western-dominated, agencies is a little problematic in that Angola is not, at least not yet, a member of key organisations such as the Lomé Convention and the IMF, although there has been persistent speculation that she is about to join the former.[98] But failure to join Lomé, so far, has been causing problems with aid towards repairing the Benguela railway, since, strictly, assistance to Angola (as opposed to Zaire and Zambia which are members) can only be granted under the 'Non-Associates Budget'. Similarly non-membership of the IMF has meant that Angola is not eligible for World Bank aid.[99] Aid has thus been received, in the main, from individual Western countries, as we have seen. But the strength of the present trade flows with the West, and the dominant position of Western culture (among the non-indigenous cultures) in the country will probably ensure that Angola's links with the West in general will continue very strong in the foreseeable future. In that light, a prediction that Angola will join both Lomé and the IMF seems justified. What Ethiopia can do she can do.

On the statistics for foreign aid and commercial capital from various sources see Table 1.2. The West is of course enormously ahead.

A prediction that links with South Africa will continue strong for a while can also be ventured. South Africa comes, of course, under both the 'Western' and the 'regional' heading. But South Africa's position in the West is an uneasy one and individual Western countries might choose to support black African states, like Angola, in a possible confrontation with it. A recent statement by Brazil's Foreign Minister, Guerreiro, during his recent five-country tour of Southern Africa, that Brazil might offer 'humanitarian aid to national liberation movements in Africa' highlights an interesting case in point. Brazil, whose own regime cannot be ranked as among the world's most 'liberal' at the present time, is already providing support to SWAPO, but does not feel 'intimate' enough with South Africa to mediate in the settlement of border disputes.[100]

That leaves us to consider lastly the fourth possible orientation outlined earlier, i.e. Angola's position as an oil producer. Oil presents both an internal and an international problem for Angola. Internal, in that most of it seems to be in the northern province of Cabinda, which is separated from the main body of the country by Zaire's corridor outlet to the Atlantic Ocean. Inevitably perhaps, a separatist movement (FLEC) has sprung up in Cabinda. While essentially defeated at present, together with the other anti-MPLA movements, FLEC still poses a threat of sabotage to Cabinda's oil wells, administered by Gulf, as we have seen. The remnants of UNITA also appear to have their sights set on this possibility,[101] although UNITA does not support the separatist claim. Angola's longer-term development may thus be jeopardised by loss of control in that sensitive area.

But oil is also posing an international-political problem in that rises in its price may be alienating certain of Angola's potential friends, i.e. the oil-consuming Third World in Africa and elsewhere. Oil may also alienate her from CMEA if she should come, for example, to regard it as more important to her development than CMEA aid. Angola has not yet joined OPEC but has been following OPEC's pricing policy. It is hardly inconceivable that she may also join OPEC in the near future. Here of course everything depends on the size of oil discoveries in the country and oil developments elsewhere. The present strength of Angola's oil exports may just be sufficient to induce something of the vision of a mainly oil-exporting state. That might mean a longer-term identification and alignment mainly with the oil-producing (and thus mainly not Marxist or African) countries. But that might in turn entail, for some time, a continued connection with the West, even if one limited mainly to co-operation with the oil multinationals.

Is Angola, in conclusion, a Marxist-Leninist state? The commitment of the leadership cannot be doubted. So the answer must be 'yes' if we use that as the main criterion. The conclusion must be confirmed by our foregoing analysis of the development of its political institutions. If the internal economy still looks, in parts, somewhat like a mixed one that can probably be explained in terms of Angola's underdevelopment. How soon she will make a serious attempt at planning remains to be seen. If she is strongly pragmatic in her international economic relations, that is probably inescapable in modern conditions. Angola knows that she needs the multinationals, to develop her natural resources, the trade with and the aid from the West, and a *modus vivendi* with South Africa for the near future. Pragmatism in general is eminently Leninist, anyway. The best generalisation is then, perhaps, that Angola is an STE in the making, currently passing through its NEP stage. It is most certainly not a case of 'War Communism', although she has been continually at war throughout her period of independence.

That is not to deny, and indeed we have suggested already, that there must be a large element of speculation in any prediction about the eventual shape of Angola's polity and economy in the long run. There are considerable attractions (and dangers) in several alternative paths, as we have seen, although these are not mutually exclusive in every case. Angola's diplomacy, in the circumstances, will need to be selective and agile. But she does seem to be firmly set on precisely such a course.

Notes

1. Kravis *et al.*, 1978.
2. See Table 1, World Bank, 1980.
3. Table 4, ibid.
4. Estimate available from private sources. But the World Bank (1980) also gives the growth rate as 9.1 per cent between 1960 and 1970.
5. See MAGIC, 1980, p. 6.
6. See *Marchés Tropicaux*, 23 April 1976.
7. But we must take note also that the traditional way in which balance-of-payments figures have been compiled by the Angolan Government is on a 'settlement' basis, i.e. from the records of external payments and receipts, which

generally differ from the value of actual flows of goods and services during the period covered. Thus the balance-of-payments figures of Table 2.3, made available to the author from private sources, do not reflect the big trade surpluses given for 1973 and 1974 by the UN data. The same picture emerges from Schümer (1977) p. 409 on figures taken from the *Boletim Trimestral* of the Bank of Angola.

8. Private sources.

9. See P. Fauvet in *People's Power*, no. 15, Winter 1979. The old colonial division between the *liceu* and the technical branches has now been replaced with free and compulsory education for all children between six and 14.

10. These three dates are from the pro-Cuban Garcia, 1977.

11. Incriminating correspondence is said to exist between J. Savimbi, UNITA's leader, and Portuguese generals. The claim is that the Portuguese were building up UNITA in the early 1970s as an irregular force for fighting against the MPLA in the Eastern provinces. See MAGIC, 1980, p. 11.

12. For a thorough analysis of the Angolan civil war see C. Legum in *Africa Contemporary Record*, 1975/6.

13. See MAGIC, 1980. Also various issues of *People's Power*.

14. See MAGIC, 1980.

15. See *People's Power*, no. 11, January-March 1978.

16. Seventy members of the council were to remain as members of the 200 Assembly and E. dos Santos was to stay President and Commander-in-Chief. See SWB ME/6566/B3, November 1980.

17. See MAGIC, 1980. Also various issues of *People's Power*.

18. See *ARB*, Political, Social and Cultural Series, August 1980.

19. Ibid.

20. Meeting with diplomatic representatives in Luanda on 24 February 1977, reported in *People's Power*, nos. 7-8, June 1977.

21. Among the various reports see, for example, the *Guardian*, 30 June 1980, 1 July 1980 and 3 July 1980. The damage only for the period between May 1978 and July 1979 was put at $100m by the Angolan government in a document presented to the UN Security Council. See MAGIC, 1980.

22. See *Africa Contemporary Record*, 1976/77.

23. MAGIC, 1980.

24. MPLA, 1979.

25. Ibid.

26. MAGIC, 1980.

27. *Marchés Tropicaux*, 23 April 1976.

28. I.e. state take-over of control. The term tends to imply that legal ownership will be settled later.

29. See MAGIC, 1980.

30. MPLA, 1979.

31. MAGIC, 1980.

32. See *People's Power*, no. 12, Autumn-Winter 1978.

33. See *People's Power*, no. 14, Summer, 1979. Also *ARB*, June-July 1979.

34. *Nachrichten fur Aussenhandel*, 27 September 1978. Also MAGIC, 1980.

35. MAGIC, 1980.

36. *Marchés Tropicaux*, 25 May 1978.

37. A particularly scathing attack on inefficiency in state enterprises accompanied a set of resolutions issued by the Political Bureau on 23 June 1979. See *ARB*, June-July, 1979. It is particularly deplored that shortages of goods lead to black markets and 'speculation'.

38. See MAGIC, 1980.

39. *Informazioni per il Commercio Estero*, 18 August 1979.

40. See *ARB*, June-July 1979.

41. *SWB*, ME/W1035, 12 June 1979. This use of currency reform against exciles is Cuban, not Soviet.

42. *To the Point*, 3 August 1980.

43. MAGIC, 1980. This shareholding is thought to entitle the foreign interest to a dividend, and so not to be fictitious.

44. *ARB*, February-March 1978.

45. *ARB*, January-February 1979 and October-November 1979.

46. *ARB*, August-September 1980.

47. See the *Guardian*, 7 November 1979.

48. See *Informazioni per il Commercio Estero*, 18 July 1979.

49. Alternative Bank of Angola estimates, as reported in *Informazioni per il Commercio Estero*, 18 July 1979, put the 1977 exports as $910m and imports at $680m. The corresponding estimates for 1978 are: exports $950m, imports $750m.

50. See also *Marchés Tropicaux*, 23 April 1976.

51. FES *Bericht*, I/1978 and I/1979.

52. *SWB*, ME/W1045/21, August 1979. Also FES *Bericht*, I/1978.

53. *SWB*, ME/W1032/22 May 1979.

54. *SWB*, 12 February 1980.

55. *ARB*, October-November 1979.

56. CEPII, 1979. Also FES *Bericht*, I/1978.

57. FES *Bericht*, I-II/1979.

58. FES *Bericht*, I-II/1979. See also NFAC, 1979, where the number of non-military Cuban personnel present in 1978 is given as 8,500. Many of these were teachers and medical personnel.

59. *SWB*, ME/6550/B/4, 16 October 1980.

60. See *South*, Nov. 1980. (New journal published from New Zealand House.)

61. CEPII, 1979. Also FES *Bericht*, I/1979.

62. CEPII, 1979, *SWB*, ME/1074, 5 June 1979, and FES *Bericht*, I/1978.

63. *SWB*, 23 January 1979. Also 5 August 1980.

64. FES *Bericht*, I/1979, reports considerable deliveries of transport, cargo handling, etc., equipment from East Germany, as well as a visit to Angola by the East German President. See also CEPII, 1979.

65. *SWB* ME/W1044, 14 August 1979. Also FES *Bericht* II/1979.

66. CEPII, 1979. Also FES *Bericht* II/1979.

67. FES *Bericht* I-II/1979.

68. CEPII, 1979, and FES *Bericht* I/1979.

69. CEPII, 1979.

70. *SWB*, 20 February 1979, ME W1030/8 May 1979, and ME 1041/24 July 1980.

71. *SWB*, W1042/31 July 1979.

72. Fishing vessels among them. See *ARB*, March-April 1979.

73. *SWB*, ME W/1040/17 July 1979. Also 5 February 1980.

74. *ARB*, June-July 1980.

75. *SWB*, 28 July 1979.

76. *SWB*, ME/W1095/12 August 1980.

77. See the *Guardian*, 20 September 1980.

78. *SWB*, ME/W1095/12 August 1980, and ME/6547/B/3, 13 October 1980.

79. The $ value of the EUA is not fixed but it has tended to fluctuate around 1 SDR = $1.25 approx.

80. *SWB*, ME/W1037, 26 June 1979. See also report in *To the Point*, 13 July 1979.

81. *ARB*, April-May 1980.

82. NFAC, 1979.

83. See *People's Power*, no. 12, Autumn-Winter 1978.

84. See *To the Point*, 24 October 1980.

85. *South*, November 1980.

86. Angola's President, E. dos Santos, has recently reaffirmed this support. See the *Guardian*, 4 November 1979.

87. See the *Guardian*, 22 October 1980. Also MAGIC, 1980.

88. See the *Guardian*, 1 November 1980, and 4 November 1980.

89. *People's Power*, no. 12, Autumn-Winter, 1978.

90. *To the Point*, 24 October 1980.

91. See MAGIC, 1980.

92. Joint Communiqué after Mobutu's visit of 3 July 1980. See *ARB* (Political/Social/Cultural Series), August 1980.

93. See the *Guardian*, 24 November 1980.

94. Ibid.

95. *ARB*, May-June 1980.

96. *SWB*, ME/6550, 28 October 1980.

97. *ARB*, August-September 1980, and *Garcia*, 1977.

98. The *Guardian*, 4 November 1980.

99. See MAGIC, 1980.

100. *ARB* (Political/Social/Cultural Series), June 1980.

101. *To the Point*, 22 February 1980.

3 ETHIOPIA

Barry Lynch

Introduction

Ethiopia (that remains its official name) is bordered by Somalia on the
east, Kenya on the south, the Sudan on the west and Djibouti and the
Red Sea on the north-east. The country covers an area of 1 million
square km. It is mainly a mountainous country, volcanic in origin.
The lowlands are semi-arid, the land being used mainly for grazing; the
highland plateaux are well watered and have a genial climate.

The population of Ethiopia is estimated to be 32,187,000 (January
1980) and has been growing at an average annual rate of 2.5 per cent.
The population comprises many ethnic groups, none of which is in the
majority. The culturally dominant group is the Amhara and Tigreans
(32 per cent of the population). The Amhara peoples inhabit the
central highlands. The Tigreans, an ethnically similar (of mixed Hamitic
and Semitic origins) but linguistically dissimilar group, live to the north
of the Amhara.

The Galla are the most numerous group – 40 per cent of the
population. They are a pastoral and agricultural people of Hamitic
origin. The Somalis, another Hamitic people, comprise six per cent of
the population and inhabit the southeast of Ethiopia, especially the
Ogaden desert region.

The two major religions of the country are Christianity (the
Ethiopian Orthodox Church) and Islam, each claiming adherents of
about 40 per cent of the population. Fifteen to twenty per cent of the
population are pagan. The basic distinction is between the peoples of
the highlands, who are generally Orthodox Christians and farmers,
and those of the lowlands, who are mostly Islamic and nomadic. The
population is also linguistically heterogeneous. The official language
is Amharic, but many other languages are spoken. The currency of
Ethiopia is the Birr (until 1976, the Ethiopian dollar). Its rate of
exchange with the US dollar was 2.5 throughout the 1960s. The rate
fell to 2.11 by 1974 and 2.09 by 1980. The foreign-trade participation
ratio is about twelve per cent (IFS, various issues). If judged by GDP
per capita, Ethiopia is one of the least developed countries in Africa.
In 1970 it was approximately $190.[1] As is characteristic of the

countries in early stages of economic development, primary production is of overwhelming importance with 45 per cent of production assumed to take place at the subsistence level. The level of general education is low, with 95 per cent illiteracy. There has been a shortage of skilled labour of all kinds and an abundance of unskilled workers which is disguised in agricultural unemployment.

The economy revolves around agriculture. Over 50 per cent of GDP and 90 per cent of employment are directly attributable to agriculture and agri-business, but the country is barely self-sufficient in food. In addition, nearly 90 per cent of external trade revenue is derived from agricultural produce; and three-quarters of industrial activity relies on agriculture for inputs.

The Revolution

The revolution began, after much university unrest, in 1974 with a military movement against the feudal rule of the Emperor, Haile Selassie. In February, there was labour unrest in Addis Ababa which was paralleled by mutinies in most units of the armed forces. The government of Aklilu Habte Wold, the Prime Minister since 1961, resigned and a new Prime Minister, Lij Endalkatchew Makonnen, was appointed with a mandate to carry out reforms, including constitutional changes. By June, the effort to institute reforms had stagnated and the newly formed Co-ordinating Committee of the Armed Forces, Police and Territorial Army took action. The Emperor was deposed (12 September), the constitution abrogated and Parliament dissolved.

A provisional military government — the Dergue or Provisional Military Administrative Council (PMAC) — was set up in place of the imperial regime. Some of the previous civilian ministers were retained to run the administration. The aim of the new government was to aid the poverty-stricken country in a campaign for 'national unity and economic salvation'. Lt-General Aman Andom was appointed the Head of State and chairman of the Dergue, which comprised 120 elected members from the Army, the Air Force and the Police. Internal power struggles began between a new ruling group of 'revolutionary cadres' and an amalgamation of disaffected groups, such as urban revolutionaries, middle-class elites and feudal interest groups. These struggles led to the assassination of Lt-General Aman and two other members of the Dergue in November 1974. At the same time 57

former high-ranking military and civilian officials were summarily
executed without trial. This moment, then, was the real revolution.
Brigadier-General Teferi Banti was chosen as the new Head of State
and figurehead chairman of the Dergue. Two vice chairmen, Major
(later Lt-Colonel) Mengistu Haile Mariam and Lt-Colonel Atnafu
Abati, were the real power in the Dergue.

The new rulers were of Marxist-Leninist persuasion. The Dergue
began to see itself as the vanguard of the Ethiopian revolution. Under
the influence of left-wing intellectuals returning from abroad, it opted
for a socialist model of government and development. Ethiopia was
declared a socialist state on 20 December 1974. Ethiopia was to apply
socialism on the basis of a ten point programme:

1. maintenance of national unity without ethnic, religious, linguistic
or cultural differences;
2. establishment of an economic, cultural and social community
with Kenya, Somalia and the Sudan;
3. 'equality, the right to guide one's own destiny and the right to
work and earn' — definition of 'Ethiopian socialism';
4. self-sufficiency at regional and village level;
5. establishment of a political party — the Supreme Progressive
Council — based on the revolutionary philosophy of 'Ethiopia
first' (nationalism) and socialism;
6. complete state control of the economy;
7. the right to own land restricted to those who work on it; state
land to be cultivated collectively; private farmers to be given
government directives;
8. industry to be managed by the state;
9. the family to be the basis of society;
10. unchanged foreign policy.

Domestic Policy

With the declaration of socialism, the new government soon initiated a
series of economic and social reforms. On 1 January 1975, six banks, all
mortgage corporations and fourteen insurance companies were
nationalised, with combined total assets amounting to $10 million.
Compensation was to be paid at a future date. On 3 February, 72
enterprises in the manufacturing and distribution sectors were
nationalised and state participation acquired in 29 others. Firms

affected included Shell, Agip, Mobil and Total.

On 3 March 1975, the Land Reform Proclamation made all rural land the collective property of the people (note the exact parallel with Lenin's 1917 land decree: the land was not nationalised). The reform abolished the landlord-tenant relationship and gave each peasant up to 10 hectares (25 acres) of land. The use of hired labour was prohibited. The peasants were organised into Peasants' Associations, each of which could farm up to 800 hectares commercially and would have a legal status with self-government and judiciary powers. The reallocation of land was extended to the urban areas in July of the same year. Businesses and rented houses were seized by the state. Urban Dwellers' Associations were formed. The Peasants' and Urban Dwellers' Associations were established to organise the social and economic activities of the country. They were used as tax and rent collection bodies, and were placed in charge of primary and secondary education. They were also responsible for security and social functions including the distribution of consumer goods in short supply.

Alternative power centres were abolished. The Confederation of Ethiopian Labour Unions (CELU), which had been established in the 1960s by the AFL-CIO, was abolished in December. It had been in the forefront of activist groups which spearheaded the popular uprisings leading to the revolution. But it opposed the continued military rule and was branded as reactionary and was disbanded. It was replaced by a more centralised and controllable organisation, the All-Ethiopian Labour Union (8 January 1977).

On 12 December 1975 the Dergue issued the Proclamation on Commercial Activities. It limited the extent of a private firm's capital in industry to $250,000; in wholesale trade to $150,000; and in retail activities to $100,000. This was a continuation of government measures to place major concerns under public ownership, and to control activities still under private ownership.

On 21 April 1976, the National Democratic Revolution Programme was announced. It analysed in Marxist terms the class structure and alliances of Ethiopia. Its objective was to strengthen the economy and raise the standard of living by consolidating the gains of the revolution: the destruction of the monarchy; the proclamation of socialism; the reallocation of rural and urban land and the means of production and distribution; labour law reform; and the creation of farmers' co-operatives. The stated objective of the programme was the creation of a People's Democratic Republic through the leadership of a single party of the proletariat and other progressive parties and institutions.

Internal Politics

The Dergue's internal problems arose over the question of political activity it had promised to allow under the April 1976 programme. In mid-1976, the Dergue gave its support to the All-Ethiopia Socialist Movement (Me'ei Sone), a Marxist-Leninist group supported by Mengistu. It wanted a Soviet-style Communist party and was prepared to accept the necessity of military rule for the time being. The other more popular Marxist-Leninist party, the Ethiopian People's Revolutionary Party (EPRP), insisted on civilian rule. It had published its programme in 1975, calling for a people's civilian government and support for Eritrean independence. The party was pro-Chinese in orientation. In September 1976, the Dergue and Me'ei Sone launched a major campaign against the EPRP which led to an increase in urban terrorism, especially in Addis Ababa. A wave of assassinations of government and Me'ei Sone figures in October led to the banning of all political parties. In November, 50 EPRP members were executed. This inter-party rivalry continued throughout 1977 with the EPRP organising strikes and discontent throughout the country. The Dergue armed its supporters and initiated the 'red terror' campaign which climaxed in December 1977 and January 1978 with mass executions of EPRP supporters. Me'ei Sone itself had disappeared by mid-1977.

Afterwards, the Dergue founded its own Marxist-Leninist group, the 'Abyot Seded' or 'Revolutionary Flame' which was a Marxist-Leninist party with a strong military membership. A split developed over whether elements in the Dergue should control the party and how centralised the organisation should be. Arrests in 1978 made it clear that the Dergue would take the lead in a centralised Communist party. By mid-1977, the Dergue, despite its own divisions and opposition to it from the Ethiopian left, had gone a long way towards establishing a power base in the new institutions it had created – the peasant and urban dwellers' associations, and the All-Ethiopian Trade Union. The 'Seded', its own political party, had made itself the most likely candidate for future political power.

After the Ogaden War (see 'Foreign Policy and Aid') Ethiopia came under increasing pressure from the Soviet Union (and Cuba) to form a civilian party which would replace military rule. Mengistu has been appointed head of a commission to draw up plans for the structure of such a party. It is envisaged that this party will be the sole legal political organisation.

The Economy

Since the revolution, the economy has been fundamentally altered by domestic policies and foreign developments. The nationalisation of private financial institutions and the reallocation of rural and urban land and rented buildings transformed the structure of ownership to a socialist basis. The aim of the wholesale nationalisation of the economy was the establishment of a self-reliant centrally planned economy. The immediate effect was a redistribution of income in favour of the rural poor.

As the economy began to adjust to these fundamental ideological and organisational changes, it was crippled in 1977 and 1978 by large-scale warfare and crop losses. The war fought with the Somali forces in the defence of the Ogaden region and nearby highlands required the diversion of resources and manpower from productive purposes, and was accompanied by major destruction of the economic infrastructure in that area. The Ogaden War was followed by an intensification of the Eritrean and other insurgencies in the north of the country. Many manufacturing firms were idled and the production and movement of export crops disrupted. The area was not made secure until the second half of 1978. Meanwhile, the recurrence of drought in some parts of the country and pest-infestation resulted in a serious loss of agricultural production, particularly of cereals, and in the reappearance of food shortages. The end of major hostilities after mid-1978 permitted a shifting of national effort to the task of revitalising the economy. Meanwhile the movement of GNP per head has been estimated by the OECD (1980) as follows: 1975 = 100, 1976 = 100, 1977 = 100, 1978 = 97, 1979 = 100.

Agriculture

Agriculture is the principal economic activity, accounting for about one-half of GDP in recent years (see Table 3.1) and the employment of nearly 85 per cent of the labour force. The bulk of the cultivated land is in the highlands. The lowlands are used mainly for nomadic livestock-raising, except in areas where irrigation systems have been built. Agricultural techniques before the revolution were rudimentary and of low productivity, although some modern commercial farms were started during the 1960s. These accounted for only 7 per cent of total agricultural production.

Table 3.1: Gross Domestic Product by Industrial Origin: Percentage of Total at Current Factor Cost

	1960	1965	1970	1971	1972	1973	1974	1975	1976
Total ($m)	890	1275	1704	1765	1770	2001	n.a.	n.a.	n.a.
Agriculture	64.8	61.3	54.8	54.5	54.8	54.7	47.5	49.5	51.9
Mining	0.1	0.3	0.2	0.2	0.2	0.2	n.a.	n.a.	n.a.
Manufacturing	6.1	6.9	10.1	10.1	10.1	10.1	6.1	5.7	5.3
Construction	5.6	5.2	5.6	5.6	5.6	5.6	4.6	4.0	3.9
Electricity, gas, water	0.4	0.4	0.6	0.6	0.6	0.6	n.a.	n.a.	n.a.
Transportation and Communication	3.0	3.7	3.7	3.7	3.7	3.7	5.3	5.5	4.9
Trade	6.9	8.5	9.6	9.6	9.6	9.6	10.2	10.0	9.4
Public Administration and Defence	3.8	4.9	5.3	5.3	5.3	5.3	6.8	6.6	7.0
Other	9.2	8.8	10.2	10.2	10.2	10.2	n.a.	n.a.	n.a.

Source: *UN Statistical Yearbook*, 1978.

The land reform of March 1975 abolished private ownership of rural land and eliminated all tenant farming. Farmers' associations were formed, each covering an area of about 800 hectares. The commercial farms were taken over by the state. Individual farmers were granted user rights on the land they were already farming or had acquired through the associations. A limit of 10 hectares — compared with a national average of about two — was set as the size holding of any one family. The user rights could be bequeathed but not sold. The hiring of labour was, in general, prohibited. By the end of 1978, more than 25,000 associations had been established with nearly 7 million members. In addition, some 2,300 service co-operatives were formed by the associations to facilitate the marketing of their produce and to gain access to loans. The State Farms Development Authority oversees the nationalised commercial farms which have been grouped into regional corporations. The acreage under state farm control has increased since 1976 through the acquisition of unused land. This followed a decline in size after the revolution because of the redistribution of land to the farmers' associations.

There are, in addition to the associations and the state farms, collectively farmed holdings. Forty have been registered as producer co-operatives since the revolution. The state farms are generally mechanised, which has led to higher productivity than on farms within the associations. While state farms account for less than 4 per cent of the volume of agricultural production, and only two per cent of food crops, they contribute nearly a quarter of marketed food crops. Over half of their acreage is devoted to non-food export and industrial crops, mainly cotton. They have also received a large share of investment in the agricultural sector in recent years.

Since the revolution the growth of food production has been lower than the rate of population growth. This has necessitated increased grain imports. Much of the shortfall has been made up by international donations to the Relief and Rehabilitation Commission to assist victims of drought. But an increasing amount has had to be covered by imports on a commercial basis. Such imports have been controlled through the Agricultural Marketing Corporation, a state trading agency, which purchases grain from domestic and foreign suppliers for sale in the domestic market. A separate agency deals with the marketing of commercial coffee production — the Coffee Marketing Corporation.

The outlook for agriculture is bleak. A large-scale return to subsistence farming has occurred following the land reforms and the nationalisation of the commercial farms, transport difficulties and the farmers' inability to move cash-crops to the markets. There is, however, considerable potential. Almost 70 per cent (approximately 83 million hectares) of the land area of the country is cultivable. Currently only 13 per cent is productive. With a significant increase in investment and transport infrastructure, Ethiopia could become at least self-sufficient in food.

Manufacturing and Industry

The modern manufacturing, the small-scale industrial and the traditional handicraft sectors account for just over ten per cent of GDP. The handicrafts sector, accounting for about half of all industrial production, covers a quarter of a million cottage enterprises which provide substantial employment. Manufacturing constitutes just over five per cent of GDP (see Table 3.1). This is due mainly to the failure to build up export-oriented industries. As a result, manufacturing is basically import-substituting and has been viable only with heavy protection. Manufacturing is centred around two principal cities: Addis Ababa and Asmara. Textiles and the processing of tobacco, beverages and food (mainly sugar) account for 60 per cent of all manufacturing output. Other products are shoes, mineral water, cement and bricks.

Before 1975, manufacturing was generally in private hands, although the state did have substantial investments in the sector. Nationalisation established government control over basic industries: those producing primary goods and creating production linkages, and consumer industries. The private sector was allowed to continue to engage in food processing, metal products fabrication and other activities. 'Sector corporations' were established by merging the wholly nationalised enterprises within each branch of industry and placed under the overall policy direction of the Ministry of Industry. As a result, manufacturing is dominated by the public sector with wholly and partially government-owned firms accounting for nearly 90 per cent of output. Despite nationalisation, little has been done by the government to expand the industrial and service sectors. Within the sectors, corporations and plants have autonomy in day-to-day management. They must present annual budgets and projected output, sales and investment targets to the Ministry for approval. Investment and budgetary control have been centralised. The increase in state intervention in the economy has caused the size of the public sector to increase. In the early 1970s budgetary expenditure accounted for twelve per cent of GDP while now it is more than 20.

Economic Development

Ethiopia recognised the need for development planning in the late 1950s with the introduction of the first development plan (1958-63). Agriculture was recognised as the mainstay of the economy, and agricultural land the main national asset. In February 1979, Ethiopia launched an economic development campaign, the National Development Campaign, with the declared long-term aim of laying the foundation of a socialist community. This was to be achieved through effecting a radical change in the economic structure of the country. The economy — presently based on farms and small-scale industry — is to be expanded by increasing the productive capacity of existing farms, introducing heavy industry and providing modern agricultural implements. Agricultural production is to be increased by eleven to twelve per cent over recent levels, an increase of 600,000 tons; manufacturing output is to rise by 45 per cent over the 1977/8 level; the distribution of goods is to be rationalised; foreign exchange earnings are to be increased; and exports of coffee, oilseeds and hides increased by 33 per cent. The objectives for the agricultural sector are to be met through more than doubling the area cultivated by state farms (an increase of 8,200 hectares), a small increase in acreage held by smallholders and an increase in the number of peasant co-operatives. The aim of establishing new co-operatives is to promote socialism in the rural areas. The means of production — oxen, cattle, farm equipment and land — are to be owned by the co-operatives which are to reimburse their members for all their inputs. The harvest, less debt and reserves, will be shared on the basis of 'from each according to his ability, to each according to his work'. This is a fundamental change in the constitution of the co-operative as it presently exists, where the means of production are pooled and the harvests shared more or less equally, while the peasants retain ownership rights to their inputs. The new co-operatives appear to be similar to Soviet kolkhozy. Agricultural yields are to be improved through the increased provision of fertiliser, pesticides and improved seeds to farmers (the Minimum Package Programme). In addition, to reduce crop losses and improve the marketing of agricultural produce, substantial additions to storage capacity are to be built. A major problem is severe land erosion in the north and north-central highlands, where population pressures have extended cultivation to steeper land and denuded it of its natural cover. The government has begun a major resettlement and reforestation programme to combat this. The goal is to close the gap between an increasing population — 2.5 per cent per year — and decreasing food production. Agricultural output decreased by 800,000 tons between 1976 and 1978, from 5.5 to 4.7 million tons, due to drought and the Ogaden war. The plan is to increase production to 5.3 million tons by the 1979/80 harvest.

The effort in the industrial sector concentrates on the raising of productivity of existing plants, starting industrial training programmes and reducing bottlenecks in the flow of imported inputs. In the distributive sector, the focus is on establishing more public sector organisations.

Foreign Trade

As can be seen in Table 3.2 four-fifths of exports are based on agricultural products, mostly coffee. Manufactures constitute the second largest category (about one-fifth of total exports) but three-quarters of these are food, beverages and tobacco (i.e. agricultural) products. Ethiopia's most important export markets have been the advanced capitalist countries (see Table 3.3). In 1970 they accounted for 80 per cent of total exports. This proportion declined to just over 70 per cent in 1973. After the revolution, trade with the advanced capitalist countries continued at about the pre-revolutionary level after an initial fall in 1974 and 1975. It was not the Communist countries which benefited from this decline, however, but rather the developing market and OPEC economies. Exports to Communist countries did not increase until 1977 and 1978, the years of the Ogaden War.

Raw materials are the major category of civilian imports (see Table 3.2), accounting for just over a third of total imports. Fuels and lubricants, machinery, transport and consumer goods have each accounted for about 15 per cent of the total since 1974. As with exports, the advanced capitalist countries have been the principal countries supplying Ethiopia's imports (see Table 3.4). In 1970 they supplied 80 per cent of total imports, the EEC, EFTA and Japan being the most important sources. By 1973 the proportion had declined to three-quarters and continued to fall after the revolution.

Table 3.2: The Commodity Structure of Ethiopian Trade

Exports by industrial origin: percentage of total value

	1970	1971	1972	1973	1974	1975	1976
Agriculture	82.2	80.6	75.0	72.7	80.3	79.1	79.1
Mining and quarrying	0.4	0.5	0.3	0.3	0.5	0.4	0.1
Manufacturing	17.3	18.9	24.7	27.0	19.2	20.5	20.8
of which foods, beverages, tobacco	14.0	15.7	21.6	23.3	15.1	14.6	16.5

Civilian imports by economic category (SITC): percentage of total value

	1970	1971	1972	1973	1974	1975	1976
Foods and beverages	8.5	7.3	5.8	6.1	5.3	4.0	5.2
Raw materials	33.1	31.9	32.0	35.6	36.8	36.3	30.2
Fuels and lubricants	7.1	9.4	5.9	8.1	12.8	16.4	14.2
Machinery	20.1	21.6	24.2	16.1	15.2	13.2	12.1
Transport	17.6	17.8	19.6	19.4	15.3	15.0	21.4
Consumer goods	13.3	11.2	11.7	13.8	13.8	14.6	15.5

Source: *UNYITS*, vol. I, 1976, 1979; Ethiopian and IMF sources.

Table 3.3: Exports (f.o.b) by Principal Country: Percentage of Total Value

	1970	1971	1972	1973	1974	1975	1976	1977	1978	1979
Advanced capitalist	80.6	76.7	75.1	73.1	67.8	55.8	71.8	n.a.	n.a.	71.2
United States	48.7	43.9	35.2	30.1	19.5	19.5	32.6	25.8	31.0	29.1
EEC & EFTA	22.4	22.7	25.7	30.2	32.3	23.2	27.8	23.3*	27.0*	27.9
of which Italy	6.2	5.3	8.2	7.8	6.7	4.5	6.9	4.8	5.9	11.2
FRG	7.3	7.9	7.3	8.8	11.4	7.8	6.0	8.6	11.8	6.4
Asian	7.2	7.4	9.1	7.6	10.5	11.1	8.1	n.a.	n.a.	6.1
Middle East	9.8	10.2	9.3	9.6	15.0	17.5	11.3	n.a.	n.a.	11.7
Saudi Arabia	6.2	6.4	5.8	6.2	8.9	13.3	7.4	8.6	11.2	8.6
Developing capitalist	8.2	9.7	10.0	11.6	13.3	23.3	14.0	n.a.	n.a.	7.5
Djibouti	5.1	6.3	5.8	6.9	6.9	11.7	8.5	4.8	1.3	5.8
Egypt	0.2	0.1	0.1	1.1	2.2	8.6	3.9	1.5	0.3	
Communist	1.2	3.2	5.5	5.7	3.9	2.6	2.9	n.a.	n.a.	9.5
CMEA	0.6	2.5	2.5	2.6	3.1	1.9	1.8	16.7	15.9	9.4
of which GDR	–	–	–	–	–	–	0.1	14.5	7.7	0.1
China	0.6	0.7	3.0	3.0	0.8	0.6	1.1	n.a.	n.a.	

Sources: *UNYITS*, vol. 1, 1976, 1979: Ethiopian and IMF sources.

* EEC only.

Table 3.4: Civilian Imports (c.i.f.) by Principal Country: Percentage of Total Value

	1970	1971	1972	1973	1974	1975	1976	1977	1978	1979
Advanced Capitalist	79.2	79.1	77.6	76.5	72.6	68.2	69.6	n.a.	n.a.	64.8
North American	8.6	9.3	9.2	8.6	5.8	7.7	17.9	10.2	5.9	12.0
EEC & EFTA	51.2	49.8	50.0	51.0	50.3	45.4	35.9	33.4*	45.1*	39.3
of which Italy	17.6	16.1	16.4	14.8	15.5	11.3	8.8	11.1	15.0	9.8
FRG	13.6	11.1	10.7	11.6	12.1	10.3	8.8	9.0	13.8	9.9
Asian	16.6	16.6	17.0	15.6	15.4	14.0	14.1	n.a.	n.a.	11.8
Middle East	7.0	8.4	7.1	8.5	9.5	16.8	14.0	n.a.	n.a.	16.5
Saudi Arabia	0.2	0.5	0.1	0.2	0.7	14.9	12.9	4.1	0.2	0.1
Iran	6.0	6.6	5.9	6.7	7.4	1.0	0.8	0.4	0.1	0.4
Developing capitalist	8.1	7.5	8.9	8.8	10.6	8.8	10.5	n.a.	n.a.	8.8
Asian	4.8	5.0	5.2	5.1	6.3	6.1	7.2	n.a.	n.a.	6.4
Communist	5.5	4.7	6.2	5.9	6.0	5.5	4.9	9.3	8.7	9.0
CMEA	4.0	3.5	4.6	3.9	4.0	3.8	3.3	6.5	6.3	7.8
of which USSR	–	–	1.0	1.1	1.7	1.5	1.3	1.8	0.8	1.9
China	1.5	1.2	1.6	2.0	2.1	1.7	1.6	2.8	2.4	1.1

Sources: *UNYITS*, vol. I, 1976, 1979: Ethiopian and IMF sources.
* EEC only.

The revolution had a direct influence on its trade with the OPEC countries. Before 1974, Ethiopia bought most of its oil from Iran. This trade ended in 1974 but was picked up by Saudi Arabia until 1977 when Ethiopia became more closely aligned with the Soviet bloc. In that year imports from the bloc, probably including oil, nearly doubled, although oil imports have not been itemised in the trading accounts with the USSR.

Soviet-Ethiopian trade is shown in Table 3.5. Imports and exports increased only slightly after the revolution. The trade balance shifted in favour of the Soviet Union in 1975 but it was not until 1977 that Soviet exports increased significantly. In that year they increased six-fold, most of the increase arising from exports of machinery. Exports were treble and double the 1977 level in 1978 and 1979 respectively. In 1978, half (31.5 million transferable roubles) of exports comprised heavy vehicles. Over the two years the unspecified residual increased from 1.1 to 37.2 million roubles. This may be masking military hardware shipments to Ethiopia.

In terms of foreign trade the period 1974-6 could be characterised by 'free-market' Marxism-Leninism. Although Ethiopia had declared itself a socialist state, gained observer status within the CMEA and sought aid from the Communist countries, it was not until 1977 that trade patterns began to reflect this change of policy. The seemingly strange point 10 (see page 91) of the declaration of December 1974 (unchanged foreign policy) reflected the high but already declining level of US support (see below).

The internal institutional arrangements also began to change. As part of the transition to a centrally-planned economy the role of the public sector in foreign trade was expanded. The Coffee Marketing Corporation increased the proportion of coffee exports it handles. The role of the Agricultural Marketing Corporation, in addition to its role in imports, was expanded to cover the exporting of agricultural commodities.

Foreign Policy and Aid

During the rule of Haile Selassie, the United States was Ethiopia's main ally. During the 1950s and 1960s, Ethiopia was the largest recipient of US military and civilian aid in Africa. Over the period 1952 to 1961, American civilian aid amounted only to a little over $99 million: $12 million in the form of grants and the remainder in loans. The 1974

Table 3.5: Soviet-Ethiopian Trade (millions of transferable roubles)

	1970	1971	1972	1973	1974	1975	1976	1977	1978	1979
Exports	1.3	1.3	1.6	1.6	2.6	3.2	3.6	22.4	64.2	44.6
Imports	0.8	2.9	2.1	2.2	3.6	2.1	0.7	1.5	4.3	18.6
Trade balance	0.5	−1.6	−0.5	−0.6	−1.0	1.1	2.9	20.9	59.9	26.0
Exports to Ethiopia										
Total given	1.3	1.3	1.6	1.6	2.6	3.2	3.6	22.4	64.2	44.6
Specified	1.2	1.1	1.6	1.3	2.2	2.7	3.0	21.3	55.1	7.4
Machinery/equipment	0.5	0.5	1.1	0.8	1.3	1.0	1.5	20.1	55.0	7.3
Oil, oil products	0.3	0.3	0.1	0.1	0.1					
Chemicals, fertilisers		0.1	0.1	0.1	0.1	0.2	0.3			
Industrial consumer-goods	0.4	0.2	0.4	0.4	0.7	1.5	1.2	1.2	0.1	0.1
Unspecified	0.1	0.2	–	0.3	0.4	0.5	0.6	1.1	9.1	37.2
Imports from Ethiopia										
Total given	0.8	2.9	2.1	2.2	3.6	2.1	0.7	1.5	4.3	18.6
Specified	0.8	2.9	1.9	1.7	3.4	1.5	0.6	1.3	4.1	18.4
Hides	0.5	0.4			0.6					
Sesame seeds	0.3	0.5	1.5	1.2	1.5	1.3		1.3		
Pulses		0.5	0.4	0.5	1.3	0.2				
Coffee		1.5					0.6		4.1	18.4
Unspecified	–	–	0.2	0.5	0.2	0.6	0.1	0.2	0.2	0.2

Source: *VT*, various years.

revolution came at a time of declining American influence in and support for Ethiopia. First, American interest in the area dwindled after 1973 when the basis of its international military communication network changed. At the end of 1973 the two countries agreed to the closure of the US communications base at Kagnew, near Asmara. Secondly, American interest in the balance of power in the Horn of Africa was lessened by an increase in activities in the area by Saudi Arabia, Egypt and Israel. Since the 1969 Somalia *coup*, the United States had been arming Ethiopia purely to check the Soviet build up in Somalia. In spite of Ethiopian requests for additional military aid after the left-wing military take-over in Somalia, the United States steadily reduced its military shipments from an average of $12 million over the previous years to $10 million in 1973/4.

Ethiopia's foreign policy after the revolution was similar to that during the reign of Haile Selassie. Attacks made on 'Western imperialism' and 'CIA interference' did not reduce the country's dependence on the US for arms and economic assistance. The Marxist ideology of the new government and the socialist restructuring of the economy and society did not lead to a closer relationship with the USSR, Eastern Europe or China. The US came to be seen as an unreliable source of arms, however. United States military aid was completely cut off in November 1974 with the execution of Haile Selassie's supporters, but shipments already agreed on continued to arrive. In 1974-5, total American military aid amounted to $7 million. By the end of 1975 the US had agreed to resume military shipments and promised $300 million over the next five years: a substantial rise. As late as March 1976, the United States again agreed to provide arms, partially to check the Soviet build-up in Somalia. Ethiopia requested $30 million of military aid but the US provided only $7 million.

In late 1976 the discrepancy between ideology and foreign policy began to disappear. In response to the insufficient aid offered by the United States, Ethiopia approached the Soviet Union for military and economic aid. But it was not until February 1977 that the Dergue publicly announced that it would in future seek arms from countries more in sympathy with its political ideology. Arms were to be supplied by the CMEA countries, ending Ethiopia's total dependence on the United States. The decision reflected not only the Marxist orientation of the Dergue, but also the need to break out of the country's growing isolation. At the same time the United States again reduced its aid because of violations of human rights in Ethiopia. They were not to receive previously-agreed military grants of $6 million, but would still be eligible for $10 million in military sales credits.

In mid-1977 USSR and Cuba took over military aid. Ethiopia's switch in foreign policy was formalised with the signing of a 20-year Treaty of Friendship and Co-operation with the Soviet Union in November 1978. This closely followed an agreement on economic and technological co-operation which began the Ethiopian campaign for development and centralised planning. The Supreme Central Planning Council was founded with the aim of speedily raising the level of agricultural and industrial output. The USSR was to provide aid for the construction of grain elevators, granaries, refrigerators and agricultural machinery overhaul shops; to improve livestock breeding, expand existing oil processing capacity, carry out geological prospecting and set up a modern ore-mining industry. In terms of trade, Ethiopia was to buy Soviet motor vehicle technology, oil and petroleum products and concrete in exchange for agricultural produce.

Relations with Somalia and the Ogaden War

At independence, Somalia claimed all Somali-speaking areas of Ethiopia, Kenya and Djibouti. There were clashes along the Ethiopian-Somalian border throughout the 1960s, rising to a peak in 1964 when an undeclared war broke out. Fighting flared again in 1973. As internal security in Ethiopia weakened in 1975/6, Somalia took advantage of the opportunity to increase its provision of arms and training of the Western Somali Liberation Front. In March 1977 Fidel Castro attempted to mediate, but in July Somali regular army units crossed the border and established control over the Somali-speaking areas of southeast Ethiopia. It is from this point that Fidel's personal sympathy for Mengistu may be dated. His troops were by now little needed in Angola. Ethiopia turned to the Communist countries for aid. On 15 August 1977 the USSR pronounced itself in her favour. Cynics have seen in this sudden and flat reversal the simple calculation that 32 million allies are nine times as numerous as 3.5 million allies. And so indeed they are, but a perverted kind of romanticism must surely have played its part.

The Russians are a very traditional people, and nowhere more so than in diplomatic and military matters. The dominant Slavic nationalities of USSR (and the Georgians and in a way the Armenians too) are traditionally Orthodox, and in military circles perhaps actually

Orthodox. Moreover ethnic Russians, who dominate foreign policy, have, as part of the folklore, romanticised links with Ethiopia. Peter the Great had a negro slave, later General Avram Petrovich Hannibal, who claimed to be 'Ethiopian', a word politely used then as now to mean 'negro but respectable'. Hannibal's great-grandson was, notoriously, Alexander Pushkin. Then too, stories had long circulated of Prester John, 'tsar and priest, before-dinner tsar and after-dinner priest'. In the sixteenth century the myth of Prester John was relocated from Cathay to Ethiopia, and the Coptic church became widely known to be non-Catholic. Though unfortunately Monophysite, it at least believed in the Single Procession of the Holy Ghost. The Moscow Patriarchate dreamed of union with the 'Black Orthodoxy'. The Slavo-philes almost treated Ethiopians as Slavs. A military/religious expedition, small and wholly disavowed by the state, landed and failed in 1888/9. The poet Gumilov (1886-1921) gave Ethiopia some very favourable publicity, until the Bolsheviks shot him for different reasons. After 1917 there was a considerable émigré colony in Addis Ababa.[2]

Somalia on the other hand is a Moslem country, and Central Asians are but weakly represented at the centres of Soviet power. Fortified by these various claims on Soviet affection, in September 1977 Ethiopia broke its relations with Somalia, and a massive influx of Soviet weapons and Cuban troops, reportedly up to 16,000 men, followed. Soviet military advisors were expelled from Somalia, the USSR's closest African ally until then, in November 1977.

Table 3.6 outlines the international attitudes to the Ogaden conflict. Support for Ethiopia came from the Communist countries except China and, to a certain extent, Yugoslavia. Somalia received support from the middle eastern countries, other than those with leftist, pro-Soviet governments — Libya and South Yemen. The Western powers remained neutral. Arms were supplied to the combatant states almost exclusively by the Communist countries and most of these supplied Ethiopia. By March 1978, the Somali army had been beaten although no formal peace was declared. Cuban troops remained in the Ogaden throughout 1978 and into 1979 to guarantee the frontier. The Ogaden war polarised attitudes in the Red Sea area. Somalia received support from Saudi Arabia, Iran, Egypt and the Sudan; Ethiopia, from Libya, Kenya and the PDRY.

The war hurt agricultural and industrial production primarily because of transport delays and a lack of vital spare parts. It necessitated massive imports of arms which have shifted Ethiopia's political alignment further east because of the West's reluctance to

Table 3.6: International Attitudes to the Ethiopian-Somalian Conflict

Countries and Organisations	Attitude to Ogaden Factions	Motives for attitude	Economic and Financial Aid	Military Aid — Arms Supplied	Military Aid — Instructor and/or Troops sent
UN	Neutrality	Desire for conciliation			
OAU	Neutrality/pro-Ethiopia	Desire not to divide Africa and respect for colonial borders			
Western Powers					
United States ⎫ Great Britain ⎬ France ⎭	Neutrality/pro-Somalia	Hostility towards Marxist Ethiopian regime but desire to avoid antagonising African states	Normal economic relations with Ethiopia and Somalia	Deferred promise of arms supplies to Somalia	
Socialist countries					
China	Neutrality/pro-Somalia	Ideological affinity with 1974 Ethiopian revolution, but anti-Soviet	Normal economic relations with Ethiopia and Somalia	Arms, especially to Somalia	
Yugoslavia	Neutrality/pro-Ethiopia	"Positive neutralism" and "Third Worldism"	Normal economic relations with Ethiopia and Somalia	Arms, especially to Ethiopia	
Cuba ⎫ Soviet Union ⎭	Declared and material support for Ethiopia	Ideological affinities with Ethiopia and strategic imperatives (Red Sea, Indian Ocean, Middle East, Africa . . .)	Privileged economic co-operation with Ethiopia	Arms to Ethiopia	Instructors, pilots and troops to Ethiopia Instructors to Ethiopia
Middle East					
Israel	Declared and material support for Ethiopia	Hostility to transformation of the Red Sea into an "Arab Lake"	Privileged economic co-operation with Ethiopia	Arms to Ethiopia (2)	Instructors and pilots to Ethiopia
South Yemen	Proclaimed neutrality, but material support for Ethiopia	Soviet alliance	Privileged economic co-operation with Ethiopia	Arms to Ethiopia (2)	Instructors, pilots and troops to Ethiopia (2)
Libya		Hostility towards Riyadh, Khartoum and Cairo	Financial aid to Ethiopia	Arms to Somalia	Instructors and pilots to Somalia
Iraq ⎫ Syria ⎬ PLO ⎭	Declared and material support for Somalia	Pan-Arab and progressist solidarity with socialist Somalia	Financial aid to Somalia None	Arms to Somalia (3) None	None Training of pro-Somali guerrillas Instructors and pilots to Somalia (3)
Egypt ⎫ North Yemen ⎬ UAE ⎭	Declared and material support for Ethiopia	Pan-Arab, pan-Islamic solidarity; in particular, desire to assure security in Red Sea	Privileged economic co-operation with Somalia Economic co-operation and financial aid to Somalia	Arms to Somalia (3) None	None
Saudi Arabia			None	Arms to Somalia (3)	None
Jordan	Undeclared		None	None	None

Countries and Organisations	Attitude to Ogaden Factions	Motives for attitude	Economic and Financial Aid	Military Aid: Arms Supplied	Instructor and/or Troops sent
Morocco		Pan-Arab, pan-Islamic solidarity, anti-Sovietism and rejection of inviolability of frontiers.			
Mauritania Tunisia	Declared support for Somalia	Pan-Arab, pan-Islamic solidarity and anti-Sovietism.			
Algeria	Absolute neutrality	Respect for inviolability of frontiers, affinities with both sides.			
Djibouti	Neutrality/pro-Somalia	Majority of population and leaders are Somalis, but economic links with Ethiopia	Economic relations, especially with Ethiopia		Militant pro-Somali Djiboutis fight in Ogaden (2)
Arab League	Undeclared	Sympathy with member state Somalia, but desire not to upset Arab-African co-operation	Financial aid to Somalia		
Iran	Declared and material support for Somalia	Hostility towards Marxist Ethiopian regime, anti-Sovietism	Financial aid to Somalia	Arms to Somalia	(1) Sudan hesitates in taking a firm attitude. President Numeiry wishes to normalise relations with Ethiopia but would be under pressure from Egypt, Saudi Arabia and Iran, tend to oppose actively Soviet initiatives in the Horn of Africa. (2) Official Somali information, unconfirmed by other sources. (3) Official Ethiopian information, unconfirmed by other sources.

Source: *ARB*, Political, Social and Cultural Series, vol. 15, no. 2, 15 March 1978.

support the country. As a result, Soviet influence extended to virtually all sectors of the economy.

Eritrea

The Federation of Eritrea and Ethiopia came to an end in 1962 when the Eritrean legislative assembly voted itself out of existence. Four years earlier the Eritrean Liberation Front (ELF) was founded and had turned to armed struggle in 1961 to gain independence. By 1969 they were making a major impact. Martial law was declared in 1971. The ELF's big military campaign began in February 1975. By the end of 1977, Ethiopian troops were confined to the large garrison towns — Barentu, Asmara, Massawa and Adi Careb — all of which were under siege, and the port of Assab. The Dergue offered immediate regional autonomy for Eritrea in May 1976, but the ELF demanded full independence. The Dergue declared that Ethiopia was indivisible and attempted to regain control of the region. On 15 May 1978, it launched an attack with the aid of Soviet-supplied arms and Cuban, non-combat, support troops. By early 1979, the war in Eritrea was once again a protracted guerrilla struggle.

There were three reasons for the Ethiopian attempt to regain control. First, without Eritrea, the remainder of Ethiopia would be landlocked, denying the country access to seaports for the trans-shipment of goods; secondly, the economy would have suffered serious setbacks without Eritrea's contribution, as its agricultural and industrial base is more developed than Ethiopia's as a whole; and thirdly, continued Soviet economic support is linked to Ethiopia's ability to offer the USSR a stable military base on the Red Sea, i.e. in Eritrea.

Foreign Aid

Since the revolution, relations with most Western countries have deteriorated. Diplomatic links have become strained and the flow of aid interrupted. Canada's $8 million water and irrigation project, Sweden's aid programme and the European Development Fund's agricultural settlement, fishery and irrigation projects have all been delayed or suspended. Other Western nations have also backtracked on economic support. Table 1.2 shows the geographical distribution of financial flows from Western governments and multilateral bodies since 1973. Official net receipts increased by half between 1973 and 1977 but the proportion from governments fell from two-thirds to half of the total. Only Sweden and the EEC countries increased their contributions. The proportion of receipts from multilateral bodies has increased mainly from aid from the UN and IDA. Ethiopia is a member of the African Development Bank and the International Bank for Reconstruction and Development, but has received little in aid from them since the revolution. Ethiopia is also the largest single recipient of EEC aid under the Lomé Treaty and has received significant levels of aid since 1974.

Since 1977, aid flows from the West have continued to decrease. The United States budgeted $37 million in economic assistance and relief activities for 1979 and agreed, in principle, to provide $21 million towards a $92 million four-year rural development package being planned with the World Bank and Sweden. Failure by Ethiopia to compensate foreign companies nationalised in 1975 has held up this aid. The United States has threatened to veto any loans to Ethiopia until this has been settled. American claims involve less than twenty companies and $20 million. The World Bank has taken a similar stand, blocking at least $150 million in planned projects for the next few years. The EEC Development Fund has gone ahead with its $120 million programme. World Bank loans to Ethiopia are 'soft', that is, at extremely low rates of interest over long periods. American economic aid, since 1976, has all been on a grant basis because Ethiopia is rated among the world's poorest countries.

Ethiopia's relationship with the USSR is based, as we saw, on the Soviet military assistance and technical support programmes. The present economic aid programme, also shown in Table 1.2, is still drawing on $100 million in credits provided in 1959. There was speculation that a September 1978 economic and technical assistance agreement included new credits, but this is unlikely. It is more a general framework to study the need for increased aid. Aid for new projects will be provided on an individual basis. So far, no new major projects have been announced.

Table 3.7 supplements the Communist data in Table 1.2 with details of the promised civilian aid from all Communist countries. Since 1954 China has promised as much aid as the Soviet Union. Most of this aid was promised even before the revolution. Since 1974 it has been the Eastern European allies of the USSR which have promised aid. In November 1978, Mengistu toured Eastern Europe to seek $200 million

Table 3.7: Promised Civilian Aid from Communist Countries

Year	Country	Amount $ M	Grant Element %	Purpose
1971	China	85.5	n.a.	Agricultural development
1974	USSR	2.0	100	Hospital
		0.7	100	Relief assistance
	GDR	0.2	100	Emergency assistance
	China	1.9	100	Relief aid
1975	USSR	0.6	100	Drought relief
		0.1	100	Education equipment
1976	Bulgaria	2.4	37.7	Agricultural development
	China	0.2	100	Relief aid
1977	Bulgaria	0.8	100	Relief aid
	GDR	3.5	100	Relief aid
		19.2	34.0	Purchase of complete industrial plants
1978	Bulgaria	n.a.	n.a.	Agricultural development
	Czechoslovakia	46.0	41.0	Various development projects
	GDR	1.0	100	Emergency assistance
		0.3	100	Emergency assistance
	Poland	n.a.		84 tons of medical equipment
1954 to	USSR	105		
1978	Eastern Europe	95		
	China	102		

Sources: The Aid Programme of China, OECD, Paris, 1975. The Aid Programme of the USSR, OECD, Paris, 1977. The Aid Programme of the East European Countries, OECD, Paris, 1977.

to $300 million in economic assistance. It is uncertain whether he achieved this target. He did receive 1,000 tractors and 50 combine harvesters from the East Germans for the state farms and a $2 million loan for port expansion at Assab. Most of the equipment was apparently given in exchange for 20,000 tons of coffee exported to East Germany several years previously.

Conclusion

We feel that Ethiopia can be classified as part of the NCTW.[3] Its commitment to Marxism-Leninism does appear to be genuine even though not all of its policies support this. On the one hand it has observer status within CMEA, but on the other it does not persecute religion. Efforts are clearly being made to bring the Coptic Church, in its new disestablished role, into the mainstream of development activity rather than to suppress it. Above all Mengistu has not encouraged the formation of a Communist Party. But both these points were for a long time features of Cuba too (indeed religion is still tolerated there); and it is safest to predict further evolution on Cuban lines. The foreign troops on the ground are, precisely, Cuban. Yet Mengistu's basic motivations are all too blatantly military. Indeed the Dergue remains the revolutionary part of the old imperial officer corps, with the old imperial military task: to hold the ramshackle empire together. Just possibly, then, Mengistu could and would still throw out the Russians if military considerations demanded it. After all Somalia next door has set this bad example, and the Dergue itself began with a pro-American foreign policy — on military grounds.

Meanwhile, although it receives its miliary aid from the Soviet bloc, most of Ethiopia's economic assistance continues to come from the West and China, despite its strained relations with both. Out of $117 million in loans listed in the 1979 budget, more than three-quarters comes from the West, particularly the World Bank and the EEC. But this too is standard practice in the NCTW.

Notes

1. Kravis *et al.*, 1978.
2. All this is mainly drawn from Jesman, 1958.
3. It has, surprisingly, been referred to as 'Socialist Ethiopia' in an unattributed article in *Mezhdunarodnaya Zhizn'*, no. 1, 1979. This appears again in the CMEA communiqué of 2 July 1981. Doubtless the laudatory adjective is a *pis aller* for a proper Communist country title.

4 THE PEOPLE'S REPUBLIC OF MOZAMBIQUE: PRAGMATIC SOCIALISM

Nicos Zafiris

1. Introduction

Mozambique has a land area of 784,961 square km. and a population of approximately 11,750,000. It is thus the largest in population and second-largest in area of the former Portuguese colonies in Africa. The big land area and a relative lack of mineral resources have resulted in a predominantly agricultural economy, in which the agricultural sector employs around 80 per cent of the population and contributes some 45 per cent of the GNP.[1] An especially long coastline of 2,500 km. and the country's geographical position as the nearest sea outlet for much of the southern African hinterland has made it an important transit link, and has ensured the development of a significant service sector which accounted for some 40 per cent of GNP in 1978.[2] Mozambique's *per capita* GNP has been estimated at $594 for 1970.[3] It is thus, by any standards, a 'less developed country', although not one of the very poorest in Africa.

Agriculture comprises both a subsistence and a cash-crop sector, the latter producing mainly for export. Cashew nuts (of which Mozambique is the leading world producer), sugar, cotton and vegetable oils are the main exports.[4] The fishing industry is also fairly developed, although mainly for the needs of home consumption. Around two-thirds of the potentially cultivable land is at present unoccupied and the potential in fishing is also considerable in view of the country's long coast. But apart from coal and small known deposits of iron ore and natural gas, there seems to be little in the way of minerals. The industrial sector is small, although it has grown from 9 per cent of GNP in 1960 to 16 per cent in 1978.[5] The main activity is the processing of food and other primary products, including oil-refining, although there is also cement and textile production. The service sector has traditionally been more important, in the form of rail, port and tourist facilities for the neighbouring countries of South Africa, Zimbabwe-Rhodesia, Zambia and Malawi. In general the economy has traditionally been very trade-dependent, with trade representing around 30 per cent of GNP before independence. Furthermore, the country's status as a

114

Portuguese colony has been responsible for a high degree of probably disadvantageous complementarity with the economy of Portugal, as well as for other key structural features which we shall be discussing later. But the annual rate of growth of GNP was, at 4.6 per cent between 1960 and 1970, among the highest in Africa.[6]

Mozambique is, ethnically, rather diverse. In the north there are a number of tribes of Zulu origin. Some of these, in the coastal districts, have been exposed to Arab influences which have accounted for considerable linguistic change and conversion to Islam. There are some 2 million Moslems living in Mozambique at present. The central and southern population mostly consists of non-Zulu and Bantu-speaking tribes. Most of Mozambique's native population is animist, if not christianised or Moslem, and Bantu is spoken by most Africans, although not necessarily as a mother-tongue. Mozambique also has a considerable minority of whites (now much diminished), half-castes and Indians, the majority of them Portuguese or Portuguese-speaking. Although Portuguese has been the country's official language, many Europeans have traditionally also been English-speaking. Portuguese is still the official language in the country's present regime as an independent People's Republic. This is governed by the FRELIMO (Party) under the Presidency of S. Machel. Mozambique's currency unit is now the *metical* which has recently replaced the Mozambican escudo. The official rate of exchange was in September 1980 $1 = 29.44 *meticais*.[7]

Among the 'target' countries studied in this volume, Mozambique has, perhaps, attracted the most attention from economic researchers. Having been influenced by several fairly distinctive ideological currents and having had to cope both with the usual constraints of under-development and with factors unique to itself, the Mozambican revolution has been the scene of intense political struggle and a field of considerable economic experimentation. Five years after independence Mozambique appears firmly embarked on a programme of socialist development. But the continued presence of certain key economic constraints is dictating a pragmatic and flexible attitude in the conduct of policy. At least some of the main features of Mozambican socialism do not thus appear to have taken a very stable form, and its longer-term course can make an interesting case of politico-economic forecasting.

2. The Colonial Background

We have already mentioned that Mozambique's economy has traditionally been trade-dependent. Tables 4.1 and 4.2 show the pattern of exports and imports in 1974 (the last year before independence). Mozambique's merchandise trade has typically been in deficit, partly made good by a surplus on invisibles. Thus in 1974 (a fairly typical year) a deficit of $123 million on visible trade was offset by a surplus of $120 million in the invisible account. In 1973 (also fairly typical) the visible deficit of $86 million had similarly been offset by $92 million of surplus on the invisible items.[8]

The economy's dependence on trade reflects, fundamentally, the country's more general condition of economic dependence. Two aspects of overall dependence can be distinguished: (a) colonial dependence on Portugal and (b) geographic dependence on neighbours. Whereas the former has, perhaps, been the more important influence before independence, it is the latter that is likely to prove decisive now.

As a colony Mozambique had to develop mainly as an agricultural (and to a much lesser extent mineral) producer with much of its production geared to the needs of a fairly closely integrated escudo zone. Cultivation of cash crops was developed in this century largely on the basis of forced labour and at the expense of peasant food crops. Peasants would often be required to produce a specified amount of a cash crop on their own land, which would generally be acquired by a concession company at very low prices. Alternatively peasants might be required to perform wage labour on the plantations. Most of the cash crops would be exported to some part of the escudo zone, the best example of this being, perhaps, the almost total exportation of cotton to Portugal by 1946. In addition to Portuguese capitalists and settlers many of the concession companies which came to dominate Mozambique's agriculture were foreign, as indeed was the case with much of the industrial capital which flowed into Mozambique since 1960. Portugal was after all only a 'sub-metropolitan' colonial power herself in terms of the world economy. Being unable to undertake on her own a complete colonial development in her dependent territories, she had to act largely as a '*rentier* state', renting land and labour, that is, to foreign capitalists.[9] It is this weakness of Portuguese capitalism, in fact, which explains Portugal's tenacity in holding on to her colonies long after the abandonment of colonialism by the other former colonial powers. The benefits of continued possession of the colonies were too great for Portugal to lose,[10] but

Table 4.1: Mozambique: Principal Exports

	1974		1975	
	Value Contos[a]	Value %	Value Contos[a]	Value %
Cashews	1519	20	1221	24
Tea	283	4	177	4
Vegetable oils	946	13	393	8
Sugar	1651	21	575	11
Petroleum derivatives	396	5	369	7
Timber	324	4	374	7
Cotton	841	11	439	9
Sisal	238	3	200	4
Other	1362	9	1302	26
Total	7500	100	5050	100

[a]   A conto = 1000 Moz. escudos (the Mozambican escudo was pegged to the Portuguese escudo before independence).
Source: *Doc. Inf. CEDIMO*, Série A (24), 1978, pp. 12-30.

Table 4.2: Mozambique: Imports by Broad Economic Category

	1974 (%)
Food and beverages	9.3
Ind. supplies	14.3
Fuel/lubricants	9.6
Machinery	31.8
Transport	25.8
Consumer goods	6.0
Other	3.2
Total	100.0

Source: *Yearbook of International Trade Statistics 1977*, UN, New York, 1978.

they could not be guaranteed under conditions of open competition with foreign capitalism. Only direct political domination could ensure the admission of foreign capital on terms advantageous to Portugal. The policy was only relaxed in the 1960s when Portugal 'opened the door' to foreign industrial capital[11] in a bid to secure political support for her efforts to retain her empire.

Apart from colonial dependence Mozambique's economy has exhibited, especially this century, a peculiarly strong regional dependence, particularly on the Republic of South Africa. As already mentioned, Mozambique is the main international freight transit-link for Zimbabwe-Rhodesia (through the port of Beira) and for the Transvaal region in the north-east of South Africa (through the port of Maputo). But in addition to railway, port and tourist facilities to these two countries, Mozambique has also developed as a migrant labour reserve for South African (and to a lesser extent Rhodesian) mines. Portugal acted here once again as a *rentier* of labour for these two countries. Many of the peasants in the South in particular were heavily dependent on contract labour in South Africa. Estimates put the numbers at over 100,000 immediately preceding independence.[12] The vast majority worked in South Africa's gold mines and had for a long time 60 per cent of their wages remitted in gold valued at the official price of $42 an ounce through the Bank of Mozambique. This was hardly remarkable until free market prices rocketed in the 1970s. But then the Bank used to resell on the free market and realise a considerable gain. This 'gold deal' with South Africa, dating back to 1897 but discontinued at the end of 1977, became of enormous significance for Mozambique's balance of payments in the few years after independence. Its worth is usually estimated at between $100 million and $150 million per annum,[13] representing up to one-third of total foreign exchange receipts for these years. It could well be described as aid from South Africa, although it is probably not unrelated to agreements which guaranteed South Africa an effective monopoly of direct recruitment of migrant labour during the colonial period.[14] The 'gold deal' also continued, however, for three more years after independence, although on a steadily declining scale.

Mozambique's development up to the time of independence was thus somewhat unbalanced: agricultural predominance, but with great inequality in the distribution of the land[15] and many poor peasants, many of them without a secure foothold in agriculture; some development of transport and commercial services but considerable dependence on labour migration; a small and mainly foreign-owned industrial sector. Above all, there was little integration of the various sectors of the economy with one another, since each was more integrated with the rest of the Portuguese Empire and the economies of its neighbouring countries.[16] There was, for example, no equipment industry to service agriculture, there was heavy regional concentration of the small industry sector while the main communication arteries ran east/west rather than north/south, being, that is, more geared to the South African and Rhodesian than to the Mozambican economy. The usual signs of underdevelopment, such as urban migration and unemployment, excessive concentration of investment resources on civil construction, and an over 90 per cent illiteracy rate, were certainly there. Finally a crucial aspect of under-development, i.e. lack of skills, was dramatically worsened overnight at independence with the departure of some 250,000 Portuguese settlers who represented, of course, the most skilled element in agriculture, industry and administration.

An overview of Mozambique's international trading partners reflects the economy's low degree of diversification as well as its relations of dependence. In 1961 73.5 per cent of the value of imports came from and 64 per cent of the value of exports went to only seven countries, namely Portugal, France, Britain, West Germany, the United States, Japan and South Africa. In 1973 these percentages had increased to 79 and 71 respectively. Portugal and her colonies alone accounted in 1961 for around 35 per cent of the imports and over 44 per cent of the exports as against South Africa's circa 11 per cent and 4 per cent respectively. After that South Africa and West Germany gained a strong position as exporters while Portugal's export share declined, and she was eventually overtaken by South Africa as the main exporter in 1973.[17] Concentration of trade with the South African Republic, among all African countries, is in fact a notable feature of the colonial trade pattern and a consequence, of course, of the isolation to which the country (and the rest of the Portuguese Empire) had been condemned by Africa. Among the other countries, some were mainly or exclusively trading in one product only; for instance, India imported cashews only, Saudi Arabia and Iraq exported oil only.

Table 4.6 in section 11 shows trade with the main trading partners in 1974 and 1975 (and later), thus completing the picture around the time of independence. As can be seen, the three main exporting countries and the only ones to account for more than 10 per cent of total Mozambique imports were South Africa, Portugal and West Germany. But Portugal remained by far the biggest recipient of Mozambican exports, followed by the USA and, once again, South Africa.

Within the limitations mentioned, Mozambique's balance of payments position was essentially stable until the time of independence. But the outflow of Europeans around that time and the consequent flight of capital (a net outflow of $62 million in 1975)[18] brought the country's position to a perilous point on the eve of independence. The accumulated foreign debt was around $640 million,[19] reserves barely covered two months' imports, and the 'gold deal' with South Africa was no longer certain. All in all the prospects appeared very dubious indeed.

It is against this economic background that the revolutionary socialist government came to power on 25 June 1975. The colonial heritage contained one point of compatibility with it: a considerable amount of *dirigisme*. The state already owned and ran transport, communications and municipal services, and co-operated actively with private capital in both industry and agriculture.

3. The Liberation Movement

Given the predominantly rural character of Mozambique's economy the liberation movement of FRELIMO started as a peasant 'nationalist' one. As the struggle progressed, more 'revolutionary' elements began to appear within it and gradually to gain ascendancy. The internal battle was fought through the 1960s, essentially between the 'traditional nationalists' and the 'revolutionary socialists'. But there were other early divisions also, particularly between a racial and a class view of the war, and even between Christian and Moslem elements in the country. It was not until 1970 or later that the battle was won by the revolutionary camp. But the movement's commitment to the 'abolition of exploitation' at that time can be said to have defined it as fundamentally Marxist at that point. The commitment took in 1972 the more specific form of a ban on wage labour for private employers. The 'class' view thus came to dominate the 'racial' or 'national' one, and its universalist character gained it wide support from all sections of the population throughout the country. Only the Moslem minority appears to have been the exception, at least according to one report.[20]

An initially broad anti-imperialist alliance of racial and class forces, such as FRELIMO, within which the peasant element was predominant, need not, however, have developed into a Marxist movement. Such a development can be expected much more readily in conditions in which the intelligentsia plays the leading role and where the working-class element is strong. But a number of important contributing factors were at work in Mozambique.

There was, first, the Chinese paradigm, with its worker/peasant or, rather, peasant/worker revolutionary alliance at the origin of the Chinese People's Republic. We are bound to say that the availability of that paradigm must have been of crucial importance in lending credibility to the views of the genuine Marxists within FRELIMO who eventually came to be its leaders. It will be remembered here that China during the 1960s was pushing much more forcefully than nowadays its model of socialist development, and was offering a serious and effective ideological challenge both within a somewhat confused Communist camp and in the world in general.

But the availability of ideological paradigms alone cannot explain why a peasant anti-colonialist revolution should have turned Marxist. Material support is also needed. But, once again, the Communist countries, particularly China, were there with military assistance. That was not unexpected, of course, both in terms of their general anti-imperialist stand and in terms of the Chinese/Soviet competition for world leadership of national liberation/revolutionary movements.

The key, however, to the question of why Mozambique's liberation should have turned Marxist may lie in the prolonged and tenacious stay of old-fashioned Portuguese colonialism in the country long after the majority of former colonies in Africa had been decolonised. While these countries were engaged in building new 'sovereign' links with their former masters and carefully incorporating whatever seemed useful in the colonial regime into their new and, in general, not particularly 'radical' politico-economic structures, Mozambique (like Angola and Portuguese Guinea) found itself fighting a crude and universally condemned form of imperialism. The fact that the imperialist power involved was, nevertheless, a member of the Western community of nations and of NATO in particular, and the long inability of that community to prevail on one of its weakest members and to ensure an honourable termination of the colonial wars in Africa, cannot but have discredited attempts to swing the movement in a westward direction and, indeed, pushed it towards Communist-guided socialism.

4. Evolution of Mozambique's Marxism

Soon after the start of the war of independence FRELIMO was becoming something bigger than a guerrilla organisation, developing rapidly into an administration for the growing number of its liberated areas. The foremost task of administration was, of course, the maintenance of the areas' production and trade. This fundamental task seems to have been accomplished with considerable success with production showing surpluses which the movement was able to export. Direct participation in production was seen by FRELIMO as an integral part of the militants' political education, alongside teaching programmes to inculcate Marxist principles as well as literacy. The movement has thus aimed since the early days to create its version of the 'New Man' in a fairly typical Marxist mould. Early attempts by individuals within the movement to establish themselves in quasi-capitalist merchant roles in the reorganised liberated areas are now officially seen as manifestations of class struggle and denounced as opportunist. The section of the movement which finally won was that which advocated nationalisation of the land, collectivisation of production, state control of distribution and, as we have seen, the abolition of wage labour in agriculture. The policy of ensuring that every militant also participated directly in production can be seen as an attempt to prepare for a society in which the ban on 'exploitation' would be observed. As already hinted also, the view came to prevail within the movement that there could be black exploiters as well as white. It was each one's social and economic role that mattered and not the colour of skin, and the war was defined in terms of class and not of race. FRELIMO sought to prevent the development of a black class of new exploiters who might have replaced the white colonialists in that role.

The Central Committee Report to the Third Congress of February 1977 (the most authoritative, perhaps, ideological statement to date) declared that a 'workers' and peasants' state had been born with the People's Republic', thus signposting unambiguously its class perception of the revolution. Further, in laying down state ownership of land and natural resources, designating collective work as the dominant form of social production and reaffirming the leading role of the state in the national economy, the Report has produced a solid socialist blueprint. With it goes, of course, a statement against racial discrimination.

A few key statements from the Third Committee Report can be quoted to show a clear Marxist-Leninist orientation, at least at that particular moment (February 1977). Firstly, the Report speaks of the achievement, with independence, of the tasks of the 'National Democratic Revolution'. All the conditions had then been created for the transition to the stage of 'Popular Democratic Revolution'. The constitution laid down the basic principles of 'People's Democracy' with the ultimate aims of 'building the political ideological scientific and material basis of a Socialist Society'.

Then, in a blueprint outline of that 'People's Democracy' (Section 2) we read:

> People's Democracy is the historical phrase in which the labouring masses, under the leadership of the working class, strengthen their power, establish the Dictatorship of the Proletariat . . . People's

Democracy is a phase when we socialise the means of production and when we create . . . and develop the two essential forms of socialist property: state property and co-operative property . . . Taking agriculture as the base, industry as the dynamic force and the building up of heavy industry as the decisive factor . . . we build an advanced economy at the service of the people . . . We raise to a more advanced stage the struggle for the creation of the New Man . . . We create the material conditions to make work the right and duty of our citizens, and to put into practice the principle of 'from each according to his ability, to each according to his work' . . . The working class shouldering the long tradition of struggle by the Mozambican People becomes the leading force for the building of a socialist society . . . The peasantry is the fundamental ally of the working class . . . Their alliance is based on the common interest of workers and peasants in the liquidation of all forms of exploitation of man by men . . . The small proprietors and the artisans are social strata that the proletariat is gradually winning for the construction of the New Society . . . Scientific Socialism is the lantern that guides the labouring classes in the assault on the exploiting and inhuman bastions of capitalism and imperialism.

Impeccable Marxism-Leninism then is displayed by the Central Committee Report to the Third Congress under the heading of 'people's democracy'. The section on the party also reinforces the commitment:

The new stage in the intensification of class struggle and in the construction of the foundation for the ultimate transition to Socialism demands a new instrument: a vanguard party . . . With this in mind, the Central Committee is proposing to the Third Congress the creation of a vanguard party, a Marxist-Leninist party.

But

if it is to be a real vanguard force of the labouring classes, our party must be armed with a revolutionary theory. This ideological and theoretical basis is Marxism-Leninism or Scientific Socialism.

The document then goes on to denounce 'liberalism' and 'indiscipline'. The fundamental organisational principle is enunciated as 'democratic centralism' and the party 'supports and encourages the practice of criticism and self-criticism'. Of party members it says that they 'constitute the most advanced and conscious part of the labouring classes, especially of the working class and the peasantry . . . what distinguishes them . . . is above all their greater class consciousness . . . and . . . their revolutionary spirit'. But membership, normally involving a year's probation or more, is granted automatically to all those belonging to FRELIMO before 'Victory Day', 7 September 1974. It is finally stated that the 'Party leads and gives direction to all state activities', in typical Marxist-Leninist fashion. Activists must 'resolutely engage in creating Party organisations in the factories, co-operatives, offices, military and paramilitary bodies within the state apparatus, in the villages and communities, in all workplaces and residential areas'.[21]

5. Developments in Internal Politics

However, the political test of the character of the state should not be limited to initial statements. It is of more importance to examine actual political developments in the few years following independence. Early post-revolutionary policy, subject to immediate pressures, may not be fully indicative of longer-term evolution. But this is perhaps less true in the political sphere than in the economic. For the one-party form of organisation, unlike, say, agricultural collectivisation, may have certain 'efficiency' advantages from the point of view of control which may also become apparent rather quickly. Such advantages may, in fact, lead to adoption of a one-party structure by governments of almost any persuasion.

It is, perhaps, fitting, therefore, that we should begin our survey of actual policies since independence with developments in the political domain, despite the fact that we shall have much more to say later about the economy, which is our primary interest. It will also, in the nature of things, not always be possible to keep the two separate.

One area where this difficulty of separation is strongly apparent is the *grupos dinamizadores*. These originated in the period of transitional government (between September 1974 and independence in June 1975) in the areas still under Portuguese control, and represented the movement's activist units at the level of the neighbourhoods and workplaces. During that crucial period they played an important economic role in keeping hundreds of abandoned firms working and countering various forms of economic sabotage, as well as the political one of basic and political education. The groups could then have been regarded as embryo party structures but in the event were not turned automatically into party cells. The campaign for 'structuring the party', begun in February 1978, which decided the creation of party cells in workplaces all over the country, also decided that members of the dynamising groups would have to apply for party membership like everyone else. When a party cell is formed in a work organisation the group ceases to exist. But the groups were to remain, for a period, the basis of residents' organisations in the neighbourhoods — a 'democratic men's organisation on a par with the youth, women's and workers' organisations'.[22]

The actual selection process for party membership is a rather complex one and involves a number of stages. Its most interesting feature is, perhaps, that it works through a series of public meetings and includes scrutiny of the candidate by his colleagues. The same is indeed also the case with elections to parliament and local government. It is generally claimed that both party selection and elections to state organs are conducted in a spirit of openness and anecdotal evidence tends to support this claim. But, equally, there appears to be a move towards greater selectivity in party membership.

A related development which is of growing interest in the Communist world, but whose state in Mozambique is still somewhat unclear, is workers' control, or, in the Marxist idiom, 'changes in the social relations of production'. 'Production councils' were set up in many enterprises after independence, the membership sometimes nominated by the party and sometimes elected by the workers. The immediate task was to keep production going, especially in the enterprises which had been abandoned by the qualified personnel. Production councils broadly succeeded in this, although considerable inefficiency was registered in many enterprises. Apart from the factor of experience, the relations of production councils with their local dynamising groups seemed to have a crucial effect on efficiency. In some enterprises 'administrators' had to be appointed to restore efficiency. These, however, showed a tendency to rely on a small managerial team and the role of the production councils seemed to be limited for a period to that of maintaining discipline. The management of enterprises thus acquired, for a while, a very Soviet character.[23] After the 1978 restructuring of the party, however, attempts were made to re-activate production councils, albeit under the 'political leadership' of the corresponding party cell. It appears that production councils are at present developing as substitutes for the trade unions, reported dissolved[24] (see section 10).

The general organisational principle of government is described in the Third Congress Report as 'democratic centralism', a rather ambiguous term on the meaning of which we shall not attempt to elaborate further at this point. With regard to various other ideological issues also, certain themes have repeatedly appeared in public statements, albeit with varying urgency, over the five-year period. The more recent ideological statements have included attacks on the Moslem religion (President S. Machel is reported to have walked into Mozambique Island's Great Mosque with his shoes on!),[25] similar attacks on the Catholic Church[26] and attacks on 'leftism', 'anarchy', 'ultra democracy', 'paternalism', 'liberalism',[27] etc., into which it does not seem easy to read a particularly coherent overall pattern. But the recent reinstatement of certain traditional titles such as 'doctor' at the expense (among others, astonishingly) of 'comrade'[28] does seem to indicate a certain fatigue with what might be termed 'ultra-revolutionism'. The establishment more recently of an officer corps in the Armed Forces (FPLM), intended to have a clear hierarchy, wear striped uniforms and sport medals, is a sign pointing in the same direction,[29] as indeed does President Machel's appointment as Field Marshal.[30] On the other hand, the creation of 'Offices of Control and Discipline', apparently in an effort to rid the administration of incompetence and corruption, is more ambivalent, especially as it has been accompanied by open discussions of the performance of officials by their fellow workers.[31]

In general Mozambique's ideological commitment to Marxism appears to have gone somewhat lukewarm. Pictures of Marx, Lenin and Engels are still much in evidence. But the general attitude seems to have a strong touch of pragmatism about it. It is probably well epitomised in President Machel's statement in May 1979 that theory and ideas came from practice and that the party was not a 'study group of scientists specialising in the reading and interpretation of Marx, Engels and Lenin.'[32]

An important test of a regime's strength is, of course, the amount of internal resistance which it encounters, and the way it reacts to resistance is a good guide as to its general orientation. Internal resistance in Mozambique is mainly represented by the RNM rebel organisation. An alliance of diverse elements (followers and collaborators of the colonial regime, many of whom escaped from re-education camps, as well as disaffected FRELIMO fighters), it was already active in the summer of 1977 and is now continuing its operations mainly in the centre and north of the country.[33] There is to our knowledge no reliable estimate of the numbers in its ranks. RNM claims to 'control' certain areas of the country. But it does not seem to pose a serious threat to the regime, although the government has found it necessary to create over a thousand *grupos de vigilancia*, mainly in response to its activities. These have been created to supplement the army and the internal security service (SNASP) which appears to have been organised with the aid of East German security experts.[34] The executions of some saboteurs and insurgents which have taken place[35] indicate that Mozambique's political stability is not yet total. But the future appears bleak for the resistance. The resolution of the Rhodesian problem with the victory of R. Mugabe's government means that the guerrillas will no longer be able to use the territory of Zimbabwe-Rhodesia as a launching ground for their operations. The Zimbabwean government has in fact promised to help Mozambique to combat this guerrilla activity.[36] But Mozambique is still accusing South Africa of supporting it.[37]

Political evolution so far offers, as we have seen, a clear-cut picture of Marxist-Leninist advance. By contrast, developments on the economic front are a little more ambiguous and the same goes for the country's foreign relations.

6. Developments in the Economy: Early Measures and Statements

We have already outlined the parlous state of Mozambique's economy at the time of independence. Industrial production was running at around 50 per cent and agriculture at around 70 per cent of their previous levels, whereas settlement of a large foreign debt had to be negotiated (largely with Portugal) against very uncertain prospects for the balance of payments.[38] For the new government, therefore, the task was not mainly to devise and start implementing a development programme but, rather, to cope with immediate and dire necessity.

Within these constraints the government did, with its first few measures in the economic sphere, attempt to take the first steps in the direction of what it was soon afterwards to enunciate as its socialist economic philosophy. First came the 'socialisation' of the land (24 July 1975) and the first tentative steps at collectivising agriculture. There followed a further programme of early nationalisation covering all rented property (3 February 1976), all health services (including hospitals and clinics), all educational services (abolishing private tutors), all legal services (i.e. abolishing all private legal practices) and the entire insurance industry. The early measures also included the establishment of control over credit institutions and construction companies. But among other enterprises the Law of State Intervention allowed generally the nationalisation only of the abandoned ones. On the other hand, communal villages and people's shops (of which more later) began to be set up. The state moved against private appropriation of abandoned agricultural land in particular, mainly through the 'dynamising groups'.

The early economic results were not, however, happy. Agricultural production in 1976 was well down on pre-independence levels,[39] a fact attributed by many to excessively rapid collectivisation as well as the departure of white farmers.[40] But the main factor, perhaps, was the complete breakdown of the distribution with the departure of almost all the predominantly white traders who had dominated it. The biggest falls were recorded in marketed output as peasants started to consume the crops with subsistence production. The trade deficit was widening and controls had to be imposed on 'luxury imports'. Increasing quantities of food (rice, wheat, maize) had to be imported and foreign aid started to flow with Sweden, Norway, Denmark and Holland among the early donors.

Despite these unhappy experiences, however, Mozambique took in March 1976 a further step in the direction of consistency with politico-economic principle by unilaterally closing its border with what was then still the rebel colony of Rhodesia. We have already made reference to the significance of the Rhodesian link for Mozambique's transit, port and tourist industries and we shall add here that the loss of exchange earnings is put at some $100 million per annum (transit) and a further $20 million from lost tourism. Traffic through the port of Beira fell by some 70 per cent in the first instance. But Rhodesia had also provided an important outlet for Mozambique's migrant labour in its (copper) mines and elsewhere. At the time of closure of the border some 80,000 Mozambican migrants found themselves in Rhodesia and were forbidden to send back remittances.[41]

From the point of view of development planning, and quite apart from the desire to establish socialism, two economic objectives would have suggested themselves in the concrete situation of Mozambique after independence. Both correspond to the structural weaknesses of the colonial era to which we have already alluded. It would have, thus, seemed desirable to (a) create a more integrated and less trade-dependent economy and (b) to find a permanent place somewhere in the economy for the country's migrant labour. The general policy choice between industrialisation and agricultural development (or some balanced mixture of both) also had to be faced, of course. On the eve of the Third Congress (February 1977) FRELIMO was confronted with the classic developmental dilemma of industry versus agriculture.

It was no longer taken for granted, in the late seventies, that development is synonymous with industrialisation.[42] Some might have argued, in fact, that the issue of 'industry v. agriculture' was misconceived since, in the absence of unusually large endowments of exportable raw materials, only agricultural development can provide the necessary surplus for industrialisation. FRELIMO's statement on the 'Principal tasks of development' (Section 4, Central Committee Report to Third Congress) amounts to an adoption of that view.

The basic strategy in the report has already been mentioned. It is to take agriculture as the base and industry as the dynamic force in building an advanced economy. In Section 4 it is reiterated that 'our strategy for development rests on agricultural production'. It later emphasises, however, the 'building up of heavy industry, industry linked to the construction of machinery and to the production of raw materials for other branches of industry'. It is asserted that 'only by building up heavy industry will our country be able to ensure control of the production processes, free itself from dependence and increase its economic capacity decisively'. This sounds remarkably like the Stalinist development formula emphasising heavy industry. That can in turn be regarded as the extreme version of the standard development strategy of industrialisation on the basis of agricultural surplus.

A few more statements from Section 4 of the document are fairly revealing of the proposed solutions to certain key strategic questions within the overall policy. It is thus stated that 'in the short term our target is to increase production from the existing industrial capacity, so as to exceed the maximum levels attained in the past in all sectors that provide the people's basic needs, or are directed to the export market. The conversion of sectors producing for superfluous consumption is a matter of urgency'. On the usual development issue of export development versus import substitution the intention is to 'speed up the work that is already under way on mapping out our natural resources so that we have detailed knowledge of our mineral and energy potential and of the viability of exploiting them. At the same time we must begin an exhaustive study of the world market and the international division of labour, so that we can determine possible areas of development and their respective priorities'. Some domestic reorientation of production is also planned and 'factories producing foodstuffs, clothing, footwear, etc., should be organised around the real needs of the working masses, converting production lines that were designed for the luxury consumption of the colonial elites'. The policy thus seems to seek to strike a balance between efficient specialisation in terms of the world economy with an attempt to define the priority areas of consumption which should be met by domestic production.

Section 4 of the Report also deals at length with systemic and organisational matters. Fundamentally it is asserted that 'the building of Socialism demands that the economy be centrally planned and directed by the State'. Within the planned economy, 'the state-owned sector of production must become dominant . . . ' But the co-operative sector also; 'the other essential form of collective production, is actively supported by the Party and by the state'. Further still, 'in non-strategic sectors of the economy, private activity will be allowed in so far as it scrupulously fulfils its social objective and participates in national production within the framework of the aims laid down by the state'. Economic Ministries within each sector create management units to 'orient the state-owned firms, define the objectives and aims of the private firms in that sector and supervise the assessment of the results'. Finally the Report announces the intention to set up a National Planning Commission.

The document pays particular attention to agricultural organisation. The policy places heavy reliance on the 'communal villages' (*aldeias comunais*) which we discuss at greater length in Section 8. Their creation had already begun before independence and had continued in the early post-revolutionary days: 'The Communal Villages are our chosen strategy for the socialisation of the rural areas . . . The organisation of the people in communal villages makes it possible for us to achieve self-sufficiency in food relatively quickly, and also enables us to satisfy health, educational and cultural needs . . . The production of a surplus, in accordance with the national plan, is the objective to be attained . . .' The communal village is thus conceived both as a living and as a producing community. But more explicitly collective production structures can be associated with it, too. 'State-owned enterprises and co-operatives are the organisational forms in agriculture which are the basis for the communal villages'. The former, in particular, are seen as 'the quickest means of responding to the country's food requirements because of the size of the areas they cover, their rational organisation of human and material resources and the immediate availability of machinery' and are to 'form centres for research and development in agrarian techniques and science'.

The last substantial item of internal economic organisation touched on in the Report concerns the 'people's shops' (*lojas do povo*), a network of state retail outlets, many mobile, which had begun to be built up ever since independence in response to the virtual collapse of capitalist distribution. The Report does not visualise that *all* distribution will be through people's shops but the system is intended to 'ensure state control over the trading circuits'. Once again a co-operative sector is expected to co-exist with the state sector and consumer co-operatives had, in fact, been growing steadily since independence.

But the Report also has something to say about public finances pledging to 'progressively tax earnings from capital, having in view less taxation on earnings from labour'. A proportional income tax is hinted at but it is explained that there can be no radical fiscal reform before the 'transformation of economic structures'.

Of seemingly not immediate importance but of some interest in terms of novelty is, finally, a statement in the Report regarding the (already nationalised) insurance sector. State insurance is, thus, envisaged 'to insure against risks involved in production with preferential rates for priority sectors, particularly to forms of collective production'. No further details are given.

7. The Economy After the Third Congress, 1977-80

We must now review actual economic developments in the intermediate and in the more recent part of the five-year period of independence. We shall do this with a view to seeing, in particular, to what extent the young people's republic has found it possible to follow the principles enunciated in the Third Congress. To complete the picture, we shall then be surveying the field of Mozambique's foreign 'economic' and 'political' relations.

It must be emphasised at the outset that the period concerned has been a difficult one in terms of non-economic influences. Two such influences must be singled out in particular, namely floods and hostilities with Rhodesia. The first floods occurred in 1976 and then on a bigger scale in 1977 (Limpopo Valley) and 1978 (Zambesi Valley). Estimates of the extent of the damages vary, but their severity cannot be doubted. Apart from the damage to crops, over 200,000 peasants were reported displaced in March 1978.[43] The consequences of the Rhodesian border closure were also not confined to the loss of freight and tourist earnings. Air-raids from Rhodesia throughout the period resulted in considerable damage to infrastructure. Mozambique's territory harboured, as is known, R. Mugabe's ZANU wing of the Zimbabwean Patriotic Front and the raids consisted mainly of attacks on guerrilla bases. But they seem to have been directed also against economic targets. The general state of hostilities also led to an influx of refugees from Rhodesia and necessitated the creation of a number of refugee camps accommodating a total of around 60,000 refugees according to the government.[44] The total economic cost of Mozambique's Rhodesian policy since 1976 and until this year was put by Machel at $150 million a year,[45] which may, however, be an exaggeration. The war damage alone was put at around $50 million by another estimate.[46]

The official target set by the Third Congress was for all branches of production to reach in 1980 the highest level ever reached during the colonial period. But official figures (Table 4.3, figures unfortunately not available for the most recent years) show a disappointing picture for a number of key, mainly exported, agricultural products. One of the principal exports, sugar, was reported in the summer of 1978 to be barely sufficient for internal needs,[47] and exports of cashews had fallen dramatically in the previous year. A total of 300,000 tons of food imports was required, according to one estimate, in 1978,[48] while the UN Review Mission expected the total to reach 386,500 in 1979.[49] Food was imported mainly from South Africa but also from Argentina, South Korea and even Rhodesia, according to one report![50] A number of aid agreements which ensured donations of purchases of food from Sweden,[51] Britain,[51] Canada,[52] the USA[53] and Italy[54] were reported. Difficulties in distribution were compounding the insufficiencies of production and shortages and queues were being reported in November 1979.[55] In recognition of the fact that prices paid to producers had been kept fixed at too low levels since independence, substantial increases were granted in June 1980.[56] But according to the latest reports at the time of writing,[57] exhaustion of the year's crops was imminent and famine-proportion shortages were expected to occur in some of the remotest areas, which had been, however, struck by droughts.[58] Subsistence farmers seemed to be the worst affected. In conclusion, Mozambique appears to be having difficulty in restoring agricultural efficiency and it seems unlikely that agricultural targets will be met for 1980.

In industrial production, too, there have been difficulties, although it seems impossible to illustrate this with figures for the entire industrial

Table 4.3: Principal Agro-Industrial Products mainly for Export (tons)

	1974/75	1975/76	1976/77	1977/78
Sugar	279,494	223,700	215,434	159,100
Molasses	93,379	82,673	66,831	n.a.
Cashews				
Nuts	200,000	160,000	73,000	120,000 [a]
Almonds	24,616	17,190	20,197	n.a.
Oil	14,907	13,380	6,366	n.a.
Cotton				
Raw	133,210	49,890	35,000 [a]	n.a.
Fibre	44,623	16,713	11,700	n.a.
Seeds	83,254	31,929	22,500	n.a.
Tea	19,236	14,365	13,500	17,500
Sisal	18,767	13,639	13,254	n.a.

a Forecast
Source: *Doc. Inf. CEDIMO,* Série A (24), 1978, pp. 12-30.

sector (or any complete branches of it). Reports point to shortages of raw materials (particularly for firms outside the state sector, the latter enjoying priority in the allocation of scarce materials)[59] and managerial inefficiencies following the departure of the former European managers. A number of individual cases of collapse of production have attracted attention, most notably, perhaps, that of the Sena Sugar Estate plantation, whose administration was finally taken over by the government, to be managed with the help of Cuban experts, following accusations of inefficiency and economic sabotage by its British management.[60] The signs are that the industrial slump probably bottomed out around 1977/78 and that production has now begun to pick up,[61] but this generalisation is not necessarily reflected in every sector. One of the success stories seems to be the cement industry which, according to President Machel anyway,[62] has not only recovered but has also been transformed into an exporting one. Among the industrial successes also must be counted the completion of the Cabora Bassa dam (with South African assistance).

One area which has presented a dilemma has been the distribution sector. Following the frustration of early hopes in the people's shops, S. Machel was saying, already in 1978, that the state 'could not waste its energies selling needles' and that, consequently, there could well be a bigger role for private retailers.[63] In agriculture, too, the relation of the state marketing organisation with private traders remained unclear. The dilemma was becoming acute by January 1980 with growing food shortages, accusations of inefficiency and corruption in the state distribution system and surprise tours by the President of shops and warehouses.[64] The poor state of distribution finally led to the 'reforms' announced on 19 March 1980.[65] The changes marked a partial return to private enterprise in distribution. The government was to withdraw from small shops which Mozambicans abroad were invited to return and take for a capital sum. Rationing was to be introduced in the cities (with no privileges, e.g. for the military) and higher prices were to be paid to farmers. Private activity was to continue in transport and wholesale trade. Other people's shops were to be absorbed by the consumer co-operatives which had proved more successful, and more egalitarian. The nationalised sector was to run on a profit-making basis. But the recent campaign against graft was to continue, too. 'Marginal' elements among the urban unemployed were to be moved out of Maputo to take up farming in a new 'green zone' to be created specially outside Maputo.

In the months which followed a large number of shops were sold back to private traders. But demand was particularly heavy for businesses dealing in products for which controlled prices allowed the highest mark-ups, clothing shops among these. Sales were not made automatically to the highest bidders but an effort was made to give preference to people who could demonstrate their ability to run a business (and did not run businesses already). The state was still represented in retailing but mainly in the form of a chain of 'model' supermarkets competing directly with private traders. Some of the old state shops were also turned over to the co-operatives, which received additional state help. The state also withdrew to a certain extent from wholesale dealing as the role of the state distributors was to be confined to the handling of the rationed products. But it was still intended to regulate closely the activities of the private wholesalers.[66]

The changes thus seem to reflect the current state of the philosophy regarding the role of the state sector, as enunciated by President Machel in July 1979.[67] The state sector 'would only win when it supplied the goods cheaper, faster and with more variety'. They amount to a reaffirmation of the role of private enterprise in 'straightening out the country' and have made observers doubt the Mozambican leadership's commitment to the planned economy.

In sum, neither agricultural nor industrial production nor value added in distribution, the main sectors of material output, have fulfilled the Third Congress's very modest goals. Even if we allow for considerable advances in education and health (import-saving outputs in which Communist governments ordinarily succeed very well; see section 10), the Mozambican people are much poorer and less productive than in 1973. But the only national income figures appear to be those of the OECD (1980): GNP per head moved from 100 in 1975 to 92 in 1976; 91 in 1977; 89 in 1978; 87 in 1979. Note that the link, 1973-5, is missing, but it is reasonable to assume it more favourable than in Angola, since fighting stopped earlier.

A crucial difficulty, which had started to bite ever since independence, but hit conclusively about halfway through the period was, of course, the termination by South Africa of the 'gold deal' (referred to in our opening section) on 11 April 1978. South Africa revalued its gold at the free market price at that time. The contingent of migrant miners had fallen to about 30,000 at that time so the traditional windfall had already drastically dwindled.[68] But its complete disappearance meant a considerable aggravation of Mozambique's balance of payments position at a difficult moment.

Estimates of the balance of payments position since independence are only available from the latest UN Report and reproduced in Table 4.4. The figures confirm the general impression of a progressive deterioration of the overall deficit until 1978 but the position appears to have improved slightly since then. The accuracy of the figures is dubious. Table 4.4 gives figures for merchandise trade, which in particular, are in considerable disagreement with the totals given for the same year in the UN *Yearbook of International Trade Statistics* (Table 4.5) and those of the IMF (Table 4.6). Table 4.4 generally shows larger deficits on visible trade than other sources, which may be a consequence of a deliberate attempt by Mozambique's government to exaggerate the deficit to the UN in support of its requests for aid.

We must not, of course, overlook the crisis in production, discussed already, which must have undoubtedly led to increased imports. It is the extent of that increase that is in question and, consequently also, the extent of the trade deficit. The deteriorating position of the balance of payments has also put pressure on the exchange rate and has led, not surprisingly, to the devaluation of the Mozambican escudo.[69] Further, it must have worsened the foreign debt position. That is not, of course, necessarily of immediate significance, and it does indeed appear that the bulk of the repayments does not fall due until 1981 or later. The debt stood at $110.5 million on 31 March 1978, but with actual payment obligations estimated at only around $15 million annually for the period 1978 to 1980. The situation had been critical,

Table 4.4: Mozambique's Balance of Trade and Payments ($ US m)[a]

	1973	1974	1975	1976	1977	1978	1979	1980
(a) Merchandise trade								
Imports	261	323	295	396	495	485	561	697
Exports	175	200	169	147	150	162	252	385
Balance	– 86	– 123	– 126	– 249	– 345	– 323	– 309	– 312
(b) Invisible items								
Payments	71	80	92	96	90	76	72	121
Receipts	163	200	255	243	200	198	200	242
Balance	+ 92	+ 120	+ 163	+ 147	+ 110	+ 122	+ 128	+ 121
(c) Capital account								
Balance	– 12	– 19	– 62	– 52	– 50	– 19	– 28	n.a.
(d) Overall balance	– 6	– 22	– 25	– 154	– 185	– 220	– 209	– 191

a Conversion rate used: 1000 Meticais = $US 33.
Source: Government of Mozambique/UN Review Missions, 1978 and 1980; the latter as reproduced in Financial Times, 17 December 1980.

Table 4.5: Mozambique's Import and Export Totals ($ 000)

	1973	1974	1975	1976	1977
Imports	464,749	463,644	417,125	n.a.	277,697
Exports	226,551	295,999	201,747	n.a.	128,991

Source: *UNYITS*, 1978.

however, for most of the period immediately preceding that. The gross foreign exchange reserves had fallen from four months' imports in mid-1977 to around two to three months' imports on 31 March 1978.[70] Foreign aid in its various forms, however inadequate, has clearly been of crucial importance in sustaining Mozambique's economy through the whole of the period of independence and it will probably continue to be a critical factor in the foreseeable future.

The balance of payments deficits have been mirrored, although not very closely, by deficits of the government's regular budget and of other 'parastatal' organisations. The deficit was estimated at $120 million for 1978, a very sharp increase over previous years, which brought the accumulated total to $305 million by the end of that year.[71] The reasons for these deficits are largely the same as those accounting for the deficits in the balance of payments and must be regarded as largely outside the government's control. The 1978 UN Review Mission makes a vague reference to 'pressures on the price level' as a result of these deficits, but the overall impression from other sources is one of relatively effective price controls and stability.[72]

The government has thus been obliged to pursue the policies proclaimed at the Third Congress against a background of severe economic difficulties. Not surprisingly, the application of the policies has not been quite smooth or steady and it has been characterised by a number of 'turns'. At the same time, such turns need not always be interpreted as the result of immediate necessity, as they may conceivably reflect more fundamental changes of heart among Mozambique's leaders.

Firstly, on the question of the overall strategy and the balance of the economy's sectors in the development effort, we can record a gradual shift of emphasis away from heavy industry. This has implied a greater emphasis on agriculture than would have been justified in terms of the classic role of the sector as a mere procurer of a surplus for development. It is difficult to find evidence of consistent commitment to 'heavy' industry during the five years, except for strong indications of an effort to develop an industry of farming equipment. The equipment concerned appears to be of the 'intermediate technology' variety; for instance, wheelbarrows, ox-drawn carts and ox-drawn ploughs. Thus, the choice of such realistically modest lines for development is in keeping with recent trends in development economics recommending adoption of 'appropriate' rather than of the most modern technologies.

It is also contributing towards greater integration of the various branches of the economy. As we have already mentioned, some of these branches, before independence, were more integrated with the rest of the Portuguese Empire than with one another, a fact which has been widely interpreted as a structural deficiency of the colonial economy. 'Integration' appears to us to be neither good nor bad, but there may be advantages in developing an agricultural tools industry in an economy like Mozambique. These may even turn out to be 'comparative advantages' in the strict sense.

Indeed, Mozambique's relatively simple industrial goods are not only for internal use. Some ploughs appear to have been exported to Angola and there have also been plans to export 3,000 paraffin refrigerators, again to Angola and Tanzania,[73] which seems to be realistic appreciation of comparative costs. The government has also fought to cut the production of luxury varieties of other consumer goods such as furniture, in a bid to increase the quantity produced of the more basic versions.[74] These moves, coupled with efforts to become self-sufficient in coal, and to develop, among the 'heavier' lines, the country's oil refining and cement industry into substantial exporting ones, the completion of the Cabora Bassa works and considerable investment in improved port facilities (mainly with foreign aid) amount to a reasonably well-balanced industrial strategy which we can applaud on pragmatic grounds. We cannot, however, see in it much urgency about developing heavy industry.

Perhaps it could not have been otherwise in any case. FRELIMO's worker-peasant alliance has always been more 'peasant'. And despite the — doubtful — 'leadership of the working class' the sheer numerical predominance of the peasantry throughout the movement's history must mean that there are definite limits beyond which the peasant sector cannot be squeezed to provide a surplus for 'socialist accumulation'. We have already mentioned recent increases in producers' prices and a move of the 'internal terms of trade' in favour of agriculture may well become more visible in the longer term.

8. Agricultural Organisation

This has been complicated and unstable. It shows minimal Soviet influence. It will be recalled that the Report to the Third Congress contained certain very positive commitments with respect to communal villages, co-operatives and state farms. Those ideas had in turn been formulated in the context of the colonial state of Mozambique's agriculture.

As already outlined in the beginning, there were three basic sectors before independence, namely (a) peasant farming (subsistence or cash crops and consisting, on the whole, of scattered isolated homesteads); (b) plantations (European-owned, producing cash crops for export and often including processing activities); and (c) settler farms (mainly situated near the cities and supplying the cities' food requirements). The objectives of the restructuring policy seem to have been, with respect to the peasant sector, villagisation, i.e. the physical concentration of houses into communal villages, as well as collectivisation of production, i.e. producers' co-operatives and state farms. Villages were mainly formed from amongst uprooted peasant communities, i.e. former *aldeamentos* (Portuguese strategic hamlets), refugees, or peasants displaced by floods, and only experimentally from stable ones. State farms were the descendants of the plantations as well as of settler farms which had been taken over, usually after being abandoned by their former owners. Producers' co-operatives were generally formed in areas which offered reasonable prospects of peasant acceptance of significant collectivisation of production. State farms and co-operatives were thus not conceived as alternatives to communal villages but as supplementary to these, to provide village households with collective agricultural work alongside individual cultivation which would still continue in the villages. State farms in particular were to be mechanised and, through their superior efficiency, to be relied upon to secure the cities' food supply. They would also serve the purpose of disseminating advanced agricultural technology. Finally, through diversifying production they could provide stable employment for the workers living near them. Elementary health and educational facilities, on the other hand, were intended to be attached to the communal villages.

The formation of communal villages was proceeding in the early and middle part of the period with unequal speed in different parts of the country. It was faster in the north, much of which had been liberated long before independence and had thereby acquired a stronger 'political consciousness'.[75] Within the villages, the growth of collective, as opposed to individual, production was taking place rather slowly on the whole. Capitalist farming was continuing here and there 'within the national plan'.[76] But while severe production difficulties were being experienced, as we have seen, the main thrust of policy was, perhaps, the mechanisation of state farms. 1,200 tractors and 50-100 combine harvesters were imported in 1977 at a cost of $40 million.[77] The policy was, however, contested from within, especially in the light of disappointing experience. The difficulties cannot have been unrelated to the lack of technically qualified personnel who could have made more effective use of the expensive machinery. A shift of policy towards 'more appropriate technology' finally took place in August 1978. Following a Central Committee meeting, large scale mechanisation was abandoned, faith in communal villages reaffirmed and the Minister of Agriculture, J. de Carvalho, dismissed.

Since these changes development of collectivised production has not been rapid. Until recently only about 1 million of the population were organised in (around 1,000) communal villages. Of these 1,000, only about 400 had some form of collective production to show.[78] And although official policy is no doubt still against isolated peasant farming, Machel has recently reaffirmed the role of family-sector production.[79]

If we regard the communal villages as a Tanzanian-inspired and, perhaps, Chinese-supported[80] invention, and state farms as a Soviet-type organisational form, we have in Mozambique something of a Sino-Soviet institutional battle in the sensitive area of agriculture. Actually that might be a simplistic and misleading picture. But it is perhaps true to say that Mozambican agricultural organisation has been unstable, with shifts of emphasis dictated by immediate needs. Production difficulties have been severe as we have seen. Given the European exodus, floods and border raids, it is hard to determine how much of these should be attributed to the inefficiencies of collective organisation or of premature mechanisation before 1978. With regard to the latter problem it was being reported in mid-1979 that 'tractors were rusting because no one could mend punctures'.[81] Perhaps this shortage of skills has been the most crucial factor. But low fixed prices for peasant production (of which more in section 10) must also have been a serious disincentive influence.

Meanwhile, the search has been continuing for the consolidation and development of agriculture's legal framework. The Law on Land Use, approved by the National Assembly in June 1979, laid down new norms. Reaffirming the state's ultimate ownership of the land, it provided for the inheritance of the use of family plots and ruled that land was to be rent-free for individual and co-operative cultivation and, indeed, for the occupation of communal villages. But the state was to have the ultimate right of allocation of all land-use rights, including the right of moving occupants but subject to compensation.[82] Private farms could use land subject to authorisation and could be charged rent. The farm's 'record' would determine renewal or otherwise of such arrangements.

Actually, all agricultural producers, state, co-operative or private, are in theory subject to the national plan, the main practical consequence of this being the obligation to deliver plan-specified quantities to the state marketing organisations or, indeed, to the many remaining private traders, at fixed prices. First-hand observers seem to believe, however, that although price controls are generally effective,[83] there is no real plan implementation in agriculture. It is, however, significant that as regards target specification planning is of the 'from above' variety with Ministry of Agriculture officials playing the decisive role.

Of particular interest is the evolving role of the agricultural co-operatives which represent the more 'organised' form of collective production outside the state sector. The place of co-operatives in the general ideological scheme is somewhat unclear, and a recent law on them promulgated on 20 August 1979 has not made it much clearer. For although they are about 'work for mutual aid among members', they are also to 'promote the material and general well-being of all'.[84] Work in co-operatives must, of course, be 'free of exploitation', which must be interpreted as a prohibition on wage labour. The real role of the co-operatives is, perhaps, to serve as centres of collective production by the side of the communal villages. Their number, given as 500 in 1979, means that there was roughly one co-operative for every two communal villages, but the co-operatives' total membership (30,000)[85] set against the 1 million inhabitants of communal villages implies that only a small minority were co-operative members and, thus, that only a few participated in organised collective work. True, a number of 'villagers' are also employed in state farms, but the fact remains that the majority are mainly cultivators of family plots with little or no participation in collective production.

A recent case study by Harris (1980) bears out this conclusion, and actually goes much further to show that the members of the particular co-operative studied formed a distinct socio-economic sub-group within the corresponding communal village. The leadership and most active membership of the Ed. Mondlane co-operative in the Gaza province was found by Harris to have originated from a class of rich peasants who had been developing into small capitalists before independence. The co-operative seemed also to have pre-empted the best part of the available land which had previously belonged to the active ex-capitalist co-operators.

The financial arrangements at least throw up many Soviet parallels. Agricultural co-operatives are subject, of course, to state intervention in the form of targets, fixed prices and financial rules for the allocation of the sales revenue. These normally require a minimum percentage to be retained towards forming a farm development fund, which can be used only with the joint agreement of farmers and local authorities. The rest is shared among the members in proportion to the work performed.[86] Low distribution levels thus mean that any capitalist accumulation must take place 'socially' within the co-operative rather than privately by individual members. This was what happened in the co-operative studied by Harris (1980), who also found the decisions on product plans and revenue distribution to be under 'exclusive' rather than popular control, i.e. control by the active co-operators in conjunction with the state service rather than by the wider co-operative membership.

Harris further discerned the effective continuation, in many co-operatives, of elements of the wage system. Although co-ops did not formally pay their non-active 'members' wages but what they regarded as *avanços*[87] against expected revenue, the recipients' lack of influence over financial decisions put them in a position of employment rather than co-operative participation. Harris misses the fact that the extreme poverty and uncertainty of the peasant's life makes any sort of predictable wage a huge benefit. He concludes that agricultural co-operatives did not by themselves produce fundamental changes in the 'relations of production' on the land and that they were often developing against the spirit of the programme of communal villages.

Current policy appears to be to encourage, often with subsidies,[88] the formation of co-operatives so that peasants come to join them voluntarily. The discussion of the previous paragraph, however, may cast doubts on the desirability of this in egalitarian terms; i.e. if co-operatives typically come to be dominated by what used to be the better-off peasants, it might be better, paradoxically for a socialist state, to extend special assistance to individual peasant cultivators! But we would not seriously expect such a thing to happen in view of its political implications.

We may begin to discern, on the whole, and after the various twists and turns of policy, an 'eclectic Afro-Marxist' organisational development in Mozambique's agriculture. The state farms, which are Soviet, are still important. The communal villages are Tanzanian *ujamaa* villages with their individual holdings, and the associated co-operatives or state farms. The co-operatives may have the makings of a Soviet *Kolkhoz* but are not repeating the historical sequence of its development. The hiring of machinery from specialist state enterprises is Soviet. There are even internal movement restrictions, recently instituted, according to a report in a usefully unfriendly publication,[89] which we might call a Soviet institution were it not a Portuguese one (and a Tanzanian and a South African!). Such restrictions, aimed, of course, at stopping poor peasants from drifting into urban unemployment, are consistent with the overall aim of stabilising agricultural employment and community living. In view of the commitment to raise rural standards, they are also consistent with the declared and more ambitious usual Communist aim of 'eliminating the differences between town and country'. The momentum is nevertheless surely in the direction of Soviet-type collectivisation and nationalisation but without much compulsion, and the current state of development could, perhaps, be located, in Soviet terms, somewhere in the NEP period. It has all moved substantially from the early days of independence when the Chinese inspiration still lingered on, and when students and teachers were on occasions mobilised to work in the fields (but that also happens, in a minor way, in USSR to-day).

9. Planning, Industrial Ownership

We have already made brief reference to planning in agriculture, pointing out the determining role of Ministry officials in setting targets. We have also indicated the ineffectiveness of agricultural planning due, according to Harris (1980), to the officials' general incompetence, but also to the partial nature of the planning exercise and, in particular, to the absence of a marketing plan for the disposal of the produce. But how far is the rest of the economy a 'planned' one?

The ambiguities of definition regarding planning are well known. There is on the one hand Soviet-type socialist planning and, on the other, what is known as 'development planning'. The former type of planning is easier to identify through its greater comprehensiveness (in its pure form, compulsory targets for all branches of the economy operationalised through annual directives) and through the extensiveness and sophistication of its administrative mechanisms. 'Development planning' is more elusive, on the other hand, as it generally lacks the above-mentioned characteristics and tends to apply to 'mixed economies' — itself an elusive term. In practice it may amount to little more than 'a few sectoral programs, a handful of agreed general development policies and a small number of large investment projects' (Griffin and Enos, 1970). A plan which is not backed by an effective planning machinery is more of a political statement of objectives than a technical document. Furthermore, planning under 'revolutionary development' conditions may present special problems. Myint (1967), for example, argues that since 'development planning is by definition an orderly approach while revolutionary changes are disorderly . . . we may advocate social revolution now and planning later but not (both) . . . at the same time without getting into serious contradictions.' As Mozambique must be regarded as 'revolutionary', as well as 'developing', and also potentially a Soviet-type economy, all these conceptual problems seem to apply.

As indicated already, planning in Mozambique is supposed to cover all firms whatever their form of ownership. In mid-1977 it was announced that firms would need to supply their year's plans to their corresponding ministries. They would also be expected to accept state-designated experts.[90] Formal steps were announced around the same time to set up a State Planning Commission and to work out a 'plan' for 1978.[91] But soon afterwards the then Planning Minister, M. dos Santos, was admitting the impossibility of 'global' planning especially in agriculture.[92] Later Machel stressed the 'planning of production in priority sectors' and the need to identify these in an apparent climb-down.[93] A sector-by-sector ten-year plan does, however, appear to have been drawn up, but is unfortunately still unpublished at the time of writing.[94]

As could have been expected, planning in Mozambique seems to have been associated in practice with policy on public enterprise and nationalisation, particularly in industry. The basic criterion for nationalisation, often enunciated in the early part of the period after independence, has been that industrial firms or farms would in the main not be taken over unless they were abandoned or guilty of 'sabotage', or otherwise not in compliance with the government's social and economic objectives. The attitude to foreign-owned enterprise has been particularly tolerant. The 1977 law on foreign investments is rather vague but the Governor of the Central Bank was recently inviting foreign investment on the basis of 'mutual profit'.[95] Earlier, in 1977, dos Santos had declared that the government 'directed state enterprise, supported the co-operative sector and controlled the private sector'.[96] Gradually, however, the emphasis seems to have shifted from an essentially 'punitive' concept of nationalisation to a more 'strategic' one and more state enterprises have been created in addition to those taken over. The state sector has thus come to be represented in most branches of industry, including internal commerce and, of course, foreign trade.

The purpose of the presence of state enterprises in particular sectors seems, however, to vary and is often unclear. In some areas a virtual monopoly appears to have been established, for instance in foreign trade (several state firms such as *Empresa Nacional de Comercialização, Agência Nacional de Despacho* and others); insurance (*Empresa Moçambicana de Seguros*); petroleum (*Empresa Nacional de Petroleos de Moçambique*); coal (*Empresa Nacional de Carvão de Moçambique*); air travel (*Agência Nacional de Viagens*); 'free shops' (*Lojas Francas de Moçambique*); vehicle production and repair, etc. In others the state sector is supplementary to or even in competition with the private and co-operative ones. Examples of the 'competitive' type of relationship are, most prominently perhaps, internal retail trade (*Empresa das Lojas do Povo*); clothing (*Sociedade Nacional de Confecções de Vestuario*); pharmaceutics (*Empresa Estatal de Farmacias*); tea (*Empresa Moçambicana do Chá*) and more recently food processing in which the biggest firm (the formerly Portuguese-owned *Companhia Industrial de Matola*) has been nationalised.[97] But in fishing also a small number of state firms seem to be cast in a 'leading' role while another enterprise has been created to 'co-ordinate the activities of the cashew industry', including the entire export trade.[98]

It is obviously the state monopolies and leading firms that can be relied on most, in terms of 'planning', but the bigger private or foreign-owned firms can also play a significant role in the planning process especially if the state also holds an interest in them.[99] But despite the growth of the public sector in Mozambique, there is not as yet much evidence of consistent 'planning'. The adverse economic circumstances which have bedevilled the country since independence seem to have restricted 'planning' to spasmodic attempts at more or less controlled reaction to crises. The various constraints have finally come to be mirrored, as is often the case, in the balance of payments, and

Mozambique's planning can thus be regarded as balance-of-payments-dominated. But planning of the 'list of projects' variety has also been practised, especially in connection with the UN Review Mission and requests for aid. This again seems fairly typical of development planning in general.

Meanwhile the general issue of which activities should be private and which public has by no means been resolved. The partial reprivatisation of domestic trade in March 1980 has been massively over-interpreted abroad as a general retreat. Suspicions were intensified with the removal, a little later, of the planning minister M. dos Santos (No. 2 in the party and regarded by some as Moscow's man) from government-executive functions to concentrate on party work. But the suspicions seemed rather unfounded when dos Santos surfaced again later in the year to deliver the May Day speech. It is by now, reading subsequent pronouncements, certain that the 'mini-reform' was but another temporary twist in the NEP direction dictated by acute economic difficulties.

10. Further Significant Developments in the Internal Economy

Brief mention must be made, for completeness, of Mozambique's tax system. Reforms introduced in February 1978 included a progressive income tax for all adults, replacing all other direct taxes (the main colonial one had been a head tax). The tax could be paid in kind by peasants. A turnover tax was also levied on the sales of all enterprises and special taxes were retained (and increased) on luxury items. The rates of income taxation seem rather more substantial than those of the turnover tax. The tax system is thus developing, at least for the time being, in the opposite direction from the Soviet-type model in that respect. Neither is the tax system the only or even the main instrument of capital accumulation. A campaign to increase the rate of savings has also been underway for most of the period, by attracting more bank deposits. Seen in the context of relatively low rates of taxation the policy thus seems not to rely entirely on the budget for the finance of investment, rather unlike the old Communist stereotype. On the other hand, it has recently been announced that credit availability will be more clearly related in future, to plan priorities.[100]

Developments on the price front have, perhaps, been more significant. In the summer of 1980 consumer prices were substantially raised, effectively for the first time since independence. Prices to be

paid for peasant production were also increased while it was re-
emphasised that state enterprises should make a profit.[101] There were,
on the other hand, no rises in wages. The intention was clearly to
move the system of controlled prices to something nearer its 'correct'
level, especially a level which would ensure increased agricultural
output for the market. Certainly food shortages appeared, at the same
time, to be continuing, and indeed to be reaching hunger proportions
in the Inhambane area, where 300,000 were reported to be threatened
by starvation.[102] A little later in 1980 Mozambique was reported to be
receiving food aid from a number of countries and international
agencies.[103]

But despite continuing difficulties in agriculture progress appears
to be taking place in other areas. Of these health and education can
be singled out. Great progress has been reported in establishing a
comprehensive state health service and particularly in extending it
to the rural areas. The emphasis appears to be shifting from 'curative'
to 'preventive' medicine, especially in the rural areas. Health service
organisation in these seems to revolve around the new 'rural health
centres' which function like small hospitals, supplemented by rural
peripheral health posts (roughly the descendants of FRELIMO's
own health posts during the armed struggle) and the more elementary
services of the communal village health workers (*Agentes Polivalentes
Elementares*).[104] A tentative family planning scheme has also been
introduced as part of the general scheme of maternal and child care.[105]
Great efforts have, of course, been made to end all forms of discrimination in the city hospitals. A parallel campaign has been underway in
the educational sphere, where the emphasis has been on breaking down
the 'dual' system of the colonial era. That had consisted, essentially, of
(mission) schools for Africans in the rural areas and a small urban
(state) sector for the settlers and *assimilados*. Despite severe personnel
shortages in both health and education progress seems encouraging, on
the whole.[106]

There have also been developments in the general area of 'labour'.
The government seems to have been moving towards a policy of
guaranteeing employment for everyone, or at least of preserving
employment wherever possible, particularly in the state enterprises.
There was even the promise of state jobs for workers in the distribution
sector who were not kept on by the new (private) owners of the shops
disposed of following the reform of spring 1980.[107] But progress is
slow (and ambivalent) on the matter of trade unions. The basic
intention seems to be to create new unions after a 'profound re-

organisation' of the Production Councils which are to form the basis of some large-scale workers' organisation.[108] But the Production Councils do not appear to have a clear role at present, and their position has been weakening *vis-à-vis* the state or even private managers to whom the government has been looking to secure production increases. It is inevitable, perhaps, that there should be talk of 'bourgeois tendencies' among them and very probable that Production Councils might develop into the main instrument for checking such tendencies.

To complete the picture we must mention the currency reform of 16 June 1980, which replaced the old Mozambican escudo with the new currency unit, the *metical*. The new unit was issued at the same value as the old but the measure was mainly prompted by the existence of large amounts of the old money in Portugal and South Africa, smuggled out of Mozambique at various times. The government was thus anxious to cancel the 'illegal' money, especially as some of it had allegedly been used to fund the MNR's anti-FRELIMO activities in South Africa. The new system also included provisions for limiting the amount of cash to be held by individuals and for checking the origins of unusually large sums presented for exchange with the new ones.[109]

11. Foreign Relations and Developments in Foreign Trade

The Third Congress report was rather brief on foreign policy and mostly confined to the diplomatic rather than the economic dimension. First it affirms Mozambique's allegiance to all the countries which had helped it during the war of independence, i.e. mainly the African countries and the 'Socialist Asian and European countries'. Secondly, it promises 'relations of friendship and co-operation with all countries on the basis of mutual respect of sovereignty and non-interference' and, thirdly, it affirms its particular affection for the 'Socialist camp, the free zone of mankind . . . and the decisive force which, on a world scale, neutralises imperialism'. More significantly, however, it affirms its membership of the Non-Aligned Movement which Mozambique considers as 'part of the anti-imperialist front' but nevertheless promises 'to work to develop'. The document also emphasises Mozambique's membership of the United Nations and of the Organisation of African Unity. As regards trade, it promises to develop it 'with progressive African countries, anti-imperialist countries and the Socialist countries'. Thus the position taken in the document is fairly strongly oriented in the direction of the East, although stopping short of total alignment with the 'socialist camp'.

As we have already seen, economic relations with the West as a whole were not significantly disturbed in the first year or so after independence. By the time of the Third Congress it had become obvious that Mozambique was operating a fairly sharp division between ideological and economic matters in the conduct of its foreign relations. Speaking at the Congress, Machel is reported to have pledged 'to take as far as possible ideologies from the East and capital from the West'.[110] That seems a fairly accurate, if unduly cynical, description of the formula.

There does certainly seem to be a strong desire for independence in Mozambique's attitude. The country did, after all, achieve its independence with a home-grown revolution and without the help of foreign troops. If we also consider the unusually severe colonial oppression which the country had suffered until very recently it is not at all surprising that it should strongly wish to avoid new relations of dependence.

Yet Mozambique has been unable so far to shake off one such relation of close economic interlinking if not dependence, namely that with neighbouring South Africa. It is, furthermore, a particularly damaging one for the country's image, due to South Africa's *apartheid* policies. The continuing co-existence cannot but be interpreted as a consequence of cynicism or else of economic desperation or, perhaps, both. The fact is that Mozambique feels let down by the international community over its Rhodesian experience which cost its economy dearly, as we have seen. Although the UN had pledged sanctions-specific assistance to persuade Mozambique to participate in the sanctions and despite repeated appeals for aid (Sec. Council Resolutions 386; 17 March 1976, and 411; 30 June 1977) only about one third of the eventual cost was provided in aid, at least according to the Mozambicans.[111] The South African 'connection' has been on the contrary quite useful for the economy throughout the period with payments for food exports, Mozambican power,[112] mine labour (although to a declining extent), the use of Mozambique's railways and harbours, as well as for some traditional Mozambican exports. Given the other economic difficulties mentioned already (however self-imposed some of those may have been) we should not be too surprised that Mozambique should be leaving for others, at the moment, the economic campaign against South Africa. Indeed she is being positive about her expectation of growth in trade and transport links with South Africa.

The Planning Minister, M. Machungo, has declared recently that 'South Africa needs the port of Maputo and we cannot avoid it . . . We need them to use the port as well. We will not close it.'[113]

As regards the trade pattern by partner countries, the only complete set of figures covering both the late colonial and most of the post-independence period (until 1978) is given by the IMF *Direction of Trade Yearbook* (1979 issue). For consistency we have chosen this set of figures for our Table 4.6 although it is not always in close agreement with the country totals given in other sources.[114]

Comparing the pre- and post-independence (1974) patterns, it can be seen that the USA had overtaken Portugal by 1977 as the leading recipient of Mozambique's exports. Portugal stood in fact in third place in 1977 as Japan had moved into second place by the same year. Japan actually overtook the USA itself in 1978 as the leading importing nation. Exports to Portugal continued to decline throughout the period. Among the other countries, exports to Zimbabwe-Rhodesia, India and Singapore seem to have grown to consistently significant levels, but exports to South Africa seem to have dropped to well below their level before independence. There has been a small increase in exports to the Eastern bloc, but a large reduction of exports to Angola. Exports to Tanzania, negligible before independence, have grown to a steady, if small, level.

On the import side we notice a significant reduction, post-independence, of imports from South Africa, which has however remained a leading exporter. South Africa would have remained at the top of the table but for: (a) an amazing increase of imports from Zimbabwe-Rhodesia which was the top exporter in 1978 — and this although the Mozambican embargo began in late 1976 and ended in early 1980; and (b) a massive increase in imports from Iraq, which occupied second place in 1978, pushing South Africa to third.[115] This is clearly due to the oil price explosion. Among the other countries, imports from Japan, France, Switzerland, Brazil and Bangladesh seem to have increased significantly. But among the Communist countries only the USSR, China and Romania have recorded significant, if unspectacular, exports. East Germany is probably becoming a major trading partner, but she ceased to publish the geographical breakdown of her trade in 1975.[116] Imports from Portugal seem to have stabilised around a lower level, compared with the colonial period.

Imports from the USA have remained more or less stable, while those from West Germany and Saudi Arabia have fallen. Angola shows, once again, a considerable fall since independence, while, on the contrary, Mozambique has started to import from Tanzania.

What inferences about policy can be drawn from all this? Trading partners are, after all (unlike the overall deficit in the balance of payments), partly at least a matter of choice. But the only conclusion which seems possible here is that there has been since independence a shift in Mozambique's trade away from Portugal and the former empire[117] and towards the wider world economy, particularly towards (a) neighbouring countries and (b) the Communist world. But the shift can hardly be described as a dramatic one and Mozambique has thus remained essentially open to the world economy. The reduction in trade with Angola presumably reflects an attempt by both countries to build more rational trading relations with the rest of the world and with their more immediate neighbours in particular. Increased trade with Tanzania can perhaps be seen in the same light. The increased imports from Brazil are not surprising in view of Brazil's extensive penetration of the African market[118] and its particular linguistic and cultural bonds with the ex-Portuguese colonies. But there may also be possibilities on the export side too, as Brazil has shown an interest in Mozambique's coal. In general terms, given Portugal's weakness, Brazil may be ideally placed to inherit and exploit the former Portuguese influence.

Turning now to the commodity pattern of trade, we can report little change. The exports continue to be the traditional ones, with some increase in the proportions of coal and cement. Certain countries, for instance India, seem to be receiving only cashews. On the import side the relative importance of foodstuffs has increased since independence. Again imports from certain countries seem to be heavily concentrated on particular products; for instance, all imports from Iraq are oil. We shall not, however, attempt to provide a comprehensive table in this connection as a lot of essential information is lacking and such statistics as are available are very scattered in the various sources.

As to aid and formal trade agreements, we can distinguish three basic groups among the countries with which Mozambique deals: (i) advanced countries capable of supplying 'development goods' and technical assistance with infrastructure; (ii) Communist countries capable of the same, and (iii) neighbouring countries for 'regional co-operation'. In (i) we must include Portugal and Brazil for the purposes of this classification, and in (ii) China and Cuba, while South Africa can be seen as belonging, effectively, to both (i) and (iii).

Among the countries in (i) Portugal's place has been a special one. As has been hinted already, Mozambique's attitude to Portuguese

Table 4.6: Mozambique – Trade by Main Partner Countries (visible civilian trade)

Imports[a] ($ US m)							Country	Exports[a] ($ US m)						
1973	1974	1975	1976	1977	1978	1979		1973	1974	1975	1976	1977	1978	1979
22.6	27.1	22.5	13.4	14.0	22.0	32.9	USA	30.6	31.5	27.4	40.2	66.1	38.0	50.5
1.0	1.4	0.4	7.1	5.8	8.9	5.5	Canada	3.6	4.0	4.1	1.3	4.8	4.1	3.1
23.6	31.0	21.3	14.7	18.0	34.0	11.1	Japan	4.6	6.9	8.9	32.5	33.9	39.8	34.6
6.3	11.3	7.5	3.3	4.5	13.0	6.5	Belgium	2.8	3.0	2.8	9.9	6.6	5.9	3.2
38.9	24.6	21.2	17.2	24.1	36.3	35.7	France	4.3	3.2	1.5	12.0	8.0	8.9	11.3
62.6	65.9	43.2	50.8	50.2	34.6	18.0	West Germany	7.0	6.1	4.4	16.1	12.9	11.6	8.3
35.3	30.3	31.7	34.5	19.9	37.3	36.8	UK	12.9	13.0	8.0	36.6	8.9	35.2	21.3
12.4	13.2	9.6	4.1	7.4	8.8	6.8	Italy	5.4	4.8	2.9	8.9	1.3	5.6	11.6
5.6	8.7	7.6	6.1	6.6	7.7	4.9	Netherlands	6.1	13.6	8.1	17.9	15.1	6.7	10.4
3.3	1.5	10.3	7.4	13.2	13.4	13.0	Sweden	1.0	1.2	0.5	2.9	3.9	5.1	3.5
11.1	10.8	7.1	4.2	9.4	28.8	5.8	Switzerland	0.2	0.2	0.2	1.6	3.4	3.3	3.5
0.9	0.6	1.0	3.6	5.1	5.1	6.9	Norway	0.8	0.6	–	3.5	0.5	–	–
3.0	3.6	2.3	2.9	2.3	1.7	0.9	Spain	4.8	10.3	4.7	5.2	3.1	3.4	3.8
1.3	1.7	1.9	3.4	0.2	8.9	1.5	Australia	2.0	3.3	2.4	0.7	1.3	2.0	1.3
1.3	2.5	3.2	2.9	2.0	2.3	1.6	New Zealand	0.3	0.4	0.3	0.1	0.2	–	–
3.8	23.9	5.2	20.0	2.3	–	–	S. Arabia	–	–	0.3	–	0.6	1.3	2.6
19.1	1.1	23.5	45.9	68.4 (25.4)	65.0 (4.6)	7.3	Iraq	–	–	–	–	–	–	–
89.3	77.6	63.5	29.9	26.6	37.9	25.4	Portugal	80.3	99.5	47.4	45.4	20.0	18.7	36.8
2.5	2.5	1.8	4.4	11.2	9.2	17.7	Brazil	1.6	0.2	7.9	0.1	–	–	–
3.6	1.9	2.5	0.7	0.9	–	–	Macao	–	–	–	–	–	–	–
0.3	0.5	0.6	0.8	1.2	1.2	1.3	India	6.8	16.9	9.1	9.8	14.0	15.7	–

Table 4.6 continued

Bangladesh	1.9	2.9	–	22.3	23.3	19.3	21.3	1.6	0.3	0.2	4.4	1.5	0.3	1.3
Hong Kong	2.9	0.7	3.6	4.1	5.7	4.1	1.0	0.2	0.2	0.1	3.1	1.6	25.8	62.9
Singapore	0.3	1.1	1.1	1.3	1.9	2.3	6.4	21.0	27.8	16.0	8.0	9.0	10.0	11.0
South Africa	94.2	91.4	71.8	53.7	55.0	56.4	62.0	–	–	–	–	–	–	–
Zimbabwe-Rhodesia	–	–	22.3	44.6	66.9	73.6	–	–	–	–	5.3	10.6	5.2	5.8
Tanzania	–	–	–	1.3	2.0	2.2	–	–	–	–	0.5	2.9	1.1c	–
USSR	–	–	–	3.1c	–	26.9c	–	0.4	0.1	–	–	2.0	4.1	1.1c
China	0.3	0.3	2.5	0.8	1.8	3.9	–	–	0.1	0.1	0.1	2.0	4.1	4.5
Romania	–	–	0.9	1.9	2.8	3.1	0.4	–	–	–	–	0.1	–	–
Angola	9.2	7.0	–	3.2	1.2	1.4	–	7.9	14.1	3.4	–	0.1	0.3	0.3
North Korea	–	–	–	–	–	–	–	–	–	–	–	1.1d	–	–
Vietnam	–	–	2.7d	–	–	–	–	–	–	–	–	–	–	–
Total[b]	464.3	467.0	410.3	443.7	277.7	424.4	375.0	225.5	298.7	198.1	301.8	129.0	282.1	400.3

a. Exports fob. Imports cif. USSR figures all fob.

b. Total also includes trade with countries not shown in table. Significant trade only shown. The trade surplus shown for 1979 seems highly suspect, however. See Table 4.4.

c. Figures from *Vneshnyaya Torgovlya* given in transf. roubles. The following conversion rates have been used: 1 tr. rbl. = $1.33 (1976), $1.46 (1978). I have also converted cif to fob and vice versa as in Table 2.4.

d. Figure from *Yearbook of International Trade*, UN 1979. No other figures for Vietnam and no other significant trade is recorded against North Korea. A small amount of trade with South Korea is also recorded.

Source: *Direction of Trade Yearbook*, IMF, 1979-80.

industrial property following independence has not been any more severe than its policy towards foreign enterprise in general. Nationalisation has been selective and compensation often paid. And despite the decline in trade new areas of co-operation have been found, notably Portuguese assistance with improvements at Beira Port including the construction of a fishing dock.[119] Further consultations have taken place on the possibilities for more co-operation in the building and repairing of fishing boats.[120] Skilled Portuguese who left at independence are being welcomed back and the welcome sometimes extends to new Portuguese immigrants as well.

We have already discussed trade and aid agreements with other Western countries. But of particular significance seem to be the recent agreements with Italy and Brazil. The agreement with Italy has been hailed as the first ever comprehensive economic pact with a Western nation, giving it preferential access to Mozambique's coal, uranium, petroleum and natural gas.[121] The agreement with Brazil provides for exchanges of (refined) oil from Mozambique, for oil exploration and equipment and training.[122] But Brazil has also been exporting locomotives[123] and advising on tourist development,[124] while the possibilities have been discussed for an exchange of Brazilian buses, lorries, fishing boats and tractors for tea and coal from Mozambique,[125] as we have already suggested. Of the other Western countries, France has opened a $200 million line of credit and has signed an agreement on scientific and technical co-operation,[126] while Spain has entered negotiations on co-operation in fishing.[127] A British credit of £57.5 million has also been announced for Mozambique's sugar sector including the Sena Estate.[128] The US has also granted credits of some $10 million for the purchase of wheat.[129]

Of the Communist countries, the majority seem to be involved in substantial agreements with Mozambique. The USSR does surprisingly little trade, and provides surprisingly little civilian aid. She is, however, the almost exclusive arms supplier. In the nature of things, it is difficult to provide reliable figures of the arms shipments or of their terms of exchange, but a lot of them are thought to be for hard currency.[130] Despite a 20-year friendship and co-operation treaty with Mozambique, signed in March 1977, the Soviet Union's strictly economic programme in Mozambique remains small, apart from a big fishing concession operated by the joint Soviet-Mozambican company, *Mozapesca*, in exchange for technical aid. Soviet experts are also helping with agricultural development schemes and geological exploration and they have been advising on the production of agricultural implements.

Plans to set up a tractor assembly plant with Soviet aid were recently announced.[131] But the Soviets also have a number of doctors and other experts in Mozambique and maintain active cultural contacts.[132]

Of the other East European countries, East Germany shows exceptional cordiality and generosity. She also provides the security experts! She has a fishing agreement similar to the Soviet Union's, and both agreements have been criticised by some as 'mortgaging the country's future wealth'. East Germany, like the USSR, has also sold Mozambique heavy machinery.[133] But it is East German machinery which has featured most prominently in Mozambican agriculture, and East Germany also sold 1,000 lorries, supplied electronic equipment, signed a number of agreements on mineral exploitation and made several gifts of machinery and medicines.[134] On the whole, East German presence in Mozambique has been more pronounced than Soviet, with the exception of the military field,[135] and the country must be becoming one of Mozambique's major trading partners.[136] The East Germans have even advised on the setting-up of Mozambique's foreign currency shops.[137] The East German Head of State, E. Honecker, visited Mozambique in February 1979 and a 20-year treaty of friendship and co-operation was signed during the visit.[138]

Romania is also reported to have sold a few locomotives and vehicles and has entered into a number of agreements for co-operation in fishing, oil, chemicals, banking and broadcasting.[139] Bulgaria has also entered into co-operation agreements mainly in the fields of agricultural infrastructure, civil engineering, the supply of tractors and the setting up of agro-industrial complexes.[140] The Hungarian bus company, Ikarus, is reported to have contracted the setting up of a bus assembly plant.[141] Hungary is also reported to have provided military equipment, food and medical personnel.[142] Yugoslavia, too, has sent electrical equipment and has granted financial aid.[143] Czechoslovakia has supplied a number of vehicles and agricultural machinery.[144] Finally Poland has helped to build (jointly with East Germany) a textile factory.[145]

On the whole, the Eastern European economic presence in Mozambique has thus focussed mainly on technical assistance rather than deliveries of equipment and materials, although these too seem to be significant and to be underestimated by official trade statistics. The programme of credits totalling $160 million from 1975 to 1978 has also not been a very big one. This is also reflected in the relatively small number of experts and technicians present (a total of 2,000 military and 'economic' personnel reported in 1978 from the USSR and Eastern Europe). Some 400 Mozambicans, on the other hand, were studying in 1978 in the USSR and in Eastern Europe.[146]

China's presence, although fading, has not been a negligible one, with some $60 million worth of credits since 1975, a co-operation agreement in force since September 1979, and some 120 'economic personnel' in 1978.[147] President Machel visited China in May 1978[148] and high-level Chinese delegations have been visiting Mozambique for most of the post-independence period. There is also in force a 20-year co-operative agreement with North Korea under which Mozambique has received rice and also aid for salt production.[149] But relatively the most impressive presence in Mozambique is undoubtedly the Cuban. Cuba is involved in aid and co-operation agreements in fishing, agriculture, civil engineering, transport and communications, etc.,[150] while the Cuban contingent of civilian and military experts was, in 1978, some 1,000 strong.[151] Cuba's influence appears to be particularly strong in education. Nevertheless, in sheer quantity of aid disbursements and commercial investments the West is very far ahead indeed (Table 1.2).

At the same time as developing its relations with the 'socialist world' Mozambique has been actively pursuing new relations with its neighbours. She realises the long-term importance of a successful regional association but, at the same time, wishes, for obvious reasons, to move away from her present close association with South Africa. Clearly, then, she must explore new forms of economic integration with the neighbouring black states.

One such black state which is also a socialist, although not an immediately neighbouring one, is Angola. The two countries recently announced the ratification of a trade agreement granting each other 'most favoured nation' treatment in all matters affecting bilateral commodity exchanges, except where a customs union or free trade area is involved for either country.[152] The practical significance of this agreement remains to be seen, in view of the currently small volume of trade, but the intention is clear. As regards its actual neighbours, Mozambique has been discussing the creation of a free zone and a number of joint projects with Tanzania,[153] the construction of new rail links with Zambia[154] and, of course, the repair of existing ones with what is now Zimbabwe, which were damaged during the war. It is now proposed, in fact, to electrify the line to Beira in a complex scheme involving contract work by General Electric, power from Cabora Bassa, locomotives from Brazil and finance from the USA.[155] But apart from increased trade and transport, Machel and Mugabe also committed themselves at a recent meeting to co-operation in the field of security.[156]

There have also been attempts to get regional co-operation moving at multi-national level in Southern Africa in which Mozambique has taken part. The Lusaka Summit Conference of nine nations was convened in April 1980[157] to examine the possibilities of reducing dependence on trade and transport links with South Africa. The need for this was clearly voiced, but the meeting did not commit the participants to any immediate confrontation. The longer-term intention of increasing the integration of the black African states was announced in the broadest possible terms. The intention was confirmed at the Addis Ababa meeting a few months later.[158] It would seem, however, that the majority of the states, Mozambique included, cannot realistically be expected to take any great strides towards regional integration until they have mastered their immediate economic problems individually. The present pattern of integration with the economy of South Africa, on the other hand, at least has the advantages of being known and tried. It can be expected to continue in the foreseeable future. The 'nine' might, of course, grow into something of a rival for the Republic but that could only happen in the longer term.[159]

This general feeling was echoed again at the Second Southern African Development Co-ordination Conference which opened in Maputo on 27 November 1980. The main purpose of that appears to have been the co-ordination of various schemes involving foreign aid in connection with the overall objective of reducing links with South Africa. Mozambique is well placed geographically in this respect. She was in fact allocated 40 per cent of the total post-improvements budget, which will facilitate the re-routing away from South African ports of goods destined for the land-locked members of the group of nine.[160]

But overall it is perhaps global rather than regional groupings which are likely to be of more interest to Mozambique at present. Some of these are of immediate importance, namely the 'Western' Lomé Convention, IMF and World Bank on the one hand, and the 'Eastern' CMEA on the other. Both the Western and the Eastern alignments hold out the prospect of a sustained flow of aid. If the view is taken that aid is what Mozambique needs most of all it is not inconceivable that she may be the first country to become a member of all these organisations.

There has been persistent speculation about Mozambique joining Lomé.[161] But she is refusing to join at present, since Lomé requires recognition of Berlin as part of West Germany and Mozambique is strongly supporting East Germany on this issue. But apart from admission to Lomé, Mozambique's stand on Berlin may be depriving her from aid from other sources such as the EEC or the USA. It seems to have blocked, in particular, Mozambique's share of a $2 billion EEC plan to overhaul the transport system of the black Southern African states.[162] The matter is likely to continue to cause problems especially with West Germany and the USA.

But there is also the CMEA. Mozambique was an 'observer' in 1979 and in late 1980 there was a spate of official claims in Maputo that membership would follow.[163] President Machel and a high level delegation then visited Moscow for talks. Brezhnev's speeches, and the final communiqué,[164] leave the Soviet attitude unknown, though it was obviously cool. There was only a 'coincidence of views', not an 'identity of views'. The word 'CMEA' did not occur in any account of the visit published in USSR. But the strong Mozambican wish remains clear, as evidenced by Machel's references to the 'need for tight co-operation with other brother socialist states' and his belief that 'by uniting our diverse resources we have the possibility to develop and strengthen our economy, to attain mutual profits'.[165]

Apart from CMEA membership there is also the question of whether she will become an actively pro-Soviet member of the 'Non-Aligned' Movement; whether, in short, Mozambique will eventually become another Cuba. It is, unfortunately, another question to which we do not feel confident enough to venture an answer at present. The Movement is merely a diplomatic sounding board, while CMEA membership *may* carry a prospect of reliable and sustained aid, as we showed in Table 1.2, and may perhaps by itself not be too costly in terms of alienating either Western or Southern African connections. Mozambique's pragmatist rulers will no doubt try to evaluate very carefully (although not necessarily successfully) all these probable consequences before abandoning their present somewhat eclectic stance.

Mozambique has indeed been eclectic in the conduct of its general diplomacy. President Machel has travelled extensively to meet other leaders in Africa and also to Scandinavia, to Eastern Europe, China and the Soviet Union, and the policy has consistently been directed at maintaining good relationships with practically everyone. In terms of official pronouncements, however, with no immediate consequences, it has been a somewhat different story and the general stance has been pro-Soviet on the whole. Addressing the Sixth Conference of the Non-Aligned Movement in Havana in September

1979, Machel was explaining that 'non-alignment could not be interpreted as non-engagement in anti-imperialist struggle' and emphasising that the socialist countries were his 'natural allies'. Within that he expressed esteem for Vietnam but called for an early resolution of its conflict with China. The latter he described in turn as a friendly power which was just wrong on one issue, Vietnam. He was very damning of President Sadat of Egypt, but had some words of affection for President Tito of Yugoslavia, as well as for President Castro of Cuba. Moving towards matters, perhaps more concrete, he urged the transformation of the Indian Ocean into a demilitarised (and denuclearised) zone, a position which agrees with current Soviet and Madagascan policy. He also made a plea against oil becoming a divisive factor in the Third World. He finally reaffirmed his support for the UN as the most appropriate forum for negotiations leading to fair international relations.[166] But Mozambique's support for the Soviet position in Kampuchea and Afghanistan has been steady.

The most delicate part of Mozambique's diplomacy is the relationship with South Africa. Mozambique's pragmatism has stopped short of opening actual diplomatic relations with the Republic (although a South African trade mission is operating). More than anything else, perhaps, the amount of trade taking place in the absence of official diplomatic links and against a background of bitter differences on almost every ideological issue is a measure of the ambiguities involved. Military or guerrilla threats to either country can easily be mounted in each other's territory. Indeed they have both accused each other of harbouring hostile activities against the other at various times,[167] and probably with some justification.

But Mozambique's perception of its own economic vulnerability will probably keep it, ultimately, on its present tolerant and conciliatory course and away from confrontation with South Africa. Mozambique will continue to be flexible on foreign trade, tolerant towards foreign enterprises and, ultimately, towards foreign ideologies. Mozambique is a genuine case of pragmatic socialism, indeed of what we may call 'pragmatic Communism'. We can predict that Mozambique will continue in the foreseeable future to guarantee by law new foreign capital investment and to trade with the South African Republic. She will also continue to trade extensively with the West, even in preference to trading with the East. She will continue to seek foreign aid. She will finally seek to stabilise her institutions.

Notes

1. World Bank, 1980.
2. Ibid.
3. See Kravis *et al.*, 1978.
4. See Table 4.1 for more details.
5. See Table 1, World Bank, 1980.
6. See Table 2, World Bank, 1980.
7. *ARB*, September-October 1980.
8. *UN Report of Review Mission to Mozambique*, A33/178, 12 July 1978.
9. See B. Munslow, 1980. Also M. Wuyts, 1978, 1980.
10. As is, perhaps, testified by the massive deterioration of the Portuguese balance of payments since 1974.
11. Generally allowing full profit repatriation. The policy has become known as an 'open door' one.
12. See, for example, *ACR*, 1976/77 and the *Financial Times*, 18 January 1978.
13. See *ACR*, 1976/77 and the *Financial Times*, 18 January 1978.
14. See Wuyts, 1980.
15. 0.2% of agricultural enterprises are estimated to have owned about half of the total land area and that can be expected to have included the best lands! See Brum, 1976.
16. Such integration was intensified between 1926 and 1960, a period characterised by Portuguese 'economic nationalism'. See Wuyts, 1980. This mention of integration is not to be taken to imply that it is necessarily a good thing.
17. See *Estatistica do Comércio Externo*, various issues.
18. *UN Review Mission*, 1978.
19. *Guardian*, 10 August 1978. This figure seems, however, very high. It must include a lot of disputed debt with Portugal, which must have been subsequently settled with less than full repayment.
20. *To the Point*, 23 March 1979.
21. As an example of a Communist (East German) assessment, Stier and Stier (1978) also recognise Mozambique as a genuine case of a 'People's Democracy' on the dual criterion of (a) a Marxist-Leninist party and (b) a 'comprehensive and planned conception of the development process'. But certain doubts may well remain, as we shall see.
22. *People's Power*, no. 12, Autumn-Winter 1978.
23. See P. Sketchley in *People's Power*, no. 15, Winter 1979.
24. *ARB*, April, May 1979.
25. *To the Point*, 23 March 1979.
26. *To the Point*, 1 June 1979. This church has in the past been the main sufferer, as representing Portuguese imperialism (*Le Monde*, 2 December 1980).
27. *Guardian*, 13 December 1979.
28. By Presidential Edict with effect from 30 January 1980, as reported in *To the Point*, 22 February 1980. Note that this slightly precedes the great economic step 'backwards' of March 1980.
29. *Guardian*, 25 September 1980. Also *ARB*, September 1980 (Political/Social/Cultural Series).
30. *To the Point*, 17 October 1980.
31. *Guardian*, 8 October 1980.
32. Interview reported in *AIM Bulletin*, no. 39, Suppl., 1979.
33. *Guardian*, 6 November 1979. Also *ARB*, vol. 16, no. 7, 15 August 1979 (Political/Social/Cultural Series).

34. *Neue Zürcher Zeitung*, 11 February 1979.

35. *To the Point*, 1 June 1979. Also *SWB*, 24 August 1979.

36. *Guardian*, 27 May 1980.

37. *Financial Times*, 17 December 1980.

38. *Guardian*, 10 August 1978.

39. According to some estimates ouput of certain key products had fallen by 1976 to less than 50% of the 1973 level (*ARB*, various numbers, 1978). Cashews and the other main cash crops registered big falls (see Table 4.3; also *Financial Times*, 17 December 1980). *Per capita* food output is estimated to have fallen by 1978 to 79% of the 1971/74 level (see Fitzpatrick, 1981).

40. See *Frankfurter Allgemeine Zeitung*, 9 February 1977.

41. See among various sources *ACR*, 1976/77, *Frankfurter Allgemeine Zeitung*, 7 April 1977 and *ARB*, 1977, various issues.

42. For a useful analysis of the broader issues see Griffin and Enos, 1970.

43. *People's Power*, no. 11, January-March 1978. Also UN Review Mission, 1978.

44. *People's Power*, no. 11, January-March 1978. The UN Review estimate put the number at 70,000 in May 1978 and predicted an increase to 90,000 by 1979.

45. Interview reported in *AIM Bulletin*, no. 39, Suppl. 1979.

46. See *ARB* December 1979-January 1980.

47. *Sunday Times*, 6 August 1978.

48. *Marchés Étrangers*, Lausanne, 24 January 1979.

49. *Review Mission Report*, 1978.

50. *The Times*, 1 August 1978.

51. *ARB*, January-February 1979 and January-February 1980 respectively.

52. *SWB*, 9 February 1979.

53. *SWB*, 10 July 1979.

54. *SWB*, 5 February 1980.

55. *Guardian*, 12 November 1979.

56. *Guardian*, 12 June 1980.

57. *Guardian*, 30 August 1980.

58. *Le Monde*, 10 November 1980.

59. See, for example, *ARB*, February-March 1979.

60. See *People's Power*, no. 12, Autumn-Winter 1978; *Financial Times*, 12 August 1978, where the management's case is also outlined; *South*, November 1980.

61. In his May 1979 interview, reported in *AIM Bulletin*, no. 39, Suppl., 1979, President Machel claimed an increase of 20% in industrial production from 1977 to 1978. In 1979 the increase was expected to be 23 per cent.

62. Ibid.

63. *AIM Bulletin*, Report on 4th Session of Central Committee, Dossier 1978.

64. *Guardian*, 24 January 1980.

65. *Guardian*, 20 March 1980.

66. *Guardian*, 11 November 1980.

67. *Guardian*, 12 November 1979.

68. The current number is estimated at 42,000. See *Financial Times*, 17 December 1980.

69. A 15 per cent devaluation was reported in *Frankfurter Allgemeine Zeitung*, 7 April 1977. The UN *Statistical Yearbook* also moved from a conversion factor of around 3.90 US cents for 1 escudo for 1974/75, to around 3.30 US cents for 1976.

70. *UN Review Mission*, 1978. Also *Marchés Étrangers*, Lausanne, 24 January 1979.

71. *UN Review Mission*, 1978.

72. See, for example, Fitzpatrick, 1981.

73. *AIM Bulletin*, no. 39, 1979. The paraffin fridges and freezers are especially useful for rural areas without electricity.

74. Interview with S. Machel, ibid.

75. *People's Power*, no. 11, January-March 1978.

76. Ibid.

77. B. Munslow, 1980.

78. B. Munslow, 1980.

79. *AIM Bulletin*, no. 36, June 1979.

80. China herself never had such communal villages until long after collectivisation and her People's Communes had collapsed by 1962. But in Tanzania *ujamaa* villages were seriously tried as a form of (forced) collectivisation until 1975, when they were themselves abandoned for what was recognised to be overall failure. Tanzania now seems to be pursuing villagisation without collectivisation, as most production in the so-called communal villages appears to have reverted to a petty-capitalist pattern.

81. *Guardian*, 19 May 1979.

82. In Tanzania there was no compensation (and some peasants' houses were burned down) in the course of forced collectivisation.

83. Prices paid to producers seem to have been low for most of the period of independence. But they have recently been increased as we shall see in section 10.

84. *SWB*, 28 August 1979.

85. Interview with S. Machel, *AIM Bulletin*, no. 39. Suppl., June 1979.

86. *People's Power*, no. 11, January-March 1978.

87. In Mexico the *ejidos colectivos* have always paid such *avanços*. In USSR the kolkhozy went from the labour-day through such a system to what is now practically a wage plus a dividend at the end of the year.

88. There have been such subsidies in Eastern Europe, but never in USSR.

89. *To the Point*, 22 June 1979, reports the institution of a *guia de marcha* without which movement is prohibited.

90. *Neues Deutschland*, 17 August 1977.

91. *Neues Deutschland*, 19 October 1977.

92. *Neues Deutschland*, 27 October 1977, and *Unitá*, 21 November 1977.

93. Interview reported in *AIM Bulletin*, no. 39, Suppl., September 1979.

94. *Financial Times*, 17 December 1980.

95. Ibid.

96. *Unitá*, 22 December 1977.

97. *ARB*, July-August 1980.

98. *AIM Bulletin*, no. 39, September 1979. Also *Doc. Inf.* CEDIMO, Série A (24).

99. Such is the case with the Cabora Bassa Company.

100. *ARB*, December-January 1980.

101. *ARB*, May-June 1980.

102. *ARB*, June-July 1980.

103. *ARB*, September-October 1980.

104. See *People's Power*, no. 13, Spring 1979.

105. *Guardian*, 4 November 1980.

106. *People's Power*, no. 13, Spring 1979.

107. *Guardian*, 11 November 1980.

108. Statement by the new Planning Minister, M. Machungo, reported in the *Guardian*, 23 October 1980.

109. *Guardian*, 17 June 1980.

110. Quotation as reported in *Frankfurter Allgemeine Zeitung*, 7 April 1977.

111. *Guardian*, 30 May 1980. The final cost was put, according to that report, at £236m by the Vice-Governor of the Bank of Mozambique.

112. Power from Cabora Bassa is transmitted directly to Pretoria and cannot be tapped by Mozambique! This is probably not imperialism but a matter of voltage reliability. Similar arrangements govern the supply of electricity by the East to the West in Europe, since otherwise the unreliability of the Eastern network would 'infect' the Western one (cf. Keltsch, 1980). The city of Maputo relies, contrariwise, on the South African electricity authority for its own supply. But Mozambique is receiving some $13m a week for the power supplied to South Africa from the complex, and work is under way now on new transmission lines which will supply power directly to the centre and north of Mozambique. See *Financial Times*, 17 December 1980.

113. *Guardian*, 4 November 1980.

114. Such as the *UNYITS*, Mozambique Government Statistics, or the partner countries' 'mirror statistics'. Furthermore, the figures available so far do not seem to do justice to trade with East European countries. Trade with the GDR in particular seems to have grown considerably, and she is now reckoned by some to have become Mozambique's third biggest trading partner. See *Financial Times*, 17 December 1980. The GDR publishes no geographical distribution of her trade: cf. Table 8.1.

115. Both the Rhodesian and the Iraq totals are, however, given by the *Yearbook* as subject to considerable margins of error. But Iraq is reported to have been the top exporter in 1979 (*Financial Times*, 17 December 1980). Cf. the *Guardian*, 19 November 1980, *Financial Times*, 17 December 1980).

116. There are several more very small entries for imports from (and exports to) one or two of the other Communist countries.

117. Trade with Macao and Cape Verde has also declined.

118. See *South*, November 1980.

119. *SWB*, ME/W1031, 15 May 1979.

120. *SWB*, ME/W1045, 21 August 1979.

121. *ARB*, January-February 1980.

122. *ARB*, May-June 1979. The line of credit from Brazil has totalled some $120m. See *Financial Times*, 17 December 1980.

123. *ARB*, March-April 1979.

124. *ARB*, July-August 1979.

125. *SWB*, ME/W1041, 24 July 1979.

126. *Financial Times*, 17 December 1980.

127. *SWB*, ME/W1089/A2/4, 1 July 1980.

128. *SWB*, ME/W1095, 12 August 1980.

129. *SWB*, ME/W1091/A2/3, 15 July 1980.

130. FES *Bericht* I/1978 gives estimates of Soviet military equipment in service in Mozambique in 1977. These include airplanes (MIG-17 and -21), missiles (SAM-6 and -7) and tanks (T-34). A number of advisers were also thought to be present.

131. *SWB*, ME/W1105, 21 October 1980.

132. See FES *Bericht* I/1978, I/1979 and II/1979.

133. *SWB*, ME/W1041, 24 July 1979.

134. *SWB*, 26 January. Also FES *Bericht* I/1978 and I/1979.

135. Although not in the organisation of internal security, where East Germany has, again, been the source of expertise, as we have seen.

136. East German aid may also be understated, since the OECD inform us that the Solidaritätshilfe is not defined by them as aid, but disaster relief.

137. *Frankfurter Allgemeine Zeitung*, 6 November 1979.

138. FES *Bericht*, I/1979.

139. CEPII, 1979 and FES *Bericht* I/1978 and I/1979.

140. CEPII, 1979 and FES *Bericht* II/1979; also *SWB*, ME/W1092/A2/2, 22 July 1980.

141. *ARB*, July-August 1979.

142. FES *Bericht*, I/1979.

143. FES *Bericht*, I-II/1979.

144. Ibid.

145. FES *Bericht*, I/1979.

146. NFAC, 1980.

147. Ibid.

148. FES *Bericht*, I/1978.

149. FES *Bericht*, I/1978. Also *SWB*, ME/1094/A2/1, 5 August 1980.

150. CEPII, 1979. Also *SWB* ME/W1063, 1 January 1980, and FES *Bericht* I-II/1979.

151. NFAC, 1980.

152. *SWB*, 2 January 1979.

153. *ARB*, November-December 1978. Also *SWB* ME/W/1089/A2/4, 1 July 1980.

154. The road link with Zambia is now reported fully operational.

155. See *ARB*, May-June 1980.

156. *SWB*, ME/6554/B/4, 21 October 1980.

157. See report in *ARB*, March-April 1980. The 'nine' nations included two South African 'independent' homelands.

158. See *ARB*, May-June 1980, and our essay on Angola in this volume.

159. Brazil's expressed preference for trading with the nine rather than with the Republic may, however, be based on an expectation of this happening rather sooner.

160. *ARB*, November-December 1980.

161. *Guardian*, 4 November 1980, also 1 July 1980.

162. *Guardian*, 28 November 1980, also 24 November 1980.

163. *Guardian*, 18 November 1980; *Le Monde*, 5 December 1980 (plainly written a few weeks before); *The Times*, 7 December 1980 (ditto).

164. *Guardian*, 19 November 1980; *Soviet News*, 25 November 1980.

165. *Pravda*, 18 November 1980.

166. See *AIM Bulletin*, Special Issue, 1979.

167. South African commando forces in fact raided on 30 January 1981 three buildings in Maputo belonging to ANC. South Africa then accused Mozambique of responsibility for guerrilla attacks but Mozambique dismissed these accusations as 'propaganda'. See *Financial Times*, 31 January 1981; also *ARB*, February 1981 (Political/Social/Cultural Series).

5 THE PEOPLE'S DEMOCRATIC REPUBLIC OF YEMEN: SCIENTIFIC SOCIALISM ON TRIAL IN AN ARAB COUNTRY

Moshe Efrat

1. In Search of Political and Ideological Identity

The People's Democratic Republic of Yemen (PDRY) continues — since its independence in November 1967 — to live up to its reputation as the odd man out of the Arab world.

Adjacent to the Horn of Africa, and close to the straits of Hormuz, the PDRY has basically a geo-political, as well as a strategic, importance. This is due to its location between the strategic Bab al-Mandub straits and the Hormuz straits on the main route of the vital oil from the Persian Gulf to the West. The PDRY is a poor, desert and backward country, almost devoid of natural resources, where agricultural land is only 0.3 per cent of its total area and the only big industrial plant is a refinery.

With a population rate of growth of 2.6 per cent per year, the PDRY had in 1980 a resident population of 1.9 million,[1] almost all of whom were Moslem-Sunnis. The Yemen Arab Republic had at that time a population of 6 million, of whom 55 per cent were Moslem-Shi'ites (Zaidis) and the remainder Moslem-Sunnis (Shaefeis). A real *per capita* GDP of $287 in 1970 was the estimate in an international comparative study (Kravis *et al*., 1978). According to the World Bank, the GNP *per capita* was $340 in 1977.[2] The foreign-trade participation ratio is about 20 per cent or about 55 per cent, depending on one's definition (Table 5.17).

Arabic is the official language. The currency, the Yemeni Dinar (YD), is pegged to the US dollar, with an exchange rate of IYD = $2.9 since February 1973.

From National Liberation to Marxism-Leninism

The 'National Liberation Front' (NLF) emerged as the dominant political organisation when the South Yemeni army came out openly in its support on the eve of Independence, thus eclipsing the Egyptian-influenced 'Front for the Liberation of South Yemen' (FLOSY).[3]

The new state was immediately in serious difficulties, both economic and political. The underlying differences within the ranks of the NLF soon widened, intensifying the power struggle between the left and the right wings of the party. The 'Corrective Movement' (22 June 1969) put an end to this struggle by establishing the full power of the left-wing faction. In November 1970, a new constitution was promulgated (drafted by East German experts), and the country changed its name from the People's Republic of South Yemen to its present form.

From June 1965 at its First Congress, the NLF (formed after the merger of several, mainly leftist, movements — of which the most important was the People's Socialist Party) — proclaimed its credo as 'Scientific Socialism'. The success of the 'Corrective Movement' permitted the new collective leadership — a five man Presidential Council, presided over by Salim Ali Rubay — to impose absolute party control over the civilian as well as the military sectors. The new outlook of the regime was summed up by Abd al-Fattah Isma'il (then Secretary-General of the NLF and thereafter President from December 1978 to mid-April 1980) in an interview with Cuban television:

> We have chosen revolutionary thought, scientific Socialist thought, and the ideology of the working class as an intellectual position to be used as a guide in our struggle. We have chosen a clearly-defined class position, asserting that the class forces — to which the interests of the revolution belong — are the revolutionary workers, the peasants, the intellectuals and the petit-bourgeois.[4]

Turning to the policy implemented, he added:

> We were, in fact, able to realise many revolutionary economic, social, educational and military changes — beginning with the establishment of a national democratic authority that expressed the spiritual and material interests of the majority of the people, with the nationalisation of foreign monopolistic companies,[5] and with the implementation, through the struggle of the peasants as represented by their initiatives and uprisings led by our Party, of the Agrarian Reform Law[6] — and, ending with the adoption of numerous social measures at the family level, the elimination of illiteracy and the preparation of cadres.

The most important rivalry among the leadership of the regime, which was intensified towards the end of 1975, emerged between the factions of President Rubay and of the Secretary-General, Isma'il. Rubay, a thorough and successful guerrilla leader, supported a pragmatic form of socialism, looking partly to China for inspiration and favouring some improvement in the relations with Western countries and with conservative Arab states. In contrast, Isma'il, a North Yemeni by birth, supported a more rigid pro-Soviet Marxist orthodox line, both internally and externally. These controversies were interwoven with personal, tribal and regional rivalries, as well as different personal backgrounds.

Following the overthrow of President Rubay in June 1978 by Abd al-Fattah Isma'il, the NLF was transformed into the 'Yemeni Socialist Party' (YSP)[7] – making the PDRY the first Arab country to be ruled by a Marxist-Leninist party.

As in the Fifth Congress of the NLF (March 1972)[8] the YSP was declared as a 'Vanguard Party'.[9] However, in the YSP regulations the process of membership was more selective and the ideological identification demanded of members was much stricter than in the NLF.

The party-government structure was remoulded on the Soviet pattern when the Presidential Council was abolished, and the Presidium of the Supreme People's Council became the leading state organ.

Mainly internal pressures resulted in April 1980 in the deposition of the 'radical' Isma'il, and in the nomination of the 'moderate' Ali Nasir Muhammad as President (the Prime Minister since 1971). Lest one be misled into believing that 'moderates' have now taken over, the most that can be said of internal PDRY politics (since the 'Corrective Movement') is that they pit 'radical Marxists' against 'less radical Marxists' on both domestic and foreign policy issues. So far (December 1980), Muhammad has given no indications that he took over the reins of power in order to change the PDRY's domestic, regional or international policies.[10]

In spite of being a Marxist-Leninist regime, the PDRY's media and leadership avoid using officially terms such as 'Marxism' or 'Leninism'. This pragmatic approach takes into consideration the characteristics of the deep-rooted Moslem faith in the local, as well as the regional, population.

Following the First Congress of the YSP (mid-October 1978), the Supreme People's Council promulgated a new Constitution (31 October 1978), which emphasises more explicitly the radical Marxist outlook than the previous one (November 1970). Article 12 of the new Constitution pointed out:

The state will develop the national economy on the basis of scientific Socialism in order to satisfy the needs of the people; a fair distribution of the social wealth and the full implementation of the principle: *From each according to his abilities, to each according to his work* [our italics].[11]

This 'socialist' principle is included in the Soviet bloc countries' constitutions, as well as in that of Albania (Blaustein and Flanz, 1971). The inclusion of this principle in the PDRY's new constitution is unique in the Arab world. The wide and significant ideological differences between the PDRY and the other 'Socialist' regimes in the Arab World are reflected in the following relevant articles in their constitutions:

Algeria. 'The cultural, agrarian and industrial revolutions and socialist management of enterprises are the basis for the building of Socialism' (ibid).

Egypt. 'The economic basis of the Republic is Socialist, based on sufficiency and justice. Its aim is to prevent exploitation and to level up differences between classes' (ibid).

Iraq. 'The state's purpose is to establish the socialist system on scientific and revolutionary foundations' (ibid).

Syria. 'The state economy is a planned Socialist economy which seeks to end all forms of exploitation' (ibid).

Nevertheless, the PDRY's constitution, as well as those of the other Arab 'Socialist' countries, proclaims Islam as the state religion and stipulates the right of inheritance. But even here there is a significant difference. Whereas the other Arab 'Socialist' states have committed themselves to the Islamic jurisprudence as 'the main law — or a main source of legislation' (ibid), the PDRY's new constitution formulates a vague, non-binding lip service in stating that 'the state shall safeguard the Arab-Islamic legacy'.[12] It is interesting that Afghanistan's constitution of 1976 abstained from declaring Islam as the state religion, but proclaimed 'the complete freedom of the observation of the rites of the sacred religion of Islam' (Blaustein and Flanz, 1971). The same rights were allowed to the followers of other religions.

The radical Marxist approach of the ruling party in Aden was much more emphasised in the constitution in regard to women's rights, the first of its kind in the Moslem world. The constitution adopted in 1970 proclaimed explicitly: 'The state shall ensure equal rights for men and women in all fields of political, economic and social life, and shall progressively provide the necessary conditions to ensure such equality.'[13] Moreover, in 1974 a Family Law was promulgated, reflecting the importance given to the emancipation of women in this deeply traditional Moslem country. The main aim is correcting abuses that had survived under the guise of religion. This law accorded legal equality to women, including pay equal to men, maternity leave with full pay, prohibition of marriage before completion of primary school education, prohibition of unilateral divorce and abolition of the dowry system.[14] Later, the new constitution (1979) proclaimed that 'family relations are based on the equality between men and women in rights and in duties.'[15]

The Road to the Soviet Orbit

In the decade preceding the Yom Kippur War in 1973 — and especially after the Six-Day War of June 1967 — Soviet attention and aid were directed in the Middle East to Algeria, Iraq, Syria and South Yemen. But the corner-stone of Soviet strategy in this area was Egypt (Ro'i, 1979, p. 332). In the Soviet outlook Aden was then a valuable potential asset, but for the time being not yet profitable enough, in spite of the close ideological affinity of the radical regime in power after the success of the 'Corrective Movement'.

After the setback to Soviet-Egyptian relations, and still more after the Yom Kippur War, quite significant shifts were perceived in Soviet strategic interests. Among them was accentuated the geographical shift towards the Horn of Africa and the Persian Gulf, which includes mainly Ethiopia, Somalia and the PDRY (ibid., p. 75). The reopening of the Suez Canal (June 1975), and the weakening of the Soviet position in the Arab-Israeli conflict in the aftermath of the Camp David agreements (September 1978), sharply raised the strategic importance of the PDRY in Soviet eyes.

The PDRY's 'contribution' to the implementation of Soviet strategy in the region was not only expressed by supporting left-wing rebels of political opponents in the Arab Peninsula countries (Yemen Arab Republic, Oman and Saudi Arabia), but also by a direct military and political involvement in the Horn of Africa. Since 1977, and presumably even in 1976, the PDRY's troops were assisting Ethiopia in her war against Somalia. Thus, Aden's military involvement overseas — still existing in the summer of 1978 — was confirmed from various sources, including the Director of Somalia's National Security Council.[16]

The PDRY's role in the Soviet concept was in 1977, at least, even more important than that. Moscow's master-plan was the establishment of a confederation of Marxist-Leninist states between Somalia, Ethiopia, Eritrea and South Yemen in order 'to strengthen the Soviet-African Alliance on the Red Sea'.[17]

Later on, the PDRY signed with the USSR a 20-year Treaty of Friendship and Cooperation in October 1979 (a year after Ethiopia). At the same time, two additional important steps were taken in order to widen the dimensions of Soviet-South Yemeni relations: the President of the Soviet Union and the President of the PDRY signed 'a plan of contracts' between the CPSU and the YSP for the years 1980-3;[18] and the PDRY was admitted to the CMEA as an observer (although it had applied in September 1973).[19]

According to Arab sources, in an undisclosed clause of this Friendship and Co-operation Treaty, the Soviets were allowed for the first time to have permanent naval and air bases in the PDRY.[20] According to the CIA, previously, in 1978, an agreement was reached on this matter between the countries.[21] Previously, since the end of 1968, Aden had agreed to give the Soviets a temporary and not unlimited foothold by allowing the use of some naval and air facilities.[22] According to Western sources, the most important Soviet foothold in the PDRY is undoubtedly the island of Socotra (more than 500 miles from Aden), which can provide mainly naval vital facilities and a base for the Soviet Navy in the Indian Ocean and along the coast of Africa.[23]

Shortly after signing the Friendship Treaty with Moscow, Aden signed in December 1979 a 15-Year Friendship and Co-operation Treaty with Ethiopia. It seems that thus Aden took another step — inspired by Moscow — to implement the first part of the above-mentioned Soviet master plan for the region.[24]

Loyalty to Moscow is thus a corner-stone in the PDRY's policy, but Afghanistan has put it under some strain. Whether because Islamic brotherhood still means something to him, or simply to prevent Aden's isolation in the Islamic as well as in the Arab world, Ali Nasir Muhammad abstained from mentioning Afghanistan at a dinner with Brezhnev in Moscow (29 May 1980).[25] Recently (September 1980), the PDRY's loyalty has been reaffirmed by the President himself, who said: 'Our relations with the Socialist Community, headed by the USSR, are closely bound up with the struggling links founded on scientific Socialism and proletarian internationalism.'[26]

The Realities Behind Yemeni Reunification

Historically, Yemen and the Western part of the PDRY were under Yemeni control in the seventeenth century, and only for a short period. The Yemenis were ejected by the Sultan of Lahij (then the ruler of most of this Western area) in the early part of the eighteenth century.[27] At the end of that century the Yemeni Imams were hardly masters of their own country; they could claim to control only the highlands, while the Red Sea littoral remained under Turkish control until after World War I.[28] In 1839, Aden was captured by the British troops, who later expanded their control over all the Western and the Eastern parts of South Arabia.

When Turkish troops ended their occupation of the greater part of the Western Protectorate territory at the end of the First World War (today the Western part of the PDRY), the Imam of Sana'a maintained his claim to that territory and occupied some of it, eventually being expelled from it. Britain and the Yemeni Kingdom signed in 1934 the Treaty of Sana'a under which both agreed to accept a *status quo* with regard to the Aden-North Yemeni frontier, which is still the present border between the two Yemens.[29]

Basically, the idea of unity between the two Yemens is a North Yemeni concept. The emigration of Yemenis to the Aden area — in search of better economic prospects under British rule — contributed somehow to the spreading out of the unity concept also in South Yemen. But the search for the chance to fulfil such a goal had to be postponed until the independence of South Yemen. Therefore, the two Yemens have never had a common economic history of the kind experienced by the two Germanies and the two Koreas.

Actually, since the end of 1968 or early 1969, clandestine organisations, led mainly by expelled leaders of FLOSY and SAL (South Arabian League), backed by the Yemen Arab Republic and Saudi Arabia, were operating in South Yemen. Later on, Oman troops attacked border posts on their frontier with South Yemen — aiming to weaken and to defeat the Dhofar rebels organised by the Popular Front for the Liberation of Oman (PFLO) — supported by Aden. These subversive activities intensified in 1972, but through the Arab League's mediation between the two Yemens a cease-fire was reached, and an agreement for their unification — within one year — was signed toward the end of the year. Committees were set up to discuss details, but these efforts broke down partly because of ideological reasons, partly because of personal rivalries between the leaders, and mainly because the Shia-Zaidis, important tribes in the YAR (the Hashed and the Bakhil) fear any real move likely to shift the population balance further in the Sunni-Shafeis' favour.

The assassination of the YAR's President al-Ghashmi by a special PDRY presidential envoy in June 1978 increased the tension between the two Yemens, and later on a mini-war broke out in February 1979 in the mountainous region between the two countries. Whoever the aggressor was, as usual in inter-Arab affairs, the move to isolate the PDRY soon fizzled out in the name of the need for Arab solidarity in confronting the Camp David agreements. In March 1979, the Presidents of the Yemens announced, once more, their agreement to unite their states on similar lines to those worked out in 1972. The difference of attitudes was expressed immediately afterwards: while the YAR favoured a gradual implementation step-by-step with the utmost caution, the PDRY's attitude was to set up the union quickly.

So far (December 1980), very minor 'cosmetic' steps have been taken: (i) to unify tariff rates for postal and telephone services; it was also agreed — in principle — to lift restrictions on the use of airspace by each other's national airlines; (ii) to set up three common companies for overland transport, marine transport and tourism; (iii) to establish joint economic projects, and to 'coordinate' their development plans.

Détente With the Oil-Wealthy Conservative Neighbours

The most important political change which occurred in the southern part of the Arabian Peninsula in early 1976 was the *rapprochement* and détente in the PDRY's relations with Saudi Arabia. Riyad recognised the PDRY and exchanged diplomatic representatives. This basic change was the result of various developments, which influenced the reassessment of the positions of both countries: (i) the accession to power of a pro-Saudi regime in the YAR (1974), which increased Saudi self-confidence as an influential power in the area; (ii) the defeat of the Dhofar rebels (1975) by the Omani troops, supported by Iranian and Jordanian forces. Therefore, though Aden will not give up her basic support to the cause of the PFLO (refuge, as well as training for its members in her territory), it will be possible to keep the peace for the time being; (iii) the availability of economic aid from conservative Arab oil-wealthy countries in the area — headed by Riyad. Saudi Arabia hopes at least to influence the PDRY to moderate its policy towards its neighbours — if possible for the long term. On the other hand, Aden seeks to use this opportunity in order to strengthen its stand by securing better and more rapid economic and social achievements — at least for the foreseeable future.

It seems very unlikely that the PDRY will abandon its fundamentally Marxist-Leninist orientation and its close ties with the USSR. Moscow, too, would be breaking with recent practice if it simply ignored too intimate a flirtation with the Saudis, and perhaps the West. Actually, the USSR's desire to maintain its strategic, ideological and military base on the Arabian Peninsula and the Bab al-Mandub straits, will determine the rest.[30]

2. The Decade of Economic Development

Economy and Society Before Independence

After 130 years of British colonial rule, South Yemen became independent in 1967. The economy was strongly dualistic in nature.[31] At this time the population was estimated to number about 1.4 million people, of whom 35 per cent were urban (engaged mainly in service-oriented activities), 55 per cent were rural (largely agricultural or engaged in fishing), and about 10 per cent were bedouin.[32]

The 'modern' sector centred almost entirely around Aden with its position as the centre of government (which included a substantial British military base employing 17,000 workers)[33] and Aden Port activities (import and transit trade, services to passenger traffic, bunkering and refining activites). The 'modern' sector was dominated by a few large foreign firms and a number of merchants of domestic and foreign origin, largely from India or Pakistan. The foreign companies controlled banking, insurance, tourism, trade, distribution of petroleum products, shipping, bunkering, dockyards, harbour transportation and the only large manufacturing plant — the Aden Refinery. The remaining commercial activities in Aden were mainly in the hands of a few big merchants.

Outside the Aden area, the rest of the territories now comprising the PDRY by and large had experienced little change in economic or social structures. Ownership of assets was organised on traditional, largely feudal lines. Tribal rulers and related family members enjoyed ownership rights to a significant portion of the country's arable land. In the fisheries sector also, the larger traditional fishing vessels were owned by tribal chieftains or fish merchants.

The Economic Scene at Independence

The PDRY confronted substantial development problems at

Independence. The 'modern' sector of the economy was in an acute depression as a result of the closure of the Suez Canal (June 1967) and the cessation of British budgetary support as well as the withdrawal of British troops. Therefore Aden Port activities declined sharply, the new Government 'lost' a financial British support of 14 million YD (in comparison to a total of 9 million YD of current annual revenues) and an additional income from British troops which amounted to 10-15 million YD annually in foreign currency.[34] All in all, the total foreign exchange receipts declined by 40 per cent (at least). As a result of all these factors, there was a sharp decline in aggregate economic activity. It is estimated that PDRY's GDP dropped by about 20 per cent between 1966 and 1968, the sharpest drop being in the services and construction sectors, Aden being the most affected.[35] Only subsistence sectors, such as agriculture and fishing, maintained their previous output levels.

The new national Government was forced to cut its expenditures drastically.[36] All expenditures (including defence) were curtailed and wages of government employees were also reduced sharply. Government efforts to mobilise additional resources through increased tax measures failed, and the current budget continued to suffer deficits. Foreign assistance was insubstantial in this period. Consequently, there was almost no public and very little private investment in the post-independence period from 1967 to 1970.

Socialist Economic Objectives

The ideology of 'scientific Socialism' determined the NLF's economic and social objectives envisaged which had the following features: (i) production and distribution mechanisms mainly socialised by the state; (ii) orientation of the economy away from services (other than those of basic human needs; see below) to material production; (iii) equitable income distribution; (iv) provision of basic human needs, such as health, cultural and educational services.

The main instrument for extending public ownership to the largely foreign-owned sector was the nationalisations of November 1969 by the new government emerging from the 'Corrective Movement'. This nationalised almost all the 'modern' sector of the economy: eight banks (of which one was South Yemeni), twelve insurance companies, five major trading firms, all Aden Port service companies (excluding bunkering operations), five petroleum distribution companies operating in the country.[37] The only two major foreign-owned installations which were not nationalised in 1969 — the Aden Refinery

(British Petroleum) and an international communications facility
(Cable and Wireless) — were transferred by mutual consent to the
PDRY (in 1977 and 1978, respectively). The only foreign-owned
companies now operating in South Yemen are the bunkering facilities
of major oil companies in the harbour.

The nationalisation decrees laid down that compensation (at book
value) would be in the form of Dinar Bonds bearing 2 per cent interest
per year and redeemable after 20 years. Doubtless the redemption
of these bonds from 1989 onwards will not pose any significant
economic problem — if it takes place. Public sector control was
extended to domestically-owned assets in the fields of agriculture,
fishing and housing.

The first Agrarian Reform Law — limiting private ownership to 25
acres for irrigated and 50 acres for unirrigated land — was introduced
in March 1968, but actually not implemented.[38] Before the
promulgation of this law, the tenancy system — which was estimated to
cover two-thirds of the cultivated land — was more common around
the coastal regions, while cultivation by owners was more common in
the interior highlands. According to the law, compensation will be paid
in 25 years, beginning five years after the actual confiscation took
place, bearing an interest rate of 1.5 per cent per annum.

Under the amended second Agrarian Reform Law, enacted in
November 1970,[39] the size of individually-owned farms was limited
to 20 acres in the irrigated areas and 40 acres in the rain-fed lands.
The state also confiscated all land belonging to the Waqf[40] and the
deposed sultans. These confiscated lands were to be distributed thus:
12-20 acres per family in irrigated lands, or 24-40 acres in the
rain-fed areas.[41] Peasants' uprisings, somehow encouraged by the
authorities, completed this process by 1972, when almost all arable
lands were also organised into cooperatives or state farms. The
'Cooperative Law' (1972) extended to the fisheries sector, which
was reorganised so that all capital assets for fishing (boats, nets, etc.)
became the property of the co-operative (there were no fishing or
agricultural production cooperatives under British rule).

The government has sought to provide for basic needs through
various measures, the most important among them being: the
establishment of the University in 1970 (first the Education and
Agriculture Faculties and later the Faculties of Economics, Public
Administration, Engineering and Medicine); the nationalisation of all
housing (except owner-occupied dwellings) in 1972; the foundation
of an Institution for Adult Education in 1973 aiming to eradicate

illiteracy (of the total population over ten years of age 70 per cent are illiterate in the PDRY — in urban areas about 60 per cent, in rural areas 75 per cent and among the bedouin more than 90 per cent).

The assertion of public ownership over major sectors of the PDRY's economy was accompanied by considerable public sector investments rising from YD 1 million in 1970 to YD 62 million in 1978. Private investment has been minimal: YD 1 million in 1970 rising to YD 2 million in 1977, and largely confined to the construction of individual housing for family use by South Yemenis working abroad. As a result, the public sector in the PDRY now encompasses all major fields of economic activity.

Macro-economic Development

Since the country achieved independence, but especially since the 'Corrective Movement' of June 1969, the political framework of 'scientific Socialism' in PDRY has led the government to work toward comprehensive and economic planning. The major decision-making body is the Politburo, with the Economic Secretariat as its technical arm. The Politburo provides the guidelines for the preparation of the plan, as well as issuing directives on the corrections to be made if necessary. As is common in the Communist parties, the Politburo of the YSP reviews the Plan with the Central Committee of the Party, the Supreme Council for National Planning and the Council of Ministers — which formally issues the Plan.

Development Plans

The PDRY has so far implemented two development plans, and begun the implementation of a new plan — the Second Five Year Plan 1981-1985 (originally intended to cover 1979-83).[42]

The Three-Year Development Plan (1971/72-1973/74) was the country's first experience in development planning. The subsequent First Five-Year Plan (1974/75-1978) was a more comprehensive plan with estimates of sectoral output targets and investment requirements. Despite the various improvements in successive plans, development planning in the PDRY has remained essentially an exercise in the listing of investment projects selected on the basis of the availability of foreign resources. However, whereas the Three-Year Plan was primarily concerned with job-creation through labour-intensive public investment programmes, it became obvious during the First Five-Year Plan period that the shortage of manpower, skilled and unskilled (particularly in the construction sector, but also in agriculture during

Table 5.1: Gross Fixed Capital Formation (YD m at current prices)

Year	Public sector Total	Of which development plan	Private sector	Total GFCF	Aden price indices[a] (1969 = 100) Cost of living	Wholesale
1969	0.3	–	0.7	1.0	100	100
1970	0.3	–	0.7	1.0	105	106
1971	3.7	3.1	0.8	4.5	111	117
1972	8.9	7.8	0.7	9.6	116	120
1973	13.0	11.7	0.6	13.6	135	163
1974	20.1	18.6	1.0	21.0	167	229
1975	26.7	24.3	1.5	28.2	187	271
1976	42.2	39.2	1.8	44.0	194	287
1977	60.0	57.0	2.0	62.0	204	305
1978	62.0[b]	59.7	2.0	64.0	215	307

a. The PDRY's government maintains a system of price controls, and since 1976 it applied not only to essential goods but also to virtually all goods and services of importance and to the entire country. These extensive price controls limit the usefulness of the existing price indices for Aden.
b. Preliminary estimates.
Source: Bank of Yemen.

harvest-time) was one of the major bottlenecks. Therefore the emphasis was progressively shifted away from labour-intensive projects. It appears that a small portion of the male manpower potential is not in the active labour market, because of income from family members abroad.

Actual plan investments have varied considerably from plan expectations because of their dependence on foreign financing. Thus the global investment targets for the Three-Year Plan (1971/72-1973/74) were YD 40 million; these had to be reduced to YD 32.4 million, and the actual investment was only YD 25 million ($76 million). In comparison with the original plan targets, the actual investment was in real terms about 50 per cent or 30 per cent of these targets by considering the cost cf living or the wholesale price index respectively. For the First Five-Year Plan (1973/74-1978) the situation has been completely reversed; the initial overall target for investment was YD 75 million, which was revised upwards to YD 276 million, while actual investment amounted to YD 196 million ($568 million). In real terms the actual investment was about 55 per cent or 40 per

cent of the original target according to the cost of living or the
wholesale index respectively (see Table 5.1). Agriculture and Fishing
received 35 per cent of total investments; industry, 17 per cent; and
48 per cent was allocated to the other sectors.

Economic Growth — Problems and Achievements

After the initial drop in the GDP following independence, and the
further fall during 1969-72 (when the basic structural changes in the
economy were undertaken), real growth of GDP accelerated and
reached a high rate in 1976/7 (Table 5.18). This latter Table — which
excludes the all-important remittances — uses the suspect Aden
cost-of-living index in Table 5.1. The 1974-based national income
deflator has evidently been abandoned by the Central Statistical
Organisation, since it does not occur in the new statistical yearbook.
It leads to widely different — and surely less plausible — results in
earlier years.

Growth, even in the GDP, is the result of import-led economic
expansion. This was made possible, it is true, by certain 'exports': the
substantial increases experienced in workers' remittances, and foreign
economic assistance. (As a matter of fact, because of the manpower
constraints, the government has discouraged emigration since 1974.
However, recognising the importance of workers' remittances for the
economy, the government eased its policy by allowing controlled new
emigration especially from rural areas with labour surpluses.)

The most significant production increases were experienced in
livestock, fisheries and construction. Also, despite Marxist prejudices,
output grew in transport and communications, finance, commerce
and Aden Port-associated activities; but this all occurred by chance,
following the opening of the Suez Canal. In contrast, agricultural
crop-production remained stagnant due to declines in the production
of major crops, such as cotton, sesame, coffee, tobacco and wheat
(resulting from institutional changes).

The production of the Aden Refinery (which employs 1,800
workers) declined sharply from 6.4 million tons in 1970 to 2.7 million
tons in 1974 and to 1.7 million tons in 1976. Since its transfer to the
PDRY authorities (May 1977), Aden increased its efforts to extend
production. By 1977 these efforts had not yet been realised when 1.8
million tons of crude oil were processed (whereas the capacity is 8.5
million tons a year). The political détente with the conservative Arab
oil-wealthy neighbours began to be 'productive' only in 1979, when 3.4
million tons of crude oil were processed. Output will reach, according

Table 5.2: Summary of National Accounts (YD m)

	1973	1974	1975	1976	1977
1. Population (million)	1.59	1.60	1.64	1.68	1.73
2. Workers' remittances	11.5	14.2	19.3	39.8	61.9
3. GDP (current market prices)	84.2	97.6	99.9	128.9	150.3
of which Agriculture	(17.8)	(18.9)	(19.2)	(26.8)	(n.a.)
Aden refinery	(4.7)	(10.1)	(2.2)	(1.9)	(n.a.)
Other manufacturing	(4.3)	(6.1)	(8.0)	(12.1)	(n.a.)
Services	(57.4)	(62.5)	(70.5)	(88.1)	(n.a.)
4. GDP (constant 1974 prices)	93.1	97.6	96.1	115.2	123.2
5. GNP (current market prices)	92.2	103.7	118.1	162.1	202.0
6. GNP (constant 1974 prices)	97.7	103.7	104.5	134.0	154.2
7. GDP/capita (YD constant 1974 prices)	58.6	61.0	58.6	68.5	71.2
8. GNP/capita (YD constant 1974 prices)	61.4	64.8	63.7	79.8	89.1
9. GDP/capita (YD current prices)	53.0	61.0	60.9	76.7	86.9
10. GNP/capita (YD current prices)	58.0	64.8	72.0	96.5	116.8
11. GNP deflator on a 1974 base (deduced)	.94	1.00	1.13	1.21	1.31
12. Inflation rate (deduced from the above, %)	–	6.3	13.0	7.1	8.3

Source: Bank of Yemen, Central Statistical Organisation, reproduced by IBRD (December 1978) and OECD (1980).
Note: For the apparently revised series c.f. Table 5.18. The use of the Marxist methodology of the Material Product System was introduced for the first time in the PDRY in the Second Five-Year Plan. See *The First Congress*, YSP, 1978, p. 345.

Table 5.3: Composition of Domestic Uses 1973-7 (as percentage of GDP)[a]

	Fixed investment	Changes in stocks	Public consumption Total	of which defence	Private consumption	Deficit on goods and non-factor services as % of GDP[b]	Factor services income, net, as % of GDP[b]
1973	16	4	26	n.a.	90	36	12
1974	22	24	26	13	81	53	12
1975	28	6	31	12	85	50	18
1976	34	5	30	13	82	51	26
1977	41	5	28	13	81	55	35

a. Excess of total expenditure over 100 per cent equals the deficit in Goods and Services and Non-Factor Services (NFS).

b. NFS comprise services such as transportation, insurance; but exclude Factor Services such as investment, earnings of citizens working abroad.

Sources: Bank of Yemen, Central Statistical Organisation.

to the Refinery officials, 5.4 million tons in 1980, due not only to the goodwill of the neighbours, but also to the Iraq-Iran War.

Significant mineral deposits have not yet been found in the PDRY and industrial strategy has therefore concentrated mainly on agro-based industries (vegetable and grain processing, textiles, leather products and fish processing) and some import-substituting industries (tools, paints, plastic products, soft drinks, etc.).

The growth of output in the various industries has shown divergent trends reflecting mostly fluctuations in the supply of raw material to the agro-based industries as a result of the declining crops. Industries less dependent on local supply conditions have grown steadily. Nevertheless, overall performance was very disappointing indeed until 1976 (Table 5.18). But the rapidly widening flows of workers' remittances even contributed to a higher, and indeed sometimes spectacular, increase in the real GNP *per capita*.

Domestic Uses of Resources

The small resource-base of the areas comprising the PDRY, and the centring of economic activity around the Port of Aden, resulted in an economy which was mainly dependent on external resource transfers throughout the period of British rule. Government investment in this period was minor, and private sector investment (except for the Aden Refinery) was largely confined to residential and commercial buildings (mainly in Aden). The current expenditures of the authorities were mainly on their bureaucracy, and the provision of social services (such as health and education) was minimal, and concentrated in Aden. Private consumption expenditures were distinguished by their wide regional and social disparities.

Developments in the economy of the PDRY since independence have not reduced the country's dependence on external transfers of resources. However, there is a significant change in their origin (more than half is now contributed by South Yemenis abroad, the rest being foreign economic aid), and in the uses to which they (with domestic available resources) are put. Public consumption expenditures, which experienced drastic cuts in earlier years, are increasing. However, salaries in public service are low (they have been reduced twice since independence), and the main increase of current expenditures has been directed to the extension of social services. But the most impressive change has been the rapid increase of investments, which were stepped up to 41 per cent of GDP in 1977 in comparison with only 16 per cent in 1973. However, the defence expenditures have remained too high for so poor a country: 13 per cent of GDP and 10 per cent of GNP in the period 1974-7 (see Table 5.3). According to provisional estimates, defence spending was an even higher burden in 1978: 17 per cent of GDP and 13 per cent of GNP.

The Balance of Payments Developments

Over the past decade, the balance of payments developments reveal three important characteristic aspects (see Table 5.4):

(1) Commodity Trade. The imbalance in commodity trade has continued, whereby the commodity exports cover only less than 10 per cent of commodity imports. Presumably, this is the consequence of the meagre resource base of the country, growing development needs and the increase of international prices (especially foodstuffs and oil).

(2) Service Receipts. Mainly workers' remittances, and partly Aden Port activities, having grown rapidly and contributed considerably to strengthening the PDRY's foreign finances. The total foreign exchange earnings allow the country not only to import minimum subsistence needs (as was the case since independence until 1975) but also to import a significant amount of capital goods for development.

(3) External Assistance. While South Yemen received in 1969 a total of $6 million of external aid ($1 million as grant and $5 million as development loans), this assistance increased considerably to $127 million in 1978 ($36 million as grants and $91 million in development loans).

The important conclusion from the developments during the period 1969-78 is that the PDRY's balance of payments is vulnerable without the income from workers' remittances. However, if this income can be strengthened and sustained, the PDRY can use these resources to maintain the pace of economic growth. Even so, official external assistance – the difference between the last two columns in Table 5.3 – is over 20 per cent of GDP, a situation that cannot last.

Composition and Direction of Trade

Commodity trade performance has been mixed (see Table 5.5):

(1) Commodity Exports. There has been a substantial increase in fish

Table 5.4: Summary Balance of Payments ($USm)

	1969	1973	1975	1976	1977	1978
Domestic exports, f.o.b.	8	14	8	26	29	19
Retained imports, c.i.f.	-87	-120	-165	-267	-324	-359
Trade deficit	-79	-106	-157	-241	-295	-340
Invisibles, net	80	54	76	145	205	283
Workers' remittances	57	33	56	115	180	258
Others,[a] net	23	21	20	30	25	25
Balance of goods and services	1	-52	-81	-95	-90	-57
Official unrequited transfers (grants)	1	–	10	46	55	36
Official medium & long-term capital	5	25	31	58	68	91
Gross disbursement	5	25	32	60	69	95
Repayments	–	–	-1	-2	-1	-4
Miscellaneous capital, net	-13	23	16	-21	7	18
Overall balance	-6	-4	-24	-13	40	88

a. Including services such as transport, travel, insurance.
Source: IMF, *Balance of Payments Yearbook*, various issues.

Table 5.5: Civilian Commodity Trade (YD million)

	1969	1973	1975	1976	1977	1978
Commodity exports and re-exports	59.7	6.9	3.9	15.5	15.8	12.2
Fish	(0.4)	(1.4)	(1.5)	(3.9)	(5.8)	(2.1)
Cotton	(2.1)	(2.1)	(0.5)	(3.6)	(1.3)	(1.4)
Coffee	(0.4)	(0.5)	(0.7)	(1.2)	(1.2)	(0.6)
Petroleum products	(44.5)	(0.1)	(–)	(5.3)	(5.8)	(5.2)
Commodity imports	90.9	36.0	62.1	85.1	121.3	134.1
Food and beverages	(19.9)	(17.8)	(22.9)	(23.4)	(29.7)	(49.2)
Machinery and transport equipment	(5.5)	(2.9)	(10.3)	(20.1)	(42.2)	(30.9)
Petroleum and products	(33.8)	(3.1)	(11.6)	(21.2)	(22.1)	(18.1)

Sources: Central Statistical Organisation; UN, *International Trade Statistics*, 1978.

exports which contributed in 1978 30 per cent of the total non-oil exports (3 per cent in 1969), while the major agricultural export in the past — cotton — remained stagnant, 20 per cent in 1978, as a result of the increased domestic consumption requirements of a newly installed textile factory. The coffee export sharply increased its relative share of the non-oil exports to about 9 per cent of the total.

(2) Commodity Imports. Commodity imports for the South Yemeni population have grown considerably compared to the pre-independence period. (Obviously, at that time, a large part of the imports was necessary to meet the needs of the colonial administration.) It is interesting to note that:

(i) Food imports continue to be a large share of the non-oil total imports — 36 per cent in 1978 — presumably because of the stagnation of the PDRY's agricultural crop sector.
(ii) Imports of machinery and transport equipment — heavily oriented to meet the development needs of the economy — sharply increased their share from 10 per cent in 1969 to more than 25 per cent of the non-oil imports in 1978.

We turn to the direction of the PDRY's *non-oil* trade (see Table 5.6).

(3) Direction of Exports. Over the period 1973-7:

(i) The bulk of South Yemeni non-oil exports are absorbed by the advanced capitalist countries — from 44 per cent in 1973 to 55 per cent in 1978. Japan is still the most important single buyer of PDRY's exports, mainly fish (17 per cent in 1973 up to 44 per cent in 1978).
(ii) The Soviet bloc increased its share in South Yemeni exports from almost no export in 1973 to 11 per cent in 1978.
(iii) There was an increase in the relative importance of the Arab markets which absorbed 22 per cent in 1978 (7 per cent in 1973). There were almost no exports to China since 1973 when Peking's markets attracted 19 per cent of the non-oil exports, and there was a sharp decrease in the importance of all other countries to 12 per cent in 1978 (in comparison with 30 per cent in 1973).

(4) Origin of Imports. The rapid increase of the South Yemeni non-oil imports, resulting mainly from the needs of economic development, have had an impact on their origin. The main changes are:

Table 5.6: Direction of Visible Non-Oil Trade (per cent)[a]

	Destination of exports						Sources of civilian imports					
	1969	1973	1975	1976	1977	1978	1969	1973	1975	1976	1977	1978
Advanced capitalist countries	37	44	51	62	77	55	49	44	51	52	60	50
UK	(4)	(9)	(3)	(2)	(1)	(5)	(9)	(13)	(16)	(13)	(12)	(13)
Japan	(13)	(17)	(33)	(35)	(63)	(24)	(20)	(10)	(9)	(14)	(21)	(11)
Others	(20)	(18)	(15)	(25)	(13)	(26)	(20)	(21)	(26)	(25)	(27)	(26)
Soviet bloc	0	0	5	2	5	11	7	9	10	12	11	11
USSR							(4)	(2)	(5)	(5)	(6)	(5)
Others							(3)	(7)	(5)	(7)	(5)	(6)
China	0	19	0	0	0	0	4	12	9	7	3	7
Arab countries	28	7	10	5	6	22	7	8	4	5	2	4
Others	35	30	34	31	12	12	33	27	26	24	24	28
Total	100	100	100	100	100	100	100	100	100	100	100	100

Note: a. As to oil, there were substantial re-exports in 1969; and oil imports are about one-fifth of all imports, all from OPEC.
Sources: Bank of Yemen, *UNYITS*.

(i) The advanced capitalist countries increased their share in the PDRY's non-oil imports to 50 per cent in 1978 (44 per cent in 1973). Japan and the United Kingdom maintained their share in this market — 11 per cent and 13 per cent respectively in 1978.

(ii) The Soviet bloc increased its share of the South Yemeni non-oil civilian imports to 11 per cent in 1978 (9 per cent in 1973). While the USSR tripled her share to 5 per cent in 1978 (2 per cent in 1973), the other Soviet bloc countries maintained their share, 6 per cent in 1978.

(iii) The PDRY's imports from China experienced a sharp decrease from 12 per cent in 1973 to only 7 per cent in 1978.

(iv) The Arab countries decreased their share in non-oil imports to South Yemen from 8 per cent in 1973 to 4 per cent in 1978.

Foreign Economic Aid

The actual flows of external economic aid to the PDRY amounted to $450 million during the period 1970-8 (only very small amounts were given before in the two first years of independence), from which $149 million were in grants and $301 million in development loans. The grants — almost all given by Arab oil-wealthy countries — are a new feature in Aden's external finances mainly starting after 1973. As to the loans, 40 per cent was from the Soviet bloc (the USSR 25 per cent), China 23 per cent, Arab oil-producing countries 25 per cent and about 3 per cent from the IDA, OPEC Special Fund and Denmark (see Table 5.7).

The total *committed* economic loans amounted in this period to $753 million: 45 per cent from the Soviet bloc (the USSR 31 per cent), more than 17 per cent from China, 30 per cent from Arab oil-wealthy countries (excluding grants) and the remaining 8 per cent from IDA (World Bank), OPEC Special Fund and Denmark (the only Western country allowing economic aid to Aden). Those commitments were formulated in the framework of *signed* agreements between the PDRY and its donors. While $82 million of aid (10 per cent from the overall total) were committed during the period of the Three-Year Development Plan (1971/72-1973/74), a sum of $671 million was committed over the First Five-Year Plan period (1974/75-1978), 90 per cent of the total amount.

It is of some interest to note that during the Three-Year Plan, the PDRY received $52 million or 68 per cent of its total actual

Table 5.7: Disbursed Economic Development Aid 1971/2-1978 ($USm)

	Three-year plan 1971/72-1973/74		First five-year plan 1974/75-1978		Total 1971/2-1978	
	amount	%	amount	%	amount	%
Soviet bloc	17	33	102	41	119	40
of which USSR	(12)	(23)	(63)	(25)	(75)	(25)
China	16	31	53	21	69	23
Arab oil countries	12	23	65	26	77	25
Others	7	13	29	12	36	12
of which IDA	(1)	(2)	(22)	(9)	(23)	(8)
Denmark	(1)	(2)	(2)	(1)	(3)	(1)
OPEC special fund	–	–	(2)	(1)	(2)	(1)
Total	52	100	249	100	301	100

Sources: Bank of Yemen; *Middle East Economic Digest, London Weekly*, 28 September 1979.

investments in aid. During the first Five-Year Plan it got $249 million or 44 per cent. The remainder was financed by workers' remittances from abroad and the Arab grants. However, in this period the Soviet bloc supplied $102 million (41 per cent), including the USSR $63 million (25 per cent); China $53 million (21 per cent); the Arab countries $65 million (26 per cent); the remaining $5 million (2 per cent) came from other sources. In the Soviet-Chinese competition for Aden, under the rubric of economic assistance, Moscow is ahead.

While Chinese assistance was mainly allocated to highway construction, textile plant and health facilities, the USSR concentrated in the agricultural sector (eight dams, three rental machine stations, seven state farms, agricultural surveys) and fisheries (a port for fishing, a fish cannery).[43]

Structural Changes in Ownership and Output

As described above, PDRY's economic policies have been aimed especially at developing and consolidating important segments of the economy under state control and ownership. The implementation of the development plans has contributed also to a wider structural change in the ownership and activities in the various sectors of the economy.

As reflected in Table 5.8 the institutional changes are as follows:

(1) Industry. The manufacturing sector is very limited in the PDRY. In addition to the Aden Refinery, it consists of a textile factory (1,300 workers), about 40 small plants (employing 4,000 workers) and a large number of very small-scale private industrial units (tailoring, bakeries, etc.) employing about 13,000 men. This private sector contributes only 14 per cent of the value of industrial production, while the large-scale plants are in government hands contributing 50 per cent. The remaining 36 per cent is contributed by the 'mixed sector' in which private capital (local and foreign) joins the public sector in establishing new industries. This policy towards private capital is emphasised not only by various investment laws but also, and for the first time, in the 1978 Constitution.[44] As a result, eight 'mixed' industrial establishments were formed (employing 700 workers).[45] As a matter of fact, no new wholly private industrial plant has been added since 1972 in the PDRY.

(2) Agriculture. The agricultural crop production sector is actually entirely in the hands of co-operatives and the state (75 per cent and

Table 5.8: Sectoral Production[a] by Type of Organisation (per cent)

	Private	Cooperatives	Mixed sector[b]	State	Foreign	Total
Industry[c]						
1973	51	–	7	6	36	100
1976	38	–	24	28	10	100
1978	14	–	36	50	–	100
Agricultural crops						
1973	–	81	–	19	–	100
1976	–	71	–	29	–	100
1977	–	80	–	20	–	100
1978	–	75	–	25	–	100
Livestock						
1973	97	–	–	3	–	100
1976	93	–	–	7	–	100
1978	93	–	–	7	–	100
Fisheries						
1973	–	51	10	–	39	100
1976	–	26	9	16	49	100
Transportation						
1973	43	1	–	56	–	100
1976	58	–	–	42	–	100
Retail trade						
1977	50	50	–	–	–	100
Construction						
1973	22	–	–	42	36	100
1976	19	–	–	60	21	100

a. Gross value of production at market prices.
b. State and private.
c. Including the Aden Refinery.
Source: *The First Congress*, YSP, 1978, pp. 241-349.

25 per cent respectively). The average cropped area amounts to 120,000 acres, half of the cultivated area in the country. The Second Agrarian Reform Law was fully implemented by 1973: the confiscated lands amounted to 137,000[46] acres (57 per cent of the total cultivated land).

The agricultural sector now includes 44 agricultural co-operatives with about 38,000 members and 214,000 acres of land, as well as 39 agricultural state farms with 30,000 acres, employing 5,000 workers (60 per cent permanently).[47] These co-operatives and state farms are served by Machine Renting Stations and eight Technical Repairs stations.[48]

The state's direct involvement in livestock is, however, limited (except in poultry). There are only four Livestock State Farms (with about 9,000 cattle, sheep and goats), whereas the main breeders still remain in private hands (one-third of which are bedouin). The poultry governmental sector consists of 81 state farms employing about 600 permanent workers.[49]

In order to encourage productivity in the co-operative sector in agriculture (as well as in fisheries), the Central Committee of the YSP decided recently to allow the members to market 40 per cent of the production.[50]

(3) Fishery.[51] When the 'Corrective Movement' took the reins of power in 1969, the fishery sector employed 13,000 private fishermen controlled by merchants and tribal chiefs. Since then the government implemented a structural change, and in 1980 the fishing sector comprised[52] 14 co-operatives with more than 7,000 members, which mainly meet the domestic consumption and account for 26 per cent of the total value of production; a large-scale fleet owned by the Ministry of Fish Wealth, employing about 4,000 people and producing 16 per cent; a joint PDRY-USSR fishing venture for export, producing 9 per cent; and, most important, the fishing activities undertaken by the Japanese Nichiro Company operating under royalty agreement and producing 49 per cent (in 1977 the PDRY's income from this royalty amounted to more than $8 million).

(4) Transportation. This sector is largely private — mostly individual freight-lorry operators under government regulation.

(5) Retail trade. Fifty per cent of the retail trade sector is consumer co-operatives and the other half is private small-scale retailers.

Table 5.9: Sectoral Structure of Domestic Production (per cent)

	1969	Value Added 1973	1976
Agriculture	16	16	13
(Plant)	(9)	(11)	(7)
(Livestock)	(7)	(5)	(6)
Fisheries	4	6	10
(Domestic and Joint Venture)	(4)	(4)	(5)
(Foreign Co.)	(−)	(2)	(5)
Manufacturing	26	10	8
(Refining)	(22)	(5)	(2)
(Other)	(4)	(5)	(6)
Transport and Communications	7	8	12
Commerce	24	17	17
Other Sectors	23	43	40
Total	100	100	100

Source: *Middle East Record*, various issues; *Middle East Contemporary Survey*; *UN Statistical Yearbook*, various issues; *First Congress*, YSP, 1978.

(6) Construction. Government capacity to undertake substantial construction activity has been rapidly increased, although the 'foreign' sector (mainly Chinese and Soviet) remains important.

The overall picture is that whilst the state dominates economic activity, small-scale individual enterprise is allowed, perhaps in order to minimise the bureaucratic complexities of a socialist system (at least at this stage). The socialisation of the economy has affected all major sectors profoundly. The largest traditional sector, agriculture, has experienced the deepest and the greatest structural change. It is not surprising that the production of some major crops has declined, despite considerable investments in agricultural infrastructure. On the other hand, fishing has grown rapidly because of the introduction of a modern fleet.

The non-refinery manufacturing sector, mainly new and modern, has shown a high rate of growth: 15 per cent p.a. in real terms in 1973-6. Commerce, transport and communications, after recovering from the depression brought about by the closure of the Suez Canal and the withdrawal of the British forces, have shown impressive growth (7 per cent and 12 per cent p.a. respectively). The effects of these developments on the sectoral structure of the economy are reflected in Table 5.9.

Education Development

The PDRY leadership regarded education as a political, economic and social central goal. The main achievements in education are reflected in various fields. First, 7.4 per cent of GDP was allocated to education expenditures during the decade 1967-77, in comparison with an average of 4.4 per cent for all development countries' GDP in the mid-seventies. The enrolment in all levels of formal and technical education increased at an annual rate of 15 per cent (girls' enrolment was much more accelerated, at 21 per cent per year). One of every seven residents in the country was a student. The government established special schools for bedouin children, with boarding facilities (while food is provided by the UN Food Programme). In 1976/7 these boarding-schools enrolled more than 29,000 pupils – more than 11 per cent of the total enrolled children in formal education in the country. In spite of social and religious obstacles to girls' enrolment – much more rooted among the bedouin – one out of every eight students in the boarding schools was a girl.

In the framework of the Literacy and Adult Education Programme (December 1973), the eradication of illiteracy was declared as a national goal, the aim being to educate adults under 45 years of age. Under the Literacy Law (1973), all the economically active population between the ages of twelve and 45 must attend a nine-month literacy programme. Until 1976/7 more than 55,000 South Yemenis – 13 per cent of the employed – were considered 'liberated' from illiteracy. In order to promote the realisation of this programme, the government offered many incentives to encourage attendance (including the promotion of public servants), and all establishments – factories, public institutions, etc. – have to hold compulsory literacy classes. Since recently, every job-seeker is required, according to a governmental decree, to have at least eight years of schooling, or should have passed a literacy examination.

Outstanding Issues and Future Prospects

The policies of the PDRY have resulted undoubtedly in substantial achievements in both social and economic development. Aden's leadership – in spite of changes and rivalries – has demonstrated in the 1970s, 'The Decade of Economic Development', significant ability in firmly pursuing the main objectives. This, despite the many resource constraints under which it operates: low *per capita* GDP,

Table 5.10: Employed Labour Force by Sector

	1969	1973	1976	1978[b]
Agriculture & fishing	138	152	181	202
Industry	8	20	27	38.5
(of which manufacturing)	(6)	(16)	(22)	(32)
Building & construction	3	15	28	33
				7[a]
Trade, restaurants & hotels	26	25	30	41
Transport, storage & communications	4	14	24	25
Finance, insurance & real estate	2	2	2	0.5
Other services (includes public, social & personal)	83	95	107	119
Total	264	323	399	466

a. Water and electricity: it is not clear where these were included in previous years.
b. Preliminary estimates.
Source: *The First Congress*, YSP, 1978, p. 251; al-Sha'ayoubi, 1972, pp. 143-240; *Statistical Year Book*, no. 1, 1980.

Table 5.11: Development Plan Departments — Planned and Actual (YDm)

	Three-year plan 1971/72-1973/4		First five-year plan 1973/74-1978	
	Planned	Actual	Planned	Actual
Agriculture & fisheries	7.6	6.7	87.3	68.7
(of which fisheries)	(0.8)	(0.8)	(34.8)	(25.5)
Industry	9.2	5.3	43.7	32.2
(of which oil & minerals)	(6.5)	(4.1)	(16.4)	(12.7)
Transport, communications & construction	12.9	10.2	76.9	58.6
Social services	2.6	2.5	67.6	36.6
Total	32.5	24.7	275.5	195.8

Source: Bank of Yemen, various issues; *Statistical Yearbook*, no. 1, 1980.

small population base (mainly illiterate), harsh natural conditions, and scarce natural resources. The government feels that PDRY's socialist system has now gained enough strength to allow and even encourage additional private ownership in certain selected sectors (excluding agriculture).

Table 5.12: Gross Domestic Produce at Current Market Prices, 1968-76 (YDm)

	1968	1973	1974	1975	1976
Agriculture & fisheries	18.5	17.8	19.0	19.2	26.9
(of which fisheries)	(n.a.)	(5.5)	(5.5)	(5.3)	(12.2)
Petroleum refining	16.9	4.7	10.1	2.2	1.9
Other industries	2.6	4.4	6.2	8.0	12.0
Building, construction, electricity, water	1.4	5.6	6.7	10.6	12.3
Commerce	12.2	13.2	15.4	15.4	19.9
Tourism	0.6	2.0	2.7	3.5	3.9
Transport, storage, communications	3.7	6.3	8.9	10.3	14.6
Financial services	1.7	5.3	6.9	7.4	8.4
Dwelling ownership	2.5	–	–	–	–
Other business and personal services	5.8	2.6	3.4	4.0	4.2
Government administration	11.4	18.0	16.5	18.3	21.5
Interest	n.a.	-1.5	-3.3	-4.4	-4.5
Sub-total	77.3	79.0	92.5	95.5	121.1
Customs duties[a]	n.a.	5.2	7.3	6.7	9.3
Production subsidies	–	–	-2.3	-2.3	-1.6
GDP at Market Prices	77.3	84.2	97.5	99.9	128.8

a. Other indirect taxes are included in data above.
Source: Central Statistical Organisation.

Table 5.13: Government Current Budget Revenue (YDm)

	1968/9	1969/70	1970/71	1971/2	1972/3	1973/4	1974/5	1975 (Apr.-Dec.)	1976	1977	1978
Taxes on income & profits	2.0	2.9	2.5	3.8	2.5	2.3	4.9	4.1	7.6	9.0	10.0
Corporations	(1.0)	(1.6)	(1.4)	(2.7)	(1.4)	(1.3)	(3.8)	(3.3)	(5.5)	(6.6)	(7.2)
Taxes on individuals	(0.2)	(0.2)	(0.2)	(0.2)	(0.2)	(0.2)	(0.2)	(0.2)	(0.2)	(0.4)	(0.4)
Wage & salary income	(0.8)	(1.1)	(0.9)	(0.9)	(0.9)	(0.8)	(0.8)	(0.6)	(1.8)	(2.0)	(2.4)
Taxes on foods & services	1.0	1.3	1.3	1.3	1.6	2.0	3.1	2.8	4.8	6.6	7.9
Import duties	2.1	2.4	3.6	5.9	4.4	4.4	5.7	3.9	6.3	11.4	14.0
Other taxes	1.2	0.5	1.1	1.5	1.4	0.6	0.5	0.5	1.0	1.3	1.6
Non-tax revenues	2.6	3.3	4.7	3.5	2.1	4.2	4.3	2.5	6.0	6.6	12.9
Total	8.9	10.4	13.2	16.0	12.0	13.5	18.5	13.9	25.7	34.9	46.5

Source: Bank of Yemen; al-Sha'ayoubi, 1972, pp. 278-83.

Table 5.14: Government Current Budget Expenditures (YDm)

	1968/9	1969/70	1970/71	1971/2	1972/3	1973/4	1974/5	1975 (Apr.-Dec.)	1976	1977	1978
General administration	0.2	0.4	0.8	1.1	1.9	2.5	3.5	3.2	5.8	6.9	2.9
Defence & security	8.0	8.2	8.1	9.2	9.8	10.2	13.2	12.1	17.1	20.0	30.8
Finance & economy	0.7	1.1	0.8	1.3	1.1	1.6	1.2	1.3	2.7	3.4	4.6
Education & guidance	1.6	1.8	2.2	2.6	2.7	3.9	4.5	4.3	6.3	8.2	11.8
Local townships	0.3	0.3	0.4	0.4	0.4	0.5	0.5	0.5	0.6	1.4	1.3
Public works & communications	1.3	1.1	1.2	1.1	1.0	1.3	1.2	0.9	1.5	0.9	1.3
Health	0.8	0.8	0.9	1.0	1.0	1.3	1.5	1.4	2.2	2.7	3.5
Others	1.1	1.2	2.2	2.1	1.9	2.2	2.0	1.8	2.9	3.9	5.2
Fifth governorate[a]	1.8	0.5	0.9	1.9	1.9	–	–	–	–	–	–
Total	15.8	15.4	17.5	20.7	21.7	23.5	27.6	25.5	39.1	47.4	61.4

a. After 1972, Fifth Governorate expenditures were included in other headings. The Fifth Governorate was separately under British rule.
Source: Bank of Yemen; al-Sha'ayoubi, 1972, pp. 278-83.

Table 5.15: Outstanding External Debt ($USm)

	Total outstanding including undisbursed							Disbursed as of 31 Dec. 1978
	1972	1973	1974	1975	1976	1977	1978	
Arab sources	30	30	57	86	96	181	226	77
Various Arab Funds	1	1	26	54	54	139	151	43
Iraq	12	12	14	15	25	25	32	20
Libya	17	17	17	17	17	17	36	14
Algeria	–	–	–	–	–	–	7	–
Soviet bloc	14	23	34	62	99	139	337	119
USSR	10	18	20	44	68	97	235	75
GDR	4	5	9	12	16	17	34	17
Bulgaria	–	–	1	2	8	15	32	17
CSSR	–	–	3	3	6	9	13	8
Hungary	–	–	1	1	1	1	18	2
Romania	–	–	–	–	–	–	5	–
China	6	15	21	37	43	59	132	69
Other sources	8	14	21	41	49	52	58	36
IBRD-IDA	1	6	11	30	38	38	53	23
OPEC Special Fund	–	–	–	–	–	2	3	3
Denmark	2	2	2	2	2	4	2	2
Others	5	6	8	8	8	8	–	8
Total	58	82	133	226	287	431	753	301

Source: Bank of Yemen; *Middle East Economic Digest*, 28 September 1979.

Table 5.16: Enrolment in Education: 1966/7-1977/8

	Primary		Preparatory		Secondary		Participation rate of age group, %			Higher education	
	Total	of which girls	Total	of which girls	Total	of which girls	Primary (7-12)	Preparatory (13-15)	Secondary (16-18)	Total	of which girls
1966/7	49,928	10,166	11,582	2,685	2,992	546	n.a.	n.a.	n.a.	–	–
1970/71	134,884	26,959	13,658	2,664	3,023	679	51.0	15.0	4.2	150	32
1973/4	183,744	47,167	23,245	4,708	6,933	1,424	63.6	23.4	8.8	n.a.	n.a.
1974/5	196,466	59,611	30,474	6,397	8,015	1,691	66.0	29.8	9.7	n.a.	n.a.
1975/6	203,617	67,964	34,348	7,725	9,767	2,199	66.5	32.7	11.7	1,262	n.a.
1976/7	206,358	71,531	43,410	10,782	10,946	2,326	65.4	40.1	12.8	1,937	479
1977/8	212,795	74,219	50,887	12,990	13,501	3,616	n.a.	n.a.	n.a.	2,517	751

Source: *Statistical Yearbook*, no. 1, 1980; UNESCO, Education Statistical Yearbook, various issues.

Table 5.17: Foreign-Trade Participation Ratios			Table 5.18: Change in GDP Per Capita (% on previous year)[c]
	(1)[a]	(2)[b]	
1969	55.6	19.9	
1970	56.6	22.0	− 7
1971	52.1	23.0	−13
1972	36.2	20.7	− 4
1973	32.8	18.5	0
1974	31.5	16.7	− 7
1975	35.5	16.1	−11
1976	51.9	20.5	+21
1977	61.3	19.2	+ 8

a. Including workers' remittances from abroad, but excluding re-exports.
b. Excluding both items.
c. In constant prices of 1969.
Source: *Statistical Yearbook*, no. 1, 1980 (for both tables).

The main outstanding issues are, in the writer's opinion: to increase productivity (mainly in the agricultural sector), ensuring a suitable labour force for the growing public sector; to remove urban/rural disparities (incomes in the rural sector are estimated to be about one-third of the level in urban areas); and to secure external resources for development — especially through workers' remittances. But whatever the outcome of these issues, it is reasonable to assume that the constraints for the foreseeable future will be more manageable than the enormous problems confronted in the last decade.

The détente with the neighbouring Arab oil-wealthy countries could not have any significant impact on the present degree of socialisation of the economy. This rapprochement cannot prevent the PDRY — firmly committed to 'scientific Socialism' as well as to Moscow — from pursuing the basic elements of its domestic and international policies.

However, the existence of this Marxist-Leninist regime and its social and economic achievements will have — presumably in the long term — an impact at least on the poor Arab countries (especially the Yemen Arab Republic) and probably on non-Marxist regimes in East Africa. As these things go, the PDRY is a success story: a secondhand beneficiary of OPEC's monopoly via remittances and aid, she has put her very considerable pickings to good use in recent years, and perhaps surpassed 1969 levels at last.

Notes

1. Excluding the South Yemeni communities abroad estimated at 150,000-200,000.
2. World Bank, *World Development Report 1979*, August 1979, p. 126.
3. Page 1972, Isma'il 1976, Kostiner, 1978, *Middle East Record*, 1967, 1968, 1969/70.
4. Interview with Cuban television on 9 September 1976, as published in *Al-Thawri*, the Adeni Arabic Weekly, 11 September 1976.
5. Mainly in November 1969.
6. The second radical one, enacted in November 1970.
7. In early 1979, the YSP had more than 25,000 adherents — members and candidates, among them 10,000 who had already received a political foundation. See *Le Monde*, 28 February 1979.
8. Isma'il, 1972, p. 110.
9. *The First Congress, the Yemeni Socialist Party, October 1978.*
10. See, for example, *Middle-East Economic Digest*, weekly, London, 25 April 1980; *Middle-East Intelligence Survey*, fortnightly report, published by the Middle-East Information Media, Tel-Aviv, vol. 8, no. 3, 1-15 May 1980, pp. 22-3, and vol. 8, no. 7, 1-15 July 1980, pp. 53-4.
11. *The First Congress*, YSP, 1978, p. 546.
12. *The First Congress*, YSP, October 1978, p. 522.
13. Isma'il, 1972, p. 162.
14. See, for example, *New York Times*, 28 May 1979.
15. *The First Congress*, YSP, 1978, p. 551.
16. *Keesing's Contemporary Archives*, London 1977, p. 28,636; 1978, pp. 28,991 and 29,358. These South Yemeni troops numbered about 2,000 soldiers and officers, including pilots, military advisors as well as infantry, tanks and artillery units.
17. *Keesing's*, 1977, p. 28,636; Legum 1978, p. 63.
18. *Keesing's*, 1980, p. 30,199.
19. Ibid. Previously Iraq had been the only Arab country admitted as an observer by the CMEA.
20. *Akhar Sa'ah*, weekly, Cairo, 20 February 1980 (in Arabic).
21. CIA, 1979, p. 34.
22. *SWB*, BBC, Soviet Union, 1 January 1969, as quoted in the *Middle East Record*, 1968, p. 50; CIA, 1978, p. 34.
23. *Keesing's*, 1980, p. 30,199.
24. *Idem*.
25. *Daily Telegraph*, London, 30 May 1980.
26. *SWB*, BBC, ME/6519/A/3, 10 September 1980, speech to the Sixth Session of the People's Supreme Assembly.
27. *Collier's Encyclopedia*, vol. 1, New York 1979, p. 119.
28. Ibid., vol. 23, p. 696; El-Zine 1978, pp. 18-21.
29. *Idem*.
30. A further advantage is that the PDRY is perhaps the only Arab country giving open support and refuge to Communists from other Arab states. For instance, the Iraqi Communist Party has a section in Aden which maintains, at the least, political activities against the present Iraqi regime for the persecution of Communists in their country — see *October*, YAR publication, June 1980, p. 3 (in Arabic).
31. For detailed background material on the social and economic conditions in South Yemen before independence, see Dr Gamal-Eddine Heyworth-Dunne, 1972; al-Abd, 1969; al-Sha'youbi, 1972.

32. al-Sha'ayoubi, 1972, p. 142.
33. *Middle East Record*, 1968, p. 708.
34. al-Sha'ayoubi, 1972, p. 277; *Middle East Record*, 1968, p. 709.
35. *Middle East Record*, 1968, pp. 707-8.
36. Ibid., p. 709.
37. *Middle East Record*, 1969/70, p. 1060.
38. al-Sha'ayoubi, 1972, pp. 210-14.
39. *Idem*.
40. Trust land bequeathed to and managed by religious endowments.
41. al-Sha'ayoubi, 1972, p. 211.
42. *SWB*, BBC, ME/W1086/A1/6, Aden, 23 August 1980; *Fourteenth October*, daily, Aden, 14 October 1980 (in Arabic).
43. *Fourteenth October*, daily, Aden, 7 October 1980.
44. *First Congress*, YSP, 1978, p. 549; *Middle East Economic Digest*, weekly, London, 23 May 1980.
45. *Al-Thawri*, weekly, Aden, 9 August 1980 (in Arabic).
46. Isma'il, 1979, p. 62.
47. *First Congress*, YSP, 1978, p. 242.
48. *Idem*.
49. *Al-Thawri*, weekly, Aden, various issues (in Arabic).
50. *Al-Thawri*, 9 August 1980.
51. al-Sha'ayoubi, 1972, p. 218; *Middle East Economic Digest*, 30 May 1980; *Fourteenth October*, 7 October 1980.
52. With the exception of certain subsistence fishermen.

PART TWO:

THE 'MARGINALS'

6 THE PEOPLE'S REPUBLIC OF BENIN

Andrew Racine

The People's Republic of Benin (the former Republic of Dahomey) is to be found on the west coast of Africa between Nigeria and Togo. Its 125 km. of coastline along the Gulf of Guinea widens further inland to over 300 km. near the northern borders with Niger and Upper Volta. This 112,600 square km. is home to 3,377,000 people[1] (50 per cent under 15 years of age),[2] over two-thirds of whom live along the southern coastal stretch, where their density exceeds 120 per square km. (as compared to only 10 per square km. in the northern reaches).[3] The World Bank's estimate for GDP *per capita* for the Beninese reached $200 p.a. in 1977 (though according to Kravis *et al.*, 1978, it was already $208.8 by 1970), having risen on the average only 0.2 per cent p.a. for the period 1960-77[4] (and this in comparison to a population growth rate of 2.8 per cent per year).[5] These estimates should be regarded from the perspective that 86 per cent of the population is rural, where most are engaged in non-market subsistence farming and local trading.

The latest figures concerning religious belief estimate that 65 per cent of the population are animists, 15 per cent Muslim and 15 per cent Christian[6] (Benin is represented at the College of Cardinals in Rome by the Archbishop of Cotonou). The President of the country, Mr Mathieu Kérékou, recently (7 September 1980) changed his name to Ahmed when he officially converted to Islam in the presence of Libya's Colonel Gaddafy.

French is the official language of Benin,[7] the CFA franc is the official currency with a fixed parity of 50 CFA francs per French franc. The 1975 average value was 245 CFAF to the US dollar.[8] The foreign-trade participation ratio is about 20 per cent.

The following pages, through a consideration of the politics and economics of this small country, will attempt to place in perspective its designation as a marginal (or more appropriately, perhaps, potential) Marxist-Leninist state.

Domestic Politics

On the 30 November 1974 the chief of state of what was then the
Republic of Dahomey, Lieutenant-Colonel Mathieu Kérékou, declared
in an address delivered in Abomey on the second anniversary of his
coming to power that, from that moment, Dahomey would be
following a socialist path of development with a Marxist-Leninist
orientation as this was the sole, historically just path for the Dahomean
people.[9] He had completely changed his mind within 17 months
(below), and had neither prepared public opinion nor developed a
Communist Party. This and his subsequent conversion to Islam (above)
amply justify our qualification of Benin as marginal!

Any serious attempt to understand the meaning of this event must
begin with a consideration of the historical development whose
culmination was to be found in this declaration.

From Independence to 1972[10]

The first 12 years of independence in Benin were marked by six
separate *coups*, as the three principal regional-ethnic blocks of the
country tried unsuccessfully to reconcile themselves to living in and
governing an arbitrary piece of land poor in natural resources: their
inheritance of close to three-quarters of a century of the exercise of
French authority in the region. Several elements contributed to these
years of turbulence. To begin with, the indigenous inhabitants of Benin
are divided ethnically and geographically into five or six major clusters,
of which three principal communities (the Fon, the Gown and the
Bariba), corresponding to three traditional kingdoms, emerged as
politically dominant. Political traditions of independence for each of
these three were not conducive to the formation of a modern nation-
state under a single authority chosen from among them. This ethnic
diversity, coupled with the size and relative educational sophistication
of the country's literate elite, meant that Benin would have a
multiplicity of politically-schooled personages and groups vying for
influence throughout its post-independence history.

There are, in addition, the destabilising effects of imposing a
framework of institutions drawn from a society where legitimacy, in
Weberian terms, is of a rational-bureaucratic type on a society where
actual legitimacy derives from a mixture of paternalistic and
charismatic authority. It is individuals not offices or institutions which
exercise command in such a context. No political leader is viewed by
his constituency as simply a man fulfilling the functions of an office.
He is seen rather as someone who by virtue of personal qualities (often
tied to ethnic background) is owed allegiance. Political parties become
organs for transferring traditional rivalries on to an alien structure for

the express purpose of fulfilling the formal requirements of the
electoral process, at the conclusion of which they, as often as not,
disappear altogether. Not surprisingly, then, the balkanisation of
French West Africa instituted by the *loi cadre* of 1956 added the final
impetus to movements in the general direction of post-independence
chaos.

Almost from the outset each of the three regions had their ethnic
identities incorporated into a separate political personage, each with
his own political party. The period between the enactment of the *loi
cadre* in June 1956 and the first government of independence, elected
in December 1960, constituted a continually fluctuating series of
alliances of two of these men against the third.

At independence, the government was a coalition between Hubert
Mago, a Northerner, and Souvou Migan Apithy, a Gown, under a
combined party (resulting from a fusion of the Parti des Nationalistes
du Dahomey with the Rassemblement Démocratique Dahoméen),
the Parti Dahoméen d'Unité. Mago assumed the office of President,
Apithy that of Vice-President. This coalition began to deteriorate
almost from the moment of its inception, and three years and three
months after Independence Day a series of strikes and student protests,
in which supporters of Justin Ahomadegbe (central tribes) were cast
in a not inconsiderable role, the Mago government was forced to
resign. Colonel Christophe Soglo of the Armed Forces mediated the
transition of power to a new Apithy-Ahomadegbe coalition, suitably
inaugurated with the formation of a new party of convenience, the
Parti Démocratique Dahoméen (PDD). A new constitution was
adopted in January 1964.

Exclusion and persecution of the northerners (Mago was detained
under house arrest), a continuously deteriorating economic outlook,
and constant jockeying for political advantage between President
Apithy and Vice-President Ahomadegbe led inevitably to a second
military intervention in November 1965, engineered again by Colonel
Soglo. An interim government led by the Speaker of the National
Assembly, Tahirou Congacou, lasted approximately one month
before continuous political manoeuvring by the three ousted leaders
(each formed his own new political party once more in December)
convinced Colonel Soglo that a protracted period of military
government was necessary to restore order, and put the economy back
on a stable course of development. Soglo's government of ten
technocrats lasted from December 1965 until December 1967 before
being overthrown by a group of young army officers headed by

Maurice Kouandété. While Lt.-Colonel Alphonse Alley assumed responsibility as Head of State, another new constitution was drafted, designed around a strong Presidency, and new elections were scheduled for May. All previous office-holders were declared ineligible to run, the result of which was a minuscule turnout of 26 per cent of voters, as the three convinced their followers to boycott the elections. The military consequently nullified the results and appointed Emile Zinsou President in July.

Zinsou's government was finished after 16 months when the young officers again stepped in, this time installing Lt.-Colonel Paul Emile de Souza as Chairman of a Military Directorate. Elections were called for yet again with the three previous office-holders invited to participate. These elections proved abortive and a compromise solution, consisting of a three member Presidential Council with a two year rotating chairmanship, was instituted. It was from this government, despite the unexpectedly smooth transition of authority from the first President, Mago, to the second, Ahomadegbe, that Mathieu Kérékou and a group of four young officers, Major Michel Alladaye, Captain Hilaire Badjogoume, Captain Michel Aikpe and Captain Janvier Assogba seized power on 26 October 1972.

The Kérékou Régime

From Kérékou's first statement to the nation, through a radio renamed 'The Voice of the Revolution', it was clear that a turning point in Dahomean politics had been reached. Although Kérékou was originally thought to have been included in the *coup* only at the last moment, in order to benefit from his popularity among the military rank and file (in particular the gendarmerie),[11] he was, it seems, from the outset, the prime mover in the regime's orientation. His address to the nation on 30 November[12] stressed the role of foreign domination (implicitly the French) in maintaining the 'backwardness' of the Dahomean economy; concentrated on developing the indigenous powers of Dahomey as the key to full economic and cultural evolution; and emphasised the role of the peasantry in the future development of the society. Each of these themes differed substantially from the thrust of the previous twelve years of political management.

The period 1972-4, punctuated though it was by a number of plots, attempted *coups* and intrigues, may be characterised as a gradual attempt to implement the ideological commitment of Kérékou and his government under the constraints of extreme dependence and relative resource insufficiency. The Military Revolutionary Government of twelve officers all under the age of 40[13] assumed control of the state. A Military Council of the Revolution consisting of young officers and NCOs was established as an advisory and overseeing board. In the months following the takeover, Dahomey established relations with the People's Republic of China,[14] North Korea, the German Democratic Republic and Libya,[15] and expressed its support for the liberation movements of South Africa, Zimbabwe, Namibia, the Portuguese colonies and Vietnam.[16] Enthusiasm for the French-dominated West African Economic Community (CEAO), which Dahomey had joined the previous June under Ahomadegbe's leadership, gave way to plans to institute a Benin Union with Nigeria and Togo. The regime announced plans for the state to take over the processing and marketing of the main export commodities (particularly cotton, palm oil and tobacco); to assume control of other vital sectors of the economy; and, in general, to extend its influence at the expense of foreign private enterprise. Agriculture became the new focus of financing projects. French was replaced in the schools by local indigenous languages.

Yet at the same time there were indications of moderation on the part of the new government. No attempt was made to withdraw from the French currency zone. No precipitous policy of nationalisations was begun. No moves were made to substitute aid originating from France, West Germany and the USA with other sources of support. Indications of moderation continued through 1973 as Kérékou withstood internal threats from the left (notably the fierce anti-French demonstrations in February, led by the United Democratic Front)[17] as well as from the right. In an interview in the *New Nigerian*, on 9 June 1973, Kérékou summed up by stating, '. . . we don't want communism, capitalism, or socialism. We have our own Dahomean social and cultural system, which is our own.'

Having rejected demands by the United Democratic Front to establish a mass party of workers, students, intellectuals, trade-unionists and progressive factions of the military, the regime did move to broaden and deepen its support through, first, the establishment of a National Council of the Revolution (CNR), including civilian participants for the first time, and later through the creation of elected revolutionary councils in the villages. The full system of political restructuring, adopted in February 1974, was designed to replace the neo-colonial French system of communes and prefectures. It comprised four levels: (1) the six provinces of the country, each headed by an appointee of the CNR; (2) the districts run by a centrally appointed district chief, along with an elected District Revolutionary Council;

(3) the rural or urban communities each with an elected Revolutionary Committee; and (4) the village or township with its locally elected Revolutionary Committee.[18] In retrospect one might view this administrative restructuring as a prelude to the 'ideological restructuring' which was around the corner. The new administrative structure, by allowing the head of state to appoint the first two levels of authority, secured Kérékou's command over the length and breadth of governmental machinery. The establishment of a 13-member Politburo, above the CNR, in November further centralised control. Kérékou also had been prudent in the use of constant cabinet reshuffles and rotating appointments to prevent any potential rival members of the CNR from consolidating their positions. All of these moves served to prepare the way for the implementation of an ideological treatise which would govern the nation from the time of its proclamation.

The discourse of 30 November 1974 was the first comprehensive statement by Kérékou of his world-view and his future plans for the nation. As a Dahomean political statement it was uncharacteristic in at least three respects: it was universal rather than regional in appeal; it was expressly ideological; it was radically left-wing. Declaring Marxism-Leninism to be the future guide of the revolution, Kérékou outlined eight tasks to be faced: eradication of foreign domination (including its indigenous bourgeois representatives); active struggle against all forms of exploitation, including tribalism, racism, etc.; unification of thought behind Marxism-Leninism; 'lifting' of the economy according to the prescriptions of scientific socialism; reviving of indigenous culture; mastering of scientific and technological skills necessary for modernisation; mastering of knowledge of the revolution; scientific organisation of the productive masses to defend the revolution.[19] As if to emphasise the seriousness of the commitment, the address was followed within one month by nationalisation of the insurance industry, two major banks and a French telecommunications company; declaration of state monopolies in automobile credit and the transport and sales of petroleum products (effectively nationalising interests of BP, Shell, Mobil, Texaco and AGIP);[20] and the assumption of half-ownership of all freight carriers.

In succeeding years political developments continued, as did ideological pronouncements, to be engineered from the top downwards. The primary commercial and industrial enterprises have all come under public ownership of some degree or another. The state assumed control of all previously private or religious education. Provincial institutions (called CARDERs) to help farmers and fishermen increase their yields and rationalise their marketing techniques came into being in 1975. The limit to these innovations has been with the agricultural producers, among whom only small regional attempts have been made to collectivise the production process.

Governmental restructuring also proceeded apace as the leadership gradually strove to replace an essentially military structure with the semblance of a civilian one. A new single political party for the country was formed in November 1975 to coincide with the renaming of the country as the 'People's Republic of Benin'. The First Extraordinary Congress of the Benin People's Revolutionary Party (PRPB) in May 1976 elected a central committee of 27 and a Politburo of 6 members (all close allies of President Kérékou). At that time the party also resolved to draft a charter for the establishment of a 'lay revolutionary state'. Public discussions and debates concerning the proposed new constitution took place throughout 1976-7 at all levels of the government down to local revolutionary committees. Finally on 30 November 1977 the *loi fondamentale* was approved. The document of eleven Chapters and 160 Articles is the product of an extensive debate filtered through the party's top echelons. It provides for a supreme legislative body, the National Revolutionary Assembly, composed of People's Commissars elected not from a regional but from a class-based constituency for three-year terms. The supreme executive organ, the National Executive Council (cabinet), is appointed by the President, who himself is elected for a three-year term by the National Revolutionary Assembly from among nominees put forward by the Central Committee of the PRPB. He is Head of State, Chairman of the National Executive Council, Supreme Commander of the Armed Forces, and also Chairman of the CC of the PRPB.[21] It was this structure which replaced the Military Revolutionary Government when in February 1980 the CNR dissolved itself, the National Revolutionary Assembly convened for the first time, and promptly elected Mathieu Kérékou the first President of the People's Republic of Benin.

While Kérékou has been busy for the past six years widening and deepening his administrative control in an effort to establish his legitimacy, plenty of others have been hard at work to accomplish his removal. In the year following his famous discourse on socialism there were no less than three separate *coup* attempts. In January 1975 his former co-conspirator Captain Assogba attempted to attain power by force, allegedly with the backing of exiled leader Emile Zinsou. Both were sentenced to death later in the year, the second *in absentia*. In June Michel Aikpe, member of the Marxist 'Ligueur' group, was shot,

having been discovered 'committing adultery' with Kérékou's wife.
The more prosaic explanation at the time involved an attempt to
overthrow the government. As Aikpe was extremely popular among
the trade-unionists, his killing was followed by a wave of strikes,
demonstrations and repression. In August of 1975 Zinsou, together
with other exiled Dahomeyans, formed in Paris the Front for the
Liberation and Rehabilitation of Dahomey. It was this group which was
allegedly behind a plot to unseat Kérékou uncovered in October. 1976
passed relatively serenely for the government, while 1977 opened with
a bang as, in January, the capital was literally invaded by 100 armed
European and African mercenaries who, while failing in their mission
to oust Kérékou, met little local resistance and managed to do $28
million dollars' worth of damage before they made their getaway. A
subsequent UN investigatory commission ascertained that the group
was trained in Morocco, under the leadership of a Frenchman named
Gilbert Bourgeaud, and later launched from Gabon. France, Morocco
and Gabon all denied involvement, but Kérékou remains convinced
of their connection with the attempt. As late as one month before the
institution of the new civilian government another group of military
men inside the regime, including long-time associates Azonhiho and
Alladaye, tried unsuccessfully to prevent the switch-over to civilian
rule.[22] Throughout it all Kérékou remains in control, if not firmly in
control, at least continually so.

Domestic Economics[23] (Table 6.1)

Benin's domestic economy is, at the moment, fairly typical of a small,
largely rural, resource-poor society, administratively over-burdened,
substantially integrated into the international capitalist structure
through both aid and trade relations, yet attempting through various
mechanisms to reduce its dependence and re-orient its domestic
economic priorities. The structure of GDP with primary, secondary
and tertiary shares at 37 per cent, 12 per cent and 42 per cent has
changed little since 1975 (see Table 6.1). Growth in real GDP,
enormously dependent on climatic conditions by virtue of the
preponderant influence of agriculture, was 3.8 per cent in 1977 but
jumped to 5.5 per cent in 1978. It is thought that an increase in
output from the primary sector, with acknowledged spill-over effects
on industry and commerce, was largely responsible for the upturn.

Table 6.1.[c] **Benin: Gross Domestic Product (in billions of CFA francs)**

	1973[b]	1974[b]	1975	1976[a]	1977[a]	1978[a]
Gross domestic product (at current prices)						
Total	85.6	95.5	112.8	130.2	146.1	161.6
of which agriculture (% of total)	42.3	42.3	34.6	36.6	37.6	37.3
industry (% of total)	9.4	8.9	13.5	12.6	12.1	12.0
services (% of total)	48.3	48.8	43.4	42.3	31.8	42.3
Per cent change in nominal GDP	7.5	11.8	4.8	15.4	12.3	10.6
Per cent change in real GDP	6.1	−7.5	−1.0	4.3	3.8	5.5

a. Estimates.
b. World Bank Document, pp. 131-2 and p. 157.
Source: Whole table reprinted from *IMFB*, p. v.

Agriculture

The main thrust of much of the government's domestic policies since 1974 has been toward rationalising production and distribution in this sector and extending government control over it. Insofar as 70 per cent of the population, 38 per cent of GDP and 90 per cent of foreign exchange earnings are dependent upon this sector (1977 estimates),[24] such a strategy can only be described as prudent.

The Ministry of Rural Development and Co-operative Action has, through a number of semi-autonomous state enterprises, assumed overall responsibility for the financing and marketing of a wide variety of goods. Only those agricultural commodities produced for local trade or consumption (i.e. chiefly maize, millet, yams, cassava, etc.) remain beyond their jurisdiction. These state boards are organised along commodity lines (e.g. forestry is managed by SNAFOR, rice milling by SONIAH, cotton by SONAGRI, fish by SONAPECHE, and so forth). Regional production efforts are in the hands of CARDERs established in 1975 (see above) which provide certain agricultural inputs, manpower and managerial skills and marketing services. Financing for the agricultural sector is achieved through three supporting agencies: la Caisse Autonome de Crédit Agricole, which extends credits both to state enterprises, such as SONIAH, and to individual CARDERs; le Fonds Autonome de Stabilisation, which ensures agricultural producers against extreme fluctuations in the price of their commodities and is itself financed via a similar arrangement with the EEC's STABEX. and the Société Nationale de Commercialisation du Benin (SONACEB), which markets most agricultural exports. Attempts are currently being made to group individual farmers into larger, more economically efficient units called *groupements villageois*. Co-operative production methods are being urged on those who have contiguous plots and whose holdings are increasingly being organised into *groupements révolutionnaires à vocation cooperative* (GRVCs). One known state farm of 1,100 hectares is being undertaken experimentally under Soviet auspices in the northern district of Borgou.[25]

Commodities of the agricultural sector may be divided into food crops of which maize, sorghum and cassava are the most important; cash crops dominated by palm products, cotton and groundnuts; and the relatively less important livestock, fishing and forestry divisions. Production of food crops is still dominated by traditional ownership and production methods, with yearly variations in output, reflecting climatic conditions and extensions of area under cultivation. Those food crops of some domestic marketable potential (for instance, sugar, rice, fruit, etc.) show greater penetration by state agencies, while the largest bulk are still marketed in the traditional sector. Cash crops, on the other hand, are marketed almost exclusively through SONACEB, which receives credits from the Banque Commerciale du Benin and advances these funds to CARDERs to pay for harvest, which it then sells to foreign buyers. Market prices, albeit with government subsidisation, remain the major motivation for choosing between food and cash crop cultivation from the view-point of any individual farmer. Much of the decline in output of cotton over the years 1974-8 has been attributed, for example, to the low price paid to producers for this product and the relative labour-intensity of its cultivation in comparison to most food crops.

A deliberate policy of holding down wages in the tertiary sector, combined with burgeoning opportunities to market agricultural produce in neighbouring Nigeria, have diminished the urban-rural income differential since 1974 and restricted to a minimum the problem of swelling urban unemployment, endemic to many LDCs.

Industry

The degree of Benin's underdevelopment and dependence on foreign capital is better revealed in the secondary sector than in agriculture. Bearing in mind that all industry represents less than 15 per cent of GDP and 2 per cent of the workforce,[26] its make-up is still of considerable interest. The industrial economy is precariously devoted to the processing of certain agricultural commodities. The manufacturing sector, averaging 3 per cent of GDP over the period 1975-7, is hampered by the fact that over 50 per cent of its value added is contributed by only two industries: oils and fats (mostly from palm products) 36.8 per cent, and textiles 18.0 per cent.[27] The top four industries created over four-fifths of total value added.

Oil products are processed by two state agencies: SOBEPALH and SONICOG, whose combined pre-tax operating profits for 1976/7 of 93m CFAF represented 9 per cent of total public enterprise profits for that year. For textiles, the industry consists of two firms, SOBETEX and IBETEX, the former 51 per cent owned by private interests (Niger, Togo, Ivory Coast and France) and the latter 52 per cent controlled by private French and Dutch interests. Overall state control of modern industry (i.e. equity shares weighted by sales) increased from 30 per cent in 1972 to 75 per cent in 1976. The smaller manufacturers of food processing, baking, printing and furniture-making industries are all still in private hands, as is a full 60 per cent of local trading.[28]

Mining and energy, both small in terms of share of GDP, are also jointly owned with foreign private capital. Of the two large mining concerns, both involved in cement production, one is 51 per cent French, the other 41 per cent Nigerian and 10 per cent Danish. The recent discovery of oil offshore, though relatively small in amount, should go far toward easing the burden of import financing. Of the total cost of exploiting this field 90 per cent is to be financed by Norwegians.

Commerce, Transport Services, etc.

Next to agriculture, improvement of the transportation infrastructure has received highest priority from the Beninese government, and foreign financing has played a substantial role in these plans. The Fonds D'Aide et de Coopération, USAID, IDA, the CCCE (Caisse Centrale de Coopération Economique), and a variety of individual countries, have contributed heavily to the reconstruction and maintenance of Benin's 3,360 km. of paved and all-weather roads. The railway system as well, especially the segment connecting Benin with Nigeria, has benefited from foreign assistance.

The deepwater port of Cotonou, managed by an autonomous port authority, is another key element in infrastructural development. The bulk of Benin's seaborne trade is shipped through this port. The importance to the government of this traffic is staggering. Of total government revenues of 24,429.7m CFAF in the first eleven months of 1978, fully 55 per cent came from duties on imports and exports — enough to cover the costs of all economic, health and general public services provided by the government for that year.[29] It is hardly surprising, therefore, that the government has embarked on a 9.6 billion CFAF renovation and expansion of port facilities. The project is being financed via a combination of credits from the IDA, the African Development Bank, and the Arab Bank for Economic Development in Africa, and French, Canadian and Norwegian banks.[30]

Prices and Wages

Prices of imported and locally manufactured goods are controlled by the Beninese government for the purpose of containing increases in the cost of living. Existing inflation (11 per cent in 1976, 8 per cent in 1977, and 5 per cent in 1978, calculated on the basis of an implicit GDP deflator) has resulted mainly from crop failures or transmission from abroad through imported manufactured goods. Of an active population of 1.6 million in 1977, 3.5 per cent were wage earners.

Less than half of these are skilled or semi-skilled, yet, paradoxically, on the management side the ratio of executive to middle-level managers is high, reflecting the priorities of the old educational establishment. The differentials between the controlled wages of government workers and those in private enterprise are said to remain in the ratio of 1:3.5-4.[31]

Three Year Plan 1977/8-1979/80

The declared aim of this $1 billion three-year investment programme is that it be democratic, independent and scientifically planned. The scheme concentrates on improving the level and equality of distribution of income of Beninese citizens while simultaneously establishing the country's economic self-sufficiency. Reduced economic dependence on both imports and exports is to be achieved through the vertical integration of existing agricultural processing, both 'upstream' and 'downstream', trying at one time to encourage, and benefit from, an authentic Beninese market in both raw materials and finished goods. Industrial development is to receive the largest single commitment of resources (44 per cent of the total) and infrastructural improvements (irrigation, roads, storage and marketing facilities) are a second area of intensive investment. Local techniques of production and availability of resources govern the direction of much of the planned investment. The average planned rate of growth in real GDP for the three years is 10 per cent. Benin is the only one of our first seven countries to have made serious progress in recent years (Table 6.1) – if we dismiss the PDRY's performance as the product of subsidies.

Foreign Economics[32] (Tables 6.2-6)

Despite the radical features of Beninese ideological statements since 1974, and its insistence on the development of economic self-sufficiency, the links between the small West African country and the major western capitalist powers show little or no sign of decreasing. Benin remains a member of several multilateral economic communities (e.g. ADB, ECOWAS, OCAM), none even ostensibly socialist in political orientation. The most important by far is, naturally, the West African Monetary Union (UMOA),[33] comprising Benin, Ivory Coast, Niger, Senegal, Upper Volta and Togo. Their common currency, the CFA

Table 6.2: Benin: Balance of Payments, 1974-9 (in billions of CFA francs)

	1974	1975	1976[a]	1977[a]	1978[a]
A. Goods and					
Services	−17.34	−25.84	−29.96	−34.19	−39.50
Trade balance	−13.31	−19.20	−24.82	−30.19	−37.00
Exports, f.o.b.	22.38	24.88	28.41	28.30	26.00
Imports, f.o.b.	−35.69	−44.08	−53.23	−38.49	−63.00
Services balance	−4.03	−6.64	−5.14	−4.00	−2.50
B. Unrequited transfers	10.19	14.40	18.20	19.00	23.10
Current account balance (A+B)	−7.15	−11.44	−11.76	−15.19	−16.40
C. Non-monetary capital	7.73	8.67	12.44	12.30	11.60
D. Monetary capital	−3.15	−6.58	−0.28	−0.07	0.72
E. Errors and Omissions (net)	2.66	4.79	1.00	2.80	1.37
Overall balance (A+B+C+D+E)	0.09	−4.56	1.40	−0.16	−2.71

a. Estimates.
Sources: BCEAO; and IMF staff estimates, reprinted from *IMFB*, p. vi.

franc, has a fixed parity, guaranteed by France through an agreement with their common central bank (BCEAO). The BCEAO maintains at least 65 per cent of its foreign exchange reserves with the French Treasury in French francs, in return for which France guarantees a value of 1 CFA fr. = 0.02 Fr. fr. through the use of the SDR. The degree of control this provides over West African currency and finance is considerable.

Benin continues actively to seek and receive bilateral and multilateral grants and loans for a variety of projects (see below). These are all negotiated by organs of the central government or semi-public enterprises. Direct foreign investment is permitted, either in conjunction with nationally controlled capital, or alone, provided a 'non-negligible' portion of profits is locally reinvested. Neither of these options, it would appear, is particularly attractive as average net direct foreign investment has declined from 1 billion CFAF during the period 1970-3 to zero during the period 1974-6.[34] Freeing the economy from direct foreign private ownership and control seems to have been pursued successfully in Benin. Disengaging the economy from indirect control and dependence is another matter altogether.

Trade (Tables 6.3 and 6.4)

The overall balance of payments reveals large and continually expanding deficits in goods and services, despite increasing transportation receipts since 1976 due to expanded trade with Niger and Nigeria. Over half of this deficit is financed by unrequited transfers (mainly emigrants' remittances, we presume), net government capital inflow making up a substantial portion of the remainder. This large and growing disparity is more evidence of the degree of import dependency of the Beninese economy, and the extent to which export earnings remain hostage to developments beyond the government's control (climate, economic developments in neighbouring countries, etc.).

Table 6.3: Benin: Imports by Country of Origin, 1975-9 (in millions of CFA francs)

	1975	1976	1977
European Community	25,197	29,512	32,879
of which France	(12,026)	(15,637)	(14,088)
Other Western Europe[a]	1,170	1,455	1,489
Eastern Europe[a]	344	771	956
USSR[a]	747	754	426
UMOA	1,828	1,773	1,968
Other African countries	2,527	3,112	3,072
United States	2,826	3,072	3,333
China, People's Republic of	1,895	1,724	986
Hong Kong	168	617	1,155
India	1,975	3,259	6,155
Japan	1,809	3,946	3,058
Taiwan	–	470	1,549
Other	3,855	4,954	6,199
	(1,594)[b]	(1,974)[b]	(3,328)[b]
Total	42,080	52,439	60,354

a. *UNYITS*, vol. 1, 1978.
b. When the figures (a) are added, these figures are what the residual must become.
Sources: Ministère du Plan, de la Statistique et de la Coopération Technique, Institut National de la Statistique et de l'Analyse Economique, *Statistiques Officielles du commerce extérieur* (reprinted from *IMFB*, p. 112).

Table 6.4: Benin: Exports by Country of Destination, 1975-9 (in millions of CFA francs)

	1975	1976	1977
Europe	3,582	6,185	6,350
European Community	3,361	6,015	6,220
of which France	1,850	2,157	2,496
Other Western Europe	73	170	127
Eastern Europe	148	–	3
Africa	2,334	1,744	1,735
of which UMOA	1,073	802	842
Nigeria	1,078	604	629
America	43	19	58
of which United States	20	1	26
Asia	803	1,236	1,903
of which China, People's			
Republic of	375	19	–
Japan	348	997	1,779
Other	29	–	1
Total	6,791	9,184	10.047

Source: Ministère du Plan, de la Statistique et de la Coopération Technique, Institut National de la Statistique et de l'Analyse Economique, *Statistiques Officielles du commerce extérieur* (reprinted from *IMFB*, p. 111).

The direction of trade is revealed in Tables 6.3 and 6.4. In terms of civilian imports France remains Benin's principal supplier, though her percentage of the total contribution has been shrinking steadily since 1974. The amount that Benin imports from the UK and the Netherlands, however, has steadily increased over this same period so that the European Community's overall share remains around 55 per cent. Both the UMOA states and the US have maintained their status as relatively small suppliers to Benin, while Asian trade, particularly from India, Japan and Taiwan, has increased over the years. The People's Republic of China continues to be a small supplier and figures for trade with the Soviet Union are not available but thought to be minuscule.

Benin exports to much the same spectrum of countries (see Table 6.4). In 1977 Western Europe received a large 63.2 per cent of all Beninese exports, a share which has been increasing steadily from a level of 51 per cent in 1974. As with imports, while the level of exports to UMOA and the US has not changed appreciably, trade with Asia, particularly Japan, has increased dramatically since 1974.

Table 6.5: Benin: Foreign Assistance, 1975-9 (in billions of CFA francs)

	1975	1976	1977	1978[a]
Current transfers	4.0	5.7	4.5	5.1
of which France	2.0	1.8	1.5	1.8
EC (STABEX)	−	1.9	1.0	1.3
Capital grants	6.4	8.2	8.7	10.0
of which France	0.6	0.8	1.1	0.5
EC (EDF)	2.0	0.7	0.4	1.3
UNDP	1.0	0.8	1.0	n.a.
Canada	0.6	0.4	1.4[b]	n.a.
US Aid	0.2	0.2	−	n.a.
Nigeria	−	3.3	2.8	n.a.
Loans	2.8	8.7	9.2	6.7[c]
African Development Bank and Fund	−	0.5	1.0	0.7
BADEA	−	−	0.5	0.5
Conseil de l'Entente	0.2	0.2	0.6	0.2
EIB	0.3	0.1	−	−
IDA	0.9	1.4	1.7	1.0
Special Arab Fund for Africa	0.3	0.3	−	−
Canada	−	2.7	0.2	0.2
China, People's Republic of	−	0.5	1.4	0.6
Denmark	−	0.1	0.2	0.2
France	0.4	1.4	0.4	0.8
Germany, Federal Republic of	0.4	0.4	1.3	0.9
Romania	−	−	0.3	−
United States	0.2	1.1	1.3	0.8
USSR	−	−	−	0.4
Other	0.1	−	0.3	0.4
Total disbursements	13.2	22.6	22.4	21.8
Debt service	1.3	1.0	2.4	2.2
Interest	0.2	0.2	0.6	0.6
Amortisation	1.1	0.8	1.8	1.6
Total foreign assistance net of debt service	11.9	21.6	20.0	19.6

a. Projections.
b. With effect from January 1977, all Canadian Government loans to Benin were converted to grants.
c. Projected on basis of commitments at end December 1977. For balance of payments purposes, total borrowing has been estimated at CFAF 10 billion in 1978.
Sources: IBRD, EDF and FAC (reprinted from *IMFB*, p. 113).
Note: The main difference between this and Table 1.2 is that the latter includes capitalist private net flows.

Table 6.6: Benin: External Public Debt by Creditor, 1975-9 (in thousands of US dollars)

	Drawings					Outstanding[b] at the end of			
	1975	1976	1977	1978[a]	1979	1975	1976	1977	1978
Multilateral loans	8,023	10,396	15,436	11,349	–	25,927	36,241	52,079	63,317
Bilateral loans	5,199	25,907	21,944	18,271	–	59,322	77,189	81,758	93,092
Algeria	–	–	300	230	–	–	–	300	530
Belgium-Luxembourg	–	–	–	–	–	633	661	139	–
Canada	147	11,240	680	670	–	3,452	14,457	14,001	14,671
China, People's Republic of	–	2,202	5,725	2,784	–	–	2,274	8,038	10,822
Denmark	218	265	933	692	–	2,557	2,856	3,665	4,206
France	1,898	5,936	1,736	3,518	–	16,189	18,825	17,622	16,846
Germany, Federal Republic of	1,683	1,552	5,322	3,988	–	4,364	5,990	11,611	15,381
Italy	–	–	–	–	–	20,909	17,448	7,096	6,278
Ivory Coast	–	–	–	–	–	602	181	329	311
Netherlands	305	–	124	660	–	669	523	46	629
Nigeria	–	–	–	–	–	–	–	665	–
Poland	–	–	1,000	–	–	–	–	1,000	1,000
Romania	–	–	–	–	–	1,978	1,652	–	–
Spain	–	–	284	142	–	–	–	71	893
Switzerland	–	–	–	–	–	1,691	1,541	1,164	–
United Kingdom	–	–	5	–	–	198	83	–	–
United States	948	4,712	5,469	3,598	–	4,063	8,698	13,830	17,355
USSR	–	–	–	1,649	–	–	–	–	1,648
Zaire	–	–	366	340	–	2,000	2,000	1,800	1,800
Multiple lenders	–	–	–	–	–	–	–	382	722
Total	13,222	36,303	37,380	29,620	–	85,259	113,430	133,837	156,409

a. Projected on the basis of commitments at the end of 1977. For balance of payments purposes, total gross drawings in 1978 have been estimated at US$43 million, raising the total debt outstanding at the end of 1978 to US$170 million.

b. Disbursed.

Source: IBRD (here reprinted from *IMFB*, p. 114).

Foreign Assistance (Tables 6.5 and 6.6)

In the years 1975-8 (inclusive) Benin has been the recipient of
80 billion CFAF-worth of foreign aid originating, almost exclusively,
in the West. Total foreign aid, net of debt service, in 1978 amounted to
19.6 billion CFAF, representing over 13 per cent of GDP (up from a
little over 10 per cent of GDP in 1975). This is greater than the total
central government investment expenditure for the year (19 billion
CFAF). Capital grants originating in France, the European Community,
Canada, the US and Nigeria amounted to ten billion CFAF. Projections
of current transfers for 1978 (including STABEX and FAC support to
the University) were 5.1 billion CFAF. Loans amounted to 6.7 billion
CFAF, of which 0.4 billion were from the USSR and 0.6 billion from
China. France, Germany and the USA remained the largest bilateral
creditors. The IDA provided the most substantial multilateral loans.
Most of this aid, as we have seen, has gone to infrastructural
development. Education received the next largest amount.

Figures for military assistance were unavailable. However, only 14
per cent of the government's 1978 budget was designated for defence
(2 per cent of GDP), so outright purchases may be considered rather
low. Furthermore, the magnitude of exports from Benin to the USSR
(a traditional means of disguising expenses for military purchases) does
not encourage speculation that Soviet military assistance has been of
any great magnitude. Finally the (London) International Institute for
Strategic Studies indicates no significant changes in the make-up of the
Beninese Armed Forces over the past several years.[35] This static
inventory may be further evidence of the lack of serious military
investment for this period, i.e. the major weapons remained physically
the same ones, and required only maintenance. There are no known
Soviet, Cuban or Chinese military assistants in Benin at this time,
though 25 Beninese are being trained in the USSR.[36]

Foreign Politics

In light of the degree of Benin's economic dependence on the West,
it is curious that its foreign policy should be as overtly leftist as it is.
Careful to maintain relatively good relations with France, despite the
deterioration since the 1977 mercenary raid (Kérékou continues to
send representatives to the annual Franco-African summit meetings,
for example), Benin's relations with other western states are cordial,
including, as we have seen, trade relations with Taiwan. Yet ever

since the October 1972 *coup*, which ushered in the present regime, there has been a gradual leftward shift in its posture with respect to the major issues confronting Third World states.

In the crisis in Angola it sided unqualifiedly with the MPLA, voting in the UN with the USSR in March 1976 to condemn South African interference, and sponsoring the admission of Neto's regime to the UN in June of that year. In the crisis in Afghanistan it abstained in the vote denouncing Soviet intervention in January 1980, and refused to join a boycott of the Moscow Olympics over this issue. The Kremlin's attitude toward the Kérékou regime, one of cautious but reserved approval, is visible in the pronouncements of one of its local organs, the South African Communist Party:

> The choice of the socialist orientation, the course towards increased friendly relations, and the growing mutually advantageous co-operation with the socialist countries create favourable conditions for the people of Benin to progress towards social and economic reforms, to strengthen their independence and to consolidate their economic freedom.[37]

At the same time Benin has carefully maintained good relations with the People's Republic of China, refusing to take sides in the dispute between the world's leading socialist countries. In 1976 a protocol for technical and economic co-operation was signed in China by Kérékou himself.

Within African politics, Benin has been strident in its call for a total arms embargo on South Africa, independence for Zimbabwe, Namibia and Polisario's Western Sahara, and has been cultivating good relations with the continent's more radical regimes, notably Congo Brazzaville. In sum, Benin seems content to espouse costless radical positions on international issues, placating some leftist critics of the regime at home and simultaneously attracting a modicum of aid from Communist countries. No overt economic moves, however, have been made in the direction of the CMEA, a development which would seriously jeopardise the important economic lifeline it has with the West.

Acutely aware of the possibilities of direct foreign intervention, since the infamous 1977 invasion, Benin nevertheless maintains only a modest military capability and harbours no foreign garrisons on her soil. Her most serious recent political dispute has been with Gabon (not an immediate neighbour) over alleged complicity in the mercenary affair. The expulsion of 9,000 Beninese from that country has been the only by-product of this squabble. Otherwise Benin maintains friendly relations with all her neighbours.

Conclusions

Historical evidence has demonstrated that countries become socialist by virtue of either popular revolutionary upheavals (USSR, Yugoslavia, China, Cuba); by foreign intervention (Eastern Europe); or by a combination of these (Vietnam). In all these cases the processes of socialising the means of production and converting the social institutions to Communist ones are long and never smooth. Countries do not become socialist by fiat, regardless of the degree of social control exercised by the central government to maintain itself in power. Yet in the past chapter we have considered the case of a small West African country which has purported to do just that — to become a Marxist-Leninist state by picking, from among numerous alternatives, socialism as an appropriate ideology and endeavouring to convert the society to this model over a period of, now, six years.

The evidence that Benin might be a socialist state are, essentially, the ideological pronouncements of its leadership; the centralisation of ownership and control over the economy in the hands of the one party government, with the gradual elimination of foreign ownership of industry and the encouragement of public rather than private investment in the domestic economy; and the positions it has taken on various political issues confronting the Third World. It might be said that Cuba had less auspicious beginnings as a Communist country.

As all of these data, when considered carefully, remain the expressions of a handful of men running the country, it may prove fruitful to look beyond these formal criteria at the rest of the social forces in Benin. First and foremost there is the peasantry. Characterised by a much more sophisticated political history than many of the pastoral-agricultural tribes of the eastern coast of Africa, the tribes of Benin nevertheless did not develop the elaborate systems of land tenure which are to be found among European peasantries. They never, as a consequence, formed the massive conservative social force of their European counterparts against the revolutionary movements of the nineteenth and twentieth centuries. By the same token they were never actively enlisted as revolutionary allies as in the Chinese, Vietnamese or Mozambican experiences. The Beninese peasantry either was, for the most part, politically manipulated by politicians keen to exploit tribal rivalries, or remained otherwise politically inert.

The traditional left-wing elements of students and trade-unionists are numerically small in Benin, though they are concentrated in politically critical areas of the southern cities. The evidence is that they formed a significant left opposition to Kérékou's regime, demanding more rapid and comprehensive socialisation measures, more abrupt and comprehensive limitation of relations with the old metropole, and a more embracing attitude toward the other socialist regimes of Europe and Asia. Their opposition has, so far, been effectively contained, though sporadic strikes and student demonstrations have peppered the political history of the past eight years.

The former members of the Beninese elite, the petit bourgeois executives, middle-level managers, small businessmen and professionals, seem to have had a divergence of political fortunes. Many university graduates studying abroad have found work or continued study-opportunities in other African and European societies. The friction with Gabon over the expulsion of several thousand Beninese from there in 1979 is continued evidence that the educated class of this small country still litters much of the West African scene. Many have also joined the right-wing opposition group in exile in France (Front pour la Libération et Renouvellement du Dahomey). Others have managed to find niches for themselves in the burgeoning state enterprises and governmental control agencies established by the government since 1974. Still others have maintained their existence as private independent businessmen, wholesalers and traders without any significant interference from the regime. As is their traditional posture, those who have not officially declared themselves to be in opposition remain cautiously accepting of the *status quo*, while continuing to provide a reservoir for possible right-wing resurgence should the political occasion present itself.

In the midst of all this is the military regime which, with a modest managerial-class alliance of civilians, strives to accomplish the near impossible task of independent development. Embedded in an environment of social classes either indifferent or mildly hostile to its pace (if not direction) of development, the regime must be looked at from the perspective, ultimately, of its own goals. While reducing income inequality and improving educational and health opportunities for a wide spectrum of the population are undoubtedly sincere and worthy achievements of the regime, the primary thrust of its policies from the very outset has been and continues to be the emphasis on autonomy and authenticity, i.e. the nationalistic character of the movement translated now into the solidification of the state. The party structure, the administrative apparatus, the foreign-aid policy and even the ideological positions are geared toward the strengthening of the Beninese state as opposed to the old metropole, class or tribal affiliations, or various supranational organisations.

This should not be very surprising. The foisting of modernity onto a tribal society in the space of two decades creates discontinuities unimaginable and unmodelable in terms of traditional western categories. A political entity previously non-existent, the Beninese 'nation', replete with an entire modern economy, has been created around, and in many instances in spite of, the actual inhabitants of the region and their social relations. As no single class or tribal element was intimately involved in the evolution of these institutions, nor immediately prepared to inherit them from the French, the events succeeding independence should surprise no-one. While the traditional elements of society carried on much as before (planting, herding, harvesting, trading, replanting) the modern sector, the polity and the economy, was left in disarray. A modern institution had to be erected *de novo* to manage these new sections of society. That modern institution was the state and its modern architect was the army. Despite all the declarations of Marxism-Leninism, this is a scenario Benin shares with many African states of all shades on the political spectrum. As in these other cases, the state in Benin has been constructed to manage an economy which itself retains much of its pre-independence character.

The attitudes of socialism and the formalities of authenticity have never enabled the Beninese leadership to wrest the economy from western domination. They will continue to be unable to do so. There are not the prerequisites in Benin to support a modern self-sufficient economy yet. They are too poor in human and non-human resources, too weak in the necessary social institutions and strategically too insignificant to make it worth the while of a major power to attempt to invest them with these necessities. The arm of socialist revolution may be long, even lengthening, but Benin continues, for the time being, to be beyond its reach.

Notes

1. *ASOS*, p. 173.
2. *IMFB*, p. 1.

3. *WBB*, p. 1.

4. *ASOS*, p. 173.

5. *ASOS*, p. 173.

6. *ACR* 1979, p. B619.

7. Hancock 1979, p. 116.

8. *WBB*, page directly following title page.

9. See the summary of Kérékou's address reprinted in the *Daho Express*, 5 December 1974.

10. The historical summary which follows is a synthesis from a variety of sources, most notably: Bebler, 1973; Cornevin, 1965; Pedler, 1979; Ronen, 1975; and Welch, 1970.

11. Ronen 1975, p. 229.

12. Versions of this address appear in various periodicals of the time. For a succinct encapsulation of the speech see *ACR*, 1972-3, p. B581.

13. Ibid., p. B580.

14. This diplomatic liaison was followed directly by an interest free loan of 11,250m CFAF provided by the Chinese Government. See *Daho Express*, 15 January 1973.

15. Ronen 1975, p. 231.

16. *ACR*, 1972-3, p. B584.

17. See the report of these demonstrations in *Le Monde*, 3 March 1973.

18. This summary of the structure is based on a report appearing in *ARB*, 15 April 1974, vol. 11, no. 3, p. 3328.

19. *ARB*, 1974, p. 3458.

20. *ARB*, Economic, Financial and Technical Series, 1974, p. 3328.

21. For a summary of the document see *ACR*, 1977-8, p. B616 and *Afrique-Asie*, 3 March 1980.

22. See the report of this attempt in *Jeune Afrique*, 27 February 1980.

23. The exposition in this section relies heavily on the information contained in *IMFB* and *WBB*. The tables have been drawn exclusively from the *IMFB*.

24. See *ARB*, Economic, Financial and Technical Series, 1977, p. 4490.

25. See *The Daily Nation*, Nairobi, 11 August 1978.

26. *WBB*, p. vii.

27. *IMFB*, p. 72, table.

28. *ACR*, 1978-9, p. B599.

29. *IMFB*, Tables on pp. 87, 89, and 90.

30. *Marchés Tropicaux*, 23 June 1978.

31. *IMFB*, p. 18.

32. This section, as the last one, draws heavily from *IMFB* and *WBB*.

33. The West African Currency Union, UMOA, was one of several institutions born during the era of independence for France's former African colonies. The aims of these new institutions were the formalisation of the economic relations among the various newly independent states, and between them and the former metropole. A West African Customs Union (UDEAC) was established in June 1959 (disbanded 21 May 1962) and the UMOA itself began in May 1962. The original document inaugurating the UMOA was signed by: Ivory Coast, Dahomey, Upper Volta, Mauritania (who withdrew in 1972), Niger, Senegal and Togo. The purposes of the Union were declared to be:

(i)   to establish a single currency unit, the issuing of which will be entrusted to a joint body (to become the BCEAO);

(ii)   centralisation of currency reserves;

(iii)   to guarantee the free circulation of currency notes within the union;

(iv)   to maintain the free conversion of currency into French francs (guaranteed

by France).
A similar arrangement was concluded for France's former Central African colonies. This resulted in the Central African Customs Union (UDEAC). Mali, as of 1962, and Madagascar, as of 1973, have had their own individual semi-formal arrangements with France concerning currency relations.

34. *WBB*, p. 90.
35. See *ACR*'s for 1976-7, 1977-8 and 1978-9.
36. *ACR*, 1977-8, p. C189.
37. *The African Communist* no. 81, 2nd quarter 1980, p. 79.

7 THE PEOPLE'S REPUBLIC OF CONGO

Andrew Racine

The People's Republic of the Congo (formerly Moyen Congo of French Equatorial Africa) lies on the west coast of central Africa, cradled for 1,000 km. by the Congo river and its tributary the Oubangui. A scant one and half million people[1] live in the 342,000 square km. between Zaire to the south and Gabon, Cameroon and the Central African Republic to the north. The rate of population increase between 1970-8 was 2.6 per cent p.a.[2] Kravis *et al.* (1978) estimated the 1970 *per capita* GDP to be $546 in the dollars of that year. The current figure is calculated to be 152,333 CFA francs ($758 US).[3] In 1974-8 real GDP at market prices fluctuated greatly, averaging an overall decline of 1.8 per cent for the period. The foreign-trade participation ratio is about 31 per cent.

French remains the official national language, despite the decision of the Third Extraordinary Congress of the ruling Congolese Worker's Party (PCT) in March 1979 to replace it with either Lingala or Munukutula. The official currency is the CFA franc, with an exchange rate, as of July 1980, of 206.9 to the US dollar.[4] About half the population are animists and close to half are Christian, with a small group of Muslims in the north. Though the 1973 Constitution guaranteed the freedom of religious expression in 1977, all faiths except the following were banned by decree: Catholic, Congo Evangelical Church (Protestant), Simon Kibanga Prophet, Salvation Army, Islam, Lassy Zephrin Prophet and Terynkyo (Japanese).

Domestic Politics[5]

Its long (in an African context) commitment to scientific socialism notwithstanding, the Congo has seemed content to sit back and watch as, over the past several years, former Portuguese colonies and countries on the Horn have moved past on their various paths leftward. Unstinting in its encouragement of these results, the Congo itself remains caught in a neocolonial economic relationship with the West from which it has been unable or unwilling to separate. An historical overview provides a logical departure-point for an analysis of this society perpetually, as it were, on the brink of socialism.

230

From Independence to the Fall of Youlou

The territory of the Moyen Congo which gained autonomy (under provisions of the *loi cadre*), during the territorial assembly session in November 1958, was an arbitrary geographical designation, inherited from French rule, enclosing a plurality of ethnically related but fiercely independent peoples.

The four principal ethnic communities, all Bantu, had a history of autonomy from one another stretching back hundreds of years by the time of independence. The Bakongo living in the south (and stretching across the border into present day Zaire) represented in 1962 almost 50 per cent of the population of the country. Their largest local sub-tribe, the Lari, dominated the region around Brazzaville and emerged, under the leadership of Fulbert Youlou, as the major force in the Union Démocratique de Défense des Intérêts Africains (UDDIA) after the 1956 legislative elections. The Batéké and Boubangui tribes inhabited the centre of the country where the Mbochi (a Boubangui subtribe from around the Alima river) were the earliest politically-organised cadre benefiting from the influence of early twentieth-century French missionary zeal. Part of their electoral success may derive from the tactical decision of their political leader, Jacques Opangault, to ally his party, the Mouvement Socialiste Africain (MSA), with the French Socialist Party. The coastal people, the Vili (Pointe Noire region), led initially by Jean-Félix Tchicaya, were the first to organise a wholly Congolese political party, the Parti Progressiste Congolais (PCC).

Though, as in Dahomey, political parties, indeed politics itself, began as little more than a vehicle for the expression of ethnicity, by 1960, when independence was declared, it appeared as if Youlou, through some adept political manoeuvring and the judicious use of coercive measures, had managed to forge a degree of unity among the divergent Bantu tribes of the young country. Youlou's fatal strategic error was to assume that unity, at the level of the political elite, on the questions of inter-tribal relations implied more wide-ranging agreement of the mass of people with governmental policy. This was not the case. From the very beginning of the Congo's existence as an independent state, the trade union and youth movements were recruited from among the young, well-educated urban population, and organised a coherent, formidable left-wing opposition to the government. Links between these groups may be illustrated by the close relationship of the Confédération Générale Africaine du Travail (CGAT) with the avowedly Marxist Union de la Jeunesse Congolaise

(UJC). Some of the leadership of the CGAT, which received most of its operating funds from the French CGT, also served in the UJC which had open ties to the French Communist Party. For the three years of Youlou's tenure of office the Congo remained largely a client of French business interests. The peasantry was, chiefly, neglected, while civil service rolls in the major cities mushroomed, enticing a massive rural exodus to the cities. Many were disappointed, and unemployment rates leapt up. Government officials, meanwhile, grew rich and indifferent to the politically uninfluential mass of the population. Ultimately a direct confrontation between a temporarily united labour movement and the President of the Republic brought these issues to a head. A general strike followed by three days of mass demonstrations in Brazzaville from August 13-15 1963 culminated in Youlou's resignation from the office of the Presidency. To this day these days are referred to, in the Congo, as 'les trois glorieuses'.

Alphonse Massemba-Débat, a Bakongo and the then Speaker of the National Assembly, assumed leadership of a newly created National Revolutionary Council (CNR) in an atmosphere of unity among the various opponents to the former regime. The National Revolutionary Movement (MNR) became the sole political party, and the state structure was reorganised along the lines of the French Gaullist Republic. An indirectly elected President was granted power to select and dismiss the Premier and other ministers and, under certain circumstances, to dissolve the legislature. Parliament, made up of deputies serving five-year terms, remained subordinate to the CNR, itself a Presidential instrument.

Massemba-Débat's Years: 1963-8

Almost from the moment the elections in December 1963 were completed, the executive of the new administration, Massemba-Débat and his Premier, Pascal Lissouba, found itself outflanked on the left by a radical Assembly and an even more radical rank-and-file party membership. Efforts to co-opt the nation's youth and labour movements by institutionalising the former into a wing of the party (JMNR), and the latter into an all-encompassing union, the Confédération des Syndicats Congolais (CSC), backfired, as each of these organisations became a launching-pad for attacks on the government.

The creation of state enterprises to handle the agricultural exploitation of the north, and to assume control of the national airline; the establishment of diplomatic relations with Peking, Moscow, Prague and Belgrade; the cultivation of ties with North Korea, North Vietnam and Cuba all failed to impress the MNR rank-and-file, who by 1964 succeeded in defining the party's policy as one of achieving economic independence through the application of scientific socialism. They denounced, at the same time, the free enterprise system, and demanded the removal of foreign control over areas of trade and agricultural development. Naturally the loans the Congo was then receiving from China and the USSR were considered to be fraternal assistance, and thus exempt from this criticism.

Though the administration was relatively powerless in the face of this leftist challenge, the Army was becoming increasingly impatient with the radicals, particularly with the militia of the JMNR, and with the civil defence corps which was being trained, at the time, by Cubans. When Lissouba resigned in 1966 he was succeeded by Ambroise Noumazalaye, the General Secretary of the MNR and a man generally considered to be a staunch Marxist. He was to discover the limits of the authority of the left in the Congo when he decided in late June to demote the popular paratroop commander, Captain Marien Ngouabi, while Massemba-Débat was temporarily out of the country. The Army responded by mutinying on 27 June, sacking the headquarters of the JMNR, kidnapping its commander-in-chief, and forcing the Noumazalaye government to take refuge in the Brazzaville sports stadium. Notice had been served. Ngouabi was quietly reinstated though the JMNR militia and the civil defence corps remained, for the time being, intact.

The final reckoning between the Army and the left had to wait another year and a half, until the increasingly conservative policies of Massemba-Débat's regime had widened the rift between the government and its leftist critics sufficiently to provoke a serious incident. When the congress of the Union Générale des Elèves et Étudiants Congolais met in July 1965 to denounce Massemba-Débat as having capitulated to the imperialists, he responded by arresting dozens of alleged 'Maoists' (including, curiously, Ngouabi), dissolving the legislature and the Politburo of the MNR, and announcing that until new elections were held, he would rule by decree.

This decision effectively alienated him from the Army, which lost no time in promptly freeing Ngouabi and establishing its own control over the government via a twelve-man directorate within the CNR, allowing Massemba-Débat to remain nominally Head of State. The organised left, sensing a *putsch*, erupted. Fighting broke out on 29 August and Massemba-Débat withdrew altogether to allow the Army to settle accounts with the JMNR radicals. When the dust settled three days later, the Army emerged victorious, arrested what was left of the JMNR leadership, impressed its militia into the regular Armed Forces along with the civil defence corps and, for good measure, dismissed the CSC executive leadership. Local military Committees for the Defence of the Revolution were set up throughout the country alongside local organs of the MNR. A new era in Congolese politics had begun.

Ngouabi's Reign 1968-77

The chairman of the new directorate within the CNR, Marien Ngouabi, was said to have begun his education in Marxian thought while he was paratroop commander in Brazzaville during the period 1963-6. Unlike many other African leaders, Ngouabi's ideological perspective was socialist in a classically European mould. His statements on the subject are instructive.[6]

> There is only one socialism — scientific socialism, the foundations of which were laid by Marx and Engels . . . One can speak of African ways to socialism, but certainly not of an African socialism.

As if to emphasise the difference between scientific socialism and African socialism, Ngouabi deliberately embraced that aspect of classical Marxism shunned by African socialists, i.e. the class struggle:

> Our analysis is always premised on historical materialism, the basis of which is the law of class struggle, the motive force of history . . . In the Congo, the most exploited classes, in the framework of the confrontation between the people and imperialism, are the working class and its ally, the peasantry. That is why they are more interested than any other class in winning independence and refashioning society.

'Refashioning society' began only a year and a half after Ngouabi acceded to power, when the name of the country, the party, the design of the flag and the structure of the constitution were all changed in one stroke at the turn of the year 1969-70. The new party, the Congolese Worker's Party (PCT), with its 30 member Central Committee and eight member Politburo, would exercise control over the government through a Council of State chaired by the President of the party who was empowered to appoint and dismiss members of the Council. The Constitution of the People's Republic of the Congo declared all

sovereignty to belong to the people, though it contained no provision
for a National Assembly since, according to one member of the
Council, the people 'can entrust to the Central Committee of the Party
... the formulation of laws and rulings'.[7]

Though proclamation of the People's Republic inevitably frightened
off foreign investors fearful of subsequent nationalisations, the
country's economy as the 1970s commenced was still dominated by
large foreign companies which benefited from an exceptionally
tolerant system of fund-transfer authorisation. The state's participation
was restricted to the export of certain commodities such as coffee and
cocoa and the marginally significant trade with eastern bloc countries.
When nationalisations eventually began, they were confined to infrastructural concerns (the ports of Brazzaville and Pointe Noire along
with the rail links between them, and the civil aviation company);
the unprofitable northern timber concerns and, most notably, the four
major French sugar-producing concerns (in 1970). Concurrently (that
is, in the period 1970-3) Ngouabi's government negotiated to receive
over 8,333 million CFAF-worth of aid from the European Community
and deliberately encouraged foreign exploitation (albeit with 20 per
cent state participation) of Congo's offshore oil deposits. European
firms were also engaged to participate in a variety of commercial
ventures, ranging from fishing (Italians) to oil refining (Belgians).
No one remained more aware of the nature of the Congolese economy
than Ngouabi himself, who declared in 1973 that the Congo was 'still
a neo-colonialist state today, in its institutions, administration and
management. It therefore serves the interests of the French bourgeoisie
and strengthens the positions of the local lackeys of imperialism.'[8]

Despite all this, the Congo, like Benin, felt free, indeed obliged to
pursue leftist political avenues. It established diplomatic relations with
the GDR (1970), Hungary (1970), the PRG of South Vietnam (1969),
and set up headquarters in Dolisie in the southern part of the Congo,
for the Angolan MPLA. It even signed economic and military agreements with the USSR, Cuba, Bulgaria and China, none of which
inhibited Ngouabi from maintaining a firm control on the domestic
leftist movement, and of flouting its wishes when it was convenient to
do so. Though Ngouabi ordered participation in the boycott of the
Montreal Olympics, due to the presence of South Africa in the Games,
he also continued to trade with the white-ruled regime and to remain
on good terms with the more conservative black governments in the
region, notably Ivory Coast and Zaire. Ngouabi even went so far as to
complain of the alleged establishment of a Central African Communist

Party, designed, he stated, for the purpose, among other things, of overthrowing the PCT.[9] Statements such as that, plus frequent purges of the labour movement and student groups (particularly when the former threatened to exert political power in a general strike), combined ultimately to provoke an attempted *coup* by disaffected left wing elements of the government in February 1972. That it took another year of determined governmental effort to track down the *coup*'s leader, Ange Diawara, while he remained at large in the region surrounding Brazzaville, might testify to the degree of mass discontent with some of Ngouabi's policies.

Certainly the Army felt itself incapable of trusting the rank-and-file of the party and its popular constituency. When Ngouabi was assassinated in 1977, the Army immediately abrogated the major attempt of his regime to establish a popular base — the 1973 Constitution, which had provided not only a National Assembly, but an Assembly Speaker who was nominally second in command to the President, and designated to succeed him if the office was, for some reason, vacated prematurely. The motives (for instance, ethnic rivalry, political differences, personal ambitions) and circumstances surrounding Ngouabi's murder in the Presidential Palace have never been satisfactorily explained. But the result was the rapid consolidation of the already dominant position of the Army in the government, and an abrogation of Articles 3, 4 and 5 of the 1973 Constitution which had provided for the existence of representative assemblies at the national and local levels, and the principle of election by universal suffrage and secret ballot of all organs of the State.[10]

Since 1977

Brigadier-General Joachim Yhombi Opango, who assumed chairmanship of the eleven-member military committee of the Central Committee of the PCT established in the wake of Ngouabi's death, inclined, given the precarious balance the Congo had been striking between leftist form and actual Western economic dependency, toward the economic exigencies of the moment and opted for closer ties with the West. He re-established relations with the US after a twelve-year hiatus, brought back the moderate Finance minister, Henri Lopes, and invited the French to build a brewery in Brazzaville (privately owned) and explore the possibilities of a third offshore oil field. Notwithstanding these moves he took care, in the name of his predecessor, to maintain a correct (i.e. leftist) foreign policy posture: he signed friendship and co-operation treaties with Angola and Benin,

extended recognition to the Polisario movement and continued close
ties with USSR, GDR, Cuba and China. His past history as the
commander who quashed Diawara's attempted leftist *coup*, coupled
with his lavish lifestyle and lukewarm enthusiasm for leftist policies,
led, inevitably, to his removal, this time in a democratic 'palace *coup*',
which brought the First Viçe-President and Defence Minister, Denis
Sassou Nguesso, to power in February 1979. At the same time the
military committee was dissolved and the 1973 governmental structure
with representative assemblies was reinstituted.

Nguesso may be the first representative of the rank-and-file of the
left to come to power in the Congo. His close ties with the radical
student movement and the November 1971 uprising may have been
responsible for his having been purged from the Politburo the
following month. A career Army officer, he is also known to have close
personal ties to the union movement and to have been a frequent
visitor to Moscow and Havana, as well as the man who received General
Heinz Hoffman as head of the visiting East German military delegation
in 1978. Like Ngouabi before him he stresses, in his ideological
statements, the importance of class struggle.[11]

> The PCT considers that there are real social classes in Africa which
> are fighting among themselves. This struggle is the basis for the
> development of African society and other societies . . . Our party
> is convinced that there is no African socialism, nor can there be any.
> There is one socialism, which is scientific socialism, Marxism-
> Leninism.

He, as well, acknowledges the importance to the Congo of other
socialist countries:

> The very existence of the socialist community enables such peoples
> as ours . . . to advance to socialism with support from the socialist
> community.

During the Third Extraordinary Congress of the PCT, held one
month after Opango's removal, resolutions were adopted to break
away, on an economic level from the 'international capitalist division
of labour'. The question remains whether or not Sassou Nguesso will
find it possible to implement such a policy. Already in 1979 agreements
were signed with AGIP of Italy for uranium prospecting and exploitation, and with US and Canadian oil companies for further offshore oil

exploration. Franco-African summits have also continued to be duti-
fully attended, despite verbal hostility to French imperialism. Socialism
for the Congo seems no closer than the horizon and, like the horizon,
recedes with each forward step.

Domestic Economics[12] (see Table 7.1)

The decision to pursue a socialist path of development was, happily for
the Congo, complemented by the discovery of offshore oil in 1969.
These two developments allowed the leadership to flirt with unprofitable state-controlled enterprises in agriculture and manufacturing, and
to do so on a scale which, over the years, generated powerful pressures
toward urban migration and increased private expenditure. Yet there
was no simultaneous investment in agricultural or other infrastructure,
necessary to maintain those economic trends. The latter half of the
1970s was marked by a general stagnation following the oil boom of
1973-4. There were fiscal crises resulting from a combination of the
marked expansion of an inefficient public sector, the rise in civil service
outlays, the lack of sufficient managerial manpower and the
uncertainty of oil revenues due to technical difficulties of extraction.
The government has recently begun to overcome these by the
rescheduling of external debt and the re-establishment of secure oil
production.

The Primary Sector

Half the Congolese earn their living in agriculture, where nine out of
ten continue to farm small, private plots using traditional methods.
Despite the number of people involved, only 11 per cent of GDP
originated in agriculture (this when forestry is added to its
contribution) over the period 1974-8,[13] and for that same time the
amount of food crops marketed in urban areas, where fully 40 per cent
of the population resides, increased by only 1 per cent p.a.[14] Given
substantial net urban migration, and a population growth rate of 2.6
per cent p.a., it is no surprise that Congo remains an importer of food,
particularly the favourite urban staple, rice.

The traditional governmental neglect of private farmers in favour
of support for large-scale state farms (like the one built in 1971 with
Chinese technical assistance and costing 300 million CFAF) has, since
1978, begun to give way to schemes designed to boost the incentives
of the private farmer. In that year a fund, established from taxes levied

Table 7.1: Congo: Gross Domestic Product (in billions of CFA francs of current prices)

	1974	1975	1976	1977	1978	1979[a]
Gross Domestic Product	137.0	159.6	173.4	181.7	202.2	228.5
Total of which						
agriculture and forestry	15.0	18.1	19.4	22.9	25.6	28.7
mining	32.6	25.8	31.0	27.3	33.8	40.9
industry and construction	21.6	27.1	28.3	26.9	33.7	38.2
transport and communications	28.6	33.2	33.6	38.0	41.7	47.0
commerce	17.4	21.2	22.4	25.3	27.6	31.4
government services	14.1	21.8	21.9	24.3	24.7	27.2
import taxes	7.7	12.4	16.8	17.0	15.1	15.1
Per cent change in						
nominal GDP	33.5	16.5	8.6	4.8	11.3	13.0
real GDP	15.9	−1.9	−0.1	−5.3	7.4	5.6

a. Forecast.

Sources: IBRD (1974-6); and IMF staff estimates, 1977-9, taken here from *IMFC*, p. 57.

on salaried workers, was begun with the aim of stabilising producer prices and providing credit for agricultural development. Collective production and marketing techniques are encouraged through a food crop agency (OCV) and a cash crop agency (OCC), but these efforts are not stressed too enthusiastically.

ONCPA, the public board responsible for marketing cash crops (notably coffee and cocoa), has, over the past five years, reaped enormous profits by setting producer prices well below actual export prices for these goods (for instance, the estimated 1978-9 producer price for coffee was 150 CFAF per kg, while the export price for it was 550 CFAF per kg; the comparable prices for cocoa were 200 CFAF per kg and 685 CFAF per kg).[15] Some of these profits, in order to boost agricultural efficiency, have been ploughed back into the sector in the form of road improvements and the provision of farm inputs, but very little of ONCPA profits find their way back to the farmers. Output of coffee and cocoa has consequently declined and the latter is being smuggled in increasing volumes over the border to be marketed in Cameroon.

Forestry, the principal export earner of the pre-oil era, still accounts for 10 per cent of export revenue (less than 5 per cent of GDP)[16] even though it has yet to recover from the effects of the severe 1975 recession in the wood industry. Today with most of the accessible southern forests depleted, the industry is more and more plagued by the infrastructural inefficiencies associated with exploration of the northern redwood groves. Of the four types of firm in the industry (state-owned, domestic private, foreign private and mixed) the latter two account for 70 per cent of the industry's output.[17] Since 1975 the Congolese Wood Office (OCB), a state board, has had a monopoly on the export of wood, buying logs from foreign and domestic producers at a 'beach price' at Pointe Noire and selling them to European buyers with representatives at the port. Sales to local expatriate producers are at preferential f.o.b. prices, taking into account their domestic investment effort.

Despite recent efforts, with Cuban and Soviet technical assistance, to increase production on the large state cattle farms, 75 per cent of beef domestically consumed must be imported.[18] Commercial fishing is carried out by SICAPE (a mixed state and private Italian concern). Local consumption of 30,000 tons annually exceeds the catch by 50 per cent, necessitating the importation of salted fish. Nevertheless the entire catch of tuna is annually exported to a US customer.

Manufacturing and Mining

Since the late 1960s the state has been increasing its participation in the manufacturing sector (representing 10 per cent of GDP)[19] in an effort to maintain employment levels and expand state control of the economy. The results, in general, have been dismal. While the private sector (confined to activities such as brewing, soap-making, shoe production, etc.) grew at a steady 7 per cent p.a. in 1967-76, textiles, sugar, flour milling, cement and glass production all evidenced severe signs of deterioration. Sugar production had, by 1977, become so critical (down to 10,000 tons from 95,000 tons in 1969 before the nationalisation)[20] that SIACONGO, the state enterprise for agricultural processing, was forced to reorganise and divide into three subsidiaries. The state textile company SOTEXCO (begun in 1968 with Chinese assistance) was forced to shut down in 1977. The following year a Swiss consortium was engaged to finance recovery plans for state enterprises. According to the arrangement, CIDOLOU, the state cement plant at Loutété (established in 1968 with a grant from the GFR), received an infusion of 400 million CFAF, and SICAPE, the fishing company, received 200 million CFAF. Since 1977 when capacity utilisation in state firms was running between 25 and 40 per cent,[21] some improvement has been noted in providing new capital, trimming work-forces and improving management, occasionally with foreign assistance (as the 1979 contract with a French management company to restart the Pointe Noire glass factory illustrates).

The mining sector (petroleum and non-petroleum) represented, by 1978, 17 per cent of GDP and a full 69 per cent of export earnings.[22] Since the disastrous flooding of the French-owned potash mines at Hollé in 1977, non-petroleum mining has been dominated by USSR, principally in the M'fouati lead and zinc mining and enrichment plant, and the Sounda-Kakamoueka gold mine. Both have experienced production problems since 1977, the former due to inadequate fuel supply, the latter to depletion of reserves.

Two European-dominated mixed enterprises, Elf Congo (80 per cent French, 20 per cent Congo) and Agip Recherches (Italian-Congolese), work the three offshore oil deposits. At present all three fields are productive (yielding a combination output of 2.6 million tons in 1979), but estimates are that the Emeraude field has already been nearly depleted of extractable reserves (11.6 million of a possible 15 million tons had been pumped out by 1979);[23] the Loango field will have dried up by 1985; and the new Likouala field will only provide an annual 1.5 million tons a little beyond 1985. The entire current output of crude is exported to Brazil, US, Spain and the GFR. Since the Belgian-built oil refinery at Pointe Noire has yet to begin operations, the Congo continues to have to import refined petroleum products for domestic use.

Commerce, Transportation and Credit

Certain vital consumer commodities (salted fish, rice, tomatoes and salt), whose retail prices are fixed by the government, along with several less important commodities, are imported and distributed in a monopoly arrangement accorded to the National Office of Commerce (OFNACOM). This office competes with private wholesalers for the distribution of other goods.

A monopoly of the importation and distribution of petroleum products has been exercised by HYDROCONGO since 1973, when the government effectively nationalised the activities of Shell, Mobil, Texaco, Total and Transcogaz. The government also fixed the retail prices of these products. Financial difficulties plaguing HYDROCONGO and OFNACOM over the past five years have led them to default on their tax payments to the central government, which itself has been unable to meet its subsidy allocations to them due to its own liquidity problems. SNE, the state electricity producer, is able to meet requirements for the Niari Valley with the added output of the Chinese financed and constructed dam on the Bouenza River, but some of Brazzaville's electricity needs must still be met by imports from Zaire.

Commercial transport throughout the river, rail and port system of the Congo has been consolidated in the Transcongolese Communications Agency (ATC) which, since its creation in 1969, has been the recipient of large quantities of Western aid (chiefly from the World Bank, France, Saudi Arabia, Canada and Kuwait) directed at modernising its equipment (this has amounted to over 21,000 CFAF since 1971).[24] The timber recession of 1975 and the Hollé mine closure of 1977 severely decreased revenue from rail transport, while large debts from the investment programme remain outstanding.

Congo shares a common central bank, the BEAC, with four other francophone states in the region: Chad, Gabon, Cameroon and the Central African Republic. As members of the Communauté Financière Africaine, these states share a common currency — the CFA franc, whose value is pegged to that of the French franc by agreement with the French Treasury at a rate of IFF = 50 CFAF. Two commercial banks, the Union Congolaise des Banques (capital of 700 million CFAF of which the government holds 51 per cent) and the Banque Commerciale Congolaise (capital of 850 million CFAF, of which the government holds 57.8 per cent) operate in the country, in addition to the Central Bank and the National Development Bank (BNDC). Of the BNDC's capital, 73.6 per cent is held by the government, 18.1 per cent by the French aid agency CCCE, and 8.3 per cent by the BEAC.[25]

Prices and Wages

A two-tier price control system has been in effect since 1972. Certain basic commodities (for instance, meat, rice, cement, petroleum, salt) are subject to fixed retail prices determined by the government. Increases in these prices are rare. A two-year experiment with uniform, fixed retail prices for the entire country proved untenable, as OFNACOM was constantly undersold by private traders in areas where transportation costs were low. Now fixed retail prices vary regionally. The second type of control is one of fixed profit margins ranging from

20 per cent to 35 per cent. Prices for luxury goods are exempt from these controls. Despite these price controls, calculation of trends in a CPI based on Brazzaville upper-income consumption patterns shows an increase of 14.1 per cent in 1977 and 11.6 per cent in 1978, due mainly to sizeable increases in food and energy prices. A new CPI calculated on low and medium income-group consumption patterns indicate for 1978 a more modest 5.6 per cent increase.[26] The guaranteed minimum wage, graded in terms of skill level, received its last increase in 1975, the same year that public sector salary-scales were last upgraded. For those employed by the government civil service, income advancement has depended, since that time, on biennial promotions. Negotiations between management and the sole trade union, CSC, every two years, set the salary scales for employees in state enterprises and private companies. The militance and independence of the CSC has led to salary increases in keeping with augmentations in the cost of living, but far outstripping productivity increases in the state sector.

Planning

Though the state plays a substantial role in the production and distribution activities of the Congolese economy, rather than elaborating formal development plans the country has, since 1968, relied on a series of *ad hoc* investment programmes directed primarily at maintaining or rehabilitating the sagging public sector. Foreign loans provide most of the financing for these programmes, as the government itself, notwithstanding increased revenues from crude oil sales, is in a chronic liquidity crisis.

Foreign Economics (see Tables 7.2-7.4)

The Congo economy's two principal relationships to outside communities may be characterised as financial indebtedness to the West and military dependence on the Communist world. Of these two mortgages, the former is the more immediately burdensome. The fountain of oil may have nourished, but it has also blackened the landscape. While the deficit in civilian trade figures has been improving, thanks to crude oil revenues, from a net deficit of 19.6 billion CFAF in 1975 (a record high) to one billion CFAF in 1978, service payments required for the development of this oil miracle have helped keep the total current account deficit steady at about 60 billion CFAF. At the same time capital accounts have steadily deteriorated, despite increases in external public borrowing, as inflows to the private and state enterprises declined from 32.5 billion CFAF in 1975 to 26.5 billion CFAF in 1978. Since 1976 the government has been forced to finance its growing budget deficit first through payment arrears, and subsequently, where possible, through debt rescheduling. As of 1978 the overall budget deficit had grown to 10.6 billion CFAF, of which the government was simply unable to meet 5.1 billion.[27]

Foreign Trade

UDEAC statistics show the Congo's largest supplier and purchaser to be the European Community, which, for the latter half of the 1970s, continued to provide approximately 70 per cent of annual imports (70 per cent of these goods came from France). Exports to the EEC have been much more erratic in value, as increases due to oil sales have been offset by declines in sugar, timber and potash exports. From 1974 to 1975 the proportion of exports going to the EEC jumped from 29 per cent to 64 per cent, illustrating the effects of oil price rises. The following year, a disastrous one for timber and a mediocre one for oil production, the proportion fell back to 37 per cent. In 1978, 70 per cent of Congo's export goods went to the European Community, only a fraction of which were destined for France.[28] Remarkable trends in trade with other western partners include: simultaneous increases in imports from, and decreases in exports to, other African countries over the past five years; an extraordinary leap in the value of exports to the US, explainable in terms of shipments of crude oil to the US Virgin Islands, and the resumption in 1978 of exports to Israel, with which the Congo had severed relations in 1973.

The People's Republic of China remains a modest but constant supplier, having sold 845 million CFAF-worth of civilian goods to Congo in 1978 and simultaneously having purchased 637.1 million CFAF-worth. Figures given by the Soviet Union and the UDEAC on trade between the Congo and the USSR differ both in magnitude and occasionally in direction of trend over the past several years. Soviet estimates of the value of imports and exports generally exceed the equivalent figures published by the UDEAC. Notable by way of exception, the large jump in Congolese exports to the USSR in 1976-7 (96.1 million CFAF-524.3 million CFAF), an increase which probably represents compensation for large military acquisitions that year, appears as a much more modest increase in the Soviet figures.

Table 7.2: Congo: Balance of Payments, 1975-9 (in billions of CFA francs)

	1975	1976	1977	1978[a]	1979[b]
A. Goods & services	−52.0	−56.9	−50.5	−56.0	−64.2
Trade balance	−19.6	−16.5	−6.3	−1.0	−3.0
Exports, f.o.b.	49.5	52.9	61.5	66.5	73.4
Imports, c.i.f.	−69.1	−69.4	−67.8	−67.5	−76.4
Services (net)	−32.4	−40.4	−44.2	−55.0	−61.2
B. Unrequited transfers (private)	−5.3	−5.5	−6.7	−0.6	−
Current account balance (A + B)	−57.3	−62.4	−57.2	−56.6	−64.2
C. Unrequited transfers (official)	7.4	8.8	5.4	7.7	8.5
D. Non-monetary capital	41.8	37.0	36.6	42.0	48.8
E. Monetary capital	3.0	2.9	1.1	−2.3	1.5
F. Errors and omissions	1.7	8.9	3.9	−2.5	−
G. SDR allocation and trust fund	−	−	0.4	1.1	1.4
Overall balance	−3.4	−4.8	−9.8	−10.6	−4.0
Financing	3.4	4.8	9.8	10.6	4.0
Debt rescheduling	−	−	1.5	3.2	4.3
Postal debt	0.7	1.0	2.1	0.7	−
Arrears	0.5	2.8	4.3	5.1	−1.0
Reserves & related items	2.2	1.0	1.9	1.6	0.7

a. Estimate.
b. Forecast.

Sources: Central Bank; CCA; IBRD; and IMF staff estimates, taken here from *IMFC*, p. 45.

Military Agreements[29]

The three principal suppliers of military training, advisors and equipment to the Congo are France, China and the USSR. Throughout the 1970s France has maintained a low profile, supplying packages of military equipment, including tents and troop transport vehicles, and providing the Congo with a community of military 'coopérants' of indeterminate number. China has signed no less than three military agreements with the Congo over the period 1971-5, with provisions concerning troop training and equipment. The main force of Congo's

Table 7.3: Congo: Foreign Trade, 1974-9 (in millions of francs)

IMPORTS FROM							EXPORTS TO				
	1974	1975	1976	1977	1978	1979	1974	1975	1976	1977	1978
Total[a]	n.a.	69,100	69,400	67,800	67,500		n.a.	49,500	52,900	61,500	66,500
EEC	20,486	23,766	27,314	32,573	38,761		15,800	24,400	16,300	25,300	18,700
of which France	15,308	17,531	18,835	24,857	28,233		5,000	10,300	6,900	5,800	3,200
USSR[b]	(629)	(679)	(886)	(738)	(1,055)		(544)	(668)	(616)	(882)	(854)
Switzerland	337	178	99	248	267		395.7	308	96.1	524.3	39
	93	278	115	379	509						
USA	1,873	1,851	2,022	2,560	2,613		1,153.8	5,007.6	17,123.9	3,576	2,309.5
Israel	–	–	–	–	–		43.6	4.5	–	–	50.1
Japan	599	666	1,170	1,522	1,494		498.6	398.1	422.3	643.0	134.0
People's Republic of China	758	1,207	1,155	512	845		288.4	–	–	249.2	637.1
Africa	1,952	2,294	2,189	2,335	3,573		2,278.6	2,851.4	2,886	2,378.4	1,084

a. *IMFC*, p. 89.

b. Numbers in parentheses derived by converting statistics from *Vneshnyaya Torgovlya* (years 1974-9), converted to CFA francs by c.i.f./f.o.b. shifts of 7.5% and by the exchange rates published in *UN Monthly Bulletin of Statistics*, vol. 34, no. 9, September 1980.

Source: Union Douanière et Economique de l'Afrique Centrale, *Bulletin des Statistiques Générales*, no. 1-2, 1979, unless otherwise stated (taken here from *IMFC*, p. 57).

tanks is comprised of 14 Chinese T62s. Between 1975-6 and 1976-7 the Congo also added three Chinese ex-Shanghai river patrol boats to its Navy. Over the past several years the Congo has been engaged in a sizeable increase of its military arsenal, and indications are that the Soviet Union has been its principal supplier. Beginning with the outright gifts of five Ilyushin-14 transport aircraft in the early 1970s, the Congolese Armed Forces have been further bolstered by a near doubling (24-44) in the number of its Soviet BTR-152 armoured personnel carriers, and the additions of 76 and 100 mm anti-tank guns, several T-59 medium-weight tanks and, most importantly, over the past three years, 10 MIG 15/17 fighter aircraft.

With the exception of a brief peace-keeping role in Chad early in 1980, Congo has had little use for this new weaponry and its relations with all its immediate neighbours (including the powerful Zaire) have been and remain cordial. One cannot but wonder to what extent these 'capital improvements' do more than enhance the prestige and *esprit de corps* of Colonel Sassou Nguesso's most influential constituency.

Foreign Aid (see Table 7.4)

Foreign assistance to the Congo is in the form of grants and loans. The West, principally France, provides grants of merchandise and technical assistance. The proportion of all grants to the Congo which were French in origin reached 68 per cent in 1977.

Communist countries give assistance in a variety of forms. Both China and the USSR have built and currently maintain hospitals in the Congo, and both provide technical assistance in areas as diverse as mining, agriculture and hydroelectric power-stations. Cuba provides equipment and technical assistance to the national sugar company, state cattle farms and the state poultry company. In addition there are hundreds of Congolese students at present being educated in Cuba under a 1964 cultural exchange agreement, and others on similar exchanges in China and the USSR. Altogether for the period 1975-7 Communist countries averaged 15 per cent of all foreign grants, mostly in the form of technical assistance.

Loans to the Congo have steadily increased over the decade, until the accumulated outstanding (including undisbursed) external public medium and long term debt represents close to 90 per cent of the annual GDP (1978 GDP 202.2 billion CFAF; 1978 accumulated external public debt 181.74 billion CFAF). By far the largest percentage (about 57 per cent of the 1978 total) of these loans come directly from other governments, France being the largest creditor.

Table 7.4: Congo: Foreign Aid 1974-9 (in millions of CFA francs)

	1974	1975	1976	1977	1978	1979[a]
GRANTS:[b]						
of which merchandise	781	2,401	1,265	861		
ASECNA	29	48	29	38		
France	–	906	924	240		
EEC	–	709	283	550		
UN/WHO	752	738	29	33		
of which technical assistance	2,661	4,158	5,817	3,341		
ASECNA	463	154	17	20		
France	1,851	2,354	2,601	2,821		
China (People's Republic)	n.a.	n.a.	1,400	n.a.		
Other socialist	n.a.	n.a.	1,255	n.a.		
UN/WHO	347	1,641	490	455		
other	2,080	583	2,272	1,141		
ASECNA	29	13	24	88		
France	549	323	545	597		
Socialist	345	...	785	...		
UN/WHO	145	–	38	20		
EEC	1,012	247	880	436		
total	5,522	7,142	9,354	5,343		
LOANS:[c]						
Suppliers & private banks	25,583	29,624	32,668	44,509	47,315	53,940
International organisations	12,636	12,650	12,201	26,991	30,067	36,885
Governments	45,999	56,741	66,240	94,512	102,362	105,806
Total						
outstanding (including undisbursed)	84,218	99,015	111,109	166,012	181,744	196,631
service payments	5,013	7,427	6,397	8,714	8,307	22,239

a. Forecasts.
b. Source: Central Bank and IMF estimates.
c. Source: Caisse Congolaise d'Amortissement & World Bank estimates (*World Bank Document*, June 1979, pp. 55-6).

Many recent loans have gone to develop the infrastructural network, particularly the Congo Ocean railroad linking Brazzaville to Pointe Noire. A portion of the French loans pays for French teachers and technical assistants, who promptly repatriate most of these funds.

Foreign Policy

Since the Army's coming to power in 1968 the Congo has become something of a bellwether for leftist non-aligned foreign policies in Africa. This may be the area of least cost and greatest practicability in which the military government feels it can make concessions to a well-organised urban alliance of workers and students, besieged as it is by demands for fiscal conservatism from its Western creditors.

Congo was one of the first black African nations to open relations with Eastern European socialist states, China, Cuba and the PRG of South Vietnam, and to sign agreements of cultural exchange with the Soviet Union. The Congo gained for itself in the late 1960s a reputation for independence and radicalism. It confirmed its image of independence by refusing to take sides in the Sino-Soviet dispute for leadership in the Communist world. In some instances it followed China's lead, as when it recognised Prince Sihanouk's Cambodian government in exile in Peking; in other instances it took its cue from the USSR, as when it broke relations with Chile after the 1973 *coup* while China did not. In recent years, especially since its own programme of military investment has accelerated, it may be seen to be tilting slightly in Moscow's favour. It sided with the MPLA, and decisively so, in Angola, and abstained in the vote condemning Moscow's Afghanistan invasion while refusing to join the boycott of the Moscow Olympics. The Congo's leaders, nonetheless, assiduously avoid direct criticism of China, or any socialist regime.

Relations with Western powers have ebbed and flowed over the years. Ties with the UK were dissolved in 1965 over the Rhodesian question, to be resumed again in 1968. The United States was cast in a villainous role in Congolese foreign policy statements from the mid-1960s, when relations between the two countries were broken, until 1977 when they were finally re-established. Portugal as the last colonial power in Africa was denied recognition until 1975, when all her former colonies had gained their independence. Relations with Israel were severed in 1973 before the October war and are still non-existent. Congo's general ambivalence about the West is neatly encapsulated in its attitude towards France, on which it depends for so much economic and cultural support, yet which represents, without question, the most pervasive neo-colonial interest on the continent now that Portugal has withdrawn. Most often Congolese leaders confine their critical remarks to the effect of neo-colonialism in general. France must go out of its way, as when it indiscreetly tried to encourage USA, UK, FRG and Belgium to help it establish a pan-African peace-keeping force in 1978, to incur direct attacks.

In terms of intracontinental politics, the Congo has clearly placed itself well on the left of most states. It has treaties of friendship and co-operation with its two closest Marxist neighbours, Benin and Angola. It was above all, in its most important act of foreign policy, the indispensable penultimate staging post for the Cuban airlift of operational troops in December 1975.[30] UNITA, the Jonas Savimbi-led opposition to the MPLA, has even accused the Congo of sending in troops to fight alongside Angolan government soldiers in their campaign against Savimbi's forces.[31] These accusations have never been confirmed. The year 1978, the year of agreements with Benin and Angola, also saw Opango visit Ethiopia to propose the creation of an anti-imperialist front of progressive African forces, though nothing more has been heard of the proposal. Yet despite its close ties with Moscow's African allies, the Congo has made no attempt further to solidify its ties with USSR and has even reserved the right to differ strongly with its policies on the continent, as with its relentless criticism of the Soviet client, Idi Amin. Much of the Congo's foreign policy, in Africa, as elsewhere, is of symbolic importance.

Conclusions

The Congo today is neither fish nor fowl. From an economic perspective, it is, as its leaders readily admit, a neo-colonial state. Most strategic sectors are in the hands of private foreign capital. Agricultural exports are geared toward the satisfaction of European and American consumer tastes. The country is heavily dependent on vital imports from the former metropole and is indebted to banks, aid, organisations and governments to the point where it is unable to meet interest payments that annually fall due.

Yet from a political viewpoint the country has had, for the past decade, the appearance of, if not an authentic Marxist-Leninist state, then one heading in that direction. While it is true that the Army remains in control of the government (an uncharacteristic role for it in a Communist state), it rules through a Leninist type of party which wholly subscribes to classical Marxian doctrines. Since 1968 successive administrations, furthermore, have striven to earn radical credentials in the foreign policy postures they have adopted. This dichotomy is a condition which cannot long endure. The political costs (among rank-and-file party members and the radical urban elite) of the country's present economic status are too great and the economic consequences of the political avenues that the government has chosen to walk in, too dire.

Entrusting oil and forest exploitation to West Europeans, and allocating scarce acreage to coffee and cocoa, rankles with those elements of the party and the population who wonder how long the struggle for national liberation will have to continue before it is won. These elements, the unions, the students and the unemployed all have histories of political organising and manoeuvring, and are numerous and strategically located. As with Laris and Villis, for the most part, their ethnic differences from the group of northerners who head the Army add a further dimension to their opposition. The Army has been able to avoid a direct conflict with this section of the Congolese, in part because of a deliberate policy of broadening the state's manufacturing and administrative function. These policies, paid for largely by oil revenues, have kept urban unemployment relatively low and urban incomes at an acceptable level.

The Army's effort to appease the left's appetite for socialism, however, is costing the Congo dearly. The agricultural sector, suffering from years of neglect, is hopelessly inadequate to the task of meeting the food needs of the burgeoning urban population. Characteristically ambivalent, the government pours millions of francs into inefficient state farm projects yet cannot bring itself to attempt collectivisation of the peasantry, from which it extracts a surplus through more traditional marketing mechanisms. Fortunately for the Army, the 750,000 people who work the land are politically inexperienced, geographically scattered around a countryside suffering from a frail and inefficient transport and communication network, and thus seemingly destined to confine their protests to minimising planted acreage or maximising smuggling activities. At the present time no active effort has been made by the left opposition to organise this potential source of support.

The Congo's capacity to remain as it is cannot outlast the

exhaustion of the element which makes it all possible — oil. If current projections are accurate, this resource will be depleted within the course of this decade. When that occurs, as the other resources dwindle and the debts remain behind, as opportunities shrink and unemployment escalates, a severe conflict between the ruling Army and the left opposition becomes increasingly likely. The outcome of such a confrontation can only be a matter of speculation. The Congo is unlikely ever to steer a path of strict, non-aligned autonomous development the way Tanzania does, if for no other reason than that too great a segment of the population is too committed to closer alignments with either the East or the West. That being the case, two distinct results of an Army-left struggle may be considered. Either the Army will, after a period of upheaval, abdicate, leaving the field to the real hard-line Marxists, who may cast the country's fortunes in with the CMEA (assuming the CMEA is interested in acquiring what will then be more of an economic burden than a strategic advantage), or a more conservative faction in the Army will emerge to arrest all flirtations with socialist policies and invite the West in on a much larger scale to develop whatever resources the country will still have to offer. This second option would call for a much more severe solution to the problem of urban, radical discontent than simply shipping a few planeloads of schoolchildren off to Havana for some years, every now and then.

Conditions provided by a geological fortuity have afforded the Congolese Army twelve years in which to vacillate between two kinds of society. Very soon a choice between these two will have to be made, and given Congo's historical background the decision is not unlikely to be taken easily or bloodlessly. The dry wells, unfortunately, leave the Congo little alternative.

Notes

1. *UNMB*, vol. 34, no. 9, September 1980.
2. *IMFC* p. v.
3. Calculated with GDP projected for 1979 by IMF 1979, divided by population figures from *UNMB*, and converted to US dollars using *UNMB* exchange rates.
4. *UNMB*, p. 222.
5. This section draws heavily from several excellent historical summaries: Bertrand 1975, and Gauge 1973.
6. These quotations are taken from an interview published in *World Marxist Review*, vol. 18, no. 5, May 1975.
7. Quoted in an article in *Le Monde*, 6 January 1970.

8. Quoted in *Le Moniteur Africain du Commerce et de l'Industrie*, 11 January 1978.

9. *Le Soleil* (Dakar), 25 January 1975. This was presumably a party covering more than one country.

10. For a review of the changes between the 1973 Constitution and the Acte Fondamental of 5 April 1977, see *Année Africaine*, 1977.

11. These quotations are taken from an interview with Nguesso published in *World Marxist Review*, vol. 21, no. 4, April 1978, pp. 58-9.

12. *IMFC*, 13 April 1979, and *World Bank Document*, 1979.

13. *IMFC*, p. 6.

14. Ibid., p. 7.

15. Ibid., Tables VII and V, pp. 63 and 61.

16. *IMFC*, p. 13.

17. *Marchés Tropicaux et Méditerranéens*, 10 November 1978, p. 15.

18. *IMFC*, p. 15.

19. *World Bank Document*, 8 June 1979, p. 38.

20. *Fraternité Matin* (Abijan), 8 June 1978.

21. *IMFC*, p. 16.

22. Ibid., p. 18.

23. Ibid., p. 19.

24. Calculated from figures published since 1969 in *ARB*.

25. *IMFC*, p. 39.

26. *IMFC*, p. 25.

27. *IMFC*, p. 47.

28. Calculated from total exports as quoted in *UNMB*, vol. 34, no. 11, p. 118 and exports to EEC and France, as quoted in *UDEAC Bulletin des Statistiques Générales*, no. 1-2, 1979.

29. The equipment figures for this section are quoted from issues of: *The Military Balance 1974/5-1978/9*, International Institute for Strategic Studies, London.

30. Garcia, 1977 (see bibliography on Angola).

31. News Agency Reports, 4 April 1978.

8 THE DEMOCRATIC REPUBLIC OF MADAGASCAR

Andrew Racine

Separated from the African mainland by the Mozambique Channel, the world's fourth largest island, together with several nearby islands, comprises the Democratic Republic of Madagascar (formerly the Malagasy Republic). This relatively underpopulated land (the mid-1979 population estimate is 8.51 million people living in an area of 226,658 square miles)[1] became, sometime in the first millennium, the home of a racially mixed, semi-south Asian, semi-African population. There are two official languages of the Republic, French and Malagasy; and the religious breakdown of the people also reflects a colonial heritage — 40 per cent are Christian, 31 per cent Muslims, with the rest remaining animists.[2]

The 1978 UN statistics report the *per capita* GDP to be $253[3] (although Kravis *et al.*, 1978, estimates it at $333.9 in 1970)[4] and, whereas the population growth-rate is reported to be close to 3 per cent p.a.,[5] the GDP between 1972-6 grew at only 2.5 per cent annually.[6] The currency unit in the country is the Franc Malgache (FMG), which follows the rate of the CFAF, indicating, despite Madagascar's withdrawal from the franc zone in 1973, that some arrangement remains between Madagascar and the French Treasury. As of October 1980 the value of the FMG was 217.5 to $1 (US).[7] The foreign-trade participation ratio is about 20 per cent.

Domestic Politics[8]

Before Independence

Current anthropological thinking suggests that the Great Island was initially uninhabited, and sometime during the period before about 900 AD was settled by a group emanating from a previously established south-east Asian colony on the east coast of Africa. Two characteristics of the Malagasy support this idea: (a) they all speak an identical language and have identical religious traditions, indicating a cultural uniformity probably predating settlement of the island; and (b) racially there appear to be separate groups — some with obvious African characteristics, others more clearly Asian.

Political unification of the island, attempted as early as the

seventeenth century by Sakalava kings of the north-west coast, was
not fully achieved until the Merina of the central plateau, surrounding
the present day capital of Antananarivo, assisted by the British,
consolidated their rule in the mid nineteenth century. Throughout
the classical period of Merina rule, that is until 1895, the British
presence at court predominated. Children of the elite were educated
in English schools, the army was organised along British principles, the
court was converted to Anglicanism and written Malagasy employed
English phonetics.

Revived Anglo-French competition for colonies at the end of the
1800s resulted in an agreement to cede to France a sphere of influence
in Madagascar in exchange for British supremacy over Zanzibar. This
understanding paved the way for a short period during which
Madagascar became a French protectorate. Outright military conquest
by the French and formal annexation into France's African empire
followed in 1895 and 1896. Colonial rule shepherded Malagasy society
out of its complacency into a relationship with the metropole based
on the transfer of an aggressively accumulated agricultural surplus. A
corps of French nationals, including large scale planters, merchants,
corporate managers and supporting administrators, educators and
technicians was imported to run European concerns and at the same
time preserve Merina hegemony *vis-à-vis* the coastal populations.
Coffee, sisal, banana, clove and vanilla plantations formed the hub of
Madagascar's economy. A compulsory labour system (the *corvée*)
replaced slavery as a means of mobilising peasants for the
infrastructural improvements necessary to the prosperity of European
enterprises. Beneath the upper-level owners and managers of French
origin, the old Merina elites waited for their chance to return to power.
The defeat of France in World War II ignited local opposition to French
authority. One of the first political parties to express outright
nationalist sentiments was the Mouvement Démocratique de la
Rénovation Malgache (MDRM), an instrument of the old Merina elite.
The Merinas' commitment to the goal of independence was
dramatically demonstrated in the famous insurrection of 1947.
Beginning on 29 March, this explosion cost about 80,000 lives and
resulted in the forcible dissolution of the MDRM and the suspension
of active political agitation for independence for a decade. As part of
an effort to separate the coastal populations from the radical nationalist
aspirations of the Merina, the French administration encouraged a more
conservative, *côtier*-[9] dominated party, the PADESM, to fill the void
created by MDRM's abolition.

Political activity revived with the passage of the *loi cadre* in June 1956. Spurred by this measure granting a degree of formal (if not *de facto*) autonomy to French colonies, hard line nationalists, leftist intellectuals and the remnants of the Merina activists of the 1940s coalesced into a party dedicated to rapid independence through negotiation with Paris. Richard Andriamanjato, a leftist intellectual, became the head of this movement, the AKFM. In the meantime, the PADESM had given birth to a successor party, the more moderate, social democratic PSD, inspired by the French Socialist Party and led by a lycée professor, Philibert Tsiranana. Though Tsiranana's party had largely a coastal membership, the support it received from local French administrators, concerned with the fierceness of Merina nationalism, enabled Tsiranana and his associate in the PSD, André Resampa, to gain influential positions on the newly created Council of Government. Their policy of qualified independence for Madagascar linked to continued dependence on France thus became the predominant one.

The referendum to approve the Fifth Republic's arrangement of a French Community of quasi-autonomous former colonies, with strong links to the metropole, received full support from the PSD. The AKFM, and a south-western, leftist peasant group, MONIMA, opposed the proposition. For them it did not go far enough. Madagascar voted with the large majority of former French colonies to approve the referendum. The Malagasy Republic was accordingly proclaimed on 14 October 1958, and Tsiranana became its first President. Two years later, on 26 June 1960, following Mali's lead, the Malagasy Republic gained full independence.

Tsiranana's Rule 1960-72

It would be difficult to overestimate the degree of French control over the new state. Its constitutional structure was transferred largely intact from the Fifth Republic. Two legislative assemblies, elected by universal suffrage, in turn elected a President for a seven-year term (an arrangement amended in 1962 to allow direct election of the President) who, in contradistinction to his French counterpart, was both Head of State and Chief of Government.

Military accords left France the responsibility for training Madagascar's Armed Forces and for helping to provide for the country's defence. Foreign policy understandings ensured, without actual stipulation, that French and Malagasy positions on vital international issues would be in accord. Along with Malagasy, French remained an official language and French teachers and administrators staffed the nation's schools, lycées and universities.

The newly created Malagasy franc was maintained by the French Treasury at a fixed parity with the French franc. The Mint remained in French control. Free convertibility of currencies allowed unhindered repatriation of profits from French enterprises in Madagascar. Various French aid institutions (most important of which was the FAC) provided technical assistance to a wide variety of projects around the island, and favourable trade agreements encouraged the marketing of Malagasy goods in France as well as the reverse.

Commerce and industry on the island were almost entirely under European control. The Compagnie Marseillaise and the Compagnie Lyonnaise dominated import-export activities; together with a third French company, these two giants controlled, as late as 1969, one half the total value of commercialised agricultural production and three-fourths of all exports.[10] Europeans controlled the banks, the construction industry, the manufacture of textiles, the processing of sugar and vegetable oil, the networks of shipping and trucking, and finally tourism as well.

Under Tsiranana's direction during the Republic's first ten years, government and party (PSD) policy permitted the French to consolidate their economic position on the island at the same time as it encouraged the local *côtier* petite bourgeoisie. *Côtier* children became recipients of scholarships to study in France (while the sons and daughters of richer Merina remained at home to get their degrees). *Côtier* youth enrolled in a newly created paramilitary force, trained by the Israelis (the FRS) as a counterbalance to the Merina-dominated regular Armed Forces. *Côtier* merchants and traders captured the local commerce outside the central plateau. Throughout this period advancement of the haute bourgeoisie, largely Merina in composition, was continually frustrated by the overwhelming influence of French businessmen.

Merina discontent alone would probably not have been sufficient to topple Tsiranana in 1972 without the added support of other disaffected groups. Within the ruling PSD itself there was a faction resentful of the French monopoly of business opportunities to the virtual exclusion of Malagasy entrepreneurs. This group was said to receive quiet sympathy from André Resampa. University students, seeing little return on long years of schooling so long as the economy remained in French control; urban unemployed; labour unions from all positions on the political spectrum; and, lastly and most importantly,

regional groupings of an overtaxed peasantry, each came to hold
Tsiranana's regime responsible for their stagnant or deteriorating
circumstances. The beginning of the end announced itself in 1971 in
a full-scale armed uprising against the state by the peasants of Tuléar
province who, in a stroke, destroyed not only the myth of *côtier*
solidarity but the very internal structure of the PSD itself, as Tsiranana,
now in a particularly suspicious mood, had Resampa and his followers
within the party arrested in June on a fraudulent charge of plotting
with a foreign embassy against the state.

The revolt cost 1,000 lives and, while not overturning the
government immediately, gave impetus to many discontented elements
who organised themselves over the succeeding 13 months in Tananarive,
so that when the university and lycée students, led by the medical
school enrolees, went on strike in April 1972 to protest at the colonial
orientation of their education, the seeds sown by the southern peasants
were ready for harvesting. The arrest and deportation of 400 student
leaders, the closing down of the entire educational establishment,
even the shooting of 40 demonstrators by the security forces on
13 May, could not stem the tide, as first the unemployed and
disillusioned members of the capital's population, and later the
white-collar and blue-collar workers of the city joined in the clamour
for a change in government. Finally, on 18 May Tsiranana capitulated,
dissolved the government and, acting as President, granted full
authority to General Gabriel Ramanantsoa, Chief of the Malagasy
Army.

Between the Republics 1972-5

The two fundamental aims of Ramanantsoa's regime, the restoration of
Malagasy control over the economy and the decentralisation and
democratisation of rural policy-making, were ultimately irreconcilable,
though it took time for this contradiction to become openly manifest.

Legitimisation of the transfer of power was a high priority for the
new government. A referendum was organised in October 1972 to
approve formally the transfer of power from Tsiranana and to create a
Popular National Council for Development (CNPD), with advisory
status only, to help the government formulate policy. With 144 elected
members (93 from rural districts where 80 per cent of the population
lived, and 51 from the cities) the CNPD met only twice a year, though
the standing committee had more continuous influence.

If the years of Tsiranana's rule had been marked by economic
stagnation (in the mid 1960s UN statistics portrayed Madagascar as one

of the least dynamic economies in the world) and the impoverishment of the peasantry and urban work force, Ramanantsoa's tenure marked the beginning of a transition of control of this state of affairs out of French hands and into Malagasy ones. Prodded by the leftist parties of AKFM (now, though still mainly bourgeois in composition, more openly Soviet in ideological orientation), KIM (an amalgam of students, unemployed and leftist intellectuals), MONIMA (the south-west rural party responsible in large measure for the 1971 uprising) and MFM (a Marxist outgrowth of MONIMA which allied itself with an organisation of unemployed youth called ZOAM, after the events of 1972)[11] Ramanantsoa's government began taking steps toward the Malgachisation of the economy. Though no private firms (with the exception of the water and electricity companies) were nationalised, the state gradually gained interests in all the commercial banks and the national airline. Many mixed companies (Sociétés d'Intérêt National) were created to extend government control into such areas as the collection and distribution of agricultural products (SWPA), import and export (SONACO), public works contracts (SINTP), and the like. The elite collection of noteworthy Merina bourgeois families was the greatest beneficiary of this policy, as they came to replace French managers, directors and company heads during this transition. The clearer it became that these new organs were less means of democratising the economy and more ends in themselves (for the aggrandisement of the Antananarivo bourgeoisie), the more support for these policies on the part of the left began to wane and the more frequent became conflicts within the government.

Some of the criticism from the left was, however, muted by the new direction taken in foreign affairs. Under the direction of the new Foreign Minister, Didier Ratsiraka, previous ties with France began to be loosened. This took various forms: asserting stricter control over foreign exchange transactions; withdrawing from the franc zone; replacing French administrators in business and education; reintroducing Malagasy as the language for official occasions; compelling nationals to apply for visas and other authorisations to settle and work in Madagascar. The results were dramatic in some cases: 7,000 French nationals left the island between May 1972 and October 1973, foreign investment declined appreciably (only 10 per cent of the Development Plan for 1972-4 was financed externally compared with 45 per cent for the 1964-8 plan).[12] Other initiatives included the rupture of relations with Israel and (thanks to a financial aid-package from the Chinese People's Republic allowing Madagascar to disengage from its financial commitments to Pretoria) with South Africa. Relations were quickly established with the USSR, China, North Korea, the PRG of South Vietnam and Guinea.

Despite these symbolic advances, the real thrust of much of leftist pressure was toward the democratisation of rural life. Colonel Richard Ratsimandrava, the Interior Minister and a product (albeit one with a radical populist orientation) of Tsiranana's *côtier*-dominated era, attempted a revival and renovation of the traditional Malagasy communities known as *fokonolona*. In these pre-colonial organic groupings of local participants, planning common defence, cultural and welfare strategies, Ratsimandrava felt he had found a decentralised structure to replace the old colonial hierarchy of prefectures, subprefectures and communes. Madagascar was divided into 10,498 village communities[13] called *fokotany* each of which elected a local *fokonolona* to make decisions concerning defence, taxation, local development projects, and the like. Above the *fokonolona*, in order of ascending centrality were: the 1,250 Firaisan-Pokotany (equivalent to the colonial subprefecture), the 110 Fivondronom Pokotany (equivalent to prefectures) and the six Faritany or provinces, beyond which lay the CNPD itself. Each level was elected by groups of the level below.

Objections to the new structure originated from elements as diverse as Tsiranana, who saw it as a means of compelling local communities to deal with Merina middlemen in commercial exchanges (thus entrenching further the Merina control over the economy) and the Marxist parties who felt it was a romanticisation of an atavistic institution unequipped to deal with contemporary problems of development, and particularly inappropriate for applications to urban areas. Ratsimandrava was, nevertheless, determined that this was the most efficient way to break the hold of the *comprador* bourgeoisie over the production and distribution of the country's agricultural surplus − a view which directly antagonised other members of the government, including the powerful Regular Army Colonel Roland Rabetafika, as well as Ramanantsoa himself. These two, coming from established Merina families, saw a definite need for centralised state control, as well as a definite role to be played by private enterprise.

By the end of 1974 the two sides to this struggle needed only a specific incident around which to coalesce, in order to bring the disagreement out in the open. In January 1975 the Mobile Police Group obliged them by mutinying over the under-representation of *côtiers* in the force. The left opposition within the government at that moment was formed by Ratsimandrava and Ratsiraka (supported by the AKFM, MONIMA and other leftist parties) while Rabetafika and Ramanantsoa occupied the moderate centre. Members of the standing committee of the CNPD took sides in the dispute with the left opposition thus virtually forcing Ramanantsoa on 5 February to hand over full powers to Richard Ratsimandrava. Six days later the Interior Minister (turned Head of State) was shot dead on a street in the capital.

The Government of Ratsiraka

That same night a 19-member Military Directorate (including within its company Didier Ratsiraka) took over the management of the government. After forcing the surrender of the mutinying police forces, the Directorate turned its attention toward organising a trial to prosecute those accused of complicity in Ratsimandrava's assassination. The trial extended for weeks, revealing plots and sub-plots within the army and the Merina elite, involving foreign companies, and even implicating former government officials. It ended, however, without producing any significant convictions and in June the Directorate dissolved itself, having first elected Ratsiraka as Head of State.

A 40-year-old Naval officer of *côtier* origin yet with important connections to the Merina bourgeoisie, Ratsiraka, at the time of his accession to power, had extensive experience in international affairs gleaned from his three years as Foreign Minister (1972-5), but was virtually unknown among the general public. Educated principally in France (from Lycée Henri IV in Paris right through to the Ecole Supérieure de Guerre Navale), he was without the regional or structural (i.e. party) support typical of traditional Malagasy political figures. With a newly created Supreme Council of the Revolution to help him run the government day to day, and a parallel body, the Military Council for Development (charged with reorganising the Armed Forces into a People's Army of Development to aid in implementing rural development projects), Ratsiraka embarked on a programme to democratise the Army, continue Ratsimandrava's *fokonolona* programme (with modifications) and socialise key areas of the economy. On 17 June all banks, insurance companies and cinemas were nationalised. On 30 June some petroleum refineries and maritime transport companies were taken over by the state. On 1 August the enormous Marseillaise Company was appropriated. Friendships with socialist countries were quickly reinforced, those with the Western powers cooled down.

Ratsiraka then announced a referendum for the last month of 1975 to ratify the establishment of a second Malagasy republic, to be called the Democratic Republic of Madagascar; to approve a new Constitution (based on Ratsiraka's own ideological programme as outlined in his *Boky Mena*, or *Red Book*); and finally to sanction Ratsiraka's new status as President of the Republic. The new Constitution would provide for a seven-year presidential term, a Supreme Revolutionary Council, two-thirds of whose membership would be appointed by the President, and a National People's Assembly of deputies popularly elected for five-year terms. The Assembly was to meet no more than four months of the year and would replace the CNPD in function. The referendum was overwhelmingly approved on 21 December, the new Republic proclaimed on 30 December and Ratsiraka inaugurated as its first President on 4 January 1976. Much of 1976 was spent quietly consolidating the political gains of the new regime. Preparations were made for elections to the various echelons of the *fokonolona* system.

In March the government formed its own political party, the Avant-Garde of the Malagasy Revolution (AREMA), and declared that any party wishing to run candidates for local or national office must be a member of a newly created loose assemblage called the National Front for the Defence of the Revolution. In the 1977 elections for the people's National Assembly AREMA won 112 seats, AKFM secured 16 and VONJY (a minor party) gained seven. When all the elections had been concluded AREMA had 90 per cent of all the seats at the *Fokotany* (most local) level and 94 per cent of the seats at the provincial level, giving the new party enormous control of the political structure at all levels.

Control of the economic dimension of national life proceeded at an even faster rate. By October 1976 state-ownership of businesses had climbed to 61 per cent overall. The State owned 33 per cent of all industrial concerns, and controlled 78 per cent of the exporting business and 60 per cent of importers.[14] The politics of nationalisation were pursued into 1977 and 1978, with the takeover of more import-export firms and the Madagascar Spinning and Weaving Company.

Internal dissent in recent years has not surfaced in the circles of established bourgeois families. They have found in the policies of Malgachisation opportunities to gain positions as upper-level managers and administrators in the flurry of newly created state enterprises. Dissent has emerged among students and the unemployed in urban areas, particularly Antananarivo.[15] In 1976 a strike at the Technical College was forcibly put down, and as a consequence the party MFM was dissolved and its leaders placed under house-arrest. In May 1978 students at the capital's universities went on strike to protest at partiality shown to graduates of *côtier* institutions. Those protests, however were gradually taken over by elements of ZOAM, the organisation of unemployed youth. To put down these disturbances the Army had to be called out, and 150 people were arrested. Since that time the only evidence of internal disquiet has been the references by Ratsiraka himself to various plots to assassinate him and overthrow the government. Usually no arrests are made and no evidence brought to light. As with previous regimes, the success or failure of the present one depends upon the allegiance of the peasantry or at the very least, its quiescence. Events, or the lack thereof, suggest that that, so far, has been secured.

Domestic Economics

The transition over the past few years from an economy controlled by the former metropole to one characterised by self-sufficiency, pervasive state ownership of the means of production and a concerted policy toward the equalisation of incomes among the people has done little to lift Madagascar from its status as one of the world's poorest nations. Its 1978 per capita GNP of $253 represents a 13 per cent decline in real income over the course of the last decade,[16] as the economy has been growing at a rate (2.5 per cent p.a. between 1972 and 1977)[17] inferior to its population (2.8 per cent p.a.).[18] Structural discontinuities accompanying Ratsiraka's rise to power, a strong official aversion to external sources of support or investment, lack of technical progress in improving agricultural productivity and declining private investment (secondary to uncertainty regarding the new government's policy intentions) have all been blamed for the present state of affairs.

The regime has relied, to date, on price manipulation and the creation of centralised agencies of state control to attempt to construct an authentic Malagasy economy out of its colonial inheritance. While urban poor and rural peasants seem to have derived some benefit from these policies, such re-allocation of resources cannot long disguise the underlying dilemma of an economy unable to keep pace with the growth of its population.

Agriculture

The dependence of this sector, which employs over 80 per cent of the active population and supplies 90 per cent of the country's exports,[19] on labour-intensive, inefficient techniques of production, is the greatest obstacle to Madagascar's economic growth. As agricultural production has lagged behind population increases, the importation of food over the years has increased substantially. Rice, the grain consumed at a rate of more than a pound a day per person in Madagascar, has had its level of importation jump from 25,000 tons in 1971 to 200,000 tons in 1978.[20] All told, food imports cost the Malagasy Treasury 4 billion FMG in 1978-9.[21] Nearly half the total value of agricultural output in Madagascar is accounted for by the staple rice.[22] It is cultivated by 70 per cent of the peasantry. Between 1970 and 1977 actual production of this grain increased by 11 per cent, but since most of this increase was due to augmentation of the area under cultivation (which grew at an annual rate of 3 per cent during this period),[23] the overall increase has resulted from recourse to less fertile soils so that output per unit area has, in fact, declined. As less fertile land is exploited, a greater percentage of the harvest has gone to feed the cultivators, so that the proportion of the total harvest actually marketed has slipped from 16-17 per cent in 1970 to 12-13 per cent in 1977.[24] Distribution bottlenecks also persist, despite the creation in 1973 of a national marketing board (SINPA). Production of cassava, the other subsistence crop used in the rural diet, has fared little better.

Among the cash crops, ground-nut production increased 12 per cent between 1970 and 1977 (again through increased area under cultivation) but local consumption kept pace with this use, compromising any increase in industrial processing. Cotton and tobacco production have both suffered from the flight of European planters (cotton production was down 20 per cent from 1979 to 1980, necessitating the importation of 3,000-3,500 tons simply to supply industry's needs),[25] while sugar-cane production has remained at virtually the same level for seven years as refining capacity has been saturated during that time. Coffee, the major export crop occupying the efforts of one-fourth of the population along the east coast, remains in the hands of small, private producers. Their inefficient methods restrict output to 370 kg per hectare (compared with 600-700 kg per hectare in Tanzania, for example).[26] Vanilla sales have suffered recently from the development of a synthetic substitute (Madagascar accounts for 90 per cent of the world's sales of natural vanilla) and even the Cape Pea, once a strong export commodity, has seen its production driven down by substitutes from 28,000 tons in 1972 to 11,200 tons in 1978.

Faced with these difficulties, the government has relied chiefly on the traditional weapon of price manipulation in its efforts to increase output. It has given secondary importance to the popularisation of new techniques of production, expansion of irrigation networks or even the increased importation of fertiliser (which actually fell from 30,000 tons in 1970 to 14,000 tons in 1976).[27] Rice-producer prices have increased 233 per cent from 1973-8.[28] Cassava prices are also up significantly, while prices of agricultural goods destined for export have been kept lower in an effort by the government to profit from the margin between producer price and sales price, while limiting production of goods for which marketing mechanisms are still inadequate.

Efforts at socialising production have been given even less attention. Both in crop-raising and in cattle-rearing they have met with peasant resistance and therefore have not been pursued with much vigour. In 1976-9 only some 50 co-operatives, involving about 1500 people, were established.

Industry

The state has taken a more active role in attempting to reshape the industrial sector into a form more in keeping with the declared socialist policies. This aspect of the economy continues nevertheless to be weak, and bear the marks of its colonial origins.

In May 1978 a Charter of Socialist Enterprises was promulgated applying to all 'economic units' where activities were deemed of strategic importance in building the socialist state. Co-ordination of the policies of these units in conformity to a national plan is handled now by Orientation Councils, made up of delegates from the National Assembly, the central government, the firm's management and its workers. Other areas of increased government control include the firing of workers, which cannot now be done without the (rarely granted) approval of the central administration; the raising of input factor prices, such as the minimum wage and the prices of certain raw materials; and the setting of maximum import profit-margins. The object of these policies is a sector contributing only 14 per cent to the GDP and employing no more than 25,000 people.[29] As was the case during the period of French control, the industrial sector is dominated by enterprises processing agricultural produce: cotton, cane sugar, tobacco, etc. Together these represent 70 per cent of industrial activity in Madagascar. The growth of manufacturing has been irregular since 1972, with some industries (tobacco-processing, paper production)

doing better than others (textiles and construction, for example).
Seasonal variation in the availability of raw material, restrictions on
the importation of necessary spare parts (industrial equipment imports
fell from 6.7 billion FMG – 1975 prices – in 1972, to 2.8 billion
FMG in 1976),[30] the old vintage of most machinery, the decrease in
private investment, and even in some cases the weakness of demand,
have all hampered growth.

The mining sector (0.6 per cent of GDP in current prices from
1972-7) has stagnated, along with the rest of the economy. Much of
this (in particular with respect to the exportation of chromite since
1974) is due to softening in global demand for these goods rather than
inherent problems in the extractive industries. Since 1975 the island's
mining concerns have been managed by a state company, SONAREX.

Finance, Wages and Prices

Budgetary policy over the last several years has reflected the
consequences of Madagascar's decision to withdraw from the franc zone
in 1973, and redesign the investment code. Assuming control of many
theretofore private enterprises, and at the same time expanding public
services, the central government rapidly increased its expenditure-
burden, while decreased foreign trade and the abolition of payroll and
animal head-taxes decreased revenues simultaneously. Faced with a
liquidity squeeze, Ratsiraka's reaction was to order the imposition of
restrictions on the repatriation of domestically-generated profits and to
drastically curtail imports after 1975. These policies allowed
Madagascar to remain relatively unburdened by foreign indebtedness
at the cost of severely restricting economic growth. To insulate the
population from some consequences of the stagnation the government
adopted an income and price control strategy. Minimum wages for
industrial and agricultural workers are dictated by the government, and
adjusted to generate greater equality between lower and higher paid
workers. In 1975, for example, non-agricultural workers had their
minimum wage raised 13 per cent while the minimum wage for poorer
agricultural workers rose 60 per cent.

About 84 per cent of the active workforce in Madagascar is engaged
in agricultural production of a mostly traditional type. The industrial
sector, construction, administration and other services employ 6 per
cent, the rest being engaged either in small commercial jobs, odd-jobs
or simply unemployed. Every year 100,000 youths arrive at working
age, the largest proportion of them ending up absorbed into the
seasonal, agricultural job market. Often young people deliberately

prolong their stay in the Armed Forces to avoid unemployment. A rapidly growing artisanal class has arisen to provide substitutes for previously imported commodities. Unemployment and under-employment is a sensitive issue for the government, which is publicly committed in its recent development plan to achieving full employment.

Planning

Toward the end of 1977, Madagascar's first development plan since 1968 was announced by Ratsiraka to the newly elected National People's Assembly. To achieve socialism by the year 2000 was the plan's overriding purpose, including, as specific goals, self-sufficiency in food production, the doubling of the country's *per capita* income, state control of 75 per cent of the means of production, the attainment of full employment, and finally the restriction of the growth of a consumer society. Failure to attain the 1978-80 projected annual growth rate of 5.5 per cent has been blamed on incompetence and dishonesty among the management of the island's state-owned enterprises.

Foreign Economics

As with Benin and Congo, the depth of the Malagasy economy's dependence on the capitalist centre of the industrialised West is starkly revealed in its foreign trade and foreign aid statistics. The changeover from foreign to state ownership of enterprises operating within Madagascar has had little effect on this salient fact of Malagasy economic life.

Trade

Recent attempts have been made to integrate Madagascar more fully into a trading partnership with other African countries. In May 1980 an agreement was initialled, designed to begin to set up a preferential trading zone among 18 south-east African nations (including, among others, Somalia, Tanzania, Uganda, Angola, Mozambique, Zimbabwe and Zambia). For the present, however Madagascar's trade is dominated by the flow of goods to and from the industrialised West.

A full two-thirds of Malagasy exports in 1978 went to either the European Community, the USA, Switzerland, or Japan. France alone accounted for close to one quarter of these goods. Of civilian imports, two-thirds originated from these same countries with France supplying over a third of all imports.[31] Though France's share in the receipt of Malagasy exports has, in general, declined over the past five years (it was up to 25.8 per cent in 1979 from 23.1 per cent in 1978, due to a 56 per cent drop in sales to the US over that period) the decrease has been more than made up by the other Western powers (i.e. other EEC members, USA, Switzerland and Japan) as their total share of Malagasy exports increased to 79.2 per cent in 1978 from 64.7 per cent in 1975. Import shares have remained more constant, with France supplying a continually decreasing proportion (down from 40.9 per cent of all civilian imports in 1975 to 32.5 per cent in 1979), while the rest of the industrialised West retains its share of about one-third of the Malagasy import market. Exports to the USSR are small, adding up to only 721.5 million FMG in 1978 (compared to, for example, 3,211.8 million FMG sold to Japan or 1,218 million FMG sold to the Chinese People's Republic). Civilian imports from the Soviet Union are even less, amounting to less than one-sixth of what Madagascar imports from China.

The current trade balance has fluctuated over the years since 1974, when shocks in prices, first of fuel and later of imported machinery, sent the value of Madagascar's imports up 45 per cent to 67.2 billion FMG and, the following year (despite a decline in the actual volume of imports), even higher to 78 billion FMG. It was in 1975 that the goverment instituted its policy of deliberate restrictions on the volume of imports which, to that time, had been permitted to decline gradually in response to rising prices. These regulations have helped maintain Madagascar's visible trade deficits at reasonable levels, though figures from 1978 show a sharp increase up to 3.8 billion FMG.[32]

Aid

Through ties of bilateral and multilateral aid, Madagascar, like other francophone former colonies, has maintained its dependence on the West, though the degree of that dependence has, by conscious choice, been somewhat less. As Ratsiraka himself put it, 'It's true that between 1975 and 1979 we have been prudent, on the alert. We didn't want to run into debt and preferred to stake our chances on poverty.'[33] Thus at the end of 1978 the total disbursed, outstanding external debt amounted to some 58.35 billion FMG ($258.6m), some 43 per cent of which was owed to the World Bank, mostly for loans on infrastructural projects. The servicing of this debt represents a mere 4.1 per cent of export earnings, a very low figure for Third World economy in general. Partly this results from the kinds of terms Madagascar has been able to negotiate with its creditors. A typical example was a recent loan from West Germany, to be repaid over 50 years after a ten year grace period at an annual interest rate of 0.75 per cent.[34]

Madagascar's credit-worthiness is good, and consequently countries as diverse as France, Kuwait, Israel, Iraq and the USSR have lent to it. France is by far the largest creditor, its financial aid to Madagascar having reached 12 billion FMG by the end of 1979. The European Development Fund is also a large creditor. Over the years 1976-80 they have loaned or earmarked 19 billion FMG for the Great Island. For the period 1980-5, 28.2 FMG have been set aside by this Fund for agricultural and infrastructural development projects.[35] The Soviet Union is a creditor as well, if on a somewhat smaller scale. Since 1977 they have loaned 10 billion FMG to finance economic and technical development projects, including grain storage facilities, irrigation schemes, hydro-electric power projects and prospecting ventures.[36] China, another big socialist lender had, up until 1977, committed 12 billion FMG to the Malagasy economy. Other socialist countries from Cuba and Yugoslavia to North Korea confine their aid chiefly to gifts of equipment (tractors, airplanes, mining equipment, etc.) and the provision of scholarships. For a statistical summary of aid by geographical origin see Table 1.2.

Foreign Politics

Ratsiraka characterises present Malagasy foreign policy as non-aligned. Developing, as it has, out of a strictly colonial context, this new policy has meant disengagement from previous close ties with France and a shift toward friendlier links with non-aligned African nations, and with countries of the socialist world. Tsiranana, in addition to being a confirmed anti-Communist, was initially cool toward the idea of integrating Madagascar's interests with those of the rest of the African nations, preferring to maintain the island's identity as that of primarily a south Asian offshoot. Ratsiraka, by contrast, has constructed a deliberate policy of actively identifying and pursuing links to Africa's more left-wing regimes. Having engineered the rupture of relations with South Africa in the early 1970s (relations with Israel and Taiwan were also broken during that time), Ratsiraka also procured the withdrawal of Madagascar from the French-dominated OCAM. Since then Madagascar has moved more and more in the direction of leftist African governments, as is evidenced by the early recognition of Polisario's Saharan African Democratic Republic, the hosting of a conference of progressive African nations in Antananarivo in May 1978, and its active co-operation, within the OAU, with a bloc of radical states including Angola, Mozambique, Guinea-Bissau, Benin, Algeria, Libya, Sao Tome and Cape Verde. Further evidence of Ratsiraka's concern with continental affairs is his efforts to mediate a solution between Ethiopia and Somalia over the Ogaden issue.

Among socialist nations, Madagascar has its closest ties with the Soviet Union, its ally Cuba, and with North Korea. Ratsiraka has personally visited Havana (for the conference of non-aligned nations), Pyongyang in 1978, and Moscow in August 1980. Agreements of friendship between the USSR and Africa in general were signed in 1977, and during this latest trip economic agreements were ratified. Currently close to 1,000 Malagasy students are studying in the Soviet Union and 28 Russian instructors teach in Antananarivo. Malagasy pilots are also being trained in the USSR, to man the MIG 21s that Madagascar received from the Soviets to replace the MIG 17s they had had on loan from North Korea. Despite these military links, Ratsiraka is quick to point out that he has neither made nor been requested to make any commitments to allow Soviet Naval and Air Force installations to be established on the island,[37] and that the USSR is a strong supporter of his policy directed at turning the Indian Ocean into a demilitarised 'zone of peace'. So it came as no surprise when Madagascar abstained in the vote condemning Soviet intervention in Afghanistan at the UN early in 1980.

Agreements over the presence of Cuban military advisors (estimated at 30)[38] were signed in 1977, followed by protocols governing Cuban scientific and cultural assistance in 1979. Madagascar has been generally supportive of the presence of Cuban military forces in Angola and Ethiopia, and Ratsiraka aseems to have developed a good personal relationship with Castro on his visit to Havana for the non-aligned nations conference. The North Korean presence in Madagascar has broadened since the 1978 opening of air-travel links. That year Ratsiraka signed agricultural, military and technical aid agreements in Pyongyang. A book store of North Korean publications has opened in Antananarivo, and Ratsiraka himself inaugurated a North Korean-built Pioneer Children's Palace constructed for the training of future revolutionaries. Finally, the President's personal bodyguard is said to be trained by North Koreans. The Chinese presence in Madagascar is confined to several modest development projects. One such programme, the 422 million FMG all-weather road from Moramanga to Toamasina, was the source of some conflict when the Malagasy protested about the numbers of technicians the Chinese brought in to do the topographical survey.

Of Western powers, France remains by far the most influential, despite Madagascar's withdrawal from OCAM and the franc zone, its sporadic attendance at Franco-African summit meetings and its vigorous condemnation of recent French military excursions into Zaire, Chad, Mauritania and the Comores. The two major outstanding issues between the former colony and the former metropole are (i) compensation for French concerns nationalised by the Ratsiraka regime and (ii) ownership of three small uninhabited islands in the Mozambique Channel, which Madagascar claims since she extended her continental shelf to 180 km. in 1973. These disagreements notwithstanding, relations with France have improved since Pierre Hunt has assumed the role of Ambassador to the point where *Madagascar-Matin* described the co-operation between the two, in August 1980, as 'eloquent'.

The USA is considered a malevolent military giant, accused of building up its armed forces on the neighbouring island of Diego Garcia and resisting justifiable claims over outstanding rent due on the now defunct satellite tracking station at Imerinatsitosika. Great Britain, since 1975, has maintained relations with Madagascar through an embassy in Dar es Salaam. In November 1978 talks aimed at reopening the embassy in Antananarivo were begun.

Despite the call for demilitarisation of the Indian Ocean, Madagascar has seen fit to augment its own military capabilities considerably since 1975.[39] The number of individuals in uniform has increased two-and-a-half times in five years to the point where, at present, the total number of soldiers is 13,000. Emphasis has shifted from the ground Army toward what are considered the more appropriate divisions (for an island nation) of the Navy and Air Force. In the past three years Madagascar has acquired eight MIG 21 fighter aircraft from the USSR (which currently trains Malagasy pilots for these aircraft), two Mi 8 helicopters and several An 12 and An 26 (Soviet) transport planes to complement the variety of transport, light aircraft and helicopters the 350-man Air Force already possessed. The Ratsiraka regime's only declared enemy in the vicinity is South Africa (though it views with considerable suspicion Ahmed Abdallah's mercenary-installed government in the Comores), and the Malagasy leadership is quite fearful of external attempts to destabilise the government militarily. This may in part account for Madagascar's recent military investments.

Conclusions

Three-quarters of a century of French domination of Madagascar, first as a colonial occupier, subsequently as a neo-colonial sponsor, left the country in circumstances quite similar to the other former French African colonies: an essentially agricultural society with a poorly developed secondary sector, and a monumental service and administration sphere (45 per cent of GDP in 1977), trading primarily with Western capitalist countries and heavily dependent upon them as sources of external investment.

What, since 1975, has changed? In a domestic context, ownership in the secondary and tertiary sectors has shifted out of private hands into state control, some decision-making concerning agricultural policy seems to have been decentralised (though it's difficult to judge in which direction the avenues of power within the new *fokonolona* system run), and infrastructural improvement at present receives a greater proportion of national resources than previously. Externally, the spectrum of trade and aid partners has widened a little, though most changes have taken place in those areas of foreign policy that are of high symbolic importance.

What has remained the same? Agriculture, the foundation of the economy, remains in the hands of independent, traditionally-oriented peasants. Collectivisation appears nowhere on the immediate horizon. Ownership questions aside, the managers of the country's industry, the commercial interests and the military remain essentially the same – Merina bourgeoisie (carefully characterised by Ratsiraka as a 'nationalist bourgeoisie' therefore, presumably, acceptable allies during the phase of national democratic revolution) – that was trained and served under the French. Finally the overall orientation of the economy's productive capacity – what is produced and for whose consumption – has also not altered appreciably in five years.

It may, as yet, be too early to predict what direction Malagasy society will ultimately follow, but one can speculate about certain possibilities. A full-scale economic and military alliance with the Soviet Union is unlikely. No official hints from either Moscow or Antananarivo have even suggested this as a possibility, and even if

Ratsiraka himself has a secret preference for this option (and there is no particular evidence that he does) he does not command enough of an unquestioning cadre within Madagascar to enforce such a choice on a population that has, at least among the bourgeoisie, a history of fierce resistance to foreign domination of any sort. Above all, AREMA is by no means a proper Communist Party.

An independent, socialist path of the kind envisaged by Ratsiraka is plagued with difficulties. Independent economic development, socialist or otherwise, presumes some solution to the problem of feeding the national work-force from the surplus generated by indigenous agricultural production. Price incentives and periodic exhortations on the part of the central government for peasants to work harder may have marginal effects on agricultural output, but without some fundamental change in the primary sector, aimed at improving the technological level of the methods of cultivation, it is difficult to see how the island will ever be self-sufficient in food – a pre-requisite for the economic independence of the kind the regime is planning. A second obstacle to socialist development within Madagascar is the present state of class relations. For an economy to opt for socialist development, political control of economic decision-making must be harnessed by a political party or parties representing the working class, the peasantry or an alliance of the two. Normally this takes place, in a country with an established bourgeoisie, only after prolonged and bitter social unrest often culminating in civil war.

The declared aim of decentralising and democratising the economic decision-making process in Madagascar through the mechanism of the *fokonolona* system raises the issue of how the established relations between a centrally-located Merina business and managerial class, an equally concentrated urban proletariat, and a peripherally located peasantry will ultimately be resolved. Should the latter two combine in a serious attempt to exploit the new system in the interests of seizing control of the economy, redressing income differentials, redirecting investment priorities, and so on, confrontation with the ruling classes is not out of the question. Here Ratsiraka's own intentions are important. The military, riddled as it is with sons of the Merina upper class, is probably willing to support his 'socialisation' plans only so far. Alienation of these men could presage a pre-emptive right-wing return to power, circumventing any ultimate confrontation with the peasants and workers.

None of the foregoing scenario is inevitable. The major alternative

Table 8.1: Gross Domestic Product (current prices in billions of FMG)

	1972	1973	1974[a]	1975[a]	1976[b]	1977[b]
Agriculture	86.0	100.3	143.0	145.1	151.2	170.0
Industry	52.3	60.2	66.7	70.6	76.0	86.1
Services	86.6	91.8	100.1	107.8	112.4	120.8
Public administration and defence	40.9	40.6	41.8	42.5	44.0	48.1
GDP at market prices	279.7	304.7	364.8	380.9	400.1	443.1
GDP at factor cost	249.3	275.8	331.0	344.0	360.4	394.5
Foreign-trade participation ratio[c]	0.21	0.18	0.19	0.22	0.20	0.21

a. Preliminary.
b. Provisional.
c. Visible and invisible exports from IMF *Balance of Payments Yearbook*, vol. 31, December 1980.
Source: *EBM*, Table 2.1, p. 82.

Table 8.2: Foreign Trade (millions of FMG)

	1974	1975	1976[a]	1977	1978	1979[c]
Exports f.o.b.						
EEC	26,710.3	20,228.3	n.a.	36,401.2	31,181.8	13,771.5
of which France	19,802.5	12,646.8	19,367.3	21,976.9	20,150.2	8,068.0
GFR	2,695.0	4,269.2	4,909.3	6,986.2	n.a.	n.a.
USA	12,060.3	7,346.6	10,962.5	18,500.3	21,879.7	6,629.6
Japan	3,468.5	2,240.6	4,958.3	7,008.3	3,211.8	2,130.4
Indonesia	n.a.	13,479.3	1,878.0	1,003.9	11,950.9	7,060.9
USSR	372.2	138.6	996.6	3,898.7	721.5	220.6
Other East Europe[b]	1,399.0*	1,361.2	2,659.3*	1,296.4	425.6	60.3
China (People's Republic)	196.0	37.4	24.7	1,300.6	1,218.0	24.6
Total	58,503.9	63,043.6	66,043.9	89,926.7	87,214.0	41,331.6
Imports						
EEC	33,999.4	43,510.8	38,097.5	50,352.8	57,609.9	27,048.1
of which France	24,094.4	31,953.7	25,508	33,549.6	34,730.6	16,489.3
GFR	5,879.7	6,538.7	6,189.0	7,069.9	n.a.	n.a.
USA	4,734.1	3,082.9	3,038.6	2,816.4	3,382.1	1,575.5
Japan	3,323.4	3,025.8	2,507.0	4,414.0	4,723.7	3,842.5
Indonesia	58.8	141.8	136.2	101.8	1.8	
USSR	23.1	28.7	321.9	138.9	792.3	627.0
Other East Europe[b]	107.9	374.0	262.9	429.7	374.7	217.3
China (People's Republic)	7,041.4	2,524.9	2,520.3	3,449.4	6,215.7	3,842.5
Total	67,256.9	78,046.6	68,399.2	85,216.9	99,632.2	50,708.3

a. The figures for 1976 were derived by multiplying the figures for *UNYITS* by the exchange rates given in *EBM*.
b. Including Poland, Romania, Yugoslavia, and GDR.
c. For first 6 months of 1979 only.
* Including Bulgaria.

Sources: *Bulletin Mensuel de Statistique*, nos. 282-3, 286-7, March-April 1979; July, August 1979 (Ministère Auprès de la Présidence de la Republique Chargé de la France et du Plan), *UNYITS*, 1978.

to an independent, socialist path of development is its affirmation in word accompanied by its avoidance in deed. That is to say, present Malagasy policy. Now that the apparatus of the present, state-directed economy has been formally identified as socialist, no further democratisation or collectivisation need take place for quite some time. Given the historic strength and resiliency of the Merina bourgeoisie, whose position in the economy has yet to be seriously challenged, the all-out investment policy Ratsiraka has recently announced (presuming the world-economy remains strong enough to continue to divert a certain amount of resources in Madagascar's direction) permits, even without a return to outright private ownership of industry and commerce, the Merina to gradually strengthen their control over the state sector. Fulfilment of the aspirations of the underproductive peasantry may possibly be deferred, so long as new supplies of land continue to be made available as a means of increasing output and absorbing a politically volatile excess labour force. A centralised, state-controlled industrial and commercial sector (providing some room for continued private investment in privately-owned concerns), based on a broad quiescent agricultural population, has a definite future in Madagascar: the foreseeable one.

Notes

1. Population estimate is from *UNMB*, vol. 34, no. 12, December 1980. Land area estimate from *EBM*, p. 1.
2. *Africa South*, . . . 1980, p. 613.
3. *UNMB*, vol. 34, no. 12, December 1980.
4. Kravis *et al.*, 1978.
5. From a document from Ministère de la Coopération, France, December 1978, p. 143.
6. Ibid.
7. *EBM*.
8. Information for this section was obtained from a variety of sources, the most important of which were: a series of articles by Nicholas Ashford and Maurice Bloch appearing in *The Times*, 26 June 1978; Archer, 1976; Kent, 1979; Ostheimer, 1975; *ACR*, various editions, esp. 1980.
9. *Côtier* is a term used to designate coastal populations.
10. Kent, 1979, p. 318.
11. For a good historical summary of Malagasy political parties see Archer, 1976, annexe 2, pp. 192-9.
12. Ostheimer, 1975, p. 54.
13. This original number was derived from Ostheimer, 1975, p. 63. Since the original plan the number of fokonolona has increased to close to 12,000.
14. *Le Monde*, 31 December 1977.
15. In 1978 many names of Malagasy cities were changed to become more in keeping with their original pre-colonial appellations. Thus Tananarive became

Antananarivo, Majunga became Mahajanga, etc.

    16. *EBM*, p. 4.

    17. *Africa South*, . . . p. 603.

    18. *The Times*, 26 June 1978.

    19. *Africa South*, . . . p. 600.

    20. The 1971 figure is from *EBM*, p. 6 and the figure for 1978 from *Financial Mail* (Johannesburg), 9 June 1978.

    21. *Africa South*, . . . p. 600.

    22. Ibid., p. 600.

    23. *EBM*, p. 6.

    24. Ibid., p. 6.

    25. 21 March 1980.

    26. *EBM*, p. 8.

    27. Ibid., p. 9.

    28. Ibid., p. 10.

    29. Percentage contribution to GDP is from *EBM*, p. 13, the figure for the number employed comes from *Africa South*, . . . p. 601.

    30. *EBM*, p. 15.

    31. These and other figures calculated from Table 8.2.

    32. *ACR*, 1978-9, p. B301.

    33. From an interview with Didier Ratsiraka published in *Afrique-Asie*, 23 June 1980 (author's translation).

    34. News Agency Reports, 7 June 1980.

    35. Calculated by applying the most recent exchange rate of 217.5 FMG per US dollar to a figure received from News Agency Reports, 13 April 1980.

    36. *Bulletin d'Afrique*, 19 August 1980.

    37. *Afrique-Asie*, 23 June 1980.

    38. *Daily Telegraph*, 18, 19 November 1977.

    39. The figures quoted here are from *The Military Balance*, International Institute of Strategic Studies, London, 1980.

9 THE SOMALI DEMOCRATIC REPUBLIC. THE ONE THAT GOT AWAY[1]

Barry Lynch

Introduction

Somalia is a republic formed in 1960 from the former British Somaliland Protectorate and the Italian Trusteeship Territory of Somalia in the Northeast Horn of Africa. It is bounded on the West by Djibouti, Ethiopia and Kenya, on the north by the Gulf of Aden and on the east and south-east by the Indian Ocean. Somalia covers an area of 637,140 square km. Thirteen per cent of the land is arable, although only 0.3 per cent is cultivated; 32 per cent is suitable for grazing, but the remainder, more than half, consists of scrubland and forest (14 per cent) and semi-desert (41 per cent).

The currency of the country is the Somali Shilling. Throughout the 1960s its rate of exchange with the US dollar was constant, at 7.1213 Somali Shillings per dollar. Its value fell in the early 1970s, to 6.325 in 1974, and has fallen since to 6.02 (1980). The foreign-trade participation ratio is about 29 per cent (IFS and Table 9.1).

The population of Somalia is estimated to be 3,510,000 (January 1980). It has been growing at an average rate of 2.4 per cent per annum, but as there has never been a census this can only be an estimate. Seventy-five per cent of the population are rural, and of this 35 per cent are nomadic herdsmen. It is a very homogeneous population, both ethnically and religiously, which makes for a nationalism quite unusual in Africa. Ninety per cent are of the Somali ethnic group (Hamitic), which has a strong sense of cultural identity despite internal (clan) distinctions. The remainder consists mainly of Bantus and Arabs. The predominant religion is Islam, which is still strongly practised by the majority of the population. Somali is the official language. The country is a member of the Arab League.

Somalia is classified as one of the least developed countries in Africa. Its *per capita* GNP is low — approximately $220[2] in 1970 — and it has a limited natural resource base. There is heavy emphasis on livestock activities which reflects the fact that most of the country is arid and only suitable for grazing. Only 9 per cent of GNP is derived from manufacturing.

In 1969, a left-wing military *coup d'état* brought the Supreme Revolutionary Council to power, with General Mohammed Siyad Barre as President, and the Democratic Republic of Somalia was formed. The former parliament was dismissed, the constitution suspended and the Supreme Court dissolved. The Revolutionary Council took over all legislative and judicial powers. The Supreme Revolutionary Council disbanded itself in 1976 (the peak period of Soviet influence) in favour of a 'scientific socialist' party with strong Islamic commitments – the Somalia Revolutionary Socialist Party. Somalia became a one-party state. The party has since been disbanded (October 1980) and the Council reinstated. Scientific socialism was interpreted as a pragmatic adaptation of Marxist-Leninist principles to local conditions. It was an attempt to blend the official ideology of the state and the party with the beliefs of the state religion, Islam. It specifically rejected the atheistic basis of Marxism, claiming that the basis of scientific socialism was to be found in the ideology of Islam and the teachings of the Koran, with their emphasis on equality, justice and social progress. In general, 'scientific socialism' put great emphasis on self-reliance, popular participation and public control, and ownership of the essential means of production. The policy was to develop the economy along basically socialist lines, although private enterprise was encouraged on a small scale.

The Economy

The Somali economy is totally dependent on pastoral and agricultural products and, to a modest degree, food processing. The economy has traditionally been based on the raising of cattle, sheep, goats and camels. The development programme initiated by the new government in 1969 aimed at the long-run objectives of raising the living standards of the population, securing full employment for the work force, and attaining an equitable distribution of national output within the framework of a socialist economy. To attain these objectives, the strategy pursued during the programme period entailed maximising resource-use through strengthening the basic economic infrastructure, forming co-operative societies in the main economic sectors, and decentralising the social and political management of the economy. Thus, after the *coup*, schools, banks and electricity supplies were nationalised. In 1972, all means of transport, the import and distribution of consumer goods, medicines and films and the distribution of funds were taken into public ownership. Nationalisation was extended in 1974, when the shipping agencies were taken over, and again in 1975, when land was taken into common ownership.

Through the development programme the government has attempted to achieve self-sufficiency in food and basic consumer goods, which could provide a basis for industrial development. Somalia's five-year development programme, from 1974 to 1978, placed particular emphasis on crops. The agricultural sector was expected to increase its share of exports and provide employment and income for an increasing proportion of the population. The government's major objective was to attain self-sufficiency in staple foodstuffs by 1981, and thereafter to produce surpluses for export. As part of its agro-industrial policy the government intended to expand production of sugar, cotton, oilseeds, vegetables and fruits.

Crops. Settled agriculture engages about 20 per cent of the population. It consists of a relatively small commercial sector — bananas being the main crop — and a larger subsistence sector, which engages more than 80 per cent of the population in this industry. The major crops for domestic consumption are cereals, oilseeds and sugar cane. Bananas are the principal cash-crop and the second largest export commodity (after livestock). Although its share of total exports has been declining over the past decade, bananas still accounted for 12 per cent of total exports in 1977. Production is undertaken for the most part on private farms. The National Banana Board, however, is responsible for marketing all banana exports. It purchases the bananas from the producers at the prevailing producer price.

The main staple crops are maize and sorghum, produced almost entirely by small-scale subsistence farmers who are required to sell their marketable surpluses to the Agricultural Development Corporation (ADC). The ADC markets all the main domestic food crops. It purchases grain from the farmers at fixed prices and sells it to the consumers at a uniform price determined by the government. If domestic production falls beneath requirements for domestic consumption, the ADC is also responsible for importing grain.

Cotton is produced both on state-run farms and by private firms whose output is sold to the ADC. The entire output is absorbed by the state-owned textile factory — SOMALTEX.

Animal Husbandry. Raising livestock is the principal economic activity and source of livelihood for nearly two-thirds of the population. A 1975 estimate placed the livestock population at nearly 34 million — 25 million sheep and goats, 4 million cattle and 5 million camels.

Most of the livestock production and trade is conducted privately. The Livestock Development Agency purchases cattle for both export and supplying the Kismayu meat-processing plant, but such purchases account for less than 10 per cent of the total livestock trade. Prices for domestic consumption of livestock and livestock products are determined by supply and demand conditions within Somalia. Domestic supply, however, is strongly influenced by export prices.

Exports of livestock account for the bulk of export earnings — 67 and 83 per cent respectively in 1977 and 1978. In previous years the 1973-5 drought affected the pattern of exports and the size of the herds. A large number of young animals died, and the proportion of off-take was increased to maintain an appropriate ratio of animals to grazing land. Exports in 1976 and 1977 were, therefore, reduced.

Fishing. The fishing industry was established with the help of foreign (Soviet) aid. In its efforts to develop the fishing industry, and as part of its resettlement programme for nomads displaced by the droughts of 1974, the government has taken measures to reorganise the traditional fishermen into co-operatives, provided modern fishing equipment and training, and established a new company — the Somali Fishing Company (SOMAL-FISH) — for deep-sea fishing and the exporting and domestic marketing of fish. Twenty-one co-operatives were formed and played a major role in the five-year development plan, and were given priority in the 1979 budget. Although commercial fishing has been undertaken for several years, Somalia's fishery resources and their potential have not been adequately explored. Note that being under native ownership fish figures as a commodity export — whereas in Angola it is 'invisible' since a Soviet company pays a royalty on it and exports it. Angola's fish is indeed invisible on shore, and the arrangement is not popular.

Manufacturing. Somalia's manufacturing sector is relatively small and reflects the government's policy of establishing import-substitution industries and export industries based on the processing of livestock, agricultural products and fish. The most important import-substitution industries are SOMALTEX, producing textiles, and the Societa Nazionale Agricola Industriale, producing sugar. A petroleum refinery, processing imported crude oil, began operations in February 1979. Other such industries include grain-processing and the manufacture of

Table 9.1: GDP by Use: Percentage of Total (Current Market Prices)

	1966	1967	1968	1969	1970	1971	1972	1973
Total (US $M)	153	161	170	178	187	197	213	256
Imports	38.1	38.1	n.a.	n.a.	33.1	33.6	42.6	48.4
Exports	25.2	23.5	n.a.	n.a.	23.0	24.5	31.1	28.4
Total resources	112.8	114.5	111.2	112.9	110.1	109.2	111.4	120.0
Private consumption	65.0	64.8	62.4	62.2	61.6	57.3	53.2	47.3
General government consumption	19.3	19.0	20.6	20.9	21.9	25.2	26.2	30.0
Gross domestic investment	15.7	16.2	16.9	16.9	16.5	17.5	20.7	22.8

Source: *UN Statistical Yearbook*, 1978.

Table 9.2: Exports by Industrial Origin: Percentage of Total Value

	1970	1971	1972	1973	1974	1975	1976	1977	1978
Agriculture	83.3	77.8	83.9	83.5	83.2	80.1	76.4	78.5	91.4
Mining & quarrying	–	0.2	–	–	–	–	–	–	–
Manufacturing	16.7	22.0	16.1	16.5	16.7	19.9	23.6	21.5	8.6
of which food, beverages, tobacco	10.4	16.6	14.9	14.1	15.4	14.7	20.6	13.0	5.0

Source: *UNYITS*, vol. I, 1976; Somali and IMF sources.

edible oil, cigarettes and matches, packaging materials, leather and footwear, aluminium utensils, pharmaceutical products, electrical fittings and detergents and soap powders. Heavy industry has not played a role in the country's development plans.

GDP is not recorded by sectoral origin. Table 9.1 shows GDP at current market prices, the proportion comprising imports and exports and how total resources have been divided among private consumption, general government consumption and gross domestic investment. Since the 1969 revolution, government general consumption and gross domestic investment have increased markedly at the expense of private consumption. Over the same period imports have risen more rapidly than exports. Measurement of the real growth of GDP and GDP *per capita* are unreliable. From 1966 to the oil crisis in 1973 it is estimated that real GDP was growing by just over 3 per cent per annum, or by just under 1 per cent *per capita,* but it has fallen since.

Foreign Trade

As can be seen in Table 9.2 exports are based almost entirely on agricultural products. Throughout the 1970s agricultural products never accounted for less than three-quarters of total exports. The proportion fell in 1976 and 1977, due to the drought. Manufactured products accounted for the remainder of exports. Two-thirds of these comprised food, beverage and tobacco products.

Table 9.3 shows the distribution of exports by type of economy and principal country. The proportion of exports to the advanced capitalist economies has fallen over the period from 1966 from nearly half. The EEC, and Italy in particular, has been the major market in this category. The main beneficiary of this decline has been the Middle Eastern countries, most notably Saudi Arabia which has taken more than half of Somalia's exports since 1968. The Communist economies, which after the 1969 *coup* became the main sources of economic and military aid to Somalia (see **Foreign Policy and Aid**), increased their trade but the former colonial ties with Italy and ethnic and religious ties with the Middle East have proved to be stronger influences on export trade patterns. This contrasts with the Soviet Union, the main Somali ally until 1978. Although the figures are not sufficiently recent to be able to discern the effect on trade of the break in relations between the USSR and Somalia, the table does show that in terms of export trade, the Soviets did not play a very large role even at the height of their good relations with Somalia.

Table 9.3: Exports (f.o.b.) by Principal Country: Percentage of Total Value

	1966	1967	1968	1969	1970	1971	1972	1973	1974	1975	1976	1977	1978
Advanced capitalist	45.0	39.4	32.2	30.7	30.2	25.9	20.5	19.0	13.2	8.4	30.1	14.6	8.0
North American	2.9	0.5	0.4	2.1	0.7	0.1	0.1	0.1	0.1	0.1	0.0	–	–
EEC	41.7	37.7	31.3	28.1	28.4	25.6	20.2	18.2	13.1	8.0	29.2	14.6	8.0
of which Italy	40.8	37.5	30.6	26.7	26.1	22.4	18.2	16.5	10.2	6.5	28.3	14.6	8.0
Middle East	49.6	58.5	65.5	66.8	63.9	60.0	66.2	70.4	74.2	79.3	58.5	72.8	89.9
Saudi Arabia	35.0	42.9	50.2	56.1	52.4	49.6	53.2	57.0	56.6	64.1	51.2	66.5	85.7
PDRY	14.4	13.4	12.5	10.7	10.3	6.6	5.0	–	3.1	2.2	0.5	0.6	0.0
YAR								7.7	3.1	4.9	0.5		
Oman					1.2	3.8	6.8	3.8	7.5	0.3	0.1		
Communist	0.2	0.4	0.3	0.4	2.5	8.4	10.0	5.7	9.3	8.3	9.5	4.1	0.9
CMEA	–	0.2	0.1	0.1	1.5	7.0	8.9	2.8	5.4	5.5	7.0	3.5	0.0
of which USSR	–	0.2	0.1	0.1	1.5	6.3	6.4	2.7	5.4	5.5	7.0	3.5	0.0
China	0.2	0.2	0.1	0.4	1.0	1.5	1.1	3.0	3.9	2.8	2.5	0.6	0.9

Source: *UNYITS*, vol. 1, 1976, 1979; Somali and IMF sources.

Table 9.4: Civilian Imports by Economic Category (SITC): Percentage of Total Value

	1970	1971	1972	1973	1974	1975	1976	1977	1978
Food and beverages	31.3	30.8	23.9	22.0	19.7	16.6	17.2	n.a.	n.a.
Raw materials	30.3	36.8	32.3	31.6	40.6	35.8	35.0	n.a.	n.a.
Fuels and lubricants	6.2	4.2	4.1	5.1	6.7	6.1	6.8	n.a.	n.a.
Machinery	5.9	5.1	13.3	13.1	11.2	15.6	11.9	n.a.	n.a.
Transport	12.0	9.0	13.0	12.3	10.3	15.5	18.1	n.a.	n.a.
Consumer goods	13.8	13.6	13.1	16.3	11.2	10.2	10.6	n.a.	n.a.

Sources: *UNYITS*, vol. 1, 1976, 1979; Somali and IMF sources.

Somalia's imports are much more diversified both by economic category and country of origin (see Tables 9.4 and 9.5). Raw materials are the most important class of import, with food and beverage second. Italy has consistently been the major source of imports, accounting for between a quarter and a third of the total. The advanced capitalist countries in general have accounted for a declining proportion of imports. In 1969 they supplied nearly two-thirds of imports; this proportion has declined since to about half. The USSR was the main but not the sole beneficiary of this shift in the pattern of imports — Third World countries also increased exports to Somalia. The USSR was the second major source, however. Recent developments in that country's relations with Somalia have reportedly led to a switch to alternative sources.

Somalia maintains bilateral trade and payments agreements with the USSR and China. The trade account with the Soviet Union is shown in Table 9.6. The account has moved into increasing deficit through the 1970s. Soviet exports consisted mainly of manufactured goods and, most importantly, oil from 1974; imports consisted of hides and processed meat. The unspecified residual in Soviet exports to Somalia, as shown in the Table, has been consistently small. All trade between the two countries was terminated in 1978, when the Russians were expelled over the Ogaden War.

Foreign Policy and Aid

Following independence in 1960, Somalia maintained relations with Western and Eastern bloc countries and received substantial aid from

Table 9.5: Civilian Imports (c.i.f.) by Principal Country: Percentage of Total Value

	1966	1967	1968	1969	1970	1971	1972	1973	1974	1975	1976	1977	1978
Advanced capitalist	62.0	59.6	68.0	71.1	64.2	58.6	56.3	55.4	48.6	55.4	54.4	45.7	56.2
North American	7.2	6.6	9.5	10.8	7.9	6.8	6.6	2.7	2.3	3.3	4.5	0.8	2.5
EEC	46.1	43.3	48.2	51.2	47.5	45.5	42.8	46.9	39.6	46.9	44.0	44.0	51.1
of which Italy	30.9	29.2	32.7	30.9	29.5	27.1	29.5	31.3	27.7	32.0	25.7	28.3	30.2
FRG	4.6	5.7	6.0	8.4	9.1	7.5	4.5	5.2	3.7	6.2	6.9	5.2	10.5
Asian	7.5	9.2	9.8	8.2	7.4	5.2	5.7	3.7	3.6	0.6	1.1	0.9	2.6
Middle East	10.0	7.5	4.9	6.5	7.9	5.0	4.4	3.9	5.9	6.4	3.3	4.8	13.5
Developing capitalist	14.0	12.8	7.7	8.0	9.0	17.3	12.3	4.4	13.1	13.3	9.8	9.7	2.5
Communist	5.7	12.1	9.7	5.8	9.6	9.6	16.9	28.9	20.9	14.6	21.1	18.7	4.0
CMEA	4.0	8.2	6.8	4.0	7.8	8.1	11.1	11.1	14.3	8.4	13.8	12.2	0.6
of which USSR	3.4	7.9	6.1	3.5	6.7	6.5	9.8	9.4	12.7	7.6	12.2	12.2	0.6
China	1.7	3.9	2.9	1.8	1.7	1.5	5.8	17.7	6.3	6.2	7.3	6.5	3.4

Source: *UNYITS*, vol. 1, 1976, 1979; Somali and IMF sources.

both. In July 1962, Somalia received a firm commitment of $95 million for its development plan capital expenditure for the period 1963 to 1967. This comprised aid primarily from the USSR, Egypt and the United States. A long-term interest-free loan of $17 million was received from China.

An agreement on military co-operation with the USSR was first concluded in 1961. By 1963 the Somali government had decided to accept Soviet military aid. Somalia had been offered $18 million in military equipment from the United States, West Germany and Italy. Western aid was turned down, however, as it was offered on the condition that such aid was not accepted from any other source. The Soviet aid of $30 million was accepted and was sufficient to equip an army of 20,000 and a small air force.

In November 1963, Somalia entered its first trade agreement with China. Under the agreement China was to export textiles, metal products, machinery, chemicals, medical instruments and tea. An agreement was also signed to build a 600-mile all-weather road between Mogadishu and Hargeisa, in the north, at a cost of $95 million, to be financed by China. In total, during the four years to 1964, Somalia received $150 million in aid. In addition to the $30 million in promised military aid, the USSR promised $45 million as economic aid, Italy $45 million, the United States $23 million and Egypt $12 million. After 1964, Somalia came increasingly to rely on the CMEA countries and China for aid.

Trade between Somalia and the USSR grew during the mid-1960s, particularly in terms of exports to Somalia as the Soviet aid programme began. Relations with China were strengthened with the signing of a technical agreement in 1966. In the same year more arms were received from the Soviet Union. By 1967 there were reported to be 200 Soviet military advisers in the country. So even before the 1969 *coup*, Somalia had close relations with the Soviet Union. The first agreement on economic assistance was signed shortly after independence in 1961; by 1963, Somalia was accepting Soviet military aid; and by 1967, military advisers. This aid was increased after the 1969 *coup*, until by 1976, with the signing of a treaty of friendship, the Soviets had established a military presence, including a naval base at Berbera, and had become the main source of military aid and equipment for Somalia. From 1969 aid from the Soviet bloc as a whole increased relatively and absolutely. This increase was partially due to a reduction in Western aid following the nationalisation of foreign investment in Somalia in May 1970. Although most of the investments affected were Italian, the

United States terminated its aid programme in protest. The reduction in Western aid was to a limited extent replaced by aid from the Communist countries. In November 1971, an agreement to increase co-operation with the USSR was signed. By the end of 1972, USSR had pledged $ 68 million in credits. But she remained a less active trader with Somalia than Italy, the United States or the United Kingdom.

Somalia also continued to accept aid from China and the West after 1969. China kept a low, non-political profile, assisting in the construction of roads and rural development projects. Close relations with the EEC were cultivated. The EEC provided important outlets for Somali exports and economic support. Somalia was made an associate member of the EEC under the Lomé Convention.

Large amounts of aid did continue from multilateral organisations. In March, 1973, the IDA gave Somalia an interest-free 50-year credit of nearly $ 13 million. During the same period the European Development Fund, funded by the EEC, gave a grant of $ 14 million for the construction of a deep-water port at Mogadishu. Somalia was made a member of the Arab League in February 1974. Little aid was received, however, because of Somalia's close relations with the Soviet Union. Aid was given by Kuwait and the Arab Fund for Economic Development, but not by Saudi Arabia. Saudi aid was tied to a breaking of ties with the USSR. Libya and the United Arab Emirates also became increasingly important sources of aid after 1974.

Relations with the Soviet bloc were strengthened right up to the Ogaden war in 1977. In 1976, a new cultural agreement was signed with the USSR and further technological and economic co-operation agreed in 1977. A similar agreement was reached with East Germany. Somalia also continued to receive military aid. In 1976, additional Soviet military hardware was received, including 250 tanks and 50 fighters, some being Mig-21s. Table 1.2 shows the net flow of official development assistance from 1973 to 1979 from the West. Total official assistance increased seven-fold over the period. Bilateral aid has generally accounted for the bulk of official aid, particularly from Italy (the former colonial power) and the USA in the early 1970s. These sources decreased in importance thereafter, with the OPEC countries becoming by far the largest contributors by 1977.

On a multilateral basis, increased flows of aid, particularly from 1975 onwards, came from the EEC, IDA and the UN. The most important source, accounting for more than two-thirds of the total by 1977 was the OPEC bilateral total. Two-thirds of the OPEC aid was as loans, whereas EEC and UN aid was predominantly as grants. Bilateral aid, in general, was in the form of grants.

Table 1.2 also shows the rise and fall of aid from Communist countries, while Table 9.7 shows Communist aid promises to Somalia by country, type and purpose since 1963. Over the period 1954 to 1978 aid promises amounted to $164 million from the USSR, $155 million from China and $6 million from the Eastern European countries.

The Ogaden War

Since independence Somalia's foreign policy has been determined by its desire to unify all Somali-speaking peoples in Somalia, Ethiopia, Kenya and Djibouti. Through the 1970s, Somalia increased its military strength with military aid from the Soviet bloc so that by 1976 it was in a position to press its territorial claims. The *quid pro quo* for this military support from the USSR was the provision of naval facilities at Berbera, on the Gulf of Aden coast.

In July 1977, Somali military forces crossed the border with Ethiopia in an attempt to secure the Ogaden region, claiming by their account, not territory but self-determination for the inhabitants. The USSR, which since late 1976 had been supplying Ethiopia with arms, shifted its full support to the Ethiopians. As a result, Somalia renounced its treaty of friendship with the USSR and expelled all Soviet advisers in November 1977. Arms shipments from the Soviet Union were ended and its military advisers sent to Ethiopia. The USSR did not support Somalia in its war with Ethiopia, as it would have damaged its image in Africa as a whole. She did not wish to appear to be supporting an action that was in open violation of the Organisation of African Unity's policy on the inviolability of colonial borders.

Somalia turned to the United States for military aid. It was agreed that economic aid could be supplied but military aid was withheld. Somalia's search for alternative sources of arms yielded few results. The Western countries would not supply military hardware. Economic aid increased, particularly after the withdrawal of Somali troops from the Ogaden in early March 1978, with Western countries and China taking over many of the unfinished Soviet projects. The EEC provided $70 million in emergency aid. West Germany provided $25 million of aid. China, which supported Somalia throughout the Ogaden conflict, agreed to take over many of the aid projects started by the Soviets.

In April 1978, President Barre visited Peking to request emergency military aid and economic assistance. The Chinese offered training and technical assistance, but only nominal amounts of military hardware.

While not completely filling the gap left by the departure of nearly 1,000 Soviet and East European technicians, China maintained its 3,000-man presence and agreed to provide $18 million of aid to finish the abandoned Soviet projects. Romania was the only East European country still active in Somalia, providing assistance with agriculture and fisheries. Saudi Arabia also began to supply aid. The Saudis supported Somalia in the Ogaden War after the rupture in Soviet-Somali relations. Aid was given to cover Somalia's foreign trade imbalances and has amounted to nearly $400 million.

In January 1979, Somalia expressed its willingness to negotiate the re-admission of Soviet diplomats. This was probably because the United States and its allies offered insufficient economic aid and refused to supply any military aid. By the end of the year, with the seizing of the American diplomatic hostages in Iran, Somalia had gained a new importance in Western — and particularly American — foreign policy. Negotiations between the USA and Somalia on increased economic and military aid in exchange for the use of the port at Berbera have recently been concluded with Somalia receiving nearly $50 million in credit.

Conclusion

Following the Ogaden War the future path of development of Somalia remains uncertain. It has broken relations with the USSR and has been actively seeking US military and civilian aid. The establishment of a US military presence in Somalia (at Berbera) as part of the rapid deployment forces will ensure American financial support for Somalia for the immediate future. The breaking of ties with the USSR has brought, and very likely will continue to bring, increasing amounts of aid from members of the Arab League.

It is extremely unlikely that Somalia will follow the path of development of those countries that we have classified as the NCTW. Internally its commitment to Marxism-Leninism was never strong since it clung officially to Islam. There is a question of the strength of the commitment to Marxism by an Islamic country, and this deserves a short *excursus*. Moslem faith as a whole has been much less eroded than the Christian faith by rationalism, libertarianism and permissiveness;

Table 9.6: Soviet-Somali Trade (millions of transferable roubles)

	1970	1971	1972	1973	1974	1975	1976	1977	1978	1979
Exports to Somalia	2.8	5.5	11.7	11.5	16.8	22.2	18.7	20.1	0.0	0.0
Imports from Somalia	0.4	1.8	2.9	1.1	2.0	4.3	4.7	2.9	0.0	0.0
Trade balance	2.4	3.7	8.8	10.4	14.8	17.9	14.0	17.2	–	–
Exports										
Total specified	2.5	4.6	10.7	11.3	16.2	21.7	17.7	17.3		
Machinery/equipment	0.8	2.3	8.4	8.1	9.2	11.4	8.3	7.2		
of which trucks, cars	–	1.3	6.7	2.0	1.6	4.2	0.7	0.8		
communications	–	–	1.7	3.1	3.3	–	0.1	0.2		
hydroelectric	–	–	–	–	0.7	3.5	3.5	3.2		
Oil and oil products	1.4	1.7	1.9	1.9	4.3	8.6	8.8	10.1		
Chemicals, fertilisers	–	–	0.1	0.1	0.1	–	0.4	–		
Building materials	0.2	0.4	0.2	0.2	0.9	1.1	0.1	–		
Industrial general goods	0.1	0.2	0.1	0.8	1.7	0.6	0.1	–		
Unspecified	0.3	0.9	1.0	0.2	0.6	0.5	1.0	2.8		
Imports										
Total specified	0.4	1.8	2.9	1.1	2.0	4.3	4.5	2.9		
Hides	–	–	–	0.2	0.2	–	–	–		
Processed meat	0.4	1.8	2.9	0.8	1.8	4.3	4.5	2.9		
Processed fish	–	–	–	0.1	–	–	–	–		
Unspecified	–	–	–	–	–	–	0.2	–		

Source: *VT*, various years.

Table 9.7: Promised Civilian Aid from Communist Countries

Year	Country	Amount $m	Grant element %	Purpose
1963	China	3.0	100	Budget support
		19.0	71.7	National hall & purchase of Chinese goods
1971	USSR	0.2	100	Food aid
		5.5	n.a.	n.a.
		2.2	100	Debt relief
		17.2	n.a.	Agricultural equipment
	GDR	42.8	37.7	n.a.
	China	110.0	n.a.	Road construction
1972	Bulgaria	1.5	35.0	n.a.
1974	USSR	45.0	60.0	Debt relief
	China	0.9	100	Relief aid
1975	USSR	59.6	n.a.	Development projects, fishing
	China	0.4	100	Relief aid
1976	GDR	1.3	n.a.	n.a.
		0.3	100	Agricultural equipment
	Bulgaria	5.0	n.a.	Hides, textiles
1977	GDR	0.6	100	n.a.
1978	China	18.0	n.a.	n.a.
1954-78	USSR	164		
	Eastern Europe	6		
	China	155		

Sources: *The Aid Programme of China*, OECD, Paris, 1979; *The Aid Programme of the USSR*, OECD, Paris, 1977; *The Aid Programme of the East European Countries*, OECD, Paris, 1977.

it also governs many more details of everyday life. In the Stalinist period Islam succumbed nevertheless, like any other religion. In Central Asia it is persecuted and has diminished almost but not quite to the same degree as Christianity in the Slavic lands. In Albania, which has remained Stalinist, even private prayer has been abolished. All churches and mosques closed in 1968, and the constitution of 1977 makes atheism compulsory. This is the most draconic anti-religious legislation in the world.

More recent policy has been much more circumspect. It is interesting to compare the policy towards Islam of three Marxist Moslem countries: the PDRY and Somalia, members of the Arab League, and the non-Arab Afghanistan. The latter proclaimed in her constitution of 1976 the freedom of observation of 'the rites of the sacred religion of Islam' — rights allowed also to the followers of other faiths. Whilst the PDRY and Somalia both proclaimed Islam as the 'state religion', only the PDRY (like Afghanistan) implements a policy aiming to alter fundamentally the traditional basis of Islamic society. The roles of men and women have been put on an equal footing, not only as citizens of the state but also as members of the family with equal rights and duties. The dowry has been abolished. In Somalia such radical changes were attempted, but they caused an Islamic backlash already in 1975, and were abandoned. For this reason we would question the strength of the commitment to Marxism in Somalia. The new doctrine had no time to establish itself in the country before the Ogaden war intervened.

It must not be thought that Somalia's history has been happy since the expulsion of the Russians — though there was at that moment the proverbial dancing in the streets. The weight of the Ogadeni refugees upon the economy is enormous, and international aid to them is of course channelled through President Barre. He supports them and his power rests on them, causing much domestic resentment. Foreign policy is frozen in an anti-Ethiopian stance, and the economy stagnates. Somalia's external relations will necessarily be affected by the fact that it has fought a war with another socialist country receiving Soviet assistance. It is the quintessential 'one that got away', joining the select but disparate group of eastern Austria, Persian Azerbaijan and possibly Finland (see Chapter 1, Group 4).

Notes

1. Prof. Ioan Lewis (LSE) has been extremely helpful.
2. Kravis *et al.*, 1978.

PART THREE:

THE INDEPENDENT STALINISTS

10 THE SOCIALIST PEOPLE'S REPUBLIC OF ALBANIA

Adi Schnytzer

1. In terms of output levels, the Albanian economy has remained the least developed in Europe throughout its modern history. Since the Second World War, however, the economy has been transformed by the rapid developments of an industrial sector which had contributed only 4.4 per cent to net material product in 1938, but which now accounts for well over half thereof. The following table shows the changes in a series of major indicators between 1938 and 1973.

Table 10.1: Growth Indices for the Albanian Economy (1938=1)

	1950	1960	1970	1973
Net Domestic Material Product	1.7	4.0	8.3	10.7
Global Agricultural Production	1.2	1.7	3.1	3.5
Global Industrial Production	4.0	25.0	65.0	86.0
Retail trade turnover	1.4	6.0	10.0	13.0
Population (millions)	1.2	1.6	2.14	2.3

Source: *30 vjet Shqipëri socialiste*, Tirana, 1974, pp. 21, 56, 112, 177, 183.

Albania's GNP *per capita* in 1970 has been estimated [1] as $350 US. Vinski (1976) puts it, from neighbouring Zagreb, at $372 US for 1970, or one-third of Yugoslavia. Kosovo-Metohija, the adjacent Albanian province inside Yugoslavia, was also at one-third of that country's average; and both our sources claim to have tried to calculate a genuine purchasing power parity (this emerges as about 9 leks to $1 US in 1970). So this improbably low figure, putting Albania well below Angola and even Mozambique, must for the time being be accepted. One reason for this poverty must be the high rate of population growth, natural to Moslem populations: 2.9 per cent p.a. in 1950-73, 2.5 per cent in 1973-8.

Having experienced a Stalinist development strategy for more than 30 years, Albanian economic structure differs from that of these African states in that only a little less than half the population lives in towns. Nevertheless, the industrial work-force numbered only 161,000 in 1973, or about 14 per cent of the labour-force. The official rate of exchange was 5 leks to $1 US in 1970, and military expenditure in 1975 was 635 million leks – around 14 per cent of GNP – another good reason for the continuing poverty. The foreign-trade participation ratio was about 7 per cent in 1970 – an amazingly low level for so small a population.

2. The distinguishing feature of Communist Albania's development strategy is that it continues to base itself on the guidelines set out by Stalin in his *Economic Problems of Socialism in the USSR*. Nowhere in the Communist world does Stalin enjoy this kind of treatment and the following possible reasons should be noted:

(i) No member of the 1944 Politburo of the Albanian Communist Party – the name was changed to the Albanian Party of Labour in 1948 – had ever visited the Soviet Union and it is doubtful whether any of them knew any Russian. Albanian is a non-Slavonic Indo-European language. The Marxism-Leninism of the pre-war West European *salons* overstated the merits of Stalinism without allowing individuals the benefit of first-hand observation of its weaknesses.

(ii) Between 1945 and 1948 the People's Republic of Albania was under constant threat of incorporation into the Yugoslav Federation. During these three years the Albanian party was split into two groups: the smaller faction, led by Koçi Xoxe, wanted to see closer ties between Albania and Yugoslavia, while the larger group led by Enver Hoxha (First Party Secretary from the birth of the Party on 9 November 1941 to the present time), Mehmet Shehu (present Prime Minister) and Hysni Kapo (probably still number three in the hierarchy) preferred complete independence for Albania. It is almost certain that Stalin was responsible for keeping Albania out of the Yugoslav Federation and – perhaps more significantly – allowing Hoxha and company to purge all opposition in the wake of the Soviet-Yugoslav split of 1948.

(iii) For an intensely nationalistic leadership, economic Stalinism provides a path of economic development which leads to independence from the outside world after the economy has reached a sufficient level of development and if it is well-endowed with natural resources. Since the latter condition is met in Albania – the country is rich in energy and mineral resources – the leadership needed only to find suitable sources of aid to build a strong industrial sector.

(iv) Current administration has been as Stalinist as long-term development. There is a detailed, central, *a priori* plan; there are passive wholesale prices; collective and state farms absorb the whole of agriculture; there is a variable turnover tax and retail prices are extremely stable; the budget provides nearly all long-term capital and no interest is charged on it; machine and tractor stations are still in existence. Such new Soviet developments as a tax on fixed capital (similar but not identical to a rate of interest) have not been adopted.

3. Wiles has described Albania's aid procurement (at about 3 per cent of GNP annually until 1975) as a remarkable feat of diplomacy and so, indeed, it seems to have been, though $32 million per year is not such a great sum for the government of a poor but strategically placed small country to collect. Be that as it may, Kaser's 'rough estimates' of aid to Albania are as follows:

(millions of US dollars at current prices; net disbursements):

(a) UNRRA 1945-8	26	(of which USA $m20.4)
(b) Yugoslavia 1945-8	33	
(c) USSR 1947-61	156	(plus approx. $m100 technical[2] and military aid)
(d) Other East Europe 1948-61	133	
(e) China 1959-75	838	
(f) Western Commercial Credits 1965-75	94	

Note: In terms of millions of 1971 domestic leks, Albania's ability to maintain a balance of payments deficit is shown in Table 10.2.
Source: JEC, 1977, p. 1335.

Albania's invisible balance is presumably positive (remittances, military bases and a little tourism); but we have no figures.

It should be noted that when the Albanians publish trade figures (and I have this on the authority of one who spent some months in the Central Planning Commission in 1967) these are given in terms of *domestic* prices. This allows measurement of the impact of aid on investment and growth of industrial output. This analysis, which led to the 'Schnytzer thesis', is given in detail in Schnytzer, 1978. The essential point is that, because Soviet and Chinese aid to Albania took the form of resources required to complete a particular project rather than simply credit, the aid was not 'fungible'. Consequently, the impact of the aid will, in large measure, be determined by the extent to which the recipient government is able to determine independently

Table 10.2: Albania's Visible Balance (m. of 1971 domestic leks)

	Net material product	Visible exports	Visible imports	M-X
1945		2	7	5
1946		7.5	8	0.5
1947		19	121	102
1948		33	73	40
1949		24	52	28
1950	1,399	26	88	62
1951		37	159	122
1952		53	128	75
1953		45	161	116
1954		41	104	63
1955		52	172	120
1956		75	156	81
1957		117	214	97
1958		117	315	198
1959		136	342	206
1960	3,292	212	353	141
1961		211	314	103
1962		178	281	103
1963		209	308	99
1964		256	422	166
1965	4,444	270	469	199
1966		303	512	209
1967		317	523	206
1968		360	535	175
1969		368	661	293
1970	6,830	431	687	256

Source: Schnytzer, 1980, p. 101.

the nature of the aid. It seems that this was not so in the Soviet case. Whereas Soviet aid was confined to infrastructure, agriculture, food, and light industries, the Chinese allowed Albania to intensify the development of heavy industry. An examination of the structure of Mongolian exports over time reveals the Soviet freezing capability quite clearly (see Chapter 12).

4. The data on the commodity structure of Albanian trade are not easy to come by.

It should be noted that the aggregation procedure adopted in compiling the following table obscures the fact that there has been a significant change (precise figures not available) in the nature of the 'Industrial Manufactures' category: from unprocessed minerals to processed minerals and completed industrial consumer goods.

Table 10.3: The Commodity Composition of Albanian Foreign Trade in 1968 (percentages)

Exports[a]		Imports	
Oil products	24	Engineering goods	37
Minerals and their products	31	Raw materials and building	
Food industry products	15	materials	8
Agricultural produce	20.5	Fuels and metals	24
Artisan products	1.5	Chemicals	10
		Foodstuffs	11
		Manufactured consumer-	
		goods	10

Exports only (another classification)				
	1950	1960	1970	1973[b]
Industrial manufactures	63.7	56.6	60.8	58.4
Agricultural manufactures	12.1	27.2	22.7	27.2
Unprocessed farm produce	24.2	16.2	16.5	14.2

a. The categories add up to 92%. Other manufactures presumably make up the difference.
b. Discrepancy due to rounding.
Source: Kaser, 1977, p. 1338.

Table 10.4 gives some data on the geographical distribution of trade. In earlier years Albania was far more forthcoming, and the history of visible trade by regions is shown in Table 10.5.

Unfortunately there are no recent figures available for Albania's most important trading partner since 1961, China. In 1978, just before the split, trade with China was said [3] to account for 35-40 per cent of Albania's foreign trade. This is about the same as in 1970 (Table 10.5).

5. On foreign policy, ideology and foreign trade, the following points may be made:

(i) Until very recently Communist Albania has always had a major aid donor. With the exception of UNRRA, this donor has also been the major trading partner.

(ii) While the Albanian leadership has always stressed the need for aid to come in the spirit of 'proletarian internationalism', it has argued that trade needs only to be to the mutual benefit of both countries. Thus, high trade levels with first the Soviet Union, and then China, are more a consequence of the simultaneous existence of the aid, i.e. of the wishes of the other party, than of Albanian ideology. Similarly, low

Table 10.4: Albania's Visible Mirror Trade ($US 000)

	1960[e]	1964[e]	1970	1971	1973	1975	1977	1978
Exports *from* countries *to* Albania								
Yugoslavia[a]	n.a.	n.a.	2,258	4,118	7,186	14,831	10,615	12,555
USSR	46,000	0	0[f]	0	0	0	0	0
Bulgaria[a]			5,299	5,897	6,807	7,334	5,589	6,433
CSSR[a]	24,000	27,400	12,639	18,368	22,384	n.a.	n.a.	n.a.
GDR[a]			6,143	7,738	9,655	n.a.	n.a.	n.a.
Hungary[a]			2,479	2,781	5,631	9,341	4,160	2,841
Poland[a]			8,050	7,395	10,8	10,351	7,418	11,766
Romania[a]			3,117	4,483	7,884	8,592	6,257	n.a.
EEC[b]	3,700	4,400	13,844	14,990	17,204	38,800	43,800	40,900
of which Italy[b]	—	—	6,852	8,312	9,808	15,600	14,510	12,844
West Germany[b]			3,274	3,382	2,048	11,930	17,420	15,085
Rest[d]	7,600	66,200?	79,534	n.a.	n.a.	n.a.	n.a.	n.a.
Total[c]	81,300	98,000	137,400	n.a.	n.a.	n.a.	n.a.	n.a.
Imports *into* countries *from* Albania								
Yugoslavia	n.a.	n.a.	2,961	4,639	10,240	21,938	19,800	15,250
USSR	24,200	0	0	0	0	0	0	0
Bulgaria			5,897	6,325	7,107	8,676	3,586	5,273
CSSR	21,100	28,200	18,258	19,251	21,940	n.a.	n.a.	n.a.
GDR			6,310	7,095	7,126	n.a.	n.a.	n.a.
Hungary			4,226	7,338	9,607	16,008	3,193	2,959
Poland			8,050	10,049	12,849	18,000	8,824	12,460
Romania			3,433	5,067	8,143	7,746	14,745	12,460

Table 10.4: Continued

Imports *into* countries *from* Albania	1960[e]	1964[e]	1970	1971	1973	1975	1977	1978
EEC	500	3,900	7,658	10,058	13,060	2,520	32,400	29,500
of which Italy	–	–	5,531	8,318	9,893	1,484	17,680	13,490
Rest	2,800	28,300?	33,189	n.a.	n.a.	n.a.	n.a.	n.a.
Total	48,600	60,400	86,020	n.a.	n.a.	n.a.	n.a.	n.a.

a. Statistical Yearbooks, countries concerned, various years, converted to $ according to UN conversion factors. But except for Yugoslavia all figures in 1960 and 1964 are from source e.

b. METB.

c. Not mirror trade: direct Albanian data from Table 10.2.

d. This is the 'Total' item as it stands minus the other items subject to a c.i.f./f.o.b. correction of 7.5%.

e. *Vjetari Statistikor*, 1965, pp. 314 *et seq*.

f. Soviet trade, applying the 'Socialist countries residual' method, seems to have been zero in 1970 (*VT*, 1971). The subsequent zeros have been inferred from this.

Table 10.5: Albania's Visible Trade by Regions (per cent)

	1955	1960	1964	1970 (approx)
		Imports		
USSR	37.0	56.6	0	0
Rest of CMEA	58.0	29.7	27.9	30
Yugoslavia	–	0.3	1.1	1.5
China	2.5	8.6	61.2	51
EEC	2.2	4.6	4.5	11
Other advanced capitalist		0.3	0.8	?1.5
Third World	0.2	0	3.4	?5
		Exports		
USSR	42.0	50.0	0	0
Rest of CMEA	55.0	43.5	47.0	50
Yugoslavia	–	0.8	2.0	3
China	0	4.3	40.0	32
EEC	2.0	1.0	5.8	8
Other advanced capitalist		0	0.7	?1
Third World	1.0	0.5	4.1	?6
Unfavourable balance ($m) with				
USSR	21.8	21.8	0	0
China	4.9	4.9	36.0	42.5

Source: *Vjetari Statistikor*, 1965, pp. 314 *et seq*. See Table 10.4.

levels of trade with Western economies, other than France and Italy, are probably to be explained largely in terms of the poor quality of Albanian exports and the high cost of capital equipment *vis-à-vis* the poorer quality equipment of CMEA and China.

(iii) According to the new Albanian Constitution (1977):

The granting of concessions to, and the creation of, foreign economic and financial companies and other institutions or ones formed jointly with bourgeois and revisionist capitalist monopolies and states as well as obtaining credits from them are prohibited in the People's Socialist Republic of Albania.

Now that Albania no longer has a 'socialist' source of aid — Albania being the only Marxist-Leninist state in the world! — it is expanding its trade with the West, but refusing to ask for long-term credits. This is really a corollary of (ii).

(iv) Ideology and trade have only been related under the most extreme circumstances. Thus, since 1961, there has been no trade with the Soviet Union, but it was the latter that instituted the boycott; in years of very tense relations, trade with Yugoslavia has fallen off sharply, but it is not clear at whose instigation; Chinese trade has behaved like Soviet trade; trade with Italy, the ancient imperial power, has always been high for reasons of simple convenience.

(v) Albania is, however, very autarkic indeed for so small a country, with a foreign-trade participation ratio of about 7 per cent (compare Belgium with 52 per cent, Hungary with 45 per cent). It might perhaps rather be said that her capacity to export is small because of her Stalinist set-up; and her import-voracity is limited only by her amazing ability to extract foreign aid.

(vi) Albania and North Korea, and Romania in lesser degree, share innumerable political and economic traits. The main ones are:

(a) A fiercely independent foreign policy, Communist in a general way but vehemently rejecting Soviet hegemony;
(b) A refusal of all foreign aid from any quarter (but Romania takes a little aid, and this policy is quite new in Albania);
(c) A low foreign-trade participation ratio (but Romania is well-endowed with food and oil, so does not need a high one);
(d) A Stalinist development policy, emphasising heavy industry;
(e) A Stalinist economic model;
(f) A Stalinist internal security system;
(g) Diplomatic isolationism and security paranoia;
(h) Cultural isolationism and fear of tourists;
(i) The cult of personality.

It is beyond the scope of this book to analyse and explain this syndrome.[4] It is enough to refer the reader forward to Vietnam, where none of this applies. The Vietnamese example is in all ways more attractive than the Albanian to the NCTW. However, as Heraclitus noted, everything is in motion. Tourists report very differently on Albania in 1980: they no longer have their hair cut at the border (if male); *Playboy*, the *New York Times*, *The Times* and *The Economist* were allowed into the country in 1980 (nevertheless the old warnings on the first and second points are still issued in advance); an Albanian guide informed a visitor that Albanians like reading foreign material, and may do so provided they are discreet; within the ambit of the Ministry of Tourism, jokes at the expense of the leadership may occasionally be heard and social contacts between Albanians and foreigners are warming up.

It is safe to predict vast changes in diplomatic and commercial policy if these deplorable trends persist. But they have not yet been securely identified with a leadership change, so their durability is in doubt. After all, in 1974 Hoxha attacked the advocates of tourism as people 'who advise us to turn our country into an inn with doors open to pigs and sows'.[5] Further, a Turkish journalist gives the distinct impression that nothing at all has changed.[6]

Notes

1. Kaser and Schnytzer, 1977.
2. This comprises the training of Albanians in the USSR and the employment of Soviet experts on Albanian soil.
3. Dode, 1978.
4. But cf. Wiles, 1981.
5. *New York Times*, 18 May 1975.
6. *National Geographic*, October 1980.

11 THE KOREAN PEOPLE'S DEMOCRATIC REPUBLIC

Pong Lee[1]

1. Introduction

The population of North Korea was 17 million in 1978[2] (South Korea 37 million). In the division of 1945 the North took the heavy industry and the South the agriculture. Reunification is an obsession with both parts, even though a state of cold war has alternated with actual war from start to finish. Income per head in 1970 is estimated by the CIA at 110 per cent of S. Korea,[3] which was $657 in the prices of that year (Kravis *et al.*, 1978). This brings N. Korea, at $723, to the prosperous end of the Third World. Incidentally, the CIA tells us, and commonsense also urges us to believe, that South Korea has recently drawn ahead. National income per head rose at 10 per cent p.a. in 1956-67 according to official Northern statistics, thereby far surpassing the South. But then these figures were suppressed, and simultaneously the Southern boom began.

Even more than the NCTW, North Korea is definitely Marxist-Leninist. No one can dispute that the economy, polity and society are of the Soviet, indeed the Stalinist, type, with due regard to the country's poverty. The most remarkable feature of the polity is Kim Il Sung's cult of personality and nepotistic dictatorship, his son Kim Chung Il being virtually named as his successor. This is a feature of not a few Marxist-Leninist countries. It has very exact parallels in Romania and Albania, and apart from the nepotism, Stalin's USSR. One is tempted to a generalisation: the ignorance of uneducated people permits, and the desire to be independent of Soviet interference makes desirable, this sort of leadership. The USSR, of course, prefers and maintains a collegial form of government in its satellites.[4]

In 1956, on the pretext of deStalinisation, certain Korean Communists tried to unseat Kim. There was both Soviet and Chinese interference, but the whole attempt came to naught (Scalapino and Lee, 1972, pp. 510 *et seq*.). No doubt it was this experience that induced Kim to pursue his isolationist line, which we may call 'Stalinism in one country'. Indeed he was already on this line in 1955, when in a speech to a group of Party workers he outlined his vision for an independent Korea. Fundamental to that vision was a strong Korean economy, able to grow without recourse to excessive levels of economic aid from China or the Soviet Union. Thus was born North Korea's national catch-word, *chu ch'e* (literally, 'national identity'; Kaser, 1977, Foster-Carter, 1977). *Chu ch'e* can be described as near-autarky in economic terms, but simultaneously as 'psychological decolonisation'. In a later version Kim throws in Marxist philosophy too: 'The *chu ch'e* idea is based on the philosophical theory that man is the master of everything . . . [it provides] a powerful weapon to grasp the world intellectually and transform it' (Kim, 1975). *Chu ch'e* is an enormously popular concept on the left-wing of the Third World. We shall only detail events since its enunciation.

To return to the concept's original and primary meaning, sharing a common border with both China and the Soviet Union placed North Korea in a delicate situation with the advent of the Sino-Soviet split. Some slight concessions to Chinese organisational forms were made in 1958, when the collective farms were amalgamated. But this amalgamation was mainly of Soviet type: there were no People's Communes. The Chinese policy, however, of the Great Leap Forward, was adopted: under the name of Chollima ('ten-thousand-ri flying horse'), again in 1958.[5] But the Korean rider, unlike the Chinese leaper, did not fall flat on his face. Pyongyang has always attempted to maintain reasonable relations with both countries, swinging first one way in 1958, as shown, and then the other in 1963 (below).

Economically, the idea of self-reliance for North Korea, a small country with limited resources, would be most difficult, if not impossible, to implement as a policy. The participation ratio was about 13 per cent in 1966 (Lee, 1972). An economic interpretion of a *chu ch'e* economy, though hardly one put into actual practice, can be drawn from the following statement of Kim Il Sung, made at the Industrial Activists' Meeting on 4 March 1975:

> Ours is an independent and *chu ch'e*-based economy. We depend on domestic raw materials for more than 70 per cent of the materials for industry and obtain the rest from socialist countries on the principle of mutual accommodation. Therefore, our country's economy is free from the impact of the worldwide capitalistic economic crises and there is no fluctuation in production due to raw materials.
>
> Fluctuation in production is inherent in the capitalist economy . . . . Since we are well aware of the intrinsic defects of the capitalist

economy, we never depend on the capitalist market for raw
materials for industry . . . . Our economy firmly relies on domestic
raw materials and has great potential to advance independently and
confidently; immune from the impact of the worldwide economic
crises. . . .

Our machine industry produces tractors, trucks, excavators,
bulldozers and other machines and equipment, satisfactorily meeting
our heavy demand for them. We import only equipment for which
we have no great need.

This paper is primarily concerned with a brief review of how North
Korea's desire to be self-reliant has been manifested in its international
economic policy, especially in the 1970s. We shall note that North
Korea's economy, despite its professed policy of self-reliance, had been
heavily dependent on the Soviet Union and China for trade and aid,
at least until the beginning of the 1970s. For example, as late as 1970
and 1971, more than three-quarters of trade was with Communist
countries, the USSR alone constituting close to 45 per cent of the total,
while nearly 20 per cent was with China. As percentages of national
income however, these numbers fall to only five and two per cent. Of
course the particular goods imported are much more important than
such low numbers imply. From 1972, North Korea attempted to break
away from this practice and ventured into a bold new policy of
importing machinery and equipment from industrialised developed
countries of the West. In consequence, the share of trade with capitalist
countries dramatically increased from less than 25 per cent in 1970 and
1971 to about 41 per cent in 1974.

In section 2, we shall briefly review events since the 1950s to 1970,
the period when the Soviet, and to a less extent, Chinese and other
Communist countries' economic co-operation and aids were essential
ingredients to completing the series of North Korea's economic plans.
Our main topic of international economic policy in the 1970s will be
discussed in section 3, which will be further divided into two parts:
(a) trade with Communist countries; (b) trade with capitalist
countries. Because of limited space our discussion will be focussed on
trade with the Soviet Union and Japan. In section 4, we shall examine
problems of foreign debt. Concluding remarks are made in section 5.

Table 11.1: Average Annual Growth Rates in Selected Economic Series

	1954-6	1957-60	1961-3	1964-70	1971-6
Global value of social product	28.7	23.0	11.1	n.a.	n.a.
National income	30.0	21.0	10.8	n.a.	n.a.
Global industrial output	41.4	33.8	13.6	12.3	16.3
Global agricultural output	11.6	8.8	7.9	n.a.	n.a.

Source: For years before 1964, Central Statistical Board, the State Planning Commission of the DPRK, *Statistical Returns of National Economy of the DPRK, 1964*, Foreign Language Publishing House, Pyongyang, 1964; global industrial output since 1964 was estimated from various offical publications. See *Trends in Asian Countries*, 1978 and 1979.

2. Events before 1970

North Korea, being one of the most secretive countries even by Communist standards, has not published any meaningful economic data in the last 15 years. Table 11.1 lists selected aggregate series officially published in annual average growth rates.

The unparalleled growth rates during the periods of the three-year plan for post-war recovery, 1954-6, and the five-year plan of 1957-60, largely represent rapid reconstruction and expansion of North Korean economy from the devastation of the Korean War. Massive economic aid from Communist countries, estimated to be about $1.4 billion, was primarily responsible for not only the restoration of war-damaged productive capacities but also diverse new production facilities.[6] In 1957, not long after the armistice of July 1953, foreign aid was still 12.2 per cent of state revenues (Kuark 1963, pp. 60-2). But already in 1960, before our own diminished series for aid begins, it had fallen to 2.6 per cent.[7] On the general rule that Communist budgets cover 60 per cent of GNP, this is 7.3 per cent and 1.6 per cent of GNP respectively.

During the first half of the seven-year plan, 1961-7, the rates of growth in almost all economic series rapidly deteriorated and reached their lowest point around 1964 and 1966. One expects the rate of expansion to slow down, naturally, from its phenomenal post-war high. Nonetheless, 14.3 per cent p.a. growth in global industrial production, 1961-6, is impressive when compared with other Communist economies.[8] Actual economic problems, however, appear to be greater than normally expected, judging from the fact that the original seven-year plan was extended in 1966 for three additional years until 1970. Also in 1964 almost all economic data suddenly disappeared from official publications. In particular, agricultural and industrial growth are available only on the misleading 'global' basis that so much inflates Communist statistics, while the growth of the national income (necessarily on a net basis) is no longer published.

Few reasons for the economic difficulties are known. A number of writers, however, attribute the problems to the Sino-Soviet rift during the period. Since 1960, North Korea tilted more toward the Chinese side of the dispute and the Soviet Union allegedly retaliated by failing to deliver industrial and farm machinery, as agreed upon by the first long-term trade agreement between the two countries signed in 1960. These Soviet machines, of course, had been taken into account in the seven-year plan. In 1963 there was a quarrel with Khrushchev. One question — very reminiscent of his simultaneous quarrel with Romania — was North Korea's excessive plans for heavy industry (Koh, 1969, pp. 90-1). Despite some long-term loans of about $105 million from China, the lack of Soviet aid in the early 1960s might have been one of the major reasons for failure, and therefore subsequent extension for three more years, of the seven-year plan.[9] Another of the causes of economic problems hinted at by North Korean officials was the necessity to increase defence spending during this period. After the Cuban missile crisis, which North Korea regarded as a Soviet retreat under American pressure, and in view of the spreading Vietnam conflict, North Korea apparently decided to allocate a larger portion of resources to a military build-up, including underground industrial and military facilities. It is quite conceivable that such military expenditure diverted scarce resources from completing the seven-year plan in time.

Beginning in the mid-1960s, North Korea gradually shifted its posture to a pro-Soviet line while professing to pursue a policy of 'active neutralism'. The departure of Khrushchev and the start of China's cultural revolution, which considerably strained North Korea-China relations, are often cited as direct causes of the policy change (Y.S. Kim, 1971). In June of 1966 North Korea and the USSR agreed on a renewed technical and economic co-operation, and from 1967 to 1971 there was a marked increase in North Korea's imports from the Soviet Union. It seems that the revived Soviet economic co-operation (but not military aid) were indispensable to North Korea's belated completion of the seven-year plan by 1970. Nevertheless, North Korea did not attend the great conference of Communist Parties in Moscow in June 1969.

According to official accounts, the average annual rate of increase in the global value of industrial production during the decade of 1961-70 was 12.8 per cent, whereas the planned growth-rate for the original seven-year plan period was 18.1 per cent. If we subtract the high growth of 1961-6, quoted above, we arrive at only 9.5 per cent p.a. in 1966-70. This cannot be unconnected with the fact that the official defence burden was 19 per cent of budget expenditures in 1960-1, but 31 per cent in 1969-70 (and 17 per cent in the 1972 plan). The amazingly high expenditures of 1969-70 (say 20 per cent of GNP), at a moment when civilian aid was negligible, were due to the influence of modernising generals not unlike Peng Te-huai (and even in the end, Lin Piao) in China, wanting to mend their fences with USSR and import sophisticated weapons. Kim himself took a quasi-Maoist line, favouring indeed an aggressive stance, but basing it on a huge militia and a general doctrine of labour-and-morale-intensive war. There are divergent views on whether USSR ever delivered the arms, but in any case Kim purged his general staff in 1969 (I.J. Kim, 1973, pp. 52-3; Spahr, 1974).

3. New Directions in the 1970s

The period of the six-year plan, 1971-6, marks the beginning of a new era in North Korea's international economic policy. Somewhat disappointed with both the USSR and China, she embarked on a large-scale import of Western machinery, equipment and other technologies in 1972, while at the same time retaining strong economic ties with the Soviet Union and China, as we note from Table 11.5. This was also the period when North Korea was supposedly continuing the policy of active neutralism between the Soviet Union and China. In practice, however, she seemed to be more sympathetic to China politically while economically more reliant on Soviet co-operation (Teratani, 1979, p. 24). For example, between 1971 and 1976 Soviet loans to North Korea were estimated to be $630 million as compared to less than $200 million from China.[10]

A. Trade with Communist Countries

It is interesting to note that, despite North Korea's agreements with the USSR and China on economic and technical co-operations to cover the entire period of the six-year plan, her imports from the Soviet Union began to decline in 1972. The decline continued until 1977, as we note from Table 11.3, which presents selected major commodities or commodity groups that she traded with the Soviet Union in the 1970s.

Imports from the USSR reached a peak of 330.1 million roubles in 1971 and then gradually decreased until 1978 when they began to rise again. Exports to the USSR, however, continued to increase, except in the years 1971 and 1976. Among the imports from the USSR, machinery and equipment had been the major commodity group until 1976. In absolute value, Soviet machinery and equipment reached a peak value of 100 million roubles in 1971 and continued to decrease thereafter to a mere 26.6 million roubles in 1978. Starting in 1972, more modern machinery and equipment from advanced capitalist countries such as Japan, West Germany, France and Sweden gradually supplemented or replaced those from the USSR. An increase in import of Soviet machinery and equipment in 1979 appears to signify not a reversal in trend but rather the improved overall trade volume of North Korea in that year.

Petroleum and petroleum products are the next most important item and their value rapidly increased, exceeding that of machinery and equipment since 1977. The sharp rise in petroleum imports in 1976 is largely due to an increase in price rather than in actual quantity. The quantity of petroleum imported in effect decreased from 1,111,000 tons in 1975 to 1,061,000 tons in 1976, whereas the value increased from 26.6 million roubles to 43.7 million roubles. Incidentally, the Soviet trade statistics ceased to publish the quantity of petroleum exported since 1977 and retained only the export value. From being very discriminatory in 1972, Soviet prices have become quite generous, but the figures are difficult to interpret (Table 11.6).

The major items exported to the USSR were rolled ferrous metals, magnesia-clinker, rice and clothing throughout the period under study. The value of magnesia-clinker export exceeded that of any other group since 1977. We note that, despite a decrease in imports and an increase in exports, North Korea continued to accumulate a trade deficit with the Soviet Union until 1977. The total deficit between 1970 and 1977 amounted to nearly $750 million (622 million roubles).

Neither China nor North Korea publishes trade statistics and our discussion is based on South Korean sources indicated in Table 11.5. North Korea's trade with China increased in the 1970s except for imports in 1975 and 1977, and exports in 1976 and 1977. The commodity composition of trade with China is not available, except that export items included mineral ores, metals, magnesites, cement, chemical products; while imports were coking coal, raw cotton, iron ores, soy beans, sugar and salt.[11] One of the notable events of the 1970s is that crude oil import from China through a new pipeline became possible since 1974. The average annual import is estimated to be about one million tons, the amount close to the import from the Soviet Union in 1975 and 1976 (Teratani, 1979, pp. 19-22).

The share of North Korea's trade with East European countries has been relatively small, amounting to about ten per cent of the total in 1970 and 1971. The commodity composition of trade with Czechoslovakia and Poland, for example, has been very much similar to that with the USSR. Exceptions are that the share of machinery and equipment imported and exported were greater, and North Korea's exports included more non-ferrous metals.[12] The balance of trade with East European countries seems to be even in general. Only with Romania has a trade deficit been accumulating in the 1970s.

B. Trade with Non-Communist Countries

A rather dramatic shift in North Korea's foreign economic policy can be observed in Table 11.2 where trade with capitalist countries is shown. As the figures in this table indicate, North Korea's even-handed policy extended to foreign trade, levels of exports to and imports from China and the Soviet Union remaining almost equal throughout the mid-sixties. Japan was by far North Korea's most important capitalist trading partner, although the volume of trade involved was moderate. Thus, even when trade with the 'West' was relatively unimportant for the North Korean economy, the major trading partner was — as in almost every other case — the former colonial power. The geographical proximity of the two countries has undoubtedly also been an important factor in stimulating trade, while North Korea's comparative advantage in raw materials and the production of labour-intensive commodities suggests that both countries would benefit from trade.

There were, however, several impediments to the further expansion of North Korean trade with Japan in the 1960s. The Japanese government's recognition of South Korea in 1965 was accomplished by means of an ambiguously worded treaty which, to Pyongyang and many opposition politicians in Japan, implied that Tokyo was recognising the Seoul government as the legitimate government of all Korea. Consequently, North Korea accused Japan of being 'a militarist trailing behind US imperialism' and her imports from Japan fell sharply in 1966 (Koh, 1969). The increase in exports over the same period is probably accounted for by Pyongyang's assessment that foreign exchange earnings may offset the disutility arising from Japanese political insensitivity. Further, the aid being provided by North Korea's neighbours made a search for Western aid donors unnecessary – if official statistics on the country's development are to be believed.

On the other hand, the slow-down of the late 1960s was of concern to the North Korean leadership and it was decided the country's development strategy would have to be modified. The absence of reliable data on North Korea's economic development since the late 1960s indicated trouble, but makes the outline of a precise scenario impossible. However, it is clear that the leadership decided that an expansion of trade relations with the West would allow the economy to resume its former rapid rate of growth; in other words *chu ch'e* itself was questioned, much as the USSR questioned its own technological independence at about the same time. Koh suggests the tensions of the Sino-Soviet dispute led North Korea to search for a still more independent foreign policy, including better relations with the West, serving to minimise the threat of invasion from the South. Whatever the validity of this assertion, it is clear that the Pyongyang government made continued efforts to improve relations with, if not gain recognition from, Japan. These efforts have focussed largely on gaining the support of left-wing elements in Japan, mainly the Korean immigrant community, of whom the majority by long tradition are at the bottom of the Japanese social heap and so support the North. Pyongyang even supports their education in Japan quite generously.[13]

In an attempt to obtain the foreign capital necessary to meet the targets of the 1971-6 six-year plan, the North Korean Committee for the Promotion of International Trade negotiated its first-ever trade agreement with representatives of a non-Communist country. The Japanese government was not, however, the signatory to the agreement; rather, it was the 'Dietman's League for the Promotion of Japan-North Korea Relations'. The five-year agreement, which was signed in Pyongyang in 1972, made the following stipulations:

(i) Trade between Japan and North Korea should increase to about $450-500 million (both ways) by 1976.

(ii) Japan would make available deferred payment conditions (exceeding eight years) to North Korea on the latter's purchase of machinery.

(iii) Commodity fairs would be held in each other's capitals.

(iv) The Japanese mission would try to facilitate the entry into Japan of trade and technical representatives from North Korea.

(v) Trade representatives from each of the signatories' countries would be permitted to operate in the other's country (Koh, 1977).

Between 1971 and 1974, total import from developed capitalist countries increased nearly eleven times, while export increased less than four times. Percentage shares of trade with each group are shown in Table 11.2. In the same three years the value of imports from these countries increased more than twelvefold, whereas exports rose only three times. As the problems of North Korea's default became widely known, the volume of this trade rapidly decreased from 1975 until 1978, when it began to increase again.

North Korea's cumulative trade deficit with advanced capitalist countries between 1972 and 1979, according to IMF data, had reached the enormous sum of more than $1.6 billion. Official Japanese data show the total trade deficit from the period was $633 million with Japan alone (Table 11.4). Although North Korea continued to accumulate trade deficits with these countries and the non-oil Third World, it apparently made a substantial inroad into export markets in OPEC countries, especially in Saudi Arabia and Indonesia.[14] The cumulative deficit with non-Communist countries as a whole, according to IMF estimate, was $1.35 billion between 1972 and 1977, and then decreased to less than $1.1 billion by the end of 1979. After Japan the biggest capitalist trade partners have been France and West Germany, as we notice in Table 11.2. USA is quite absent because of a particularly tight application of the Battle Act to this ex-enemy.

Trade between North Korea and Japan began in 1956 indirectly through China. Direct trade between the two countries had not materialised until 1961. Of several agreements signed between North Korean representatives and Japanese trade organisations, the most important one is the accord to promote trade between the two countries signed in January 1972. The accord of 1972 cleared the way for North Korea to be eligible for credits from Japan and, therefore, for delayed payments for its large scale imports.[15] We note a sudden jump in imports from Japan in 1972, while imports from the USSR began a sharp dive in the same year. The composition of trade with Japan from 1971 to 1979 is shown in Table 11.4. A rather clear and consistent pattern emerges, North Korea exporting foods, raw materials and non-ferrous metal products, while importing machinery and equipment, chemicals, processed metals, textiles and other products of light industries. The patterns of trade with France and West Germany have been somewhat similar.

Table 11.2 : North Korea, Direction of Visible Trade ($USm)

	1960	1964	1965	1966	1967	1968	1969	1970	1971	1972	1973
Exports to											
Communist countries											
Soviet Union	75	81	82	92	108	121	127	143	136	156	180
China	n.a.	81	82	92	88	50	55	50	65	95	115
Other Communist countries	n.a.	21	21	26	26	33	42	53	47	53	57
Total		183	185	210	222	203	223	246	248	303	351
Non-Communist countries											
Japan	0	20	15	23	30	34	32	34	30	38	72
Other non-Communist countries	6	3	8	11	19	18	23	30	38	45	59
Total	6	23	23	34	49	52	55	65	68	83	131
Grand total	n.a.	206	208	244	271	255	278	311	316	386	482
Imports from											
Communist countries											
Soviet Union	39	83	90	86	110	172	202	230	367	305	302
China	n.a.	82	89	86	81	50	55	50	70	105	135
Other Communist countries	n.a.	20	20	21	21	36	42	41	55	67	57
Total		185	199	187	212	258	298	321	492	478	494
Non-Communist countries											
Japan	1	11	17	5	6	21	24	23	29	93	100
Other non-Communist countries	4	7	17	27	27	30	72	42	31	46	184
Total	5	18	34	26	27	51	96	65	60	139	284
Grand total	n.a.	203	233	213	239	309	394	386	552	617	778

Sources: 1960-73 *Area Handbook for North Korea*, Washington, 1976, pp. 298-9; *Area Handbook for North Korea*, Washington, 1969, p. 373. The figures for trade with China have been calculated as differences. Any discrepancies in the summation are due to rounding.

Table 11.2 Continued

	1973	1974	1975	1977	1979
Total					
Exports	(495.1)				
Imports	(836.8)				
Balance	(−341.7)				
Advanced capitalist countries					
Exports	119.3	172.2	160.9	105.6	262.2
Imports	256.6	701.6	474.6	256.9	431.7
Balance	−137.3	−529.4	−313.7	−151.3	−169.5
of which Japan[a] Exports	72.3	108.8	64.8	66.6	152.0
Imports	100.2	251.9	180.6	125.1	283.8
Balance	−27.9	−143.1	−115.8	−58.5	−131.8
France Exports	17.3	29.2	38.2	8.2	26.4
Imports	68.5	106.6	24.6	6.0	8.7
Balance	−51.2	−77.4	3.6	1.2	17.7
West Germany Exports	15.5	20.8	47.0	20.3	65.2
Imports	42.5	89.1	83.3	26.4	37.1
Balance	−27.0	−68.3	−36.3	−6.1	28.1
Developing countries					
of which oil exporters Exports	3.1	58.3	105.8	183.9	435.8
Imports	3.9	6.4	7.3	10.6	20.1
Balance	−0.8	51.9	98.5	173.3	415.7
Rest[b] Exports	33.6	70.3	82.2	65.3	113.5
Imports	89.5	110.6	109.5	134.1	203.7
Balance	−55.9	−40.3	−27.3	−68.8	−90.2

Table 11.2 Continued

		1973	1974	1975	1977	1979
Communist countries of which USSR	Exports	180.0	196.5	210.4	223.0	
	Imports	302.4	256.5	259.7	224.0	
	Balance	−122.0	−60.0	−49.3	1.0	
Other Eastern Europe	Exports	47.2				
	Imports	48.4				
	Balance	−1.2				
China	Exports	112.0	120.0	192.2	164.0	
	Imports	136.0	180.0	176.5	156.0	
	Balance	−24.0	−60.0	15.7	8.0	

a. From Table 11.4 below.

b. Includes Greece, Malta, Portugal, Romania and Yugoslavia.

Source: International Monetary Fund, *Direction of Trade Yearbook*, 1977, p. 204; 1980, p. 290; Communist data from Table 11.5 below.

Trade with LDCs had been negligible in the 1960s and then rapidly expanded in the 1970s. For example, in 1970 total trade with all LDCs including OPEC was less than a fifth of that with developed capitalist countries. By 1979, however, exports to OPEC alone were 1.6 times exports to the latter,[16] whereas imports from all LDCs were still about a half. The significant increase in volume and in geographic diversity in trade with LDCs in the 1970s was the result of a strongly emphasised policy actively to befriend countries of the Third World.

One has to be reminded that, in spite of a rather dramatic change in international economic policy in the 1970s, North Korea is still trading primarily with Communist countries, about two-thirds of the total in the late 1970s. The still large share of trade with the Communist countries may be due to the problems of foreign debt with capitalist countries, especially developed ones. We shall now examine some aspects of North Korean foreign debt.

4. Problems of Foreign Debt[17]

There are a number of events that have possibly led North Korea to the drastic policy change, which in turn caused problems of foreign debt and payment default in the mid-1970s. In the early 1970s detente became a fact. That is, the European Communist countries also underwent a major policy reorientation and started to import advanced Western technologies. In consequence, several advanced capitalist countries were actively competing for markets in the Soviet bloc. China already had been trading primarily with Japan and other non-Communist countries ever since the Sino-Soviet split, culminating in a dramatic *rapprochement* with the USA in 1972.

North Korea had additional incentives to review its policy of economic dependence exclusively on the Soviet Union and China, and actively to seek out a policy of a greater independence. First was the disappointing experience with both countries during the seven-year plan period that had had to be lengthened for three more years. Secondly, the technological revolution had been advocated as one of the crucial components of success in the six-year plan of 1971-6: proof indeed that North Korea is responsive to CMEA fashions. Yet, without modernising existing productive capacity, which consisted mostly of outdated Soviet and East European machinery and equipment and domestic copies, the technological revolution would have been simply an empty slogan. Thirdly, pressure may have been exerted from South

Korea. The South Korean economy had been rapidly developing for some time by 1971 and forecasts were extremely optimistic. Fourthly, and perhaps a more direct reason, was North Korea's decision to complete the six-year plan by more than a year earlier than the original plan date of December 1976. The push for an earlier completion of the plan was apparently designed to coincide with the commemoration of the 30th anniversary of the Liberation of Korea and of the Party in autumn 1975.

North Korea extolled the successful achievement of most targets set for the six-year plan by a year and four months earlier than planned. Yet the price of the premature completion appeared to be very high indeed, both internally and externally. Internally, not only the remaining months of 1975 and 1976 had to be devoted to catching up with yet uncompleted segments of the plan, but also 1977 was designated as the year of 'readjustment' or of 'shock absorbing', suggesting that the economy was in considerable disarray. In the December of 1977, the second seven-year plan for 1978-84 was finally adopted.

Externally, the ambitious push for an earlier completion of the six-year plan contributed to excessive imports, while export capacity was not expanding fast enough to maintain the deficit within a manageable range. There was a combination of variables that adversely affected North Korea's balance of payments. One of the leading factors was the oil crisis of late 1973 and the ensuing world-wide 'stagflation'. Since the crisis, the Soviet price for oil eventually increased considerably, as we noted earlier, though we do not know whether North Korea pays the CMEA price or the world price, which is always higher. On the other hand, the world-wide recession apparently caused a sharp decline in the prices of non-ferrous metals and pig iron, the kingpins of the country's exports. An official explanation of the debt problem hinted at was the shipping, rail and other transportation bottle-necks that prevented North Korea from delivering her export products in time. It is quite conceivable that there was a lack of modern ports and other transportation capacities to accommodate a rapidly expanding international flow of commodities. There are other factors that might also have aggravated the balance of payments problem: a constant emphasis on heavy and military industries, lack of experience in trade and finance with the West, and agricultural failure. Certainly the balance of payments crisis has been very severe. Diplomats in Scandinavia were even caught dealing in drugs, evidently on official instructions to finance themselves in this manner (*The Times*,

20 October 1976).

From the commodity breakdown of trade it became clear that North Korea's comparative advantage is not yet in machinery and equipment and other producer goods. Nevertheless, like most other Soviet-type economies, she continues to channel resources into heavy and military industry. Maintaining a large force under arms also drained labour from the productive sectors of the economy. The overly optimistic expectations of the policy-makers in the early 1970s may have largely stemmed from their lack of experience in trade with the West, especially in payment mechanisms and credit conditions. Prolonged drought in the mid-1970s, combined with lack of material incentives to farmers, forced a large and continued import of grains from abroad. According to an estimate of the US Department of Commerce, total wheat and wheat flour imported from the West in 1974 alone reached $139 million.[18]

Few official publications on the exact magnitude of North Korea's debt are available from the countries involved. However, the various estimates seem to converge around the total debt of about $2.3 to $2.4 billion by the end of 1976. About $900 million is owed to the USSR, $100 million to China and the rest to the 'West'. France, Japan, West Germany and Sweden are considered to be the leading creditors.[19] There are no indications that the total amount of debt has been decreasing since 1976. In fact, North Korea has been seeking renegotiations with many capitalist creditors in recent years. An accord with Japan signed on 25 October 1979 may provide an example. The new accord prescribed that North Korea (i) complete payment of unpaid interest by June 1980; (ii) pay ¥85 billion (about $390 million) with interest in equal instalments during the next ten years; (iii) the rate of interest is to be set at LIBOR plus 1.25 per cent.[20]

The total debt is not big by South Korean standards (about two-thirds as much per head; Foster-Carter, 1980). The trouble is that the service of the capitalist part of it is a much higher percentage of hard currency exports, and there has been actual default on some of it.

5. Conclusion

At times, North Korea managed to walk on a tight-rope between the Soviet and the Chinese influences and was able to maintain political independence. Most of the time, however, North Korea has tilted to one side or another, despite its active participation in the non-aligned

Table 11.3: North Korean Visible Mirror-Trade with USSR in Selected Commodities and Commodity Groups, 1970-8 (in million roubles, percentages in parentheses)

	1970	1971	1972	1973	1974	1975	1976	1977	1978	1979
1. Exports to USSR										
Total	128.9 (100)	122.2 (100)	128.4 (100)	133.3 (100)	148.9 (100)	151.4 (100)	118.7 (100)	164.0 (100)	201.6 (100)	256.4 (100)
Machinery & equipment	7.1 (5.5)	4.9 (4.0)	11.1 (8.6)	8.3 (6.3)	15.1 (10.1)	12.3 (8.1)	4.7 (4.0)	4.0 (2.4)	7.4 (3.7)	14.0 (5.5)
Non-ferrous metals	2.8 (2.2)	2.9 (2.4)	3.8 (3.0)	4.1 (3.1)	5.2 (3.5)	5.4 (3.6)	5.5 (4.6)	7.9 (4.8)	8.4 (4.2)	10.9 (4.3)
Rolled black metals	32.5 (25.2)	28.8 (23.6)	31.5 (24.5)	35.9 (26.9)	39.0 (26.2)	41.2 (27.2)	23.1 (19.5)	32.2 (19.6)	41.1 (20.4)	55.3 (21.6)
Cement	6.0 (4.7)	4.7 (3.9)	5.6 (4.4)	6.4 (4.8)	4.5 (3.0)	6.5 (4.3)	5.6 (4.7)	4.8 (2.9)	4.5 (2.2)	4.4 (1.7)
Magnesia clinker	10.6 (8.2)	19.1 (15.7)	17.6 (13.7)	19.5 (14.7)	18.3 (12.3)	19.1 (12.6)	26.7 (22.5)	41.1 (25.0)	58.0 (28.8)	62.5 (24.4)
Rice	11.3 (8.8)	13.2 (10.8)	11.3 (8.7)	12.1 (9.1)	17.0 (11.4)	15.8 (10.5)	15.5 (13.0)	33.6 (20.5)	31.0 (15.4)	35.1 (13.7)
Clothing	12.1 (9.4)	14.9 (12.2)	12.3 (9.6)	11.0 (8.3)	7.5 (5.0)	10.9 (7.2)	7.3 (6.2)	7.1 (4.3)	9.0 (4.4)	11.6 (4.5)
2. Imports from USSR[a]										
Total	207.0 (100)	330.1 (100)	251.6 (100)	224.0 (100)	194.3 (100)	186.8 (100)	181.8 (100)	164.7 (100)	176.5 (100)	235.4 (100)
Machinery & equipment	89.4 (43.2)	100.4 (30.4)	95.8 (38.1)	81.1 (36.2)	83.9 (43.2)	75.6 (40.5)	50.0 (27.5)	34.0 (20.6)	26.6 (15.1)	49.8 (21.2)
Equipment for production of cast iron, steel & rolled metals	—	—	31.6	26.3	24.7	14.6	4.6	2.3	1.7	2.8
Coal and cokes	12.4 (6.0)	12.8 (3.9)	9.8 (3.9)	8.0 (3.6)	6.8 (3.5)	7.3 (3.9)	11.3 (6.2)	12.4 (7.5)	18.2 (10.3)	15.3 (6.5)
Petroleum & ITS prod.	27.7 (13.4)	23.4 (7.1)	13.8 (5.5)	16.8 (7.5)	24.7 (12.7)	26.6 (14.2)	43.7 (24.0)	47.3 (28.7)	56.3 (31.9)	71.6 (30.4)
Wheat	17.2 (8.3)	—	10.8 (4.2)	12.7 (6.6)	12.6 (6.5)	14.8 (7.9)	21.6 (11.9)	29.7 (18.0)	23.7 (13.4)	44.6 (18.9)
3. Trade Balance (1-2)	-78.1	-207.9	-123.2	-90.7	-45.4	-35.4	-63.1	-.7	25.1	21.0

a. Approximately a third of the total value of Soviet exports to North Korea is not specified in official Soviet statistics.
Source: *VT*, 1970, 1972, 1974, 1976, 1978.

Table 11.4: North Korean Visible Mirror-Trade with Japan is Selected Commodities and Commodity Groups, 1971-9 ($ USm, percentages in parentheses)

Exports to Japan	1971	1972	1973	1974	1975	1976	1977	1978	1979
Total	30.1 (100)	38.3 (100)	72.3 (100)	108.8 (100)	64.8 (100)	71.6 (100)	66.6 (100)	106.9 (100)	152.0 (100)
Foodstuffs	3.3 (10.9)	6.4 (16.8)	10.1 (14.0)	9.4 (9.0)	7.6 (11.7)	10.2 (14.2)	8.0 (12.0)	29.7 (27.8)	51.4 (33.8)
Fish & shellfish	2.0	4.0	7.0	6.7	4.4	4.9	3.7	17.4	38.6
Fruits & vegetables	–	–	–	1.0	1.8	3.4	2.2	5.3	9.5
Raw materials	16.9 (56.2)	19.2 (50.1)	27.0 (37.3)	38.4 (35.3)	24.5 (37.8)	18.7 (26.1)	22.0 (33.0)	30.6 (28.6)	40.0 (26.3)
Raw silk	6.4	8.9	11.8	12.0	2.8	2.5	6.0	15.5	7.4
Iron ore & scraps	4.9	5.9	6.2	5.2	3.3	–	–	–	–
Non-ferrous minerals	3.7	2.6	5.1	17.7	15.2	13.0	12.5	11.9	27.2
Magnesia clinker	1.1	.8	2.0	4.0	3.4	6.2	4.4	5.5	10.4
Natural graphite	–	–	–	.9	.4	.4	.8	–	–
Stealite	.5	.6	1.0	.8	.6	–	–	–	8.5
Talc	.7	.7	.8	.8	1.1	–	–	3.2	3.6
Mineral fuels	1.2 (3.9)	.9 (2.4)	1.0 (1.4)	1.2 (1.1)	1.2 (1.9)	2.2 (3.1)	1.9 (2.9)	1.4 (1.3)	3.2 (2.1)
Anthracite coal	1.2	.9	1.0	1.2	1.2	2.2	1.9	1.4	3.2
Manufactured products	8.6 (28.6)	11.7 (30.6)	33.8 (46.7)	52.6 (48.3)	31.4 (48.5)	40.3 (56.3)	34.3 (51.5)	43.5 (40.7)	56.2 (37.0)
Chemicals	.1	1.3	1.4	.8	.9	.4	1.0	1.1	.4
Other products	8.4	10.4	32.3	51.8	30.1	39.9	33.3	42.4	55.7
Pig iron	2.3	4.0	7.2	17.1	9.2	11.1	2.9	6.4	16.1
Non-ferrous metals	5.9	6.2	23.6	34.0	20.2	29.5	30.1	34.5	37.4
Silver & alloys	2.7	3.2	6.0	11.5	3.0	1.7	.8	–	–
Zinc & alloys	2.8	2.8	14.0	15.8	13.2	20.0	17.7	16.2	22.0
Lead & alloys	.5	.1	3.4	6.5	4.1	6.8	11.7	17.9	14.9
Machinery & equipment	–	–	–	.1	–	–	–	–	–
Re-export and others	.1 (0.2)	– (0)	.4 (0.6)	.1 (0.1)	.1 (0.2)	.2 (0.3)	.5 (0.8)	1.6 (1.5)	1.2 (0.8)

Table 11.4: Continued

Imports from Japan	1971	1972	1973	1974	1975	1976	1977	1978	1979
Total	28.9 (100)	93.4 (100)	100.2 (100)	251.9 (100)	180.6 (100)	96.1 (100)	125.1 (100)	183.8 (100)	283.8 (100)
Foodstuffs	.1 (.4)	.1 (.1)	.1 (.1)	.2 (.1)	– (0)	.1 (.1)	.2 (.2)	.6 (.3)	.7 (.2)
Raw materials & fuels	.4 (1.4)	1.0 (1.0)	1.6 (1.6)	.5 (.2)	1.3 (.7)	3.0 (3.1)	6.5 (5.2)	5.3 (2.9)	12.9 (4.5)
Light-industry products	5.9 (20.4)	25.4 (27.2)	20.3 (20.3)	57.3 (22.7)	22.6 (12.5)	21.5 (22.4)	36.9 (29.5)	45.0 (24.5)	67.8 (23.9)
Textiles	3.6	19.7	13.6	36.0	4.5	5.1	20.0	21.9	31.2
Non-metallic mineral products	–	–	–	1.5	4.5	3.4	2.2	3.1	4.0
Others	–	–	–	20.0	13.6	13.0	14.7	20.0	32.6
Heavy & chemical industry prod.	21.2 (73.3)	66.2 (70.8)	74.3 (74.1)	190.3 (75.5)	152.4 (84.4)	68.2 (71.0)	79.6 (63.6)	119.9 (65.4)	186.0 (65.5)
Chemicals	5.4	7.6	12.4	10.9	17.4	14.0	13.4	25.0	26.6
Metals	1.5	10.8	28.7	66.9	27.5	12.1	17.3	27.5	39.3
Iron & steel	–	8.8	25.3	60.4	15.3	4.4	7.3	13.7	26.9
Metal products	–	–	–	6.6	11.8	6.5	6.6	13.8	10.1
Machinery & equipment	14.4 (49.8)	47.7 (51.1)	33.2 (33.1)	112.4 (44.6)	107.5 (59.5)	42.2 (43.9)	48.9 (39.1)	67.3 (26.9)	120.2 (42.4)
General machinery	10.3	34.3	16.6	66.4	62.5	17.8	21.9	26.3	41.3
Electrical machinery	3.3	6.2	7.4	18.0	27.5	12.5	18.0	25.2	27.9
Transportation equipment	.2	5.2	7.8	23.9	14.8	9.8	7.1	13.3	46.8
Precision instruments	–	–	–	4.0	2.7	2.1	1.9	–	4.3
Others	1.3 (4.4)	.8 (.8)	3.8 (3.8)	3.5 (1.4)	4.3 (2.4)	3.2 (3.3)	1.9 (1.5)	12.6 (5.0)	16.5 (5.8)

Sources: Japan Ministry of International Trade and Industry (MITI), *Tsushohakusho White Paper on International Trade*, vol. 2, 1974, 1979, and 1980. Japan External Trade Organisation (JETRO), *White Paper on International Trade*, Japan, 1974, 1976, 1978.

Table 11.5: North Korean Visible Mirror-Trade with Eastern Europe, USSR, China and Japan, 1955-79 ($USm)

	Bulgaria			Czechoslovakia			GDR			Hungary			Poland		
	X	M	X-M	X	M	X-M	X	M	X-M	X	M	X-M	X	M	X-M
1955				0	4.7	-4.7	.1	7.6	-7.5	n.a.	n.a.	-3.7	n.a.	n.a.	-12.0
1956				.8	12.5	-11.7	1.7	8.3	-6.6	.2	3.9	-1.9	1.1	13.1	1.3
1957				1.1	16.9	-15.8	2.5	6.8	-4.3	1.0	2.9	-4.1	2.7	1.4	-1.0
1958				1.5	11.8	-6.3	2.9	5.5	-2.6	.2	4.3	-3.9	.8	1.8	-4.0
1959				6.1	23.8	-17.7	5.2	8.4	-3.2	.6	4.5	-1.3	2.5	6.5	.5
1960				3.6	11.7	-8.1	4.6	4.7	-.1	3.3	4.6	-3.5	1.9	1.4	1.5
1961				5.0	6.4	-1.4	3.3	4.1	-.8	.8	4.3	-1.4	2.9	1.4	.7
1962				6.3	5.8	.5	4.2	5.1	-.9	1.8	3.2	-1.1	4.0	3.3	-.5
1963				5.4	3.1	2.3	2.8	3.6	-.8	1.6	2.7	.1	3.9	4.4	-.3
1964				7.4	4.3	3.1	2.1	2.6	-.5	1.9	1.8	.1	3.8	4.1	1.4
1965				7.2	6.0	1.2	3.4	4.5	-1.2	3.4	1.6	1.8	6.2	4.8	.6
1966	1.6	.9	.5	10.1	3.8	6.3	3.1	3.8	-.7	3.1	.8	2.3	6.4	5.8	-4.6
1967	.9	.8	.1	6.6	3.4	3.2	1.7	7.3	-2.6	1.7	1.7	0	2.5	7.1	-2.5
1968	2.1	1.2	.9	7.1	3.7	3.4	2.2	8.7	-3.2	2.2	2.9	-.7	9.3	11.8	-4.1
1969	2.5	2.1	.4	9.5	2.5	7.0	3.2	9.5	3.3	3.2	3.2	0	8.3	12.4	1.6
1970	3.4	3.2	.2	12.1	3.1	9.0	3.7	14.7	2.4	3.7	3.2	.5	10.2	8.6	2.2
1971	2.0	4.8	-2.8	11.0	7.4	3.6	4.3	25.2	-13.2	4.3	2.8	1.5	7.2	5.0	.6
1972	3.9	6.0	-2.1	12.5	6.2	6.3	2.8	29.0	-16.2	2.8	2.9	-.1	9.3	8.7	1.5
1973	8.5	9.9	-1.4	11.4	7.2	4.2	4.2	21.5	-6.0	4.2	3.7	.5	7.6	6.1	1.7
1974				12.5	8.7	3.8	4.8	13.8	6.0	4.8	4.5	.3	12.4	10.7	6.7
1975				9.3	11.6	-2.3	9.2	9.8	-.6	9.2	9.8	-.6	18.1	11.4	
1976															
1977													n.a.	n.a.	
1978													16.0	15.0	1.0
1979													25.0	19.0	6.0

Sources: For Eastern Europe and USSR: for the period between 1966 and 1975, 'Trade of Eastern European Countries with Each Other, and with Communist Asia and Cuba,' 1966-72 and 1969-75, prepared by International Trade Analysis Staff, US Department of Commerce. Other periods based on *Puk Han Mu Yok Ron* (North Korean Foreign Trade), Research Series no. 11, Institute of Far Eastern Affairs, Kyong Nam University, Seoul, Korea, pp. 272-3, pp. 277-8, p. 284, pp. 301-4; International Monetary Fund, *Direction of Trade Yearbook*,

Table 11.5: Continued

	Romania			USSR			China			Japan		
	X	M	X-M	X	M	X-M	X	M	X-M	X	M	X-M
1955	n.a.	n.a.		40.8	44.2	-3.4	n.a.	n.a.		n.a.	n.a.	
1956	n.a.	n.a.		51.2	53.8	-2.6	n.a.	n.a.		0.5	1.1	.4
1957	–	3.2		62.6	60.0	2.6	n.a.	n.a.		2.0	2.1	-.1
1958	.4	–		47.1	58.1	-11.0	n.a.	n.a.		1.9	2.1	-.2
1959	1.1	5.4	-4.3	51.6	74.1	-22.5	n.a.	n.a.		.8	2.8	-2.0
1960	3.0	5.3	-2.3	74.7	39.4	35.3	45.0	45.0	0	3.1	1.9	1.2
1961	2.8	.9	1.9	79.1	77.0	2.1	46.0	46.0	0	4.0	4.9	-.9
1962	1.7	3.0	-1.3	88.2	80.7	7.5	47.0	47.0	0	4.6	4.8	-.2
1963	6.1	4.5	1.6	88.1	82.1	6.0	49.0	46.0	3.0	9.4	5.3	4.1
1964	5.5	5.5	0	80.7	82.9	-2.0	53.0	51.0	2.0	20.2	11.3	18.9
1965	3.5	5.1	-1.6	88.3	89.8	-1.5	53.0	53.0	0	14.7	16.5	-1.8
1966	3.1	3.6	-.5	92.3	85.6	6.7	43.0	42.0	1.0	22.7	5.0	17.7
1967	5.1	5.1	0	108.0	110.3	-2.3	44.0	46.0	-2.0	29.6	6.4	23.2
1968	6.3	7.4	-1.1	120.9	172.2	-51.3	56.0	54.0	2.0	34.0	20.7	13.3
1969	5.3	12.0	-6.7	126.6	201.6	-74.3	55.0	55.0	0	32.2	24.2	8.0
1970	6.0	8.0	-2.0	143.2	230.0	-86.8	58.3	77.8	-19.5	34.4	23.3	11.1
1971	10.7	10.0	.7	135.8	366.8	-231.0	106.3	112.5	-6.2	30.1	28.9	1.2
1972	11.2	14.4	-3.2	155.8	305.3	-148.6	112.0	136.0	-24.0	38.3	93.4	-55.1
1973	16.0	17.6	-1.6	180.0	302.4	-122.0	120.0	180.0	-60.0	72.3	100.2	-27.9
1974	19.0	28.8	-9.8	196.5	256.5	-60.0	192.2	176.5	15.7	108.8	251.9	-143.1
1975	15.0	24.5	-9.5	210.4	259.7	-51.6	190.2	196.1	-5.9	64.8	180.6	-115.8
1976	7.9	27.4	-19.5	158.3	242.4	-84.1	164.0	156.0	8.0	71.6	96.1	-24.5
1977	7.8	19.7	-11.9	223.0	224.0	-1.0	230.0	210.0	20.0	66.6	125.1	-58.5
1978	26.0	23.6	2.4	293.0	257.0	36.0	n.a.	n.a.		106.9	183.3	-76.4
1979	28.6	26.0	2.6							152.0	283.8	-131.8

1980, for Romania between 1975 and 1979. For China: *Puk Han Mu Yok Ron* (North Korean Foreign Trade), pp. 272-8 and *Puk Han Chun So* (North Korea Handbook) 1945-80; The Institute of East Asian Studies, Seoul, Korea, 1980, p. 80. For Japan: *The Kita Chosen Kenkyu* (North Korean Studies), June 1979, no. 60, p. 77 and *Puk Han Mu Yok Ron* (North Korean Foreign Trade), p. 317.

nations movement of the Third World.

Economically, the policy of self-reliance has been understandably more difficult. Before 1970, Soviet economic co-operation and aid were the major contributing factors in fulfilling series of economic plans. China and other Communist countries also played important roles at various times. In the 1970s North Korea underwent a rather drastic change in international economic outlook in an apparent attempt to reduce its dependence on both the Soviet and the Chinese economies. One of the side-effects of the new policy was a huge accumulation of foreign debt.

It is quite normal for any dynamic and rapidly developing poor country to have a prolonged deficit in the balance of payments. What is unusual in the case of North Korea is that the problem was far more serious than usual, resulting in a widespread default on the international money market. There is evidence that they belatedly recognised this and tried to rectify it by placing a greater emphasis on exports. One example is the National Foreign Trade Activists' Meeting held in October of 1979. At the meeting the foreign trade workers, among others, were urged to improve the quality and to increase the production of export goods, such as minerals, labour-intensive food products and light industry products, and to take a greater part in trade fairs abroad.

The problem of not being able to compete effectively in an open and highly competitive international market is not necessarily confined to North Korea, but rather common among the Soviet-type economies. It arises from the fundamental nature of non-market systems of central planning. North Korea, however, not only was more ambitious than others and therefore became the first Communist country to default (a very remarkable record), but also retains one of the more rigid Soviet-type economies. The future prospects of her success in achieving economic independence from the USSR and China will, to a large extent, depend on how far she is willing to be flexible in adjusting the domestic economic structure to make it more competitive in an open international market.

Any assessment of North Korean economic performance in recent years is virtually impossible because the authorities never publish any comprehensive economic data. On the other hand, our discussion of foreign economic policy and especially foreign debt may overshadow the actual achievements of the domestic economy. Relying on fragmented information, it appears that the North Korean economy has been able to sustain a rather impressive growth, although there

Table 11.6: Soviet Oil Export Prices ($ per tonne)

	To OECD	To CMEA	To North Korea
1972	22.4	18.7	42.0
1973	28.7	21.7	38.8
1974	80.5	23.9	34.7
1975	86.9	46.4	33.3
1976	91.9	48.8	53.3

Note: After 1976 total value data, and therefore implicit price data, were suppressed. The 'prices' above are the total value of all qualities and degrees of refinement of petroleum, divided by the total number of tonnes. Since the mixture varies the 'prices' can be misleading.
Source: *VT*.

have been increasing problems of efficient resource allocation as the economy has become more diversified and complex. This growth has been possible because the leadership apparently has been successful in continuously urging the people to work hard, not only with repeated battle-cries but also with some quantity of materials, and other incentives. The end result is that North Korea at present is one of the more industrialised countries in Asia, with substantial productive capacities and the potential to be competitive in the world market.

North Korea has drawn civilian aid from USSR as shown in Table 1.2. These sums are fairly small, and again go to show that *chu ch'e* has meaning. Her trade is shown in Table 11.3 here. She has in the past been an observer at CMEA, but was not officially reported as such at the conferences of 1979 and 1980. She has a few ongoing co-operation schemes: Korean lumberjacks cut Soviet trees and share the timber, Korean specialists work at Dubna on atomic energy. There are plane services to Khabarovsk and Moscow direct, and there is a transit traffic in Soviet export goods, accepted at rail terminals in the West and delivered to Soviet ships in the East (Kondrat'ev, 1978). In relating these rather commonplace facts, Kondrat'ev does not mention the CMEA.

Very little indeed is known about North Korean trade with China, or Chinese aid. How curious that the flow of aid should indeed have been from poor to rich! No Far Eastern Communist country reports its trade adequately, so we have not even mirror trade figures.

North Korea, in conclusion, is a richer and bigger country and also one that has grown faster than Albania. It has contributed a credible concept, nay even an ideology, of autarkic Stalinism, while Albanian propaganda and ideology are the merest schizophrenic snarl. But it is still a very unpleasant place, frightened to admit tourists, trying to assassinate the South Korean president, and stifling the human spirit with photographs and speeches of the leader.

Notes

1. The author, hampered by a long line of communication, has tolerated many changes by Adi Schnytzer and Peter Wiles.

2. UN estimates. The areas are 46,500 and 38,500 square miles. There is much conflict over the Northern population. *The South Korean Statistical Yearbook 1962* puts the total population of the peninsula at 25.12m. on 1 May 1944, that of the North at 9.24m. US and South Korean sources claim that about 3.2m. migrated to the South by August 1946 (1m, 1966, pp. 31-2). After the war UN (i.e. enemy) statistics were quoting a population of 3 to 3.5m. in the mid-fifties (*New York Times*, 1 March 1958); and indeed there was surely further migration while the North was partially under UN military occupation, though it certainly does not show up in Southern statistics. But nobody disputes (we shall not put it more strongly) the current level of about 17m. The official Northern figures for the controversial period are (th): 31 Dec. 1946, 9257; 31 Dec. 1949, 9622; 1 Dec. 1953 (i.e. after the armistice), 8491; 1 Sept. 1956, 9359; 31 Dec. 1966, 12,640 (Chung, 1973, pp. 146-7). If we accept the old figure for May 1944, then North-South migration in May 1944-December 1946 equalled the whole natural increase, say 300,000; and the casualties and migration in 1950-3 were about 1.7m. The official growth-rate 1956-66 is 2.7% p.a.

3. CIA, *Korea*, 1978. Using different methods from Kravis *et al.*, the CIA put the north at $590 and the South at $605 in 1975.

4. It follows that Cuba is not a proper satellite. We do not enter into this matter here. On the reasons for pseudo-charismatic leadership under independent Stalinism, cf. Wiles 1981.

5. Bulgaria also had a Chinese-type 'Great Leap Forward' in 1959-60.

6. *North Korean Foreign Trade*, pp. 414-37. Amounts of aid estimated for this period (in millions of $US): USSR 570; China 389; Czechoslovakia 200; East Germany 102; Poland 91; Romania 22.5; Bulgaria 12.5; Hungary 0.4.

7. *Area Handbook*, 1976, pp. 369-71.

8. On this period cf. Koh, 1969 and Ko, 1977.

9. Y.S. Kim, 1971, p. 44; Teratani, 1979; *North Korean Foreign Trade*, p. 425.

10. *North Korean Foreign Trade*, pp. 414 and 425.

11. *North Korea Handbook*, p. 400.

12. See annual issues of *Facts on Czechoslovakian Trade*, Chamber of Commerce, Prague, and *Rocznik Statystyczny Handlu Zagranicznego*, Warsaw.

13. *Korean Review*, Pyongyang, 1974, p. 1764; Cumings, 1974.

14. This is based on IMF *Direction of Trade*, 1980. The IMF document of 1978 and earlier editions, however, show much smaller North Korean exports to Saudi Arabia until 1977. South Korea has made a major effort to export to Saudi Arabia since 1974.

15. *Trends in Asian Countries*, 1974, pp. 95-8, and *North Korean Foreign Trade*, pp. 313-15.

16. See note 14 above.

17. The writer is indebted to the following documents for the discussion on foreign debt: Teratani, 1979, pp. 14-27; Wiechert, 1978, pp. 49-53; *North Korean*

Foreign Trade, pp. 512-27; *North Korea Handbook*, pp. 403-5.

18. 'Free-World Export to and Import from Communist Areas in Eastern Europe and Asia, and Cuba, January-December 1974', International Trade Analysis Staff, US Department of Commerce, June 1976.

19. For detailed discussion of various estimates, see *North Korean Foreign Trade*, pp. 517-27.

20. Teruo Komaki in *Ajia Toko Nempo*, Trends in Asian Countries, Institute of Developing Economies (Tokyo, 1980), p. 66.

PART FOUR:

THE THIRD WORLD ALREADY WITHIN
THE CMEA

12 THE MONGOLIAN PEOPLE'S REPUBLIC

Alan Smith and Adi Schnytzer

Outer Mongolia gained its independence from China in 1921 with the aid of Russian troops. A foreign trade monopoly along Soviet lines was established and the majority of Chinese traders were driven from the country. As a result between 1931 and 1951 virtually all of Mongolia's trade was conducted with the Soviet Union. Following Mao's victory in China and the extension of Soviet power to Eastern Europe, Mongolia sought to increase its trade with the newly emerging Communist countries. President Tsedenbal visited China in 1952 and a number of economic agreements were signed in the following years. By 1957 trade with the USSR accounted for only 75 per cent of total trade and the Chinese government began to provide Mongolia with economic aid. In particular, she supplied substantial amounts of labour which have been estimated as lying in the range of 12,000 to 20,000 workers at a time.[1] But of course the reception of such *Gastarbeiter* is better called Mongolian aid to China.

Mongolia continued to receive Chinese aid until 1964, despite the deterioration in Mongolian-Chinese relations as a result of the Sino-Soviet dispute. But finally Mongolia committed itself irrevocably to the Soviet side and apparently purged high-ranking officials who had taken a pro-Chinese line. A major determinant of this decision was probably, in addition to Soviet military influence, the extent of Soviet aid offered to Mongolia, largely under the auspices of CMEA. Mongolia was admitted to full membership of the CMEA at the June 1962 Session, which also approved the Basic Principles of the Socialist International Division of Labour. These incorporated proposals for increasing the rate of economic development of the less advanced members and narrowing the gap between the levels of development of the member countries (see Chapter 1). This was to be achieved partly through a higher level of accumulation in the less developed countries but primarily by the vehicle of technical transfer, deliveries of complete equipment for industrial plant and the granting of credits and other forms of aid.

A Soviet authority[2] on Mongolian economic development argues that three clear principles underlying Mongolia's industrialisation can be observed in this period:

(i) in the initial stage socialist industrialisation was concentrated on the establishment of infrastructure, light industry and especially the food industry, not heavy industry;

(ii) an exceedingly large role has been played by outside sources for financing capital investment;

(iii) the later stage of construction has been marked by the development of new industries primarily aimed at the export market (and in particular at satisfying demand on the socialist international market).

Analysis of Mongolia's economic development and its relations with CMEA countries and the USSR in particular tends broadly to confirm this. Mongolia has been a major recipient of long-term credits (ten years) from the CMEA countries at low interest rates (2-3 per cent, or more recently as low as 0.5 per cent) with repayment in the form of products from the newly-constructed enterprises. In the third five year plan (1961-5) 47.1 per cent of total investment in the Mongolian economy was based on such credits; the corresponding figures for 1966-70 and 1971 to 1975 were 50.3 and 49.8 respectively.[3] In the third five-year plan investment growth was primarily concentrated in the non-productive sector, largely as a result of the construction of the city of Darkan and its related industrial complexes on the basis of assistance from the USSR, Czechoslovakia and Poland.[4] In the same period the priority of the production of Group A commodities over Group B, which had been a feature of the previous decade, was reversed, and the proportion of Group A products in total industrial output fell from 51.6 per cent to 47.8 per cent.[5] Priority of industrial investment was accorded to the production of electricity and food processing, but the failure of agricultural production to keep pace with population growth resulted in produced national income per head actually falling by 8 per cent from 1961 to 1965.[6] The cessation of Chinese aid in 1964 led to a reduction in the total volume of investment and the 1963 investment level was not re-attained until 1967, following the conclusion of an aid agreement with the USSR.

An approximate estimate of the cost to the USSR and other CMEA nations of aid to Mongolia has been provided in Table 12.1. The first four rows, indicating the size of Soviet-Mongolian trade flows from Soviet sources, show that deliveries of machinery and equipment account for a rising proportion of Soviet exports and are closely correlated to Soviet surpluses in visible trade. The size of machinery and equipment exports (and the visible surplus) in the first four years of the current five-year plan is as large as that of the preceding

Table 12.1: Mongolian: CMEA Data Discrepancies (million transferable roubles)

	1961-5	1966-70	1971-5	1976-9
A. Soviet data				
Soviet exports	540	839	1265	2214
Soviet imports	261	260	481	590
Soviet surplus	279	579	784	1624
Soviet machinery exports to Mongolia	267	472	722	1484
B. Mongolian data				
Imports from CMEA	n.a.	500	743	1084
Imports of machinery and equipment	n.a.	134	238	381
C. Discrepancies (CMEA mirror trade[a] minus Mongolian data)				
Mongolian trade deficit with CMEA	n.a.	450	666	1275
Mongolian machinery imports from CMEA	n.a.	375	525	1150

a. Uncorrected for c.i.f. and f.o.b.

Sources: Rows 1 to 4 are calculated directly from *VT*, various years. Rows 5 and 6 are calculated from data provided by Mongolia to the CMEA Statistical handbook (*Statisticheskii Yezhegodnik* SEV), various years. Figures for 1966 to 1970 are estimates based on figures for total imports for each year and respective commodity/country breakdowns provided for the end years.

Rows 7 and 8 are calculated from the Foreign Trade handbooks of each individual CMEA nation. Due to incomplete data several estimates have had to be made. The figures have been rounded to indicate that they are approximate. The predominance of Soviet trade, for which accurate data are available, lends some confidence to these estimates.

fifteen years, and would appear to represent a considerable diversion of resources. It is also interesting to note that there are considerable discrepancies between Mongolian foreign trade statistics submitted to CMEA and those published in CMEA partners' national handbooks. The best explanation of the discrepancy appears to be that aid deliveries have not been included in Mongolian import statistics — a hypothesis that is supported by an article by the Mongolian Minister of Foreign Trade in a CMEA journal which distinguishes between deliveries 'based on technical and financial assistance' and those 'in the sphere of foreign trade'.[7]

Estimates of the discrepancy between CMEA partners' data and Mongolian data for the imbalance in foreign trade are indicated in row 7 in Table 12.1, which show a far higher Mongolian deficit from partners' sources than can be obtained from Mongolian sources. Row 8 similarly indicates that partners' data record a far higher volume of CMEA exports of machinery and equipment than that calculated from Mongolian sources. It can also be seen from Rows 3 and 4 that Soviet exports of machinery and equipment (equivalent to row 8) may be based on 'technical and financial assistance' while the total volume of net aid may be approximated by row 7. This indicates a considerable growth of Soviet aid in each five-year plan period and a particularly rapid increase since 1975.

This hypothesis also appears to be confirmed by a Mongolian author writing in a Soviet journal, who argues that Soviet technical and financial assistance would double over the course of the sixth five-year plan (1976-80) and would comprise 70 per cent of all Mongolian capital outlays in that period,[8] while the article by the Mongolian foreign minister refers to the construction of coal mines, a cement factory, numerous enterprises in the leather and textile industry and a considerable volume of investment in agriculture as being conducted on the basis of Soviet and CMEA assistance.[9] Primarily as a result of increased aid, investment (including houses and stocks) in the sixth five-year plan grew by 14 per cent per annum and in 1978 constituted 50.5 per cent of national income.[10] It follows from Table 12.2 that aid has recently run, excluding all subsidies and deficits in direct trade, at 35 per cent of national income, which is surely close to a world record.

The structure of investment undertaken throughout the period since Mongolia's break with China is shown in Table 12.2. Since aid is concentrated in major construction projects there have been considerable discontinuities in the branch structure of investment, but it appears that from 1966 to 1975 considerable emphasis was attached to agricultural investment while housing and social construction received a significant but declining share of investment funds. From 1966 to 1970 industrial investment was concentrated primarily in the development of electricity supply and food processing, while nonferrous metallurgy has been expanded since 1970.[11]

The most significant changes have come since 1975, and appear to indicate a closer integration of the Mongolian economy with the CMEA and with the USSR in particular. President Tsedenbal has both welcomed closer links between Mongolia and the USSR — referring to them as 'one crew in battle, one brigade in labour' — and been fulsome in his praise of the current integration measures being pursued in CMEA. These, as we saw in Chapter 1, are along the lines of improved joint planning, joint construction projects and closer plan co-ordination,[12] which can largely be considered as long-term Soviet objectives and which would considerably reduce Mongolia's room for independent manoeuvre. Tsedenbal has also argued that a more rapid growth of the Mongolian economy, based on the aid of the USSR and other socialist countries, would enable the country to achieve the economic levels attained by its CMEA partners and enter Full Communism more or less simultaneously − which in turn would lead to the strengthening of a single indestructible world socialist system.[13] The feeling that this is primarily a strategy to achieve a greater volume of Soviet aid, possibly in exchange for compliance with Soviet objectives in CMEA, is strengthened by the article of LuFsandorj, which repeats the argument that equal development levels are necessary for the simultaneous transition to communism, but adds that, although the relative gap between less developed and more developed member countries may be closing, the absolute gap is widening as a result of the higher absolute economic levels in the more advanced countries to which lower relative growth rates apply.[14] LuFsandorj continues to praise the CMEA long-term Target Programmes and joint construction projects as a major vehicle for achieving equalisation of levels of economic development.

Concrete measures to stimulate Mongolian economic development which had initially been included in the CMEA Complex Programme of 1971 were approved in the CMEA Agreed Plan of multilateral integration measures for 1976-80. These included joint-construction projects in Mongolia, the provision of favourable credit terms, favourable prices for Mongolian exports of agricultural products and raw materials, and assistance not subject to repayment.[15] These proposals do however imply that the Mongolian economy will become more closely linked to the needs of the CMEA market. A CMEA geological expedition has undertaken a survey of mineral resources, while joint Soviet-Mongolian ventures have concentrated on the development and processing of copper and molybdenum at Erdenet[16] and a joint association (Mongolsovtsvetmetal) has been established to prospect for gold and non-ferrous metals.[17] Table 12.2 confirms that the growth of investment since 1975 has been concentrated in non-ferrous metallurgy, fuel and electric energy. In the sixth five-year plan Mongolian exports to CMEA are planned to include the traditional items, meat and meat products, textiles, leather and other light industry and food products[18] (over 90 per cent of the output of plants constructed in these sectors on the basis of technical assistance

Table 12.2: Investment in Mongolia (m. Tugriks: 1 Rouble = c.4.5 Tugriks, 1961-79, by the commercial and non-commercial rates)

	1961-5	1966-70	1971-5	1976-9
A. Total	3,849	5,289	7,010	11,909
of which through aid	1,812	2,660	3,491	(8,336)
from own resources	2,037	2,629	3,519	(3,573)
B. Industry	n.a.	1,682	1,766	4,840
of which electric energy	n.a.	507	298	899
Fuel	n.a.	84	94	567
Food processing	n.a.	295	201	72
Non-ferrous metallurgy	n.a.	14	278	1,796
C. Agriculture	n.a.	1,225	1,774	1,749
D. Transport and communications	n.a.	514	967	1,167
E. Housing and social	n.a.	980	1,120	2,173

Sources: All figures calculated from *Statisticheskii Yezhegodnik SEV*, various years.

The division between aid and own resources has been calculated from the percentages provided by Tsedenbal (see text), except for 1976-9 which has been estimated on the basis of the figure given in the text for the proportion of investment planned to be undertaken with Soviet assistance.

are destined for export),[19] but also new commodities, notably non-ferrous metals and other precious metals.

Consequently although Mongolia is currently a major recipient of CMEA investment aid, the CMEA nations may expect some benefits in the form of imports of fuel and metals. However, Mongolian exports of the latter are only planned to reach a maximum of 68 million transferable roubles by 1980 and such benefits may be a long way off.[20] Currently the major cost of this investment is being directly borne by the USSR. It should be mentioned that the increased size of the Soviet commitment has been offset in intra-CMEA trade by the windfall effects accruing to the USSR as a result of the sliding world-average price system in intra-CMEA trade.[21]

Largely as a result of its geographic location it is not surprising that trade with the West has not exceeded 2 per cent of total Mongolian trade turnover for several decades. The latter figure is derived from Mongolian statistics and if the discrepancies in trade with CMEA partners are taken into account the figure becomes well below 1 per cent.

On the other basic data, given so freely and perhaps so rashly elsewhere in this book, we feel too insecure to pronounce. We do not know Mongolia's national income, national income per head,[22] rate of growth[23] or participation ratio.[24] We only feel fairly certain that the 1.6 million 'Outer' Mongols in the People's Republic are much richer than the 3 million 'Inner' Mongols in China (see Chapter 1). This, of course, is the 'name of the game'.

Notes

1. Murphy, 1966, p. 195.
2. Matveeva, 1978, p. 122.
3. Tsedenabl, 1980, p. 12.
4. Matveeva, 1978, p. 139; LuFsandorj, 1978, p. 47.
5. Matveeva, 1978, p. 138.
6. *Statisticheskii Yezhegodnik* SEV 1977, p. 42.
7. Ochir, 1977, p. 21.
8. LuFsandorj, 1978, p. 48.
9. Ochir, 1977, p. 21.
10. *Statisticheskii Yezhegodnik* SEV 1980, p. 46.
11. Dupuy, 1970, p. 294.
12. Tsedenbal, 1980, pp. 12-15.
13. Ochir, 1977, p. 21.
14. LuFsandorj, 1978, p. 50. Thus if USSR stands at $ 100 per head and grows at 2 per cent per annum she puts on $ 2; if Mongolia grows at 4 per cent but stands at $ 40 she puts on only $ 1.60. This argument is used all over the world by poor people and countries. Though not fallacious, it is of limited scope; for it is mathematically impossible for the absolute increase of the poorer party to continue lower for very long. In the case given the effect ceases in year 10.
15. Ochir, 1977, p. 20; Faddeev, 1977, pp. 11-12; *Multilateral Economic Co-operation*, pp. 55-6.
16. Ochir, 1977, p. 20; Matveeva, 1978, pp. 165-6.
17. Matveeva, 1978, p. 165.
18. Ochir, 1977, p. 22.
19. Matveeva, 1978, p. 168.
20. Ochir, 1977, p. 22.
21. Smith, 1981, *passim*.
22. Perhaps $ 700-900 in 1978.
23. Perhaps 3-4 per cent per head per annum, 1975-9.
24. Perhaps 25-35 per cent. The figures in notes 22-4 have been derived from the *Statisticheskii Yezhegodnik* SEV 1980, in very indirect ways.

13 THE SOCIALIST REPUBLIC OF VIETNAM

Adi Schnytzer

Our study of Vietnam is much briefer, since no-one ever supposed this country to be other than a Communist one, and our book can only be so long. We concentrate on foreign economic relations. In June 1978, Vietnam became a full member of CMEA. In view of the potential loss of freedom in determining domestic economic policy implied by such a decision, any analysis of Vietnam's commercial policy must seek to explain the country's drift into the Soviet sphere. It will be argued that the history of Vietnam's relations within the Communist world has been the most important factor in determining the extent of economic relations with both the Soviet Union and the Western World.

In 1970, the population of North Vietnam was 22,675,000 and the official rate of exchange with the US dollar was 3.68 dong. Her GNP in 1972 has been estimated at $1.8 billion. By contrast, the population of South Vietnam in 1970 was 18,000,000, GNP around $4.0 billion and the offical rate of exchange with the US dollar 275 piastres. The 1980 population of unified Vietnam has been reported at 60,000,000 while in 1979 GNP was around $85 billion (*The Military Balance*, IISS, various years). Income per head is thus very approximately $140. The South was and is, it seems, richer than the North.

The likely direction of Vietnamese allegiance in the contemporary Sino-Soviet split is not easily derived from the history of Ho Chi Minh's struggle for power in Vietnam. Unlike Enver Hoxha in Albania, Ho was always closely associated with the Comintern and, as a consequence, worked closely with both Chinese and Soviet Communists in Southern China before the Second World War. After the War, Ho found himself slowly filling the power vacuum left by the defeat of Japan and an uncertain France. Being aware that his Viet Minh did not have the popular support to govern without French approval, Ho argued, in 1945, that the French should rule Vietnam for a further five years. It is not unlikely that Ho's motive for this paradoxical position was the belief that the French Communist Party would win the elections of 1946. The poor showing of the French Communists in the 1946 elections had important implications for Ho Chi Minh and his small band of followers. On the one hand, it led the Politburo of the Indochinese Communist Party out of Hanoi and into the mountains to fight a Maoist-style guerrilla war against the French colonial power. On the other, poor Communist performance in France contributed to the Soviet conviction that a greater effort was required in propaganda work and the provision of other assistance to the Communists of Western Europe. Given the cordial state of relations with China, there was no compelling reason why Moscow should accord Ho Chi Minh a high priority for assistance in his struggle.

For the Chinese Communist Party, not yet in power, the matter was somewhat different. Vietnamese and Chinese comrades had fought side by side against the Japanese and — provided only that Mao's pre-eminence remained unchallenged — a Communist government was to be preferred to any other in Vietnam. The extent of Chinese aid to Ho Chi Minh has been the subject of considerable controversy. One source claims that:

> Whether the Chinese under Vo Nguyen Giap in the final campaign (Dien Bien Phu) numbered 20,000 or more or less, and whether all the Chinese were 'pioneers' and sappers or included artillerymen, is unimportant; the certain thing is that Chinese help comprised whatever Ho and Mao . . . judged to be necessary to bring victory to the revolution of Vietnam (Duncanson, 1975, p. 508).

On the basis of the foregoing political arguments, it might be expected that Chinese aid to North Vietnam in the early years of its existence would exceed Soviet aid. Unfortunately, the available sources are divided on this question. Thus, a recent paper[1] argues that, between 1955 and 1964, the Soviet Union provided $440 million, Eastern European countries $201 million and China $352 million in non-military aid. However, an earlier source[2] indicates that Chinese civilian aid outweighed that from the Soviet Union and its East European allies in the fifties, and that, by the end of 1961, aid from China represented 64.4 per cent of aid received as against the 27.8 per cent from the Soviet Union. The same source further notes that, whereas statements made by North Vietnamese officials in 1962 indicated that deliveries under aid agreements with China were slow and incomplete, North Vietnam's pro-Peking stance on the Sino-Soviet dispute led to a decrease in the level of Soviet aid from 1964. These accounts may only be reconciled if it is assumed that North Vietnam received an enormous quantity of Soviet aid in 1963 and there is no evidence on which to base such an assumption.

With respect to foreign trade, it has been argued[3] that the major aim of North Vietnam's commercial policy during this period was to import the machinery and other capital goods necessary for the rapid development of the industrial sector of the economy. North Vietnam conducted its foreign trade on the basis of bilateral trade agreements. The first country with which trade relations were established was the People's Republic of China (1952). Subsequent annual agreements between Hanoi and Peking were signed between 1955 and 1960, when a two-year agreement according to which China would supply North Vietnam with steel products, mechanical products, cotton and chemicals in return for coal, timber, cement and agricultural products was signed. Trade with the Soviet Union was conducted on the basis of annual agreements between 1955 and 1960, while a five-year agreement was concluded in 1960. According to a 1958 protocol, the Soviet Union would provide North Vietnam with, among other things, metal-working machines, electrotechnical equipment, spare parts, bearings, oil products, sheet-metal, cable, chemicals and cloth, in return for jute, hardwood products, knitwear, footwear and food items.[4]

Given her geographical situation, it is not surprising that Hanoi's initial response to the Sino-Soviet crisis was neutral. Thus, at the Twenty-second Congress of the CPSU in 1961, the Vietnamese delegation argued emphatically that the USA was engaging in imperialist intervention around the globe — a Chinese position — while noting that it considered the USSR as the 'centre' of the socialist bloc and praised the 'creative Marxism-Leninism' of the CPSU. Vietnam was not yet ready to be drawn into the Soviet bloc.

The commencement of the American bombing of North Vietnam in 1965 brought with it a considerable change in commercial policy. Hanoi was now in no position to take a radical position *vis-à-vis* the Sino-Soviet dispute, and both parties to that dispute 'united' in their determination to see a Communist victory in Vietnam. However, in material terms, it was the Soviet Union which provided most assistance to Hanoi. Thus, between 1965 and 1975, the Soviet Union provided North Vietnam with $ 1,778 million in non-military aid, as against $1,491 million from China,[5] and provided considerably more military aid than did Peking. Further, it should be noted that during the 1965-75 period relations between Vietnam and the Soviet Union improved, while those between Vietnam and China deteriorated. Three factors must have contributed to this shift in Hanoi's alignment within the socialist world. First, the removal from office of Khrushchev, in October 1964, led to a re-evaluation of the role of Asian Communist parties in Soviet global strategy. Khrushchev's preoccupation with

Europe had kept Soviet attempts to compete with China for influence in Asia to a minimum. In February 1965, Kosygin was warmly welcomed in Hanoi and offered extensive war assistance. It was reported[6] that Deng Hsiao Ping made a secret visit to Hanoi late in 1964 after the Gulf of Tonkin incident and offered the North Vietnamese government $1,000 million aid per year, provided that aid was not accepted from the Soviet Union. The offer was apparently refused.

The second factor influencing Hanoi's drift towards Moscow was Peking's actual physical interference with Soviet arms deliveries in 1965. China made no charge for the rail transit, but prohibited over-flights and delayed acceptance of these high-technology shipments at the Soviet frontier. Unbelievable as this may be, it is well attested.[7] We see again, as already in the North Korean case (see Chapter 11), the funest influence of Mao's doctrine that war is best fought by labour- and morale-intensive means, and that military technology gaps are not important. The lord of a billion people, not immediately threatened by anyone, could well enunciate such nonsense. He had won wars in such a way, even stale-mating a small US expeditionary force in Korea. But Kim and Ho had to look beyond the undeniable advantages of high morale and the *levée en masse* for poor belligerents to the actual size of the masses they could levy. For Ho in particular the acceptance of Soviet high-technology weapons was not just a matter of philosophy but of survival.

Thirdly, we must mention the Great Proletarian Cultural revolution, which introduced considerable uncertainty into China's foreign policy. Recent Vietnamese reports indicate that the current rift between Hanoi and Peking began in late 1967, when Chinese Red Guards were reported to have demonstrated outside Vietnamese consulates in Nanking, Canton and Kunming, accusing the North Vietnamese government of revisionism (Huynh, 1979, p. 342). The same source notes the Viet-namese allegation that Chinese emissaries tried to win Chinese communities within Vietnam (the Hoas) over to the Cultural Revolution: 'From the other side of the border, Chinese loudspeakers, directed towards Vietnam, started a shouting campaign against "southern revisionism" in abusive and virulent terms.'

In summary, while there can be no doubt that both China and the Soviet Union granted significant quantities of aid to Hanoi in its struggle against the Americans, political factors led to a shift in alliance, on the part of Vietnam, from Peking to Moscow.

The Americans agreed to withdraw from the South in 1974 and

Vietnam was unified by the conquest of the South in 1975. The North Vietnamese government prepared for its transition to a peacetime five-year plan with the announcement, in 1974, of a two-year economic reconstruction and rehabilitation plan. Preparations for the transition also included a significant foreign aid agreement drive.

A senior government and party delegation, led by First Party Secretary Le Duan, visited Moscow towards the end of October 1975 and secured two major aid agreements, which would underwrite the forthcoming five-year plan and assist in the reunification of the country. The two parties pledged to co-ordinate 'economic development plans', and it has been suggested that Vietnam was offered a special role in CMEA (Thayer, 1976, p. 21). On his visit to Peking a month earlier Le Duan had, according to one source, secured a long-term, interest-free loan and a protocol on the supply of general goods for 1976 (ibid.). In August, according to the same source, an economic delegation led by Le Thanh Nghi had secured Chinese agreement on aid for 1976, and an agreement on long-term economic co-operation amounting to approximately $400 million (ibid.). In May 1977 Vietnam joined the CMEA financial agencies IBEC and IIB.

A later source provides a completely different picture of Le Duan's visit to Peking. Huynh (1979, p. 344) believes the purpose of the trip was to thank China for the part it played in the Vietnamese victory and to request continued aid. It is alleged that the Chinese government demanded Vietnamese agreement upon an 'antihegemony' clause in the joint communiqué and that Le Duan refused. The Chinese response was apparently to terminate all aid agreements with Hanoi. On the basis of the available data, it is impossible to determine the accuracy of either report. However, it seems reasonable to argue that Vietnam's relations with China were continuing to deteriorate and, to the extent that Peking was withholding aid, the Vietnamese government was being driven into the hands of either Moscow or the West.

During the course of the two-year plan, North Vietnam's trade with the West increased significantly. Table 13.1 shows trade with various countries, East and West. Aid from Western sources remained modest, Japan providing $27.6 million and Scandinavia and Australia smaller amounts (Thayer, see above). But the USA offered nothing, since the South had been conquered contrary to agreement. She also did no trade, and blocked World Bank help as well. So it must have been clear to Hanoi that its major source for economic assistance for some time to come would be the Soviet Union. On the other hand, the Vietnamese leadership had continually stressed its desire for greater trade relations with the West even if aid was not forthcoming.

Sino-Vietnamese relations reached crisis point in 1978. The Kampuchean-Vietnamese conflict had been slowly escalating since 1976 and Peking was siding openly with the Pol Pot regime. Hanoi's perception of the Chinese position *vis-à-vis* Vietnam has been summarised by Huynh:

> As 1978 began, the deterioration in Sino-Vietnamese relations had reached a point where Vietnam's leaders perceived that the country was subject to a multipronged guerrilla-type attack by China, aiming at sapping its internal strength and sabotaging its economic development strategy. In addition to the military conflict with Kampuchea, the Vietnamese perceived a determined Chinese endeavour to wean Laos away from Vietnam's sphere of influence. While in the northern frontiers, the Vietnamese felt the pressure of an increasingly hostile China, within the country itself they felt that they were subject to a two-pronged Chinese attack: (a) the alleged Chinese effort in instigating the Meo, Nung and Tay highland minority people against the lowland Vietnamese and (b) the alleged Chinese attempt to secretly organize the Hoa people to sabotage the Vietnamese economic plan (Huynh, 1979, pp. 345-6).

It is difficult to assess the validity of these allegations on the basis of the vast volume of often contradictory accusations which have passed between Hanoi and Peking since 1978. It is clear, however, that Hanoi's response to its perceptions was dramatic. On 23 March 1978, a government decree to 'transform capitalist commerce' was published. This led to the immediate closure of all private business enterprises in Vietnam and the confiscation of accumulated commodities. Further, the 'capitalist traders' were offered the choice between jobs in government-operated enterprises or opportunities to make new lives for themselves in the 'New Economic Zones' — the Vietnamese Gulag Archipelago. It has been estimated that around 30,000 households in Ho Chi Minh City — mostly Hoa people — were affected (Huynh, ibid.).

While the March 23 decree was promulgated in an attempt to further the socialisation of the South, there can be little doubt that Hanoi's animosity towards Peking was an important factor in its timing. The ethnic Chinese who dominated commerce in Vietnam were thus left with few desirable options. Whether of their own accord, or possibly under pressure from either the Chinese embassy in Hanoi or the

Table 13.1: Combined Vietnam's Visible Mirror-Trade ($ US 000)

	1971	1972	1973	1974	1975	1976	1977	1978
EXPORTS *FROM* COUNTRIES *TO* VIETNAM								
Bulgaria[a]	8034	6573	8857	8041	11259	15836	19299	25943
CSSR[a]	16807	17945	25024	21584	16690	23222	26904	34277
GDR[a]	22762	22325	33626	40121	n.a.	n.a.	n.a.	n.a.
Hungary[a]	16366	17954	29344	29675	40507	18894	15316	20881
Poland	15145	7941	14674	12440	13265	17632	22772	23639
Romania[a]	3517	6672	7148	6479	8631	6298	8108	n.a.
USSR[a]	154776	113633	194087	254143	219990	308388	371870	442638
EEC[b]	75318	59406	60586	70000	13580	71000	264000	253500
of which France[b]	41391	32593	25023	27810	5430	29650	89400	92800
Japan[a,c]	165900	106580	83830	101830	79290	168850	192890	285610
USA[a]	297000	318000	314000	675000	213000	1000	–	–
Hong Kong[d]	23014	19034	18446	22732	19104	35045	64756	18132

Table 13.1 Continued

IMPORTS BY COUNTRIES *FROM* VIETNAM

Bulgaria	2136	2593	3193	2887	1240	3519	3586	9281
CSSR	6528	3016	3085	7708	8055	10571	13806	13564
GDR	4262	3669	8852	9714	n.a.	n.a.	n.a.	n.a.
Hungary	1482	1036	641	2120	3697	3122	5414	7441
Poland	2893	3973	2022	2673	3484	6972	7719	12714
Romania	350	633	80	1067	2998	3381	5131	n.a.
USSR	23889	27262	50117	57357	66261	84359	176034	220667
EEC	10196	8513	11706	19200	13780	11680	10710	12750
of which France	7314	6540	8749	12700	361	3490	4075	5330
Japan	4630	14100	28120	29480	39840	49420	80630	55660
USA	200	200	300	800	600	100	–	–
Hong Kong	3833	6712	20753	25516	19520	14725	17000	16789

Sources: a. Country statistical year books. b. METB. c. JETRO. d. Monthly trade statistics. Exports include re-exports.

Notes: While Communist countries never overtly traded with the South, capitalist ones did do some trade with the North. Thus in 1973 the Japanese totals include $ 4000 th. of exports to and $ 8000 th. of imports from the North^c; and the EEC figures are respectively $ 6570 th. and $ 1510 th. In view of the incompleteness of the table no c.i.f./f.o.b. correction has been made.

Vietnamese government, many Hoa people in the North, including old Communists, departed for China. In May, the Cholon private market in Ho Chi Minhville (mainly Hoa) was closed, and the suffering and exodus of the Boat People began in earnest. In June Vietnam joined CMEA. On 3 July 1978, Peking announced its decision to terminate all its remaining aid projects in Vietnam and recall all technical experts from the country. Thus by mid-1978 the Vietnamese government was firmly aligned to the Soviet Union in the Sino-Soviet conflict, and the decision to join CMEA was probably undertaken on the suggestion of Moscow. It is perhaps surprising that such an important decision was not given greater press coverage in Vietnam, although there is evidence to suggest that the decision was taken rather suddenly. On 29 April 1978 Hanoi celebrated the twentieth anniversary of the founding of the Ministry of Foreign Trade. According to a published report of the proceedings,[8] CMEA was not mentioned even though the emphasis of speeches was on the past and future development of the foreign trade sector.

Vice-premier Le Thanh Nghi noted that, since 1975, the resources of the South had been tapped while there had been increasing development of the North. The value of exports in 1976 had increased by 70 per cent over 1975, while the 1977 increase over 1976 was 42 per cent. Unfortunately, this citation is typical of the very few statistical statements which appear in the Vietnamese press, in that it is not made clear whether the data are in volume or value terms, or whether the reference to 1975 exports is to the country as a whole for the entire year or to the North only, before unification. Import statistics are always conspicuous by their absence, although a balance of trade deficit is often noted.

Le Thanh Nghi did, however, make some informative commercial policy pronouncements. He noted that Vietnam would focus on the export of products such as coffee, rubber, timber, shrimp, ink, frozen pineapple, *objets d'art* and clothing, whilst international aid and credits would be used to import equipment and machinery, raw materials, fuel and fertilisers. Further, to the extent that a commodity was highly priced on the world market and domestic requirements were limited, that commodity should be exported regardless of its sector of origin. The vice-premier stressed the importance of a state monopoly of foreign trade and remarked upon the generous assistance provided by the socialist countries. He argued that the failure of exports to keep up with imports was an organisational rather than an economic problem. Increased levels of exports would be forthcoming if markets were created and their existence made known to all producers.

Although it was instantly publicised in Moscow, Vietnam's June accession to CMEA was only mentioned in Vietnam at the end of a major foreign economic policy pronouncement[9] in October 1978, in a three-line passage noting that the decision would assist in 'co-operation with fraternal socialist countries on the basis of mutual benefit'. Another article which appeared in the same month[10] was entitled 'CMEA and the Forms of Specialist International Economic Co-operation'. However, while it provides an interesting summary of CMEA's history and organisation, its only reference to Vietnam notes that the economy's backwardness and war-destruction limit the extent to which Vietnam can participate in the international division of labour and co-operation, although it was hoped that membership would help accelerate economic development. On the basis of the above evidence, it seems reasonable to argue that Hanoi's decision to join the CMEA was made quickly and probably at the behest of Moscow. However, it is equally clear that by the middle of 1978 any hopes of reasonable relations with China were gone, and Western sources of economic aid were rapidly disappearing as a consequence of Hanoi's seemingly endless military adventures, especially in Kampuchea. However there was surely one other factor, though more an interesting than an important one: Cuba.

Historically Cuba and Vietnam are not so different, and the Cuban precedent is most convincing. Both countries fought their own way to a Marxist-Leninist revolution. Both are distant from the Soviet Union and poor, but there is no longer a promise of rapid economic equalisation associated with membership of CMEA. Cuba abandoned Guevarism in 1970; Vietnam unified her currency and brought the South under the Northern economic management in May 1978. Both countries, again, are threatened by hostile, neighbouring great powers; and since these powers are enemies of the USSR both are of great strategic value. Both have made a business of letting their own citizens go, on a scale quite unknown in other Communist countries. Both have sent their troops abroad, in an exportation of revolution that clearly owes more to native thrust than to Soviet initiative. It has been rumoured that Vietnam consciously imitated Cuba in all these matters.[11] It is certain that Cubo-Vietnamese relations have been very cordial ever since Cuba was the first to recognise the South Vietnamese PRG in 1972, and Fidel Castro visited the 'liberated' portion of South Vietnamese territory in September 1973.[12] He was the first foreign Communist leader to do so.

Vietnam, rather like Cuba, went through an experimental period. She could not, like Cuba, consciously imitate the Chinese, but turned right instead. In 1977 she joined the IMF and the World Bank, and is indeed the only CMEA member to be in the latter (Chapter 1, Table 1.4). Clearly she had been taking a far more pragmatical and open-minded line before plumping for CMEA: one thinks of the sale of oil rights to West European companies, and of the very liberal foreign investment law. Nay more, even after joining she showed far greater sensitivity to her neighbours than Cuba ever did. Thus she tried to obscure the military and diplomatic threat implied by her joining CMEA. From 2 to 28 July 1978 the Deputy Foreign Minister Phan Hien visited Japan, Singapore, Australia, New Zealand, Malaysia and Thailand (i.e. not Indonesia). He assured them of Vietnam's continuing independence, and her desire for close economic and cultural relations with the countries visited (Bräker, 1970, pp. 31-2). Even Soviet propaganda against ASEAN eased up considerably (ibid., pp. 41-3). Indeed until the Boat People crisis it looked as if CMEA membership would be compatible with openness to multinationals – and for this there is good Hungarian precedent. But now it is less certain.

Given the perceived relative insignificance, in the short term, of CMEA membership, it remains to analyse the Vietnamese government's official position *vis-à-vis* commercial policy. This will be done using the major statement so far to have emerged from Hanoi entitled: 'It is Necessary, on the Basis of the Experiences that have been Gained, to Perform Good Foreign Trade Work in the New Stage of the Revolution'. It was published in October 1978 (see note 9).

Dang Viet Chan begins with a brief history of North Vietnam's foreign trade and notes that in 1964 the value of exports was two to three times what it had been in 1957 whilst the volume of imports had risen 1.5 times during the same period. During the war period, 1965-1975, it is noted that exports declined seriously while import requirements rose. Due to the 'correct international solidarity policy of the Party', it is argued that generous aid was forthcoming from socialist countries and other friends. With the cessation of bombing, exports again rose, the value being 30 per cent higher than it had been in 1964. Since the author does not indicate whether his export values are calculated on the basis of constant or current prices, they are difficult to use in analysing North Vietnam's foreign trade performance.

The author then proceeds to note that unification has led to further increases in exports and that Vietnam had economic relations with 60 countries, while its trade with non-socialist countries was facilitated

through various international economic financial organisations.
According to Dang, the history of Vietnam's commercial policy
provides four lessons for the future:

*(i) The State Monopoly of Foreign Trade Must Be Maintained and
Strengthened.* During the war against France (1946-54) private
merchants had been used to open the flow of goods between liberated
and other areas. For a certain time after the complete liberation of the
North, private merchants were still used for trade with Hong Kong, but
this allegedly led to 'excessive consumer-good imports competing with
domestic production', traders demanding gold in payment for their
goods, and artificially high prices. As a consequence of these undesirable outcomes, a foreign trade monopoly was established in South
Vietnam immediately after the Communist takeover. In addition to
this pragmatic justification, Dang does not fail to note that a foreign
trade monopoly is a law of socialism but that the specific form to be
found in different economies is determined by historical circumstances.
Thus, the organisation of foreign trade in Vietnam is determined by the
fact that a significant proportion of goods for export are currently
produced by private farmers and artisans. Under these circumstances,
it is necessary to centralise foreign trade decision making within the
Ministry of Foreign Trade. On the other hand, for those commodities
produced within the state sector of the economy, notably rubber,
shrimp and frozen squid, it is more efficient to allow a measure of
decentralisation, so that individual producers are permitted direct
communication with foreign markets via the Ministry, which provides
unified management for foreign trade activities in line with Party
policy.

*(ii) Production Must Be Developed in Such a Way that Many Sources
of High-value Export Goods Are Available Within the Country.* Dang
argues for the creation of centralised, large-scale, readily mobilised
sources of exports. He asserts that, in moving from small-scale to
large-scale methods of production, exports serve the function of
stimulating production, raising its technical level, redistributing social
labour and creating conditions for the expansion of imports. Further,
the structure of export industries must be based on Vietnam's natural
resource base, and produce goods which satisfy the requirements of
the world market, while yielding a high return.

It should be noted that this stress on export-led development differs
significantly from the Albanian policy (see Chapter 10). Whereas current

exports are necessary to pay for those imports which are not provided
as grants or on long-term credits in the case of any economy, the
Albanian leadership has never accorded exports any other positive
function. In this respect, Enver Hoxha would be in full agreement with
Milton Friedman (1980, p. 41):

> Another fallacy seldom contradicted is that exports are good,
> imports bad. The truth is very different. We cannot eat, wear, or
> enjoy the goods we send abroad . . . Our gain from foreign trade is
> what we import. Exports are the price we pay to get imports. As
> Adam Smith saw so clearly, the citizens of a nation benefit from
> getting as large a volume of imports as possible in return for its
> exports, or equivalently, from exporting as little as possible to pay
> for its imports.

Both these authorities also clearly agree with Kim Il Sung (see
Chapter 11).

*(iii) Import Policy Must Be Closely Linked to the Economic
Construction Line of the Party as Expressed in Annual and Five-year
Plans.* Dang argues that since the economy is underdeveloped, it is
necessary to use the strength of foreign economies to develop that of
Vietnam by importing machines, raw materials, technical supplies and
other instruments of production. Development implies not only
rapid industrialisation but also the growth of the agricultural sector
of the economy. Thus, in development priorities a difference is
discernible between the Vietnamese and Albanian governments. For the
Party of Labour of Albania, the rapid growth of the industrial sector
remains a first priority; but then Albania is not quite so poor.

On more specific policy issues, Dang notes the importance of external
credit for financing imports but warns against the possible adverse
consequences of too great a debt. With respect to the structure of
imports, the importation of complete equipment sets is regarded as an
important priority. As to the ranking of imports, Dang argues that
cost-benefit analysis should be used whenever possible.

*(iv) Implementation of the Party's Economic Construction and Foreign
Affairs Policies Requires that Trade and Other Economic Relations
With Foreign Countries Be Expanded.* Here Dang cites the correct
policy as being:

the strengthening [of] our relationship with the fraternal socialist countries on the basis of socialist internationalism while developing economic relations with other countries on the basis of maintaining our independence and sovereignty and benefiting both sides.[13]

Dang is optimistic regarding the potential for a rapid expansion of foreign trade and consequent growth. He suggests that the socialist states are gaining in economic strength and that the 'nationalistic' states of the Third World have 'developed' their independence. These factors have led to a relative weakening of the capitalist world, imposing on it the need to find new foreign markets, make overseas investments and grant loans. For these reasons, Dang maintains Vietnam is in a position to secure, at low cost, the imports necessary for development. On the other hand, argues Dang, the crisis of capitalism means that capitalist economies must increase the level of imports and here again Vietnam is in a position to gain from an aggressive export policy.

It is difficult to assess the extent to which Dang believes his own argument, for he also indicates that the socialist states are to remain Vietnam's major trading partners in the foreseeable future. He expresses the ambitious hope that within seven or eight years (from 1978) Vietnam will have balanced trade. Finally — and again in marked contrast to Albanian policy — Dang notes the importance of expanding the tourist industry as a source of foreign currency.

Notes

1. Theriot and Matheson, 1979, p. 569.
2. Smith, Bernier *et al.*, 1967, Ch. 18.
3. Ibid.
4. Ibid.
5. Theriot and Matheson, 1979.
6. The *Guardian Weekly*, 29 October 1978.
7. *Ost-Probleme*, Bonn, 22 April and 2 December 1966.
8. *Nhan Dan*, 5 May 1978.
9. Dang, 1978. This came out in October.
10. *Nghien Cun Kinh Te*, 5/1978 (i.e. October), pp. 34-5.
11. *Far Eastern Economic Review*, 22 June 1979, p. 7. But there are substantial differences. Cuba was infinitely more humane, allowing rather free emigration of its bourgeoisie and selling only its few prisoners to USA for a properly arranged prior ransom. Vietnam takes their money for a place on a leaky boat — money she could take anyway by passing a law against private gold and currency holdings. I.e. for Cuba the currency was the main thing, for Vietnam it is the expulsion. Again the Vietnamese Communists have always been much more orthodox than Castro.
12. *Yearbook on International Communist Affairs*, Hoover Institute, California, 1974, p. 567.
13. Dang, 1978.

14 CONCLUSION

Peter Wiles

It is appropriate to conclude this book immediately after the Vietnamese section. Assume first that a country belongs to the New Communist Third World already. Then the Vietnamese experience presents it with a dramatic alternative to the Albanian and North Korean cases. The most important differences seem to be:

(i) The Vietnamese government appears to have no marked bias against Western trading partners or aid donors provided that economic advantages are apparent in the relationship.[1] The Albanians will trade with the West but refuse to accept either aid or long-term credits. This too is the basic North Korean position.

(ii) For the Vietnamese, the rapid growth of exports is seen as part of the development strategy, not only because it may provide scarce foreign currency and thus allow imports of capital goods, but also because the 'discipline' of producing commodities for an export market is argued to have beneficial spin-offs for the domestic economy as a whole. The strategy is export-led to an unusual degree among Communist countries.

(iii) The Albanian leadership on the other hand has sought to maximise the inflow of scarce resources while minimising the outflow. It has had over the years a truly astounding success in this. And it is here that North Korea has differed; keeping a rough balance of trade apart from the one great borrowing spree. Vietnam wishes to keep a rough balance, too.

(iv) Albanian criticism of CMEA and Soviet 'social imperialism' reflects, among other things, discontent with Khrushchev's attempts to steer the Albanian leadership away from a heavy industrialisation strategy following the Soviet New Course in the 1950s. Vietnam has not been a member of CMEA for a sufficient time for us to determine whether Moscow will similarly attempt to modify the Vietnamese development strategy to suit its own ends. The Vietnamese are confident that membership of the CMEA will involve no loss of freedom for them, and they are not so obsessed by heavy industry as the two smaller powers.

(v) The Vietnamese suffer less from security paranoia. In the case of tourism no other explanation is even plausible: the two independents admit very few tourists indeed, though the foreign currency earnings would be considerable.

Above all, Vietnamese behaviour is Leninist, i.e pragmatic, while Albania and North Korea are Stalinist, i.e. dogmatic. It is a real paradox that Vietnam, the CMEA member, looks outward to all the world whilst the two independents strive for autarky. The paradox becomes milder when we remember that Stalin also turned the CMEA inwards, trying to create an autarkic bloc of many countries that yet traded quite vigorously with each other. It would be mistaken to seek a rule, but the most plausible is the distinction between the Leninist and Stalinist temperaments. It is Leninist to try to join the CMEA, as Mozambique is trying to do. It is Stalinist to turn one's back on the world.

Cuba is a well-studied country, and a book already too long has no room for it. She is culturally even more open than Vietnam, and more tolerant of religion. She trades as widely with Western Europe as any CMEA member, and her economic dependence on the USSR is due to a highly special circumstance: she is cut off by the US embargo from her natural economic trade partner and source of capital, remittances and technology. The role that OPEC plays in the commercial policy of the PDRY 'should' be, but is not, played for Cuba by the USA. It is this alone that has forced Cuba into an unnatural dependence on a distant patron, a dependence strongly reminiscent of Albania's, though that was more self-imposed. The lessons we have drawn from Vietnam are thus strengthened by Cuba — which after all set her the example. Quite especially marked is the parallelism of their foreign-policy independence: both countries take initiatives up to and including invasion with merely Soviet permission. But one contrast between them really cannot be explained away: Cuba's hostility to non-Communist international organisations, and Vietnam's receptivity (cf. Table 1.4). It still cannot be said, however, that even Cuba rejects private capitalist investment (cf. Tables 1.2 and 1.3).

Mongolia is clearly a very special case indeed, by reason of her geography and her small population. She can only choose between her giant neighbours: we think she has chosen wisely. Transport costs forbid her to cultivate other trade partners seriously.

There is, actually, a third solution: to be open and not a member of the CMEA. This is the Yugoslav and Chinese way, and merely to point that out is to show how little generalisation on it is possible. Yugoslavia was the first Communist country to cut loose, and she has developed a non-Marxist ideology of self-management, whilst nevertheless retaining the Leninist style of government. This style appears to be permanent: the country is culturally and economically open but politically closed, strongly totalitarian, and stable. Tito's death has made little difference. China, the Middle Kingdom, is far too big to retain in any Communist commonwealth not run by itself. After an 'Albanian' period she is going through a 'Yugoslav' one, which is surely not stable either. Both countries must of course defend themselves against Soviet invasion. As the biggest country in the world, China can nevertheless get by on a proportionally small defence budget, but Yugoslavia's is enormous. In this respect the 'open' and the 'closed' independents have the same problem!

The 'open Communists' ' most interesting problem is how not to converge with capitalism, since they have no moral, cultural, military, ideological or economic backing from the bloc. While the CMEA members are partially open to all the world, Yugoslavia and China are not open to the CMEA. It is amazing to walk around Belgrade bookshops and find that, despite similarities of language and even script, the only Russian books are Dostoyevski's novels. China, of course, without these cultural links, is still worse off, and cultivates an official Russophobia. These countries look to the West, and Yugoslavia's non-political culture is heavily Westernised. China is naturally too big to be seriously affected by any foreign culture outside a few cities, but these are full of tourists, advertising, political discussion and other threats to national security.

It would be very rash, and altogether beyond our mandate, to make predictions. What we hope to have done is set out some of the major possibilities in a little regarded, and rapidly expanding field.

But prior to the question of 'How to Be a Good Communist' is the question of whether to be one at all. The research reported in this volume does not answer this question, but we feel more entitled than most to venture an opinion. What follows, therefore, is the editor's own 'Concluding Unscientific Postscript', for which his collaborators are not responsible, and it brings, in the words of the title of a third famous book, *Naught For Your Comfort*. Communism, especially in its CMEA variant, has some economic, many diplomatic and still more military and ideological attractions.

It is diplomatically very attractive because it enables one to cock a snook at international capitalism, and above all the ex-imperial power. That power is always hated or at least profoundly mistrusted: memories rankle. From minor pin-pricks (recognising North Korea) all the way to major historical actions (helping the Cuban airlift to Angola) there are innumerable delights in being Communist or pro-Communist. One must of course have a strong digestion to swallow every Soviet misdeed. But few politicians are even halfway honest: their stomachs are usually up to the task. So the foreign policy of the Third World as a whole is anti-capitalist and neutral *vis-à-vis* the USSR.

Militarily of course such a policy pays hand over fist. Poor in civilian machinery, poverty-stricken in food, the USSR has good, not very obsolete, arms in abundance. She is generous and quick with them, and *in extremis* Cuba will send troops. On the other side only France (Kolwezi, 1979) has so good a record. The USA was beaten in Vietnam, the USSR is winning in Afghanistan: two approximately equal tests of will. China, Vietnam, Angola, Mozambique: the list of revolutions that have been won with Soviet logistical support is most impressive. She has burned her fingers now and again, as perhaps in Kolwezi. But she has had no evident failure of a serious commitment since Greece and Korea.

Marxist-Leninist ideology is of course excellent for semi-educated people. The dialectic offers *a priori* certainty of what the future will be: morals play no part. Yet it is also profoundly moral, engaging men's passions on behalf of the poor against the exploiters, and permitting ample freedom of action within the pre-determined framework (e.g. *Operación Carlota*). A secular religion and a dedicated way of life, Marxism-Leninism is the Islam of the non-Islamic world. Whenever a semi-educated minority can dominate by force, this ideology is likely to win. A strong competing popular religion will defeat it (Somalia); combine that with substantial secondary and higher education, and the country is impervious (Poland). Only perhaps Holy Russia itself is an exception: with a full complement of well-educated cardinals and theologians whose great intellectual goal is Orthodoxy within the new religion. Their faith ᵕmakes little impression on ordinary Russian citizens, but these latter are certainly not in active disagreement (in the national minorities there are greater, but still manageable, problems). Non-disagreement, after all, is the most that any government can hope for; it is amply available in the Third World.

A word in passing on radical Islam. Islam is of its nature anti-Western, and anti-capitalist. Though the West has had few actual Islamic colonies, it has established many protectorates, and perpetrated many aggressions from the First Crusade to Israeli independence. Such relations are indeed more exacerbating than straight conquest and colonisation. Islam is in one of its periodical fermentations, and striking

out in all directions including itself. But as an ancient religion it has
many more varieties than its Communist competitor. One of these is
radical, violent, socialist Islam. In Libya and indeed in Somalia this
variety has also been expansionist. It bears many fundamental resem-
blances to Marxism-Leninism, and shares in Libya's case many
medium-term goals. The Iranian Mujaheddin and Fedayin are similar.
There are such movements in Egypt, Iraq, everywhere. With their
passions fully engaged against the West, such people have always over-
looked the persecution of Islam in Central Asia, and are now busy
digesting even Afghanistan. My fear is that the PDRY will light the way
for them, and they will abandon all but the trappings of Islam, just as
the Provisional IRA and the ETA have done to Catholicism, in favour
of a 'uniate' Marxism-Leninism, differing only in liturgy.

Economics is the weakest side of Third World Communism. In the
absence of adequate statistics for real national income, we can form no
firm judgment on the NCTW *vis-à-vis* the most capitalistic countries,
such as, say, Kenya, or *vis-à-vis* our own 'Marginals'. Merely on a
literary basis, NCTW policies seem to be counter-productive. The
collectivisation of agriculture and the nationalisation of retail trade do
only harm. State-run factories make vast losses. Only foreign capitalism
works in these countries. The CMEA gives negligible aid and engages
in negligible trade, while the West is generous — though only by
comparison. No wonder, then, that the marginals hesitate above all to
imitate the Soviet economy: why should they? No wonder, indeed, that
Benin has grown the fastest of the first nine countries in our study —
except for the PDRY which has floated up on petro-dollars.

What indeed is wrong, when Benin or the Congo continue to hover?
Real Communism will not help them internally or externally: the
present policy is simply the best thing to do. But they are tempted:
Communism does generate a feeling of activity. It mobilises (some of)
the people, even if for foolish purposes. It makes the governing elite
feel good. It prevents the corrupt accumulation of wealth on a Kenyan
scale. The 'marginals' seem silly to us: hypocritical and indecisive, they
'cannot get their heads together'. But there is another way of looking
at them. The first duty of a Third World government today is to get aid.
Their countrymen are perpetually saying to these temporary leaders, in
the words of the advertisement, 'While you are up, get me a Grant'.
A leader well-versed in this art can add a percentage point or two to the
national expenditure[2] every year of his reign. When Kérékou 'bowed
down in the House of Rimmon' with Colonel Gaddafi, he brought back

a fat cheque; Machel has precluded that, while hitherto opening up no other source of aid.

The growth of the NCTW most curiously (with a few exceptions) fails to alarm the rest of the Third World. It is very bad manners to draw attention to it, or to laugh when Cuba claims to be 'non-aligned'. Anti-imperialist solidarity, and the shared experiences of colour discrimination and colonial liberation, matter more. Development economists and Third World diplomats alike turn a blind eye to the whole phenomenon; and I cannot imagine that this book will be popular in such circles. We have seen indeed that outside the military and diplomatic sphere the NCTW is not at present a very remarkable group within the whole Third World. But this of course holds only provided that we do not look to the future.

When it comes to mortgaging or not mortgaging the future of one's country in this way one must stress the possibly arbitrary character of choice. The last colonial liberation, of the Portuguese colonies, was necessarily Communist in Mozambique: no-one else supported FRELIMO. The wonder is that in Angola and Guinea-Bissau it was not so. The West had destroyed its own position by the many years during which NATO turned its blind eye towards its single colonialist member. But in all the other places we have discussed Communism has been accepted, or flirted with, by free choice. From one day to the next the CIA can destroy an Arbenz in Guatemala, or Castro a Savimbi in Angola. But above all in that same time-span a Kérékou can take his country, peacefully and *reasonably*, a giant stride nearer to Communism. His policy is not a foolish one: his people need to be disciplined and mobilised in a new way but subsidised in an old way; and being an 'NCTW marginal' makes all that possible. But another dictator could have chosen differently, and all bets are off. One is reminded of the Khazarim of old, whose Khakan (based in Astrakhan in the eighth century) considered the various forms of Christianity that were currently being sold to the barbarians — and chose to make his people Jewish.

Of course one has to sacrifice personal freedom for ever. To those who have never had it, whose one struggle is for physical survival, this is nothing at all. Freedom is indeed a necessity, but only for those who are in an economic and intellectual position to exercise it.

It is not that Marxism-Leninism is, in comparison with other development strategies, a great success in the Third World. It is not even that the elites in the NCTW are happy with what they have done. For instance, the Russians and all their works are distinctly unpopular in Benin, Congo, Angola and Ethiopia.[3] It is rather that their *ideas* are very popular among the elite, that in practice their system as a whole is not a total disaster, and its military and security sides function very well indeed. There is then no rapid slide towards them, but since the irreversibility doctrine (see Chapter 1, 4) is probably true, this means the slow take-over of everything, as in a successful game of grandmother's steps.

In conclusion this unsentimental picture is a far cry from certain points very prominent in the Brandt report (1980). I express them in Herr Brandt's own language, inserting our own numbers (Brandt, October 1980):

> In recent months — indeed for years now — we have become increasingly conscious of the close interaction between East-West and North-South issues. We are realising that what happens in 'remote' parts of the world also has a direct impact on Europe. Events in Iran and Afghanistan — and in the Middle East, South East Asia, Southern Africa and Central America — have dramatically spotlighted the need to see that the balance of interests between North and South, between industrialised and developing countries, is just as important as détente in an active policy for the pursuit of peace. The world is starting to recognise (i) that peace is not only menaced by power rivalries and conflicts between extreme ideologies but (ii) that the future of mankind is threatened just as much by mass starvation, economic collapse and ecological disaster. (iii) It is a dangerous illusion to think that fenced-off pockets of prosperity and security can survive indefinitely in an age when one-fifth of the world's population, concentrated mainly in the Southern hemisphere, is suffering from starvation and malnutrition.

I would comment that (i) and (ii) are about disconnected subjects: peace and starvation. The struggle between the West and the East must be properly named: it is between Northwest and Northeast, where Japan and Australasia, but not Switzerland or Sweden, are defined as Northwest. It is this struggle (i) that menaces peace. Starvation (ii) is only to this extent connected, that the struggle diverts Northern money from aid into arms. But does it? If there were no struggle, there would be no competition for the South, and so perhaps less aid. It is not obvious that the very poor nations of the South would receive more aid in a world that did not need their military bases or ideological allegiance. Certainly they would have to pay for their own arms, and since they have excellent reasons to fight among themselves they might be actually impoverished by that.

But point (iii) seems to be altogether without foundation. So long as rich countries are armed there is no 'dangerous illusion' whatever. The West Germans and the East Germans are actually more likely to come to blows because of some event in Mozambique or Zaire, where they are in competition, than through an incident on the Elbe. Above all, some initiative by or against South Africa is extremely likely to endanger world peace. It is no accident that the NCTW is heavily represented in this neighbourhood, and official racism is indeed a threat to peace. So if the two Germanies fenced themselves off from the South they would be more secure. I concur that foreign aid should be multiplied, but this particular argument for it is a *non sequitur*.

Behind Brandt's reasoning, though not openly featured, is a point I fully accept: the Northwest is far more guilty of past misdeeds in the South than the Northeast. But that only means that the Northeast has until now been too weak to oppress people so far away. Where I differ altogether is over the curious notions that there there is such a thing as a unified Third World — neither the NCTW nor even really OPEC figures in the Brandt report — and that there is or might be some military tension between 'Northwest' and 'South'. There is no North-South tension, for the 'North' is divided practically into two and the 'South' into many: simply the Northeast has moved South, and the Cold War covers the globe.

Notes

1. We have no special chapter on Cuba, since there exists an excellent and easily available literature on it. But the similarities of Vietnam to Cuba (cf. Chapter 1) extend even to this point. The overwhelming Soviet position in Cuba's foreign trade is due to the overwhelming sugar etc. subsidies (Table 1.3). Cuba trades much more with Western Europe than with Eastern Europe.

2. But, we must be careful to add, perhaps not to GDP! I do not deny the kernel of truth in the strictures of Peter Bauer.

3. Walter Schwarz in the *Guardian*, 18 February 1981; Jon Swain in the *Sunday Times*, 1 March 1981; David Lamb in the *Los Angeles Times*, May-June 1980; Christabel King in the *Daily Telegraph*, 10 March 1981.

15 POSTSCRIPT

Since the bulk of this book was written history has continued to happen, information has accumulated, and we have had afterthoughts on our general evaluation.

I.   Let us begin with *recent events*.

Mozambique was not admitted to *CMEA* in July 1981, the next Council meeting after her informal application (cf. p. 158). Nor, indeed, was Laos, the failed candidate of June 1978, which would presumably have a prior claim. One reason must be that, as we saw, admission of the NCTW implies sharply increased aid, in the name of 'levelling up': but at the moment of Poland's economic collapse there are far more important things to do with spare resources. At this latest Council meeting the whole of the NCTW as defined, minus Grenada plus Laos, were observers; but not North Korea, nor of course Albania. Nothing daunted, Mozambique seems to have instantly and publicly re-applied![1] At this meeting too the NCTW received a sort of verbal recognition at last in Prime Minister Tikhonov's speech: 'Three developing countries, having chosen the path of socialist contribution – Mongolia, Cuba, Vietnam – have become members of the CMEA . . . The countries of the CMEA are also trying continuously to widen economic relations with Laos, Cambodia, Afghanistan, PDRY, Angola, Ethiopia, Mozambique. In their relations with all developing countries . . .'

The Polish events cannot but leave their imprint on the CMEA and even the NCTW. Long-term supranational planning will clearly take a back seat until such mundane problems as punctual deliveries from Polish factories have been solved. But more than that: invaded or not invaded, Poland is an ideological setback. Nay more, the economic symptoms of Poland's disease – bad labour discipline, corrupt administration, black work – are scarcely less evident in USSR or Czechoslovakia, even Hungary. This is not the moment for vast futuristic schemes.

Thus Poland has set back both the extension of the CMEA and the heightening of its powers. In *Mozambique* itself there is evidence of continuing shortages particularly in the main cities. A new rationing

system was reported as introduced in spring 1981 in three major
cities and covering eleven basic items, to be administered by private
and co-operative, as well as state trading organisations. The country
has been repeatedly hit by drought and has continued to import foodstuffs in large quantities (for example rice and wheat from the US),
she has also continued to ask for and to receive substantial aid under
various programmes, including a new British credit of $23 m.[2]

But, according to official figures at least, the balance of trade
showed a surplus in 1979, for the first time since independence. It
was partly made up of increased exports and partly of reduced imports.
New aid and co-operation agreements have also been reported including
one with Iraq to increase oil refinery capacity and with Czechoslovakia
for prospecting.[3] The position of East Germany both as a trading
partner and a donor has grown to amount to something like a 'special
relationship' which is still, unfortunately, not reflected in official trade
figures. It is amply demonstrated, however, by recent agreements on
geological co-operation, help with the setting up of textile plants and
training of personnel and also in fishing, as well as by the tone of press
reports and official statements.[4]

Despite continuing growth of trade with South Africa in 1979,
Mozambique's diplomatic efforts are being increasingly directed
towards reducing dependence on that country. The issue relates also to
the problem of controlling migration to South Africa, one that she
shares with the other front line states. Moves are under way to establish
a Southern African Labour Commission to co-ordinate policies.
Mozambique's position, summed up by its representative Justice
Minister T. Hunguana, seems to accept, however that:

> migrant labour will exist in our region for as long as economic
> relations of dependency determined by geography and under-
> development continue to exist. Migrant labour will continue under
> the different conditions we are now beginning to impose. Migrant
> labour will probably continue after the downfall of apartheid within
> the context of normal relations between countries of different social
> systems.[5]

It is still difficult, at this stage, to assess the wider significance of the
reforms of 1980, and particularly of those introduced in March of
that year. It may be said, however, that the mobilisation of and reliance
on the private trader has been consolidated for the time being. In
exactly the same way, the inevitability of seeking foreign investment

resources for major development projects is acknowledged. But in the state apparatus the role of the administrator and of hierarchy in general seems to have been strengthened, too. The bureaucracy is now supposed to be more 'accountable' especially to the Ministries and to the mass organisations, but its growing ascendancy may still shape the disorder of society away from 'self-management' in particular. But, at present, the society is, on the whole, a relatively relaxed and open one. One may actually find the English pool results in *Noticias*![6]

In *Angola* the First Extraordinary Congress of the MPLA (Workers' Party) was held on 17-23 December 1980, 'to analyse the degree of accomplishment' of the 'orientations' of the 1977 Congress over the three-year (1977-80) period and to lay down guidelines for the 1981-5 five-year one. The emphasis appears to have been on the party's practical objectives for the future, the 'antiquated' methods of 'improvisation' and 'individualism' having been 'superseded' by 'planned', 'programmed' and 'collective' work and 'criticism' and 'self-criticism'. The attacks on 'petty bourgeois' corruption, speculation, tribalism, regionalism, negligence, indiscipline and 'liberalism' (which we may better translate as 'irresponsibility'), were reiterated, reflecting, among other things, some anxiety with key aspects of economic performance. But 'elitism' and 'sectarianism' were also attacked, as was religion, especially 'those churches which opposed the laws of the state'. 'Democratic centralism' was to remain the party's guiding organisational principle.[7]

In the economic sphere, the Congress recognised the urgency of raising the worker's living standards and the need to improve the functioning of the distribution system. The practice of *'auto-consumo'*, i.e. the preferential sale of products to the enterprises' own workers, was roundly condemned, together with theft and the speculative handling of goods. The importance of bringing as much of the country's output to the 'units of production and commercialisation' as possible was affirmed. However, L. Lara, Secretary for Organisation of the Central Committee, had conceded in an interview a little earlier, that: 'the small trader is still vital in his own way, because he helps with the distribution of goods. The shops we set up are not enough in numbers and their management is not as good as it should be, so the small independent trader is still necessary'.[8] The adequacy of the state apparatus set up to replace the pre-independence Portuguese-run private distribution had thus been admitted, some five years after independence. The need to bring a greater part of the 'present surplus' to the market and to overcome present lack of faith in the currency's power to buy industrial goods appeared to be more keenly felt, as at July 1980.[9]

A further development in education seems important. The literacy campaign (conducted in Portuguese only with some success since independence) will soon start to offer classes in the main vernacular languages. Six of these have now been codified into written form.[10]

Some new figures[11] (whose accuracy cannot be guaranteed) certainly paint a bleak picture of the state of production in 1978 in relation to 1973. The drop in coffee (26,000 tons compared to 210,000) appears particularly serious, although the 1980 estimate is given as 80,000. Cotton appears to have slumped almost completely (from 79,300 tons to a mere 1,000) and the figures for a few other main products also make grim reading (maize 198,000 tons in 1978 from 700,000 in 1973, rice 3,240 from 29,340, potatoes 40,000 from 70,000, sugar 39,000 from 82,000 and sisal 15,000 from 60,330). Food imports increased by some 35 per cent in value between 1978 and 1979 and the state of the economy appeared critical in many respects. A campaign is currently under way to increase food production and improve agricultural organisation.[12]

The intention remains, however, to make more progress towards the planned economy. The Extraordinary Congress resolved to replace the National Planning Commission which had 'introduced planning' with a 'state planning committee', intended (significantly perhaps) to function as an 'organ' of the Council of Ministers.[13] But foreign trade was also to be encouraged and 'dynamised' through the direction of a Foreign Trade Bank.

On 21 June 1981 Angola applied to join OPEC (cf. p. 84).

Foreign trade continued fairly vigorously in 1979 in any case, showing a surplus of just under $½ billion. Crude oil accounted for $^2/_3$ of the exports in 1979, and oil production is expected to increase by 17 per cent in 1981. New co-operation agreements in the oil field are constantly reported and efforts are being made to increase refining capacity.[14] Trade with South Africa has increased, as has trade with the USA.

Yet South Africa's diplomatic relations with Angola seem to have worsened. South African attacks on Angola have continued through May-June 1981 and the 'undeclared war' has led to the evacuation of considerable areas in the South of Angola. Angola's Foreign Minister P. Jorge asked for an oil and arms embargo against South Africa and urged other African countries to take measures against Western powers which opposed the implementation of UN Resolution 435 (1978) on

South-West Africa.[15] Angola regards the USA as the prominent example here, especially following President Reagan's election and in view of his apparent support for the remnants of the MPLA's rival movements. Otherwise the foreign policy 'orientations' of the First Congress of 1977 were reaffirmed in the Extraordinary one of December 1980.

We left *Benin* in the text with a minor unsolved conundrum: is Colonel Kérékou's conversion to Islam genuine? Two pieces of information indicate that it is not: the general ridicule evoked in Africa by his change of name (laughter at diplomatic gatherings), and the fact that *Noticias*, the official Mozambican newspaper, on 15 April 1981, called him Mathieu not Ahmed during his visit to Maputo. But if his Islamic faith is not serious, how about his Marxist-Leninist faith? Our feeling is that his attitude to all faiths is exceedingly cynical and instrumental. It is amusing and illuminating to note that Gaddafi temporarily converted to Emperor Bokasser in the same way in 1976. Apart from this issue, all the recent signs are that Kérékou is evolving towards the position of Sékou Touré, who condemns 'imported models'.

We feel we have much underestimated the importance of *fish* in the Soviet scheme of things, and particularly of the fish it is licensed (or not licensed) to take from the seas of the NCTW.[16] Foreign fishing boats, as we point out on pp. 77, 191 and 281, tend to use a licence, and to send their catch directly home without touching shore. So *fish may not be visible*: they may only appear as a licence fee. But since invisibles are seldom published, and their geographical breakdown almost never, we have little idea of the value to the NCTW of the Soviet catch in and off NCTW waters. Indeed a fishing fleet may be partially based on, say, Luanda but work outside Angolan territorial waters. There will then not even be an Angolan licence fee, but only some minor on-shore purchases. Nay more, by international accounting convention fish is exported or imported only when a boat of country A lands it in country B. It follows that a fish caught in mid-Atlantic by a Soviet boat and eaten in Leningrad might as well have been caught in Lake Baikal for all an international trade statistician could know.

II.   The reader may have noticed that there is no single *ideological or methodological* scheme informing this volume. Contributors have felt free to select, emphasise and interpret the facts according to their own predispositions and — dare we say -- prejudices. It would be most surprising if we were all equally sympathetic to the tendencies now dominant in our countries of study. Discussion among us has led to a closer consensus but not a full one.

Over sympathies it is not necessary to be more explicit. But are we too flat-footedly empiricist? Is our perception of the NCTW too 'voluntaristic'? Is not its situation quite closely determined by deeper forces? Andrew Racine writes:

This book is a collection of attempts by different authors to approach an understanding of changes currently taking place in certain Third World societies. Though the various essays maintain a consistency of presentation, it would have been extremely unusual for all the authors to have united in a single methodological approach to the subject. As a contribution toward the clarification of some of our methodological disagreements I offer the following thoughts on the conclusions elaborated above.

A curious and fundamental feature of political writing is that the form an argument assumes often reveals as much about the underlying attitudes and assumptions of the discussant as does the actual content of the discourse. The decision to emphasise a thing is itself an eloquent statement deserving as much attention as that which is said about the thing that is emphasised.

Throughout the preceeding pages much effort has been concentrated on describing the environments in which Third World leaders make decisions and on outlining the probable results they may anticipate when choosing from among various alternatives. The reader has been urged to consider these situations of choice as the key to understanding developments in the societies comprising this study.

For my part, I would direct attention to the meaning of this singular treatment afforded to situations of political choice and then offer an illustration of a different approach. Limitations of space require an abbreviated presentation here of what is rightfully a long and difficult argument.

The characterisation of political development as the cumulative outcome of a series of strategic decisions is perfectly in keeping with an influential contemporary trend in social science having roots in the positivist traditions of the previous century. What began as an attempt to separate 'science' from 'metaphysics' has developed into a single-minded distrust of all things eluding empirical verification or direct observation. All that falls outside, between or within observable objects and events, that which might be termed relations, cannot be *directly* observed, and hence, for this approach to social science, can have no meaning beyond what may be expressed in descriptive statements concerning objects and events which *can* be observed.

The balance thus struck between things and relations has profound consequences with respect to the perceived orientation of objects in our purview. The cosmos assumes the appearance of a collection of objects and events related but contingently one to the other. If no two 'things' are *necessarily* related, and any two 'things' *conceivably* are, if every observable social phenomenon, every institution, every job, every belief, every event is thought of as possessing a degree of autonomy with respect to all other phenomena such that relations between two or more of them appear never to be more than *associations* occurring with given degrees of probability, then the ordering of social institutions and events, their cohesion, is something which must be continually reinvented and reimposed as an act of will.

Theory, in such a system, seeks to elaborate the probability distributions by which different objects in the world are associated and, where possible, to offer such descriptions in advance of the association having occurred, i.e. to predict. In general, theorists follow one of two paths in pursuit of this end. Along one route, present and past patterns of associations among observable objects and/or events are accumulated in exhaustive detail in the expectation that such patterns manifest a temporal dimension of some magnitude so that descriptive information concerning them will have corresponding predictive value. The other route consists of inquiries into the process of decision making itself, the sole indisputable (if often enigmatic) source for the existence of associations of social objects and events. The 'Conclusion' above travels this route.

I would advocate an alternative approach which regards any given object or event as the phenomenal appearance, *at a given point in time*, of what is, viewed more radically, an ongoing relation. To comprehend the orientation of objects and the flow of events in this alternative view is not a matter of cataloguing and describing apparent associations but of finding the underlying relations of which observables are the present aspects and subsequently reconstituting phenomenal appearances on that basis.

An army, for example, would be understood to be not a collection of individuals flying Russian MIGs, bearing Chinese automatic rifles and travelling in Cuban armoured personnel carriers but would be looked upon as the form assumed by propertied interests of a society in confronting perceived threats to that property originating either within or outside the community.

In general, I would argue, political events and institutions are the phenomenal forms assumed by the material relations of civil society at various points in history and are unintelligible outside the context of the anatomy of civil society. For the societies under examination in this book the predominant relations of civil society are class relations and a look at political developments in light of this overwhelming fact may help to illustrate the virtues of the approach I favour.

Class relations, in what have been termed the 'marginal' NCTW countries, did not originate with the arrival of the French bourgeoisie but rather were radically rearranged as a result. Local states predated the European colonisation of these regions, in some cases by centuries. The material superiority which the French bourgeoisie enjoyed with respect to indigenous classes permitted it to reorganise methods of surplus generation in conformity with its own needs, employing military measures to overwhelm resistance when necessary.

The principal economic activity of these outposts of European capital became the extraction of raw materials. A small cadre of the regional population was enlisted to perform and administer the performance of the necessary work, while a much larger proportion continued, via traditional methods, to cultivate enough agricultural surplus to sustain everyone.

In each of the three colonies (Dahomey, Congo and Madagascar) a local bourgeoisie emerged as a protégé of its French counterpart assisting in administrative and commercial functions and exploiting the material forces at the command of its French sponsors in establishing its own political power. Yet in comparison to their European counterparts, and more importantly, in relation to other classes in their own societies, these incipient ruling classes were weak and insecure.

They lacked the material basis which strengthens and sustains the metropolitan bourgeoisie. There was no industry to speak of in these colonies, no heavily consolidated agribusinesses, no well-entrenched secondary sectors. Hired by their French supporters, for the most part, to be local managers for French industrial concerns or to direct commercial transactions between an underdeveloped agricultural sector and the metropole, the relative personal wealth they thereby accumulated in no way altered the fact that the material basis for surplus generation in these societies remained in the hands of a freeholding peasantry or the French themselves.

Once direct French political and military forces withdrew, conflict among social classes previously suppressed in the face of those forces began to emerge, often violently. In Benin, competition within the ruling class based on tribal as well as economic interests threatened to disrupt the day-to-day exercise of business activities. In Congo, students and workers organised a nexus of urban political agitation marked by riots and mass demonstrations. And in Madagascar significant peasant unrest, particularly in the south, ultimately erupted into open rebellion.

Faced with these challenges, each local bourgeoisie did what it could to strengthen its position. The appropriation of foreign concerns represented no threat to competing indigenous classes and thus ran little risk of provoking a confrontation. The broadening and deepening of the administrative structures of the state served the dual purpose of recruiting a mass which would identify its own future with that of the government (i.e. the bourgeoisie) and strengthening control over the expression of popular discontent throughout the society. Finally, *in extremis*, each local ruling class sought refuge in its Armed Forces as an apparently neutral, highly effective instrument capable of maintaining order and preserving the conditions conducive to profit-making activity.

Yet rule by the army is more an advertisement for, than a solution to, the menace which haunts the classes in control in these countries. Their dominant position hinges upon an ability to redirect generated surplus into enterprises which continue to accumulate capital under their control. Buffeted from below by the demands of workers and peasants for a share of the surplus more congruent with their contributions to its generation and from above by demands of private foreign firms and bilateral and multilateral financial institutions for their own share, the local bourgeoisie in each country is finding it harder and harder in the context of underdevelopment to expand or even stabilise the process of accumulation of capital within their domains.

Based on this kind of analysis, my own view is that although the discovery of offshore oil, or the accession to power of a benevolent administration in France, might extend the tenure of command of the *ruling classes* of these countries, political control will ultimately pass from their hands altogether. To the extent that the three countries I have used as illustrations are of small relative importance to Western capitalism, these developments will have minor repercussions from that point of view. To the extent that the class conditions in these societies are not unique, these minor repercussions will resonate.

To which Peter Wiles, replies:

In most African countries there are no classes in the Marxist sense, and in many none by any definition. In these latter, the less developed ones, there are tribes, and also educated in-groups that have seized power. Notably Ethiopia, Congo and Benin are governed by educated *military* in-groups, themselves centred on some tribe. The relation of a given tribe to property is whatever empirical anthropologists tell us it happens to be; that of such in-groups is that, having weapons, they take the property they can lay hands on. Property is the sweetener not the base of political power; it 'grows out of the barrel of a gun', and most African countries are pretty pure kleptocracies. Only in Madagascar, Kenya, West Africa and the Mediterranean litoral (except Libya) does it begin to be possible to speak of classes and of power based on property.

But this property is often state, not private, property, and we find power in the hands of a 'state bourgeoisie', an 'administrative class' which possesses rather than owns the public property concerned via a quasi-monopoly of education and nepotistic appointment to jobs. Note that perhaps the majority of these jobs, being military, judicial or diplomatic, have no connection with tangible property at all. This very common Third World structure is strongly exemplified in Malaysia, where the dominant Malays are installing it to the disadvantage of the classical capitalism of the Chinese minority. Andrew Racine has himself convincingly shown the actual conversion of a private into a state bourgeoisie in Madagascar. This is a most striking example of the superior explanatory power of the concept: the most powerful people in the country have abandoned the one structure for the other. They see it as being more secure.

In very poor countries there is very little tangible property except land, and it is all so conspicuous, so easy to seize or destroy, so difficult to keep in good repair, that he would be foolish indeed who relied on it. Jobs and connections are the thing, preferably military jobs and connections. Given a few years of internal peace, Benin and Congo will surely develop, from the families of military officers, just such a state bourgeoisie. However each case is separate, and must be studied on its own. But Africa rubs in the lesson that, North America, Europe and Russia have already taught: Marxism has no predictive power whatever. It was the supreme merit of Marx to ask the right questions: his answers were always simply wrong.

Of course generalisation is nearly impossible, and what I have said above is intended rather to introduce some of the necessary complications than to re-order the phenomena into a new simplicity.

Above all the preceding account omits morality. There is not a little effective morality in left-wing societies, and the administrative class does not ordinarily enrich itself to the same extent as a private capitalist class. This may well be a less efficient economic policy, and it is certainly bad for human liberty, but it is none the less grounded in morality, and it does generate greater equality. In the NCTW itself the leadership has not widely different social origins from that of the 'marginals', and it certainly rests its power on no other base than guns, education and appointments; but its stronger party discipline is just such a moral force. These leaders also are a state bourgeoisie, but they will take less than the 'marginal' leaders, let alone the leaders of Kenya or Morocco, and indeed less than those of Poland or USSR, where the common ideology is by now far weaker.

Given all this I unrepentantly defend the more Althusserian concept of an arbitrary 'Khazar's choice' of regime. Furthermore if the dictator's or junta's choice favours Marxism-Leninism, and the Kremlin takes it seriously, it is irreversible. Nor is that choice yet proven to be a bad one for the subject people concerned, when we compare North Yemen or Uganda or Libya. It will *become* a regrettable choice, when with development freedom becomes a valid option for a whole people. Russians would be wise to regret 1917, Mozambicans should suspend judgement on 1974.

III. Soviet Military Aid to the NCTW, 1964-78[17]

The Soviet Union began to extend its military aid to the NCTW in the sixties namely to Somalia (1963) and, later, to the PDRY and Congo (1969). Until the mid seventies, this Soviet means of penetration and influence was on a relatively limited scale. Political and military events in the Middle East and in Sub-Saharan Africa opened new opportunities for the Soviets in extending their military aid to new clients – Angola (1975), Benin, Madagascar, Mozambique and Ethiopia (1976).

The Soviet military aid to all these countries was not limited to obsolete and unsophisticated weaponry. The USSR supplied them gradually with a wide range of advanced and sophisticated military equipment, such as fighter aircraft MIG-21s and MIG-23s, helicopters Mi-8 and Mi-24, tanks T-62s, surface-air-missiles Sam-2 and Sam-3, and the self-propelled anti-aircraft gun ZSU-23-4.[18]

According to the US Arms Control and Disarmament Agency[19] (see Table P.1) the USSR delivered military aid worth $123 million to the above-mentioned countries in Sub-Saharan Africa and South Arabia

Table P.1: Soviet Military Deliveries to the NCTW

	1964-73 (in million dollars)	1974-8 (in million dollars)	1964-78 (in million dollars)	1964-73 (in per cent)	1974-8 (in per cent)	1964-78 (in per cent)	1978 (in million dollars)[a] sustainable annual values		
							civilian imports	aid	military deliveries
Angola	—	410	410	—	16	15	15.3	3.5	100
Benin	—	20	20	—	1	1	1.1	0	10
Congo	7	30	37	6	1	1	4.1	0	neg.
Ethiopia	—	1,300	1,300	—	50	48	16.3	2.5	1,000
Madagascar	—	20	20	—	1	1	1.6	0.9	15
Mozambique	—	130	130	—	5	5	1.3	0.5	90
PDRY	47	370	417	38	14	15	2.5	6.0	210
Somalia	69	300	369	56	12	14	0	0	0
Sub-total	123	2,580	2,703	100	100	100	4,350	10	3,715
Third World total[b]	7,545	18,575	26,120						

Source: US Arms Control and Disarmament Agency, *World Military Expenditures and Arms Transfers* (Washington), various issues.
Notes: a. Extremely appropriate. For civilian imports and aid derived from Tables 1.1 and 1.2. For military deliveries deduced from ACDA data on the sub-periods 1973-7 and 1974-8. 'Sustainable' means our judgement for the next few years, assuming no big changes from 1978.
b. Excluding Mongolia, Cuba, Vietnam, North Korea and Albania but including the NCTW.

during the period 1964-73. As a result of the deepening Soviet involvement in those countries — resulting either from the wars in Angola and in the Somali-Ethiopian conflict, or the radicalisation of the regimes in the remaining countries — the Soviet military aid amounted to $2,580 million in 1974-8. While Somalia and the PDRY were the most important receivers of Soviet military aid during the decade 1964-73, Ethiopia was the most important client in 1974-8, followed by Angola and the PDRY. It will be recalled that Somalia expelled the Russians in 1974. Afterwards of course there were no economic transactions of any kind.

It appears from Table P.1 that Sub-Saharan Africa and the PDRY received 14 per cent of the total Soviet military aid to the Third World in 1974-8 compared to only 2 per cent in the preceding decade 1964-73. We have called these deliveries aid because we do not know how they were financed. But presumably in fact Benin and Congo have paid, just as Ratsiraka has claimed for Madagascar (but at what prices?), while the NCTW has not. We present in the last columns of Table P.1 some figures that very roughly illustrate the relative importance of Soviet arms, Soviet civilian imports and Soviet civilian aid.

We can hardly insist enough on the 'ball-park' nature of these estimates. But if, as is highly probable, the US figures for Soviet arms deliveries are too low military trade and aid are overwhelmingly the most important economic relation between USSR and the Third World as a whole, let alone the NCTW.

Notes

1. *Pravda,* 2-6 July1981; *Guardian,* 14 July 1981.
2. *SWB*, 28 April 1981.
3. *SWB*, 23 June 1981.
4. See *Noticias*, 17 April 1981: *Neues Deutschland, passim*.
5. *People's Power*, no. 17 (Spring 1981).
6. Yet foreign-policy paranoia continues. Current numbers of *Noticias* are displayed in the Mozambican embassy in Lisbon, as are those of its opposite number in the Angolan embassy; but no numbers at all are available in any Portuguese library (or in London anywhere). Both embassies are exceedingly inhospitable to enquirers.
7. Speech by President E. dos Santos reported in *Jornal de Angola*, 24 December 1980.
8. Ibid.
9. Interview in *Noticias,* Maputo, 11 November 1980, reprinted in *People's Power*, no. 17 (Spring 1981).
10. See P. Fauvet in *People's Power*, no. 16 (Summer 1980).

11. *ARB*, 1981, p. 5866.

12. *People's Power*, no. 16 (Summer 1980).

13. *Jornal de Angola*, 24 December 1980.

14. *SWB*, 10 March 1981.

15. *SWB*, 6 June 1981.

16. Cf. Jacques Latrémolière in *Marchés Tropicaux*, 29 May 1981.

17. A more comprehensive analysis of the Soviet Military Aid to the Third World is being carried out in a research project entitled 'A New Approach to the Economics of the Soviet Military Aid to the Third World' by Moshe Efrat under the Chairmanship of Professor P.J.F. Wiles.

18. IISS, *The Military Balance* (London), various issues; Stockholm International Peace Research Institute, *World Armaments and Disarmament Yearbook* (Almqvist and Wiksell, Stockholm), various issues.

19. This is to date (July 1981) the only available reliable Western source publishing data on the value of all the Soviet military equipment delivered to those countries: that is to say major weapons as well as other military equipment such as artillery, light arms, ammunition, spare parts, transport and electronic equipment. These American estimates are much lower than the partial information, namely only major weapons, published by the Stockholm International Peace Research Institute. The lack of detailed data from this valuable source does not allow us at this stage to make a comparative analysis of the Soviet military aid to our countries.

BIBLIOGRAPHY

Chapter 1 and General

Alampiev, P., Bogomolov, O. and Shiryaev, Yu. *A New Approach to Economic Integration* (Moscow, 1973)

Askanas, Benedikt, Askanas, Halina, and Levcik, Friedrich. *Entwicklung und Niveau der Löhne in den R.G.W. Ländern*, Wiener Institut fur Internationale Wirtschaftsvergleiche (1/1976)

Bräker, Hans. *Die Aufnahme Vietnams in den R.G.W.*, Bundesinstitut fur Ostwissenschaftliche und Internationale Studien (Cologne 7-1979)

Brandt, Willy (Commission Chairman). *North-South: A Programme for Survival* (London, 1980)

Brandt, Willy in *Euroforum*, Brussels, EEC (10 Oct. 1980)

Bukharin, N.I. and Preobrazhenski, E. *The ABC of Communism* (1921). Also Penguin edn (London, 1969)

Carrère d'Encausse, Hélène. *L'Empire Eclaté* (Paris, 1978)

Centre d'Etudes Prospectives et d'Informations Internationales (Paris, 52 rue St.Denis) *La Base Matérielle de la Présence Soviétique dans l'Afrique sub-Saharienne* (1979)

Clarkson, Stephen. *The Soviet Theory of Development: India* (Toronto, 1978)

Feis, Herbert. *From Trust to Terror* (London, 1970)

Foreign and Commonwealth Office, Foreign Policy Document no. 49, *Soviet, East European and DAC Aid 1970-78* (London, 1980)

Huang, Po-Wen. *The Asian Development Bank* (NY, 1975)

IMF, *Balance of Payments Yearbook* (Washington)

IMF, *Direction of Trade* (Washington)

Jeffreys, Ian. *The Stalinist Economic System as a Model for Underdeveloped Countries*, Ph.D. thesis 1974, in the Library of the London School of Economics

Kaser, Michael. *Comecon*, 2nd edn (Oxford, 1965)

Keesing's Contemporary Archives, Keesing's Publications (Longman Group Ltd., London)

Khrushchev, N.S. in *World Marxist Review* (September 1962)

Kolarz, Walter. *Russia and her Colonies* (1952)

Kravis, I.B., Heston, A.W. and Summers, R. 'The Real GDP *per capita* of more than 100 Countries', *Economic Journal* (June 1978)

Legum, Colin in *Problems of Communism* (January-February 1978)

Lenin, V.I. *Original Draft of the Theses on the National and Colonial Question* (5 June 1920)

Mikulski, K. *Lenin's Teaching on the World Economy and its relation to Our Times* (Moscow, 1975)

Morozov, V.I. *SEV, Soyuz Ravnykh* (CMEA, Alliance of Equals) (Moscow, 1964)

Nayyar, Deepak. (ed.) *Economic Relations between Socialist Countries and the Third World* (London, 1977)

OECD, *The Aid Programme of China* (Paris, 1979)

OECD, *The Aid Programme of the East European Countries* (Paris, 1977)

OECD, *The Aid Programme of the USSR* (Paris, 1977)

OECD, *Geographical Distribution of Financial Flows to Developing Countries* (Paris, 1978)
  Idem. (Washington, 1980)

Primakov, Yevgeni in *Gesellschaftswissenschaften* (East Berlin, 3/1979)

Stepanyan, Ts.A. in *Voprosy Filosofii* (10/1958)

US Department of Commerce, *US Trade Status with Communist Countries*, quarterly.

UNYITS, annual.

VT, annual

Wiles, Peter J.D. 'Power Without Influence', in *The Impact of the Russian Revolution*, Royal Institute of International Affairs (London, 1967)

Wiles, Peter J.D. in *Est-Ouest* (Paris, December, 1979)

Wiles, Peter J.D. *Communist International Economics* (Oxford, 1968)

Wiles, Peter J.D. and Smith, Alan. 'The Convergence of the CMEA on the EEC' in *The EEC and Eastern Europe*, ed. Avi Shlaim and G.N. Yannopoulos (Cambridge, 1978)

World Bank, *World Development Report*, (Washington, 1979)
  Idem, (Washington, 1980)

Yowev, S. in the *Bulletin* of the Institute for the Study of the USSR (Munich, 1960)

Albania

Dode, P. in *Probleme Ekonomike* (P. Dode is chairman of the State Planning Commission) Tirana 1/1978

Kaser, Michael, and Schnytzer, Adi. 'Albania — a Uniquely Socialist

Economy', in *East European Economies post-Helsinki*, JEC of Congress (Washington, 1977)

Schnytzer, Adi. *The Impact of Aid on Albanian Industrial Development in the Chinese Economy Post-Mao*, JEC of Congress (Washington, 1978)

Schnytzer, Adi. *The Albanian Economy* (OUP, 1981)

Vinski, Ivo. *Društveni Proizvod Svijeta* (Zagreb, 1976)

Wiles, Peter J.D. in *Asian Perspectives* (Seoul, Autumn 1981)

Angola

Bender, G.F. *Angola under the Portuguese* (Heinemann, 1978)

CEPII (1979)

Centre d'Etudes Anti-Impérialistes. *Angola* (1977)

Clarence-Smith, W.C. 'Class Structure and Class Struggles in Angola', in *Journal of Southern African Studies*, vol. 7, no. 1, October (1980)

Garcia Marques, Gabriel. *Operación Carlota*, Mosca Azul (Lima, 1977)

Heimer, F.W. 'Thesen zur Politischen Entwicklung in Angola and Mosambik', in *Bericht*, Deutsche Stiftung für Internazionale Entwicklung Dok 990B – IIB-E, 3/78

Heimer, F.W. *Der Entkolonisierungskonflikt in Angola* (1979)

Henderson, L.W. *Angola – Five Centuries of Conflict* (1979)

Legum, C. 'Foreign Intervention in Angola', in *Africa Contemporary Record* (1975/6)

MAGIC, *Angola Socialism at Birth* (London, 1980)

Marcum, J. *The Angolan Revolution* (1978)

MPLA, *Central Committee Report to First Congress*, MAGIC (London, 1979)

National Foreign Assessment Center. *Communist Aid Activities in Non-Communist Less Developed Countries, 1978*, ER 79 – 1041, 2U, September (1979)

Ogunbadejo, O. 'Soviet Policies in Africa', in *African Affairs*, vol. 76, 316, July (1980)

Schumer, M. *Die Wirtschaft Angolas, 1973-76*, Institut für Afrika-Kunde (1977)

Stockwell, J. *In Search of Enemies* (1978)

Benin

ACR
ARB
Africa South of the Sahara 1980/1, 10th edn (London, 1980)
Bebler, Anton. *Military Rule in Africa-Dahomey, Ghana, Sierra Leone and Mali* (New York, 1973)
Cornevin, Robert. *Le Dahomey* (Paris, 1965)
Hancock, Graham. (ed.) *Africa Guide*, World of Information (England, 1979)
Pedler, Frederick. *Main Currents of West African History 1940-78* (London, 1979)
Ronen, Dov. *Dahomey Between Tradition and Modernity* (New York, 1975)
Welch, Claude E. (ed.) *Soldier and State in Africa: A Comparative Analysis of Military Intervention and Political Change* (1970)

Congo

Année Africaine 1977, Centre d'Etude d'Afrique Noire de Bordeaux, (Paris, 1979), pp. 159-69
Bertrand, H. *Le Congo* (Paris, 1975)
Gauge, René. *The Politics of Congo Brazzaville* (Stanford, 1973)
IMFC
World Bank, *People's Republic of the Congo, Economic Trends, Current Issues and Prospects*, Report no. 2213-COB, (1979)

Ethiopia and Somalia

ACR
Africa Quarterly, Indian Centre for Africa, New Delhi
Africa Report, African-American Institute, New York
Africa South of the Sahara: *1976/77, 1977/78* and *1979/80*, London
Africa in Soviet Studies, USSR Academy of Science, Africa Institute, Moscow
The African Review, Department of Political Science, University of Dar es Salaam, Dar es Salaam
ARB
Jesman, Czeslav. *The Russians in Ethiopia* (London, 1958)

Legum, Colin. (ed.) *Africa Contemporary Record; Annual Survey and Documents* (London, 1977)

Legum, Colin, and Lee, Bill. *Conflict in the Horn of Africa* (London, 1977)

McLane, Charles B. *Soviet – Third World Relations*, vol. 3, Central Asian Research Centre (London, 1974)

Mezhdunarodnaya Zhizn', no. 4, 1979, Moscow

Quarterly Economic Review, Economist Intelligence Unit, London

UN Statistical Yearbook: 1978, United Nations, New York

Newspapers

Financial Times, London
The Times, London
Guardian, London

Madagascar

ACR
Africa South of the Sahara 10th Edition (London, 1980)
Archer, Robert. *Madagascar Depuis 1972* (Paris, 1976)
EBM
Kent, Raymond K. (ed.) *Madagascar in History*, The Foundation for Malagasy Studies, Albany, California (1979)
Ostheimer, John M. (ed.) *The Politics of the Western Indian Ocean Islands*, (New York, 1975)

Mongolia

Dupuy, T.N. *Area Handbook for Mongolia* (Washington DC, 1970)
Faddeev, N. in *Planovoe Khozyaistvo*, no. 4, 1977
LuFsandorj, P. in *Planovoe Khozyaistvo*, no. 9, 1978
Matveeva, G.S. *Sozdaniye Materialno-Tekhnicheskoi Bazi Sotsialisma v M.N.R.* (Moscow, 1978)
Murphy, G.C.S. *Soviet Mongolia* (Berkeley, 1966)
Ochir, E. in *Ekonomicheskoe Sotrudnichestvo Stran-Chlenov SEV*, no. 3, 1977
Smith, A.H. 'Economic Factors Affecting Soviet-East European Relations', in *Soviet-East European Dilemmas*, Karen Dawisha and Philip Hanson (London, 1981)

Tsedenbal, Y. in *World Marxist Review*, no. 2, 1980

Statistical Sources and Documents

The Multilateral Economic Co-operation of Socialist States, Collection of Documents (Moscow, 1977)
Statisticheskii Yezhegodnik Stran-Chlenov SEV, various years, Moscow
VT, various years

Mozambique

Brum, J.M. 'Manufacturing Industries in Mozambique. Some Aspects', in *Wissenschaftliche Beiträge*, Institut Ökonomik der Entwicklungsländer (Sondersommer II, 1976)

Fitzpatrick, J. 'The Economy of Mozambique: Problems and Prospects', in *Third World Quarterly*, vol. 3, no. 1, pp. 77-87 (January, 1981)

Frelimo: *Central Committee Report to the 3rd Congress*, MAGIC (1978)

Griffin, K.B. and Enos, J.L. *Planning Development* (1970)

Harris, L. 'Agricultural Co-operatives and Development Policy in Mozambique', in *Journal of Peasant Studies* (April, 1980)

Heimer, F.W. 'Thesen zur Politischen Entwicklung in Angola und Mozambik', in *Bericht*, Deutsche Stiftung für Internationale Entwicklung Dok 99C B IIB − E 3/78

Henricksen, T.H. 'Marxism and Mozambique', *African Affairs*, vol. 77, no. 309 (October 1978)

Henricksen, T.H. *Mozambique: A History* (1978)

Heynold, J. 'Der Umgestaltungsprozess der Landwirtschaft in der VR Mozambique', in *Asien, Afrika, Lateinamerika*, Band 7, 3 (1979)

Jemin, Panzer, U. 'Transformation der Landwirtschaft und Überwindung von Unterentwicklung in Mozambik', in *Afrika-Spektrum*, 13.3 1978

Keltsch, Erhard, in Gottfried Zieger and Azel Lebahn (eds.), *Rechtliche und Wirtschaftliche Beziehungen* . . . (Baden-Baden, 1980), pp. 305-8

Meyens, P. *Befreiung und Nationaler-Wiederaufbau von Mozambique*, Institut für Afrika-Kunde (1979)

Munslow, B. 'Peasants, Politics and Production, the case of Mozambique' in Paper presented at Annual Conference of Political Studies Association of UK (1980)

Myint, H. *Economic Theory and Development Policy*, Inaugural
    Lecture, LSE (1967)
National Foreign Assessment Centre: *Communist Aid Activities in
    Non-Communist Less Developed Countries, 1978.* ER 79–1041, 2U
    (September 1979)
Stier, E. and P. 'Some Problems of the Emergence and Development of
    People's Democratic States in African Developing Countries', in
    Economic Quarterly (East Berlin, 4/1978)
Wuyts, M. *Peasant and Rural Economy in Mozambique*, Centro de
    Estudos Africanos, University Ed. Mondlane (1978)
Wuyts, M. 'Economia Politica de Colonialismo em Mozambique', in
    Estudos Mozambicanos 1 (1980)

North Korea

Area Handbook for North Korea (Washington, 1969, 1976)
Chung, Joseph S. *The North Korean Economy* (Stanford, 1973)
CIA *Korea, the economic race between the North and the South*,
    ER 78–10008 (January, 1978, Washington, DC)
Cumings, Bruce G., in *Problems of Communism* (March-April 1974)
Foster-Carter, Aidan, in *Bulletin of Concerned Asian Scholars*, 1977
Im Ik-Soon in (ed.) Joseph S. Chung, *Patterns of Economic
    Development: Korea* (May 1966)
Kaser, M.C., in *International Currency Review*, 4/1977
Kim, I.J., in *Problems of Communism* (January-February, 1973)
Kim, Youn-Soo. 'North Korea's Relationship to the USSR: A Political
    and Economic Problem', in *Bulletin of the Institute of the Study of
    the USSR* (Munich, June, 1971)
Koh, B.C. *The Foreign Policy of North Korea* (New York, 1969)
Koh, S.K., in *Pacific Affairs* (1/1977)
Kondratev, V., in *Ekonomicheskaya Gazeta* (4 September 1978)
Kuark, Y.T., in *China Quarterly* (April-June 1963)
Lee, Pong in *Asian Survey* (June, 1972)
'North Korean Foreign Trade': *Puk Han Mu Yok Ron*, Research Series
    no. 112, Institute of Far Eastern Affairs, Kyong Nam University
    (Seoul, 1979)
'North Korea Handbook': *Puk Han Chun So, 1945-1980*, The Institute
    of East Asian Studies (Seoul, 1980), p. 400
Scalapino, Robert and Lee, Chong-Sik. *Communism in Korea* (London,
    1972)

Teratani, Hiromi. 'Relations between USSR and North Korea', in *Korea Review*, in Japanese (April, 1979)

'Trends in Asian Countries': Ajia Toko Nempo, Institute of Developing Economies (Tokyo, various dates)

Wiechert, Rainer. 'Economic Relations between North Korea and the Soviet Union as Reflected in Soviet Sources', in *The East-West Economy*, Overseas Economic Research Institute (Seoul, 1978)

Wiles, Peter J.D. in *Asian Perspectives* (Seoul, Autumn 1981)

Vietnam

Dang Viet Chau in *Tap Chi Cong San*, no. 10 (October, 1978) as translated by the Joint Press Reading Service of the US Department of Commerce

Duncanson, D.J. 'Vietnam: From Bolshevism to People's War', in *The Anatomy of Communist Takeovers*, (ed.) H.T. Hammond (New Haven, 1975)

Huynh Kim Khank. 'Vietnam: Neither Peace Nor War', in *Southeast Asian Affairs 1979*

Smith, H.H., Bernier, D.W. *et al. Area Handbook for North Vietnam* (Washington, 1967)

Thayer, C.A., in *Asian Survey*, 1/1976

Theriot, L.H. and Matheson, J. 'Soviet Economic Relations with non-European CMEA: Cuba, Vietnam and Mongolia', in *Soviet Economy in a Time of Change* (Washington, 1979)

Yemen

al-Abd, Salah. *Analysis of the social and economic conditions of the People's Republic of South Yemen* (1969)

Blaustein, Albert P. and Flanz, Gisbert H. (eds.) *Constitutions of the Countries of the World*, in progress, 14 Volumes and Supplementaries (1971)

CIA, *Communist Aid Activities in Non-Communist Less Developed Countries– 1977* (Washington DC, November 1978)

CIA, *Communist Aid Activities in Non-Communist Less Developed Countries – 1978* (Washington DC, September 1979)

Collier's Encyclopaedia (New York, 1979)

El-Zine, M. Abdallah Yahia. *Le Yémen et Ses Moyens d'Information*, Société Nationale d'Edition et de Diffusion (Alger, 1978)

The First Congress, the Yemeni Socialist Party, October 1978, Dar Ibn-Khaldun, in Arabic (Beirut, 1979)

Heyworth-Dunne, Gamal-Eddine. *Al-Yemen – A General Social, Political and Economic Survey* (Cairo, 1972)

Ismael, T.Y. *The Arab Left* (Syracuse, 1976)

Isma'il, Abd al-Fattah. *The National Democratic Revolution*, Dar Ibn-Khaldun, in Arabic (Beirut, 1972)

_____, *On the National Democratic Revolution and its Socialist Horizons*, Dar al-Farabi (Beirut, 1979)

Keesing's Contemporary Archives, London

Kostiner, Joseph. *From Guerilla to Government: the NLF and its Rivals in Struggle for Independence and Power in South Yemen 1963-1973*, unpublished M.A. thesis, Haifa University, in Hebrew (September 1978)

Legum, Colin. (ed.) *Middle East Contemporary Survey*, vol. 1, 1976/77 (New York, 1978)

Middle East Record, 1967, 1968, 1969/70, Shiloah Centre, Tel-Aviv University, Israel University Press, Jerusalem

Page, S. *The USSR in Arabia: the Development of Soviet Policies and Attitudes towards the Countries of Arab Peninsula 1955-1970*, Central Asian Research Centre (London, 1972)

Ro'i, Yaacov. (ed.) *The Limits to Power – Soviet Policy in the Middle East* (London, 1979)

al-Sha'ayoubi, Muhammad Ali. *South Yemen – Studies in Economic Development and its related problems*, Dar al Ouman, in Arabic (Beirut, 1972)

Newspapers and other publications

Akhar Sa'ah, weekly, Cairo (in Arabic)

Al-Thawri, weekly, Aden (in Arabic)

Daily Telegraph, daily, London

Fourteenth October, daily, Aden (in Arabic)

Le Monde, daily, Paris

Middle East Economic Digest, weekly, London

Middle East Intelligence Survey, fortnightly, Tel-Aviv

New York Times, daily, New York

October, weekly, Sana'a (in Arabic)

Summary of World Broadcasts (BBC, London)

NOTES ON CONTRIBUTORS

Dr Moshe Efrat is a Research Fellow at the London School of Economics and Political Science, where he attained his PhD in economics. Prior to his present position, he served with the Israel Government, lectured at the Haifa University and was a Research Fellow at the Tel-Aviv University. Dr Efrat is currently preparing a major study on the economics of the Soviet military aid to the Third World.

Pong S. Lee is Associate Professor of Economics at the State University of New York, Albany, USA, and received his graduate degrees in economics from Yale University. He has written on the economics and trade of Japan, North Korea, Romania and other East European countries. Some of his articles appear in *Yale Economics Essays*, *Soviet Studies*, *Kyklos* and *Journal of Korean Affairs*.

Barry Lynch is a Senior Researcher at the Confederation of British Industry, which he joined in 1980, and has longstanding affiliations with the London School of Economics and Political Science as a teacher and a researcher. In addition to work in the Soviet area he is also the author of numerous articles on local government finance.

Andrew Racine received his bachelor's degree from Harvard College in 1974 and is currently working on an MD and a PhD in Economics at New York University.

Adi Schnytzer read chemistry and economics at Monash University in Melbourne. He gained the DPhil at Oxford in 1978, on the economics of Albania. He is at present lecturer in the School of Social and Industrial Administration at Griffith University, Brisbane. His research interests are the Socialist Third World and Comparative Economic Systems.

Alan Smith is a lecturer in the Economics of Eastern Europe at the School of Slavonic and East European Studies, University of London, and has been visiting Professor of Economics at Dartmouth College, Hanover, New Hampshire. His publications include articles on the

Romanian Economy, Comecon and Soviet and East European Foreign Trade. He is currently writing a book entitled *The Planned Economies of Eastern Europe* to be published by Croom Helm.

Peter Wiles is Professor of Russian Social and Economic Studies at the University of London. He was educated at New College Oxford. His publications include *Price, Cost and Output*, *The Political Economy of Communism* and *Communist International Economics*.

Nicos Zafiris is currently Principal Lecturer in Economics at the London School of Economics and Political Science. He gained his BA in Philosophy, Politics and Economics at the University of Oxford and his MSc in Economics at the London School of Economics and Political Science. He has held appointments at Middlesex and North London Polytechnics and the National Bank of Greece. His specialist interests include Micro-economic Theory, Business Economics, Public Finance and Comparative Economic Systems.

INDEX

The following have not been indexed: Marx, Engels, Lenin, NCTW, USSR; many fleeting references to countries and people not at the centre of our attention; authors in footnotes, or bracketed in the text; references in tables.

In addition to names we have indexed our key concepts. They are marked with an asterisk.

'PS' means some page in the Postscript.